DARWIN'S CENTURY

Evolution and the Men Who Discovered It

by Loren Eiseley

ANCHOR BOOKS

DOUBLEDAY

NEW YORK LONDON TORONTO SYDNEY AUCKLAND

AN ANCHOR BOOK
PUBLISHED BY DOUBLEDAY
a division of Bantam Doubleday Dell Publishing Group, Inc.
666 Fifth Avenue, New York, New York 10103

ANCHOR BOOKS, DOUBLEDAY, and the portrayal of an anchor
are trademarks of Doubleday, a division of Bantam Doubleday
Dell Publishing Group, Inc.

Darwin's Century was originally published in hardcover
by Doubleday in 1958. The Anchor Books edition is
published by arrangement with Loren Eiseley.

Library of Congress Cataloging-in-Publication Data
Eiseley, Loren C., 1907–1977.
   Darwin's century: evolution and the men who
discovered it / by Loren Eiseley.
      p.   cm.
   Reprint. Originally published: Garden City, N.Y.:
Doubleday, 1958.
   Includes bibliographical references and index.
   1. Evolution—History.   I. Title.
QH361.E35   1990   90-1161
575′.009—dc20   CIP
ISBN 0-385-08141-3

To Carl Frederick Wittke
distinguished historian and friend of
those whom history has forgotten
this book is dedicated

He who calls what has vanished back again into being, enjoys a bliss like that of creating.

Barthold Niebuhr

CONTENTS

I. The Age of Discovery   1

The Voyagers—The Two Ladders and the Scale of Being—The Baconian and Humanistic Traditions in Natural History—Linnaeus—The Fixity of Species

II. The Time Voyagers   27

The Extraordinary Voyage—Benoit de Maillet—The Comte de Buffon—Erasmus Darwin and Lamarck—Early Glimpses of Ecological Adaptation

III. The Pirate Chart   57

Time and Organic Change—Pagan and Christian Time—The Chart—The Rise of Catastrophism—James Hutton's World Machine and Uniformitarianism—William Smith—Cuvier: the Magician of the Charnel House

IV. Progressionism and Evolution   91

Geological Prophecy—Sir Charles Lyell and the Re-emergence of Uniformitarianism—Non-progressionism

V. The Minor Evolutionists   117

Branching Evolution—William Wells—Patrick Matthew and Robert Chambers

CONTENTS

VI.   The Voyage of the *Beagle*   141

The Age of Giants—The Influence of Erasmus Darwin—Darwin's Intellectual Background—The Voyage—South America—The Galápagos

VII.   The Making of the *Origin*   175

"The Bridgewater Treatises"—Darwin and Malthus—The Law of Divergence—The First Essay Attempts—Darwin and Design—Darwin and Lamarck

VIII.   The Priest Who Held the Key to Evolution   205

Gregor Mendel—Pre-Mendelian Genetics—Pangenesis—Artificial Selection and the Evolutionists—Mendel's Contribution—Johannsen and Variation

IX.   Darwin and the Physicists   233

Kelvin and Residual Heat—The Biological Retreat—De Vries and Saltatory Evolution—Time and Radioactivity

X.   The Reception of the First Missing Links   255

The Evolutionists Turn to Man—Ape and Hottentot—The Microcephali—The Descent into the Past—The Java Ape Man

XI.   Wallace and the Brain   287

The Darwinian Bias—Alfred Russel Wallace—Darwin and Human Evolution—Degeneration or Development—Wallace and Human Antiquity—The Concept of Latency—Brains and Time

CONTENTS

XII. Conclusion   325

*Time: Cyclic and Historic—The Pre-Darwinian
Era—The Struggle of the Parts—Evolution and
Human Culture—The Role of Indeterminism*

Glossary   353

Suggested Reading   355

Index   361

NOTE

After their first listing, frequently mentioned sources are referred to in the footnotes by the following code letters:

D   *Charles Darwin's Diary of the Voyage of H.M.S. "Beagle,"* edited by Nora Barlow, Cambridge Univ. Press, 1933.

FO   *Foundations of the Origin of Species,* edited by Francis Darwin, Cambridge Univ. Press, 1909.

JR   *Journal of Researches* (1839), facsimile reprint of the first edition, Hafner Publishing Co., New York, 1952.

LLD   *Life and Letters of Charles Darwin,* 3 vols., edited by Francis Darwin, London: John Murray, 1888.

LLH   *Life and Letters of Thomas Henry Huxley,* 3 vols., edited by Leonard Huxley, Macmillan & Co., London, 1913.

LLL   *Life, Letters and Journals of Sir Charles Lyell,* 2 vols., edited by Mrs. Katherine Lyell, London: John Murray, 1881.

MLD   *More Letters of Charles Darwin,* 2 vols., edited by Francis Darwin and A. C. Seward, London: John Murray, 1903.

N   *Charles Darwin and the Voyage of the "Beagle,"* edited by Nora Barlow, Philosophical Library, New York, 1946 (this book contains the rough notebooks kept by Darwin during the voyage).

O   *The Origin of Species* by Charles Darwin, reprint of the first edition, Philosophical Library, New York, 1951. (Unless otherwise indicated O will stand for this edition.)

PG   *Principles of Geology* by Sir Charles Lyell, 4 vols., third edition, London: John Murray, 1834. (Unless otherwise indicated all references are to this edition.)

VAP   *Variations of Animals and Plants under Domestication* by Charles Darwin, 2 vols., Orange Judd & Co., New York, 1868.

A glossary of certain technical terms used in this book will be found on page 353.

ACKNOWLEDGMENTS

The author wishes to express his grateful appreciation to the Administration of the University of Pennsylvania for providing the leave of absence during which much of the writing of this book was done, to the Wenner-Gren Foundation for Anthropological Research for financial encouragement, and to the American Philosophical Society for the opportunity to utilize its magnificent collection of Darwiniana, including the privilege of quoting from one unpublished letter.

For the Anchor edition I have made a few minor changes and drawn attention to my recent study of Edward Blyth. Otherwise the edition remains the same.

Loren Eiseley

The University of Pennsylvania
September 16, 1960

DARWIN'S CENTURY

Chapter I

The Age of Discovery

We saw as a sign we were nearing America some great birds like crows, but white with long tails.

Abraham Kendall, 1594

When we arrive at certain lands, newly discovered, the inhabitants we find are there scarce men; they are animals with human figures, and those sometimes imperfect, but almost without human reason . . .

Bernard Le Bovier de Fontenelle, 1686

I The Voyagers

It has been remarked by historians that the discovery of the world by the great voyagers, and particularly their passage across the western seas, had made a tremendous impact upon the thought of Europe in the sixteenth and seventeenth centuries. There was nothing recondite or obscure about the discoveries of the captains. The unlettered as well as the cultivated were stirred by new facts and speculations to an increasing sophistication which spread by way of the ports and the tales of homing sailors. This broadening intellectual experience was shared by all western Europeans and it aided tremendously in ushering in the dawning age of science.

As an indirect consequence of this adventure the the-

ory of evolution, vast in its implications as a new continent, was really, in essence, glimpsed through the fogs
and sea wrack penetrated by the master mariners. Moreover, and most appropriately, it was to be a voyager-natu-
ralist, Charles Darwin, later on in the nineteenth century,
who would finally establish its reality. Like the fabulous
western isles the idea would be coasted at first through
dangerous intellectual waters. It would be termed a phantom, a figment of man's restless imagination. It would be
labeled like a sea monster "blasphemous," "illusory," and
"godless." Finally it would lie there under the lifting fog-
wisps which had so long obscured the human vision, a
country of wraiths and changelings among whom was to
be accounted man himself. Time such as humanity had
never dreamed before lay across that world. It was a land
where water wore away the shapes of mountains, and the
great bones and carapaces of vanished beasts lay hoar
and rime-frosted in deep crevices and canyons.

This wild landscape was, by the twentieth century, utterly to possess the human mind. Christian thought had
long contemplated eternity but it had been the shadow-
less, changeless eternity of God. Earthly time had been
seen by comparison as the brief drama of the Fall and
Redemption, the lowly world of Nature merely the stage
setting for a morality play. "Time we may comprehend,"
wrote Sir Thomas Browne in the *Religio Medici*, " 'tis but
five days elder than ourselves, and hath the same Horo-
scope with the World."[1]

The tight little medieval domain, with its ark full of
known animals and its Biblically accounted for humanity,
was soon to find itself theologically at grips with a whole
series of unexpected problems. Ostensibly the voyagers
went to seek lands and riches but they saw with human
eyes and they returned with observations which stimulated the curiosity of savants and stay-at-home thinkers.
"We carry with us the wonders we seek without us: there

[1] *Religio Medici*, 1635.

is all Africa and her prodigies in us" defends Sir Thomas Browne again, and this is true. Nevertheless, the curious marvels over which he exclaims are, to a marked extent, the product of that subversive and elusive thought which has begun to reach even the sedentary scholar in his garden. Intruding into the devout world of Thomas Browne comes "another secret not contained in the Scripture, which is more hard to comprehend . . . and that is . . . how America abounded with Beasts of prey and noxious Animals, yet contained not in it that necessary Creature a Horse, is very strange. By what passage those, not only Birds, but dangerous and unwelcome Beasts, came over; how there be creatures there, which are not found in this Triple Continent; all which must needs be strange unto us, that hold but one Ark, and that the Creatures began their progress from the Mountains of Ararat."

Obviously the solution to this mystery lies in evolutionary radiation and organic change. The seventeenth century does not provide an appropriate answer but it is clear that the voyagers, bringing home accounts of East Indian orangutans and Cape Hottentots, along with strange seeds from the Americas and reports of the doings of Red Indians, are providing a new and mysterious universe for examination. Old explanations no longer hold, old philosophies are fraying at the edges.

Long before the eighteenth-century naturalists began to grope toward an explanation of the odd facts of animal distribution and variation, speculations such as the one I have just quoted from Sir Thomas Browne were destined to become widespread in European thought. It would not be long until all the ingredients necessary to devise a working theory of evolution would be present in the literature. The emergence of a true evolutionary philosophy would then wait only upon the abatement of religious prejudice and the appearance of a synthesizing mind capable of taking a great body of diverse data and relating it within the confines of a single abstraction.

First, however, as so often happens in the history of a scientific hypothesis, a series of compromises were bound to be attempted between older and more recent modes of thought. It is obvious that to fully understand the evolution of the evolutionary principle itself, one must examine the preceding intellectual climate out of which it arose. The various streams of thought which, pursuing separate channels, eventually merged as one in the mind of Charles Darwin have had an intricate and autonomous existence which is not fully revealed by a mere recital of dates and names. It is my hope, in the pages that follow, to recapture from the fossil world of documents some glimpses of the living shape of thought as it flows, mutates, and transforms itself from age to age. The task has about it some of the same fascination which comes to those who pursue the related forms of animals downward through the ever lengthening vistas of the past.

To some degree it is inevitable that we should share with the paleontologist the vexation of lost documents and disconnected phylogenies. For this reason I have not attempted to treat of the speculative evolutionary philosophy of early Greek writers, nor to pursue the distantly related alchemical thinking of the Arabs. What is known of these matters has been adequately treated in the works of other authors. In this book we shall be concerned only with the last three centuries which, as I have intimated, afford us our major clues to the nature and development of the evolutionary philosophy. My treatment of the subject does not purport to be a history of biology in general. It is directed only toward the main theme and, in two chapters, is concerned particularly with problems which arose in the field of human evolution.

If I have touched lightly upon certain familiar names such as Thomas Huxley, it has not been out of neglect or ignorance, but simply because their story was not germane to the particular line of thought being followed in this work. At the risk of being deliberate and pedestrian, I have chosen to follow the intellectual currents which produced the major evolutionary synthesis and, by patient and detailed analysis, to perceive from whence and under what conditions that complex of ideas known as Darwinism has emerged. I am under no illusion that the story has been fully told. I will be satisfied if there is added to the general store of our knowledge a glimpse of the ingredients which crystallized into a new thought pattern which lies at the root of Western thinking. The period after nineteen hundred is really a separate problem in itself, complex, many-sided and demanding lengthy individual treatment. To that period, as time may permit, I contemplate devoting a second volume.

II The Two Ladders and the Scale of Being

There are two main ways by which the transmutations of organic substance, or, as we would say today, the evolution of life, can be approached: through the living world around us or by means of the record of the fossil past which is preserved, albeit fragmentarily, within the sedimentary rocks of the planet. There is, in other words, a ladder backward into time which involves the careful anatomical comparison of existing forms of life at various levels of complexity, and the use of such information in attempting to work out the major physiological and anatomical advances in the history of life. The other ladder by which we descend into the past is that of paleontology itself, the analysis, again by comparative anatomy, of the organic remains of all those once living orders which have left bones or impressions of their bodies encased in the substance of ancient land surfaces or sea bottoms. There are, of course, accessory approaches to the problem to be derived from such studies as animal and plant distributions and from embryology, that science which concerns itself with the development of the single individual from the time of his conception. Essentially, however, all of these methods are in some degree dependent upon our two major techniques: the analysis of the living organism in order that we may extrapolate into the past, and the use of the fossilized organism to determine the actual life of the past. Thus we are able in some degree to check the findings of comparative anatomy as it philosophizes from the living animal alone.

As we survey the course of scientific history it would appear inevitable that the present world would have given man his first clues to the history of life. Yet it is interesting to observe that only the existence in the West of a certain type of theological philosophy caused men to look upon the world around them in a way, or in a frame, that would prepare the Western mind for the final acceptance of evolution. Strange though it may sound, it was a combination of Judeo-Greek ideas, amalgamated within the medieval church itself, which were to form part of the foundation out of which finally arose, in the eighteenth and nineteenth centuries, one of the greatest scientific achievements of all time: the recovery of the lost history of life, and the demonstration of its total interrelatedness. This achievement, however, waited upon the transformation of a static conception of nature into a dynamic one. It was just this leaven which the voyagers supplied with their unheard-of animals, and apes that were scarcely distinguishable from savage men.

Widespread in the literature of the seventeenth and eighteenth centuries, and easily traceable into earlier periods, is the theological doctrine known variously as the *Scala Naturae,* Chain of Being, *echelle des être,* Ladder of Perfection, and by other similar titles. Before the doctrine and its history were subjected to careful analysis in Professor A. O. Lovejoy's masterly volume *The Great Chain of Being* (1942), several well-intentioned but historically naïve scholars, coming upon expressions of this philosophy in eighteenth-century literature, had mistakenly multiplied the number of Darwin's forerunners. It behooves us to examine this philosophy carefully, for if we think of our first approach, the living ladder into the past, this philosophy will be found to equate quite satisfactorily with the Scale of Being concept. There can be little doubt that the rise of comparative anatomy is inextricably linked to the history of the Chain of Being concept with its gradations of complexity in living forms. In making this observation, however, we have to keep in mind one salient fact. Strange though it may sound to a modern evolutionist this gradation of organisms implied nothing in the way of phylogenetic relationship. Equally it implied nothing in the way of evolutionary transformations and it specifically denied the possibility that any organism could become extinct. The whole scheme was as rigidly fixed as the medieval social world itself. Indeed it is to some degree a powerful mental projection of that world.

"There is in this Universe a Stair," continues Browne, "rising not disorderly, or in confusion, but with a comely method and proportion." And since the Scale of Nature runs from minerals by insensible degrees upward through the lower forms of life to man, and beyond him to purely spiritual existences like the angels, ourselves, compounded of both dust and spirit, become "that great and true Amphibium, whose nature is disposed to live . . . in divided and distinguished worlds." We exist, in short, in both the material and spiritual universes. In this respect *Homo duplex*, as he was sometimes called, occupies a place on the scale of life as a link between the animal and spiritual natures. Man suffers from this division and it contributes to his ofttimes confused and contradictory behavior.

If, however, this serried array of living forms does not denote a physical phylogenetic connection, what can it be said to represent? It is just here that we enter upon the very real differences which exist between the recognition of grades of complexity in nature and the assumption that a lower level of complexity evolves physically into that of a higher—that an ape, by way of illustration, may evolve into a man. The scholars of the eighteenth century recognized quite well that the ape stood next to man on the Scale of Nature, but they did not find this spectacle as appalling as a nineteenth-century audience listening to Thomas Huxley. There was a very simple reason for this: The *Scala Naturae* in its pure form asserts the immutability of species. The entire chain of life is assumed to have been created in its present order when God by creative fiat brought the universe out of chaos.

As we remarked earlier the scale is static. Creation is not considered as still in progress. Thus the resemblances between living things are not the result of descent with modification but rather are the product of the uniformity and continuity of the divine act. Since the world was assumed by theologians and scientists alike to be only a few thousand years old, the question of evolution could arise only with the greatest difficulty. There was literally not time enough for such a creation. Theologically it was also held that animal species could not become extinct. By and large, men eyed askance the notion that a whole order of life could disappear. Such piecemeal disappearances from the Scale of Nature seemed to threaten the confidence reposed in divine providence.

As time went on, evidences for the past existence of organisms no longer to be found on the planet began to be brought forward but were received with obvious reluctance. Few wished to believe the reports and their reception was not encouraging. Since knowledge of some parts of the world was scant, even well into the eighteenth century, one favorite resort was to accept the disappearance of certain forms of life in Europe but with the proviso that the creatures probably still survived in remote areas of the earth.

It was a convenient evasion of a question which had theological overtones. For just this reason, however, the often mentioned reports of mammoths surviving into colonial times in interior North America have to be viewed with great skepticism. The intellectual climate of the times promoted and encouraged such accounts. Always the creatures lay just a little farther on, first in the Virginia woods, or in Labrador, then deeper into the interior or "across the lakes." They were heard bellowing in the woods, or seen grazing on the plains of South America. In no case, however, is the documentation satisfactory, nor were hides or tusks from recent beasts shipped home to adorn the cabinets of eager scientists. With the acceptance of the idea of total and successive extinctions of past faunas at the dawn of the nineteenth century the sporadic reports of living mammoths or mastodons began to fade. It must also be remembered in this connection that until the great age of the world and its successive strata were grasped, no great antiquity could be attributed even to fossil bones.

It remains a curious episode in the history of science that the Scale of Nature doctrine which denied extinction should at the same time have encouraged the comparative anatomical observations which would eventually lead to the discovery of extinction. Even more important, the idea of phylogenetic relationship along the scale of life would emerge almost simultaneously. The attention which perfectly orthodox thinkers were encouraged to give to the ascending ladder of being, their eagerness to trace every degree of continuous relationship in the productions of the divine being, their zealous efforts to show that the apparent missing links in the scale could be found, enormously stimulated the study of taxonomy and variation.

All that the Chain of Being actually needed to become a full-fledged evolutionary theory was the introduction into it of the conception of time in vast quantities added to mutability of form. It demanded, in other words, a universe not made but being made continuously. It is ironic and intriguing that the fixed hierarchical order in biology began to pass almost contemporaneously with the disap-

pearance of the feudal social scale in the storms of the
French Revolution. It was France, whose social system
was dissolving, that produced the first modern evolutionists. As we look back upon the long reign of the Scale
of Being, whose effects, as we shall later see, persisted
well into the nineteenth century, we may observe that the
seed of evolution lay buried in this traditional metaphysic
which indeed prepared the Western mind for its acceptance. "Thus disguised and protected," writes Lois Whitney, "did the hypothesis of evolution have, as it were, a
happy seed time, a period in which to germinate and take
root, before the orthodox world scented the danger."[2]

III   The Baconian and Humanistic Traditions
in Natural History

The documents of the early naturalists contain scattered observations generally left undeveloped by their
originators. One finds, for example, that it was apparently
Sir Francis Bacon who first proposed the idea that the
peoples of Holarctica, that is, the northern circumpolar
land mass, tended to dominate the southern areas of the
planet because they had greater ruggedness and endur-
ance than the people of the southern continents. Whether
he ever realized it or not, Charles Darwin made use of
precisely this same idea, extended on a broader evolutionary scale, to account for the frequent dominance of
northern faunas over southern ones at such times as faunal movements radiated in a north-south direction. This
has appeared often to be the case in Tertiary and Qua-
ternary times, northward movements from southern faunal centers seeming, with occasional exceptions, to be less
successful.

Here are Bacon's own words from his essay "Of Vicissitudes of Things" written most probably in the last dec-

---

[2] *Primitivism and the Idea of Progress*, Baltimore, 1934, p. 158.

ade of the sixteenth century: "But North and South are fixed: And it hath seldome or never been seene, that the farre Southern People have invaded the Northern, but contrariwise. Whereby it is manifest, that the *Northern Tract* of the World, is in Nature the more Martiall Region: Be it in respect of the Stars of that Hemisphere; Or of the great Continents that are upon the North, whereas the *South Part*, for ought that is known, is almost all Sea; Or (which is most apparent) of the Cold of the Northern Parts, which is that which without Aid of Discipline, doth make the Bodies hardest, and the Courages warmest."

Charles Darwin's interpretation, unchanged from the first edition of the *Origin* to the last, runs as follows: "I suspect that this preponderant migration from north to south is due to the greater extent of land in the north, and to the northern forms having existed in their own homes in greater numbers, and having consequently been advanced through natural selection and competition to a higher stage of perfection, or dominating power, than the southern forms."[3] Though this is said in a context referring to plant life Darwin makes it very clear in later editions that "the same principles apply to the distribution of terrestrial animals and of marine productions." My intention in aligning these two quotations is not, of course, to derive Darwin's biology from Bacon, but to give at least a glimpse of the antiquity of some of the ideas which needed only to be developed and elaborated in order to take a legitimate place in an evolutionary system of thought. Darwin, as a matter of fact, is far more apt to have taken his idea of "polar dominance" from Lyell's *Principles of Geology* upon which he drew so much. Lyell argued that the cooling state of the earth in recent geo-

[3] Charles Darwin, *The Origin of Species*, New York: Philosophical Library, 1951, Chap. 2.

logical times had stimulated a faunal movement in a north-south direction.[4]

Ideas of this character—ideas without which an evolutionary theory could never have been constructed—are surprisingly numerous in the literature of the seventeenth century. In many instances they are confined to a paragraph or so, as when the astronomer Christian Huygens in his posthumous work *The Celestial Worlds Discovered* (1698) recognizes the principles of comparative anatomy. He is arguing for the likelihood of life basically resembling ours on other planets and, to make his point, he draws on the analogy of the new world of America. "Who doubts," he contends, "but that God, if he had pleased, might have made the animals in America and other distant countries nothing like ours? Yet we see he has not done it."

"They have indeed some difference in Shape," he goes on, "but even in this Variety there is an Agreement, an exact Correspondence in Figure and Shape, the same ways of Growth and new Productions, and of continuing their own kind. Their Animals have Feet and Wings like ours, and like ours have Hearts, Lungs, Guts, and the Parts serving to Generation. . . . 'Tis plain then that Nature has not exhibited that Variety in her Works that she could. . . ." Pondering at some length over these morphological similarities which yet contain a shade of difference —"an Argument of no small Weight that is fetched from Relation and Likeness"—we can see Huygens's thought revolving, all unknowingly, about a mystery which will be resolved only in the Darwinian maxim "descent with modification."

If we return a moment to Sir Thomas Browne whose felicity of phrase so well reveals the cultivated thinking of his era, we find him speaking of two books, two revelations, which have contributed to his religious life. "Be-

[4] Sir Charles Lyell, *Principles of Geology*, Vol. 3, 3rd ed., London, 1834, pp. 84–85.

sides that written one of God," he speaks of another, Nature, "that Universal and publick Manuscript, that lies expans'd unto the eyes of all: those that never saw him in the one, have discovered him in the other. There was never anything ugly or misshapen, but the Chaos," he continues thoughtfully as he runs a contemplative eye over a toad, a bear, and an elephant. "All things are artificial," and "Nature is the art of God." Here, superlatively expressed, is the tolerant and inquiring spirit which, arising out of a growing interest in the natural world, was eventually to soften the harsh orthodoxy of those who regarded the earth and its products as vile. In this view is incorporated that argument from design which reaches a culmination in the *Bridgewater Treatises* of the early nineteenth century. In Browne's work, however, this philosophy lacks the narrow anthropocentrism which it acquired at the hands of less gifted and more orthodox thinkers.

In English thought since the time of Bacon two influences have been paramount in the study of living nature. One stems directly from the purely scientific and experimental approach of Bacon, the subjection of nature "to the question," in the grim phrase of the Lord Chancellor. The other more gracious, humane tradition descends through John Ray and Gilbert White, two parson-naturalists, to the literary observers of later centuries, men such as Thoreau and Hudson. The two streams have at times mingled, influenced and affected each other but they have remained in some degree apart in method and in outlook. Though Darwin is generally claimed by the scientists, it is worthy of note that he did not remain uninfluenced by the literary tradition in natural history which is so strong in England. He was a devoted reader of Gilbert White and once commented to his friend Jenyns that it was a pity foreign periodicals showed no interest in this

type of anecdotal natural history.[5] There is little doubt
that he received the initial stimulus for his earthworm
studies from *The Natural History of Selborne* (1789) and
his debt may be even more extensive. It has not been generally remarked by students of Darwin's *Variation of
Animals and Plants under Domestication* that in 1780
White expressed to his friend Pennant the opinion that
the small blue rock pigeon is the ancestral prototype
of the domestic varieties of this bird. This hypothesis,
greatly elaborated by Darwin as part of his marshaling of
evidence bearing upon evolution, occurs in both the *Origin* and in his later treatise upon domestication. Darwin
does not claim originality in respect to his views on the
subject and we may well suspect that White's comments
did not go unstudied when Darwin was combing the
biological literature for proofs of his theory.

It is to the labors of innumerable scholars of White's
observational abilities that we owe the accumulation of
detail which led eventually to the erection of the major
evolutionary hypothesis. Note that in the case we have
been discussing there is already a clear recognition of organic variation within the domain of a single species. One
hundred and fifty years earlier Browne, musing over his
own palm prints, had discovered that "which I could
never read of nor discover in another." The wonder of individual variation had struck him. "Even in things alike
there is diversity." Genetics was as yet unborn but its essence is contained within that simple statement.

An earlier and greater parson-naturalist than White,[6]
John Ray (1627–1705), was a contemporary of Browne.
Ray was one of the leading naturalists of the seventeenth
century and not least among those whose attempts to clas-

---

[5] *More Letters of Charles Darwin,* ed. by Francis Darwin and
A. C. Seward, London: John Murray, 1903, Vol. 1, p. 55.

[6] Ray was not, of course, so beautiful a stylist as White.

sify and describe the living world were a necessary prelude to the discovery of organic evolution.[7]

An orderly and classified arrangement of life was an absolute necessity before the investigation of evolution, or even its recognition, could take place. Before life and its changes and transmutations can be pursued into the past, the orders of complexity in the living world must be thoroughly grasped. Comparative anatomy must have reached a point of development sufficient to permit the scientist to distinguish a living animal from one no longer in existence. Moreover, the naturalist must be able to recognize affinity and relationship in the midst of difference. He must be able to observe the likeness which reveals the interrelatedness of life across the gulf of time and yet, equally, pointing to distinctions of detail, the student must be able to say "here change is evident." Knowledge of this degree of sophistication could not come in a day. As the great Swedish taxonomist Linnaeus was to remark later, "The first step of science is to know one thing from another. This knowledge consists in their specific distinctions; but in order that it may be fixed and permanent distinct names must be given to different things, and those names must be recorded and remembered."[8] John Ray was a modern in his search for a natural system of classification based upon clear structural affinities.

In this respect Ray anticipated and influenced Linnaeus. Moreover, in his emphasis upon "natural system," in his concern with behavior, he had perhaps a more far-ranging philosophic mind than his successor. He not only helped make possible the *Systema Naturae* of Linnaeus: he was also the forerunner of Gilbert White, of Paley's *Natural Theology* and finally of the *Origin of Species*.

---

[7] Charles E. Raven, *John Ray, Naturalist: His Life and Works*, Cambridge University Press, 1943.

[8] Sir James Edward Smith, *A Selection of the Correspondence of Linnaeus and Other Naturalists from the Original Manuscripts*, London, 1821, Vol. 2, p. 460.

The Wisdom of God Manifested in the Works of Crea-
tion (1691), his best-known and most popular work,
created a pattern which, in its attempt to expound the
mysterious laws of life and co-ordinate a wide range of
phenomena, is still to be found in innumerable books of
both a vitalistic and mechanistic nature right down to our
own day.[9]

In the last decade of his life, writing to his friend
Lhwyd (1695) over some puzzling fern leaf impressions
in stone, he hesitates and confesses that such an exact
similarity to real plants seems hardly ascribable to chemical accident. Sincere Christian that he was, there is a
touch of pathos in his penetrating vision of what the full
acceptance of the real meaning of fossils might mean to
the devout. The consequences, Ray saw, might well result in challenging the whole Christian cosmology as it
was then understood. Fossils might raise questions as to
the antiquity of the world and the duration of species.
"Whatever may be said for ye Antiquity of the Earth itself and bodies lodged in it," Ray argued, retreating from
the abyss, "ye race of mankind is new."[10] Nevertheless,
he broods a little. He had premonitions that would return
to haunt Linnaeus long years later.

IV Linnaeus

Linnaeus shares, with the Comte de Buffon, whom we
will consider in the next chapter, the distinction of being a phenomenon rather than a man. This achievement,
though it demands great energies and unusual ability, is,
in reality, dependent upon the psychological attitudes of
a given period. The genius must receive extraordinary
support and co-operation in intellectual circles. Linnaeus
wrote and flourished in a time when the educated public
had become fascinated with the word, the delight in sheer

[9] Charles E. Raven, *John Ray, Naturalist,* p. 452 ff.
[10] Robert Gunther, *Further Correspondence of John Ray,*
London, 1928, p. 260.

naming. The natural world, the world of the voyagers, was being described, oriented, classified—and suddenly, for no clearly apparent reason, the public wanted to participate in the process. It wanted to send packets of seeds to its hero, Carl Linnaeus. It wanted to hear him pronounce a new rolling Latin name to which, if one were lucky, one might find one's own attached.

He was the inspiration of young men like Peter Kalm who, as one of his American correspondents wrote to Linnaeus, "has undergone such great difficulties in travelling through a great part of this vast forest, and risked such dangers in his person from its savage inhabitants, that . . . his zeal cannot be sufficiently applauded."[11] Another enthusiast writing from the island of Madeira complains that "all the rare plants grow either on high cliffs near the sea or in horrible deep chasms."[12] Ships fail to make port; precious plants wither in the months of endless voyaging; there are other dangers. "Dr. John Mitchel," reports Linnaeus in 1746, "is returned from Virginia, where he has been closely occupied for six years in collecting plants; but he was plundered in his voyage home by Spanish pirates, to the great misfortune of Botany."[13] In London the Quaker merchant Peter Collinson confided prophetically to the master, "We are very fond of all branches of Natural History; they sell the best of any books in England."[14] In the great parks of English noblemen plants from around the world were beginning to grow, plants and even occasionally animals which had been collected in the gloom of the American forests and nursed homeward in the cabins of rough sea captains. It was at last the full if early morning of the scientific age. All over the world the night was passing and strange beautiful plants were

[11] Sir James Edward Smith, A Selection of the Correspondence of Linnaeus and Other Naturalists, London, 1821, Vol. 2, p. 458.
[12] Ibid., p. 561.
[13] Ibid., p. 399.
[14] Ibid., Vol. 1, pp. 18–19.

opening their flowers to the sun. In that time of unfolding beauty the purpose of science was still largely to name and marvel. In that art there was none to surpass Carolus Linnaeus.

In 1707, two years after the aged and infirm John Ray had died at Black Notley, Linnaeus was born in southern Sweden. It was a time of marked English influence in Sweden. Many young men of family journeyed to London, and English philosophy and science exerted great influence upon Swedish culture. Linnaeus, being in modest circumstances, took his medical degree in Holland, where he came in contact with the great Dutch scientist Hermann Boerhaave and launched the first edition of his best-known work, the *Systema Naturae,* in 1735. In 1736 he visited England and made a solid acquaintanceship in learned circles. From that time onward his prestige in English science was enormous—a genuine mass phenomenon. As his recent biographer Knut Hagberg remarks, "The greatest distinction an Englishman—whether amateur or academically qualified—could dream of at that time was to be mentioned in one of Linnaeus's works, and to that end they sent him innumerable suggestions for the alteration of the classification of species in *Systema Naturae.*"[15] That the personal charm of the man contributed to the regard in which he was held, there can be no doubt. When we consider, however, that his influence reached into the New World among men who had never seen him and, moreover, that this adulation persisted into his old age so that upon his death in 1778 he was borne to the tomb like a king, it is evident that he had become in some strange manner the symbol of science itself. Not least among the ironies of Linnaeus's career is the fact that he whose taxonomy had, before his death, come to stand for the sure fixity and eternal order of relation-

[15] *Carl Linnaeus,* London: Jonathan Cape, 1952, p. 159.

ships in the world of life should have entertained discreet doubts as to its reality.

Because Linnaeus became known to the English reader as a taxonomist, as the creator of a system of ordered relationships, much of the poetry of his nature—his Whitmanesque love of the incredible variety of life—has escaped attention. Few of his great heaps of manuscripts and only some of his letters have been translated. It was basically this poetic hunger of the mind to experience personally every leaf, flower, and bird that could be encompassed in a single life which explains his gigantic labors. He was the naming genius par excellence, a new Adam in the world's great garden, drunk with the utter wonder of creation. This is revealed in miscellaneous notes and jottings where, like a poet, he catalogues for the rich joy of the words. "American falcons, divers kinds of parrots, pheasants, peacocks, guinea fowl, American capercaillie, Indian hens, swans, many different kinds of ducks and geese, gulls and other web-footed birds, snipe, American crossbills, sparrows of divers kinds, turtle doves, and other doves together with various other species of birds, with whose cries the garden resounded."[16]

Similarly it is the poet brooding over time and destiny who writes this eulogy for the great botanists: "For even if knowledge of the true and original Tree of Life, which could have postponed the arrival of old age, is lost, the plants nevertheless remain and renew their flowers, and with gratitude enduring through the years they shall always exhale the sweet memory of your names, and make them more lasting than marble, so that they will outlive those of kings and heroes. For riches vanish, the most stately mansions fall into decay, the most prolific families die out sooner or later: the mightiest states and the most flourishing kingdoms may be overthrown: but the whole of nature must be obliterated before the genera of plants

[16] Cited from Hagberg, op. cit., p. 100.

disappear and he be forgotten who held the torch aloft in botany."[17]

"The plants remain and renew their flowers"—in those simple words is the nostalgia and melancholy of a man who, even at the height of his success, knew with preternatural insight that, as he himself wrote, "fate is always against great things." Perhaps he felt, in those lines written to a far-off captain bringing him seeds, a premonition of the future—his own lapse into senile dementia and the blurring of the sharply precise and ordered system of taxonomy which had been his vision when he wrote the *Systema Naturae*.

It was Linnaeus's fate to stand on the threshold of the modern world, in fact to spend the better part of his life constructing that threshold, that entrance, to new vistas he would never see. As we have seen, the same year that he went to Holland to complete his medical degree Linnaeus published the first edition of the *Systema Naturae*. At that time it was only a summary digest of the extensive treatise it was later to become. Coincident with his rise to scientific fame and fortune, he succeeded in later editions of the *Systema* and other works in imposing the now well-known system of binominal nomenclature upon the scientific public. The naming of plants and animals before Linnaeus had been confused, unsystematic, and verbose. This is not to say that Linnaeus had not been influenced by his forerunners. He knew the work of Ray who had sought to distinguish species from larger indefinite groups and who had seen fully the necessity of rules of nomenclature. But his was the fortunate psychological moment and he had his way. Others had used such ideas before him but never with such pertinacity or success with the public.

Animals and plants were denoted by two names. The first, generic, was such as to indicate a general group of creatures visibly related, such as all doglike forms, for ex-

[17] Hagberg, op. cit., p. 10.

ample. The second adjectival name denoted a restricted specific group, a species, as the wolf among canids—thus *Canis lupus*. He also recognized larger divisions such as classes and orders. As might be expected in any pioneering attempt, his botanical classification, based largely on the sexual parts, is not totally successful. Artificial systems of arrangement were in contrast to the "natural system" through comparative anatomy which had been sought by Ray.

It should be explained that an artificial system of classification is one in which a single organ—as in the case of the sexual parts of plants—is taken as a standard by which to classify a living group. The danger in such a system lies in the fact that some adaptive variation in the particular organ being used as the standard for classification may result in a particular plant's being wrongly classified. A natural system, on the other hand, takes account of all the organ systems and avoids arbitrary arrangements. Since the rise of evolution, taxonomical efforts in both zoology and botany have striven to determine affinity, that is, the relationship of any given group of plants or animals to a common ancestor. This, of course, was not clearly grasped by the first taxonomists.

Nevertheless, it must be said in justice to Linnaeus that as early as 1737 he had commented in a letter to Haller: "I have never spoken of that [his sexual system of botanical arrangement] as a natural method; on the contrary, in my *Systema* . . . I have said, 'No natural botanical system has as yet been constructed, though one or two may be more so than others; nor do I contend that this system is by any means natural. . . . Meanwhile, till that is discovered, artificial systems are indispensable.' And in the preface to my *Genera Plantarum*, sect. 9: 'I do not deny that a natural method is preferable, not only to my system, but to all that have been invented. . . .'"[18]

That pure naming and systems of classification got a

18 J. E. Smith, op. cit., Vol. 2, p. 232.

little out of hand and took on a one-sided emphasis which persisted well into the nineteenth century need not be attributed solely to Linnaeus. He rose to fame in a period of great wonder and eagerness to explore and catalogue the products of far lands. New words were pouring into European speech. The name was all and Linnaeus, with his gift for precise definition, with his exquisite taste for order, was providing the framework necessary to science before science could proceed to other things.

Further, if Linnaeus pursued the name, the name in its own way led to things no man could foresee. It was in his time, and owing greatly to his influence, that naturalists began to be apportioned posts on voyages of exploration. Cook's voyage on the *Endeavor* in 1768, to which Sir Joseph Banks contributed so heavily, is a case in point. It set the pattern which led eventually to Darwin's voyage on the *Beagle*. A letter from John Ellis, another of the English collectors, to Linnaeus in the year the *Endeavor* sailed speaks volumes on what Linnaeus had done for science. "No people ever went to sea better fitted for the purpose of Natural History," he writes, "nor more elegantly. They have got a fine library of Natural History; they have all sorts of machines for catching and preserving insects; all kinds of nets, trawls, drags, and hooks for coral fishing; they have even a curious contrivance of a telescope by which, put into the water, you can see the bottom to a great depth, where it is clear. They have many cases of bottles with ground stoppers, of several sizes, to preserve animals in spirits. They have the several sorts of salts to surround the seeds; and wax, both beeswax and that of Myrica; besides, there are many people whose sole business it is to attend them for this very purpose. They have two painters and draughtsmen, several volunteers who have a tolerable notion of Natural History; in short Solander[19] assured me this expedition would

---

[19] Solander was a student and protégé of Linnaeus.

cost Mr. Banks ten thousand pounds. *All this is owing to you and your writings.*"[20] (Italics mine. L.E.)

Linnaeus was not the uninspired drudge that men began to regard him after the naming mania had passed. For him, as for all Christians of his era, there had been one act of creation. The modern species were as fixed as on the sixth day of God's labor. But he glimpsed, more than his fellows, the wonderful pattern of creation, the unities as well as the diversities of form that existed in the mind of God. Inspired by him men would die of fevers in Africa, or perish under the knives of Abyssinian bandits, be pounded among the wreckage on coral reefs, or wander in the cloudland of unmapped mountains. It was for the name, his students thought, the beautiful order and arrangement of the living, the glimpse, as Linnaeus himself once expressed it, into the secret cabinet of God. But to the master himself in later years there must have come secretive glimpses of a wilder and more awe-inspiring wilderness than any through which the boldest of his students scrambled.

In erecting his classificatory system in such a manner as to cover the whole range of life he was unconsciously forecasting the possibility of its physical relationship. Curiously enough, though he had been quick to express the view that there were no new species, and this view in turn had been taken up and reiterated with great confidence in theological circles, there is clear evidence that he later came to doubt his own statements but by then was held fast in a doctrine at least partially of his own making.

V   *The Fixity of Species*

Scientists have long accused the church of holding back, by its preconceived beliefs, the progress of the evolutionary philosophy. The matter is actually more compli-

[20] J. E. Smith, op. cit., Vol. 1, p. 231.

cated than this. Science, in the establishment of species as a fixed point from which to examine the organic world, gave to the concept a precision and fixity which it did not originally possess. Categories of plant and animal life, as we have previously observed, did not, in earlier centuries, possess the clarity that they began to take on at the hands of Ray and Linnaeus. As one astute but anonymous writer observed over fifty years ago: "Until the scientific idea of 'species' acquired form and distinctness there could be no dogma of 'special' creation in the modern sense. This form and distinctness it did not possess until the naturalists of the seventeenth century began to substitute exactness of definition for the previous vague characterizations of the objects of nature."[21]

As scientific delight and enthusiasm over the naming of new species grew with the expanding world of the voyagers, the conviction of the stability and permanence of the living world increased. Strict definition, so necessary to scientifically accurate analysis, led in the end to the total crystallization of the idea of order. It is true, as we have observed earlier, that the notion of the fixed Scale of Being and the Christian conception of time, as well as the Biblical account of Creation, all tended to discount the evolutionary hypothesis, but, ironically enough, it was Linnaeus with his proclamation that species were absolutely fixed since the beginning who intensified the theological trend. His vast prestige in both scientific and cultivated circles made it assured that his remarks would be heeded. Henceforth the church would take the fixity of species for granted. Science, in its desire for classification and order, had found itself satisfactorily allied with a Christian dogma whose refinements it had contributed to produce.

Yet no sooner had Linnaeus proclaimed his dogma than, while working in the botanical gardens of his patron

21 "Lamarck, Darwin and Weismann," *The Living Age*, 1902, Vol. 235, p. 519.

Clifford at Hartecamp, he grew aware of the modern "sportiveness" of nature. He saw varieties appear spontaneously, he saw "abnormal" plants derived from normal ones. Like Ray before him, but perhaps more clearly, he was forced to distinguish between the true species of the Creator and the varietal confusion and disorder of the moment, which might be artificially manipulated by the skill of gardeners. In this way he attempted to cling to his original thesis. He had assumed that all species come from original pairs created on a small island which, in the beginning, had constituted the only dry land, the original Eden of the world.

As one pursues this subject through his multitudinous writings and the ever mounting editions of the *Systema Naturae* one can trace a growing uncertainty and doubt. He sees the possibility of new species arising through crossbreeding. He confesses that he dare not decide "whether all these species are the children of time, or whether the Creator from the very beginning of the world had restricted this course of development to a definite number of species."[22] He cautiously removes from later editions of the *Systema* the statement that no new species can arise. The fixity of species, the precise definition of the term, is no longer secure. "*Nullae species novae*" had been accepted by the world, but to the master taxonomist who had drawn the lines of relationship with geometric precision all was now wavering toward mutability and formlessness. Only the natural orders now seemed stable. What this actually might have meant to Linnaeus who had placed man along with monkeys in his order of the Primates, it is far too late to determine satisfactorily, but that he toyed with ideas of strange animal mixtures and permutations we know.

There is something awe-inspiringly symbolic about the stroke that destroyed his mental competence. It savors of the divine nemesis of which he had once written and long

[22] Cited by Hagberg, op. cit., p. 202.

feared. He who in youth had beheld the beautiful radiating lines of life gleam for an instant like a spider web on a dew-hung morning glimpsed a truth which, as is true of so much human knowledge, was also an illusion. The rainbow bridge to the city of the gods had vanished, leaving an old, memoryless man. The passionate cataloguer of the *Systema Naturae* no longer knew his book. Finally, and most dreadful fate of all, there passed away from that proud, world-famous man the knowledge even of his own name. There remained in his garden only the dried husk of an old plant among new flowers reaching for the sun.

Chapter II

The Time Voyagers

The geographical novelties of the earth . . .
are now exhausted. Our voyages of discovery
have become time voyages.

Wyndham Lewis

I   The Extraordinary Voyage

The eighteenth century can be characterized as essentially Linnaean in outlook, for we find a preoccupation with the naming of new species, a limited time scale, and an assumption of the fixity of animal life. It was necessary for man to discover one great principle, one supreme generalization capable of drawing a multitude of otherwise dispersed and meaningless facts together, before biology could cast any light upon human origins. Scientifically man's oldest written records told him nothing of himself. They showed him a picture limited, at best, to a few millennia in which he had warred and suffered, changed kings and customs, marked the face of the landscape with towns and chimneys, but, for all that, he had remained to himself unknown.

Until the one great effort at synthesis—evolution—was achieved, man saw himself essentially as having emerged from an unknown darkness and as passing similarly into an unknown future. It is no cause for surprise that, trapped as he was within the ominous and enigmatic present, man became addicted to a naïve supernaturalism, nor that he peopled the nature about him with baleful or beneficent beings which were often, in reality, the projected shadows of his hopes and fears. Man was a creature without history, and for a thinking being to be without history is to make him a fabricator of illusions. His restless and inquiring intellect will create its own universe and describe its forces, even if these are no more than the malignant personifications which loom behind the face of nature in the mythologies of simple folk.

The eighteenth, however, was a relatively sophisticated century. The voyagers, and the raconteurs and philosophers who fed upon their discoveries, had done their work. Where men of today feed upon an ever growing technology and delight in space fiction, people of the seventeenth and eighteenth centuries fed upon a literary diet of extraordinary voyages—real, utopian, and imaginary. In these the fixed arrangement of the *Scala Naturae* was often confused. One could read in the numerous "voyages" of man-animal crosses, of women mating with monkeys or with bears. It is an old folklore but one which always flourishes on far frontiers where men and animals meet on a level of equality and the distinctions between them remain blurred.[1]

Moreover, as the religious traditions of foreign nations became known, as other interpretations of how the earth came into being were encountered, it began to appear possible there might be other reasonable theories of earth history beside the orthodox one. The Linnaean century, in other words, was really a divided century. Scholars were following the Linnaean lead but there was an undercurrent of doubt about the fixity of species. We have seen

[1] Geoffroy Atkinson, *The Extraordinary Voyage in French Literature before 1700*, Columbia University Press, 1920, p. 58.

it emerge in the case of Linnaeus himself, but it became most openly expressed in that nation which had been the chief producer of the form of literature known as the extraordinary voyage. France, whose revolutionary stirrings had been fed by accounts of *le bon sauvage* and accounts of democratic societies of aborigines, real or imaginary, was approaching the time when the voyages of discovery in the present would no longer suffice the hungry intellectual. He would turn to another dimension; he would attempt the most dangerous intellectual journey of all—the voyage backward into time.

II Benoit de Maillet

Among the books widely read at the midpoint of the eighteenth century—a work which achieved popularity in English translation—was a volume entitled *Telliamed: Or Discourses Between an Indian Philosopher and a French Missionary on the Diminution of the Sea, the Formation of the Earth, the Origin of Men and Animals, etc.* Telliamed, the name of the Indian philosopher, is the name of M. de Maillet, the author, spelled backward. It was something of a literary tradition in France throughout the previous century to make use of a stock character, the tolerant oriental sage, whenever one wished to advance ideas of a heretical or socially critical cast.[2] True to the tradition De Maillet addresses his sage as follows:

"I confess to you, that notwithstanding the small Foundation I find in your system, I am charmed to hear you speak with as much Assurance of what you think passes in the vast Extent of the Universe, as if from infinite Ages, flying from Vortex to Vortex you had been an Eye-witness of what you relate concerning them. . . . I hope you will also deign to give me your Opinion of the Origin of Men and Animals, which in your System, are no doubt the Pro-

[2] Geoffroy Atkinson, *Les Relations de Voyages Die XVIIᵉ Siècle et L'évolution des Idées*, Paris, n.d., p. 82 ff.

ductions of Chance, a doctrine which neither my Religion nor my Reason permit me to believe."[3]

It will be observed that the author, as a good Christian, carefully disavows belief in the theories of his fictional sage. Nevertheless, he recounts them at length and with great enthusiasm. At the close of the book the sage, with convenient discretion, departs for his Far Eastern home. The interview itself is supposed to have taken place in Cairo, a meeting place of East and West, in 1715.

Telliamed, though known to English historians of science, has passed comparatively unnoticed. Of five histories of biology which I have consulted on my shelves only one mentions *Telliamed*—and then only in a passing sentence. This neglect seems to lie largely in the fact that De Maillet was a traveler and a government official, not a professional scientist, and that his work contains elements of the fantastic. The popularizer, however, was often a very significant figure in the earlier centuries of science. His work might plant the germ of new ideas in other, more systematic minds, and the actual diffusion of his books, as represented by numbers of editions and translations, can throw light upon the ideas which were beginning to intrigue the public imagination.

Benoit de Maillet (1656–1738), for all his anecdotes of mermen attracted by the female figureheads of vessels, and similar tales which sound as though gleaned from the taverns of the ports, is worthy of serious attention. He made one of the first fumbling attempts to link cosmic to biological evolution; he anticipated a greater age for the world; he recognized the true nature of fossils and suspected that some fossil plants "exist no more." He termed a fossil quarry "the most Antient Library in the World"; he had an idea of a planet evolving by natural forces. He even grasped dimly the principle of the successive deposition of strata. He is not, of course, the original author of all these separate ideas but he picked

[3] De Maillet, op. cit., English translation, London, 1750, p. 206.

them up, combined them in his own cosmological theory, spread them and made them widely accessible. Certainly the volume played a part in the stimulation of far greater minds.

It is not surprising that beds of fossil shells began to attract attention long before the remains of vertebrate animals. In the first place they are more easily recognizable for what they are, and they occur, often, in greater profusion. The bones of extinct land vertebrates, on the contrary, demanded a detailed knowledge of comparative anatomy before they could be recognized for what they were. The presence in various parts of Europe of marine shells far from the sea or uplifted in mountain ranges raised questions as to how they had been transported into regions remote from their natural habitat. Since the great age of the earth and the transformations which its surface had undergone remained unappreciated, the fossil shells were often regarded as "sports" of nature, the product of "plastic forces" and thus as never really having lived at all. Or naturalists linked the shells to the Noachian Deluge and assumed that they had been laid down during the time when the world had been overwhelmed by water.

There was little in the way of a clear recognition of the long stratigraphical history of the planet, nor of the fact that mountains were of different ages and themselves represented dynamic forces at work in the earth's crust. The vast waters which the Christian mythology demanded were often assumed to have emerged from the interior of the earth and to have re-entered it again. As Ray remarks in the picturesque language of the time, "Ye Earth itself, I mean this Terraqueous globe, is in a forced & preternaturall state, ye earth above ye water, wch is lighter than it, so that did not ye Scripture tell us so much, one might by reason collect, that the Water was sometime uppermost & covered all."[4]

[4] R. W. T. Gunther, op. cit., p. 260.

As science began to grope toward an understanding of the surface features of the planet it was handicapped by certain erroneous preconceptions which had arisen in past intellectual climates and which even atheistic free thinkers found it necessary to explain. Shells on mountaintops demanded higher seas, for water was movable and mountains were not. As a consequence, all the "theories of the Earth," as the new geological speculations were called, were much taken up with this problem. *Telliamed* is no exception. Though first published posthumously in Amsterdam in 1748, the book is actually, in its composition and flavor, a product of the early eighteenth century. The intricate dance of the planets, which forms a major part of De Maillet's attempt to explain the shrinking water content of the earth, is based upon Descartes's theory of vortices. This idea had a wide popularity in France beyond the close of the seventeenth century.[5]

De Maillet was fully cognizant that the incorruptible celestial heavens had disappeared under the telescopes of the astronomers; stars shift their positions, fade or flare up, comets appear and disappear. This globe and "this whole System which we see, this fine Order which we admire, are subject to Changes." This world of cosmic change which he observed in the heavens De Maillet extended to the earth and to life itself. He believed that at one time the earth was totally covered with water which had slowly been receding throughout the planet's history. This great sea, however, he carefully differentiates from the localized phenomenon of the Mosaic flood. The slow recession of the seas had laid bare more and more land and promoted the emergence of life from the waters. In working out his theory De Maillet fully recognized the advantages of examining geological exposures of either a natural or artificial character, such as those made possible in commercial excavations.

[5] Charles Singer, *A Short History of Science*, Oxford University Press, 1946, pp. 224–25.

Making allowance for the state of knowledge in his time De Maillet's system is essentially uniformitarian, that is, dependent upon the known and still operating forces of nature. He speaks of "the insensible Fabrication of our soils," of the wind and the rain acting upon rock to wear its substance away; he traces these substances downward to the sea where they will form in the course of time sedimentary rock containing fossils. "You must observe, sir," he remarks, "that Brooks, Rivers, Rivulets, and even the peculiar Substance of our Soils, are things accidental to our Globe, and posterior to the Appearance of our first Ground."

He challenged the conception that the life of the sea cannot be transformed into the life of the land and he maintained that this transformation had not alone taken place in the past but is continuing at the present time. It must, nevertheless, be remarked that De Maillet's evolutionism still savors of the purely generic variability of other seventeenth- and eighteenth-century writers, except that he has introduced a change of medium, from water to air. De Maillet, in other words, labors under the illusion that the life of the land is essentially duplicated in the sea—that plants and animals quite similar to the terrestrial ones can be observed there. Flying fish, for example, are on the way to becoming birds; there are mermen and women. The legendary has become entwined with the actual.

On the other hand, De Maillet was capable of surprisingly modern observations. He noted amphibious species such as otters and seals which he rightly observed are in some manner transitional half-world creatures moving from one medium to another. In one passage he is already debating the significance of a phenomenon which was still mystifying the naturalists of Darwin's time; namely, that "in small islands far from the Continent, which have but appeared a few Ages ago at most, and where it is manifest that never any Man had been, we find Shrubs, Herbs,

Roots and sometimes Animals. Now you must be forced
to own, either that these Productions owed their Origin
to the Sea, or to a new Creation, which is absurd."[6]

In effecting the transition from sea to land, De Maillet,
in one passage, and without elaboration, strongly hinted
at what really amounts to mutation and preservation
through natural selection. "If a hundred thousand have
perished in contracting the Habitude," he said, "yet if two
have acquired it, they are sufficient to give Birth to the
Species."[7] Strange primates excited De Maillet's attention: "A human Form met with in Madagascar, who walk
as we do, and who are deprived of the use of Voice";
orangs from the Dutch Indies, creatures who resembled
men so much that "it would have been rashness to pronounce that they were only brutes." People lately come
out of the sea, De Maillet contended, had no voice and
would only acquire one by degrees through a number of
generations. A Chinese author, he asserted warily, had
maintained that "men were only a species of Apes more
perfect than those which did not speak."

As for the origin of life itself, De Maillet found it
in organic atoms which reproduced their various kinds.
Such living atoms could be seen under the microscope.
"Whether," De Maillet observed, "these Seeds have existed always, or have been created in Time, each of these
Opinions is equally agreeable to my System." This notion
of living organic atoms, different from those making up
inorganic objects, was a derivative from the microscopic
observations of the day. Sperm, protozoa—the world of
the infinitely little heretofore unsuspected by man—were
now generating almost as much interest as the universe
in outer space revealed by the telescope. These organic
atoms would pass through many hands and descend
into the nineteenth century to become the pangenes of
Darwin.

[6] Op. cit., p. 218.
[7] Ibid., p. 225.

The total system proposed in *Telliamed* may be seen as uniformitarian in essence, mutable in its parts, and self-renewing. Planets acquire heavy water content when remote from the sun. As they move inward the water content dissipates, just as that of earth is now doing. Eventually the earth will be desiccated and itself become a sun, or escape, by fortune, to become part of another solar system. Finally, a burnt-out wreck, it will perhaps pass into the vortex of another sun, regain, on the confines of that system, its water content, and begin once more its eternal circling dance through space and time. Who knows, the author muses, how many times this event has already happened, or what traces of those former worlds lie buried beneath our feet?

Elated with the symmetry of his system De Maillet writes movingly, "What Comparison could we make between a Clock-maker, who had skill enough to make a clock so curiously, that by the Disorder which Time should produce in her Parts and Movements; there should be new Wheels and Springs formed out of the Pieces, which had been worn and broken; and another Artist of the same Profession, whose Work should every Day, every Hour, and Minute, require his attention to rectify its Errors and eternal Variations?"

III   The Comte de Buffon

We have now come, at the midpoint of the eighteenth century, into a world where several ideas are beginning to emerge without quite coalescing into an organized whole—the theory which will unite them is still to be manufactured. It is thus no longer possible to pursue a single line of scientific innovators. Instead, several contemporary streams of thought must be examined. Before exploring these channels in more detail, it may serve the purposes of orientation to list some of these ideas.

1. Theories of cosmic evolution, of suns and planets

emerging from gaseous nebulae in space, appeared almost simultaneously with the first intimations of organic change. The timeless Empyrean heaven was now seen to be, like the corrupt world itself, a place of endless change, of waxing and waning worlds. Although the fact waited upon geological demonstration, the new astronomy with its vast extent of space implied another order of time than man had heretofore known. For a little while the public would not grasp what the sky watchers had precipitated. It would have to be brought home to them by the resurrection of the past.

2. Already, as we have seen in the case of De Maillet, there were those who were beginning to sense that the fossils of the planet told, like the old coins of the collector, a story that stretched backward through buried centuries and millennia. Ray and his friends had pondered the problem nervously if devoutly in the seventeenth century. There were now whispers that some of that buried life was no longer present among the living. Still, no man gazing upon the world around him dared to say its antiquity might be of the order of even a million years. A figure of a hundred thousand would have been a rash and heretical statement, though one man, the Comte de Buffon, slightly exceeded that estimate.

3. The microscope, which, like the telescope, had been invented at the beginning of the seventeenth century, had opened a new world as fascinating in its way as the vistas of space. Men began to explore the reproductive cells and to puzzle over the developmental stages of the living organism. Did a new creature grow from a microscopic but true replica of its adult form, or did it develop by degrees from a less differentiated substance? C. F. Wolff in his *Theoria generationes* (1759) took the latter point of view though it was not immediately popular. One must note, however, that to accept *development,* an emergence *by degrees,* in the case of the single individual makes it possible to accept with greater equanimity the conception

that a species itself may have come into existence by some more extended process of phylogenetic change. Thus, indirectly, epigenesis, or the developmental theory of embryonic growth, fitted, analogically, the theory of evolution, just as the older preformationist doctrine— of the fully formed but microscopic homunculus—coincided more satisfactorily with the idea of special creation.

4. In France, mismanaged and drifting toward the storms of the Revolution, an enormous interest in man, his destiny, the nature of society, the struggle of the poor and downtrodden to exist stimulated the thinking of intellectuals upon nature. The first studies of human population in relation to food supply began to be made. Analogies were drawn with wild life. Later, at the end of the century, Thomas Malthus, the English clergyman, drew heavily upon these sources in the composition of his famous *Essay on the Principles of Population.* England, in the first phase of the Industrial Revolution and frightened by the excesses of the French monarchial overthrow, would take readily to the bleak expression of the human struggle as portrayed by Malthus. The doctrine of the survival of the fittest would lie ready to the hand of Darwin. The revolt against the church promoted the spread of philosophical Deism—the elevation of the second book of revelation, Nature, to a pre-eminence over the written book. What was read in the rocks and seen in the woods would thus come to take on an importance and authority it could never have possessed for the scholastic minds of the Middle Ages.

5. The treasures that had been named by Linnaeus were being observed in royal gardens and the hothouses of English noblemen. Variation was observable, artificial selection consciously practiced. Interest in the improvement of stock had diffused among the gentry. It was partly from this source that Buffon, and after him the later evolutionists, would draw ideas of change. But no one quite

dared to say steadily that change was endless—the fossils were still too firmly locked in the Paris limestones.

In the interaction of many minds, in the letters that flowed to and fro, in the flourishing scientific societies, it is often impossible to say with much surety where a given idea originated. If one searches diligently one may find an intriguing sentence or an ambiguous hint. Only recently some forgotten books which contributed to the development of evolutionary ideas have been brought to the attention of historians of science. Thomas Malthus, for example, had long been preceded by a little French work issued in England under the self-revelatory title of *A Philosophical Survey of the Animal Creation, Wherein the General Devastation and Carnage that reign among the different Classes of Animals are Considered in a New Point of View; and the Vast Increase of Life and Enjoyment Derived to the Whole from this Institution of Nature is Clearly Demonstrated*. The work is by John Brückner (1726–1804), and the English translation appeared in 1768.[8]

Similarly the French philosopher and scientist Pierre de Maupertuis (1698–1759) had fallen into an undeserved obscurity from which he has recently been rescued by Professor Bentley Glass of Johns Hopkins University.[9] In 1745 Maupertuis published a small anonymous book titled *Venus Physique* which contains some surprisingly modern embryological and genetic observations, including a theory of particulate inheritance long prior to Mendel. In his *Système de la Nature* (1751) he advanced the view that by repeated fortuitous deviations it might have been possible for the diversity of life which we see around us to have arisen from a single source. Buffon was enor-

[8] For an extended treatment of the early students of population see J. J. Spengler, *French Predecessors of Malthus*, Duke University Press, 1942.

[9] Bentley Glass, "Maupertuis and the Beginnings of Genetics," *Quarterly Review of Biology*, 1947, Vol. 22, pp. 196–209.

mously impressed by Maupertuis and the two men had
some influence upon each other.

Linnaeus, I have said, had one great rival in the public
affection; this was the Comte de Buffon (1707-88). In
1749 he published the first volume of his huge *Histoire
naturelle*, a set of studies of the living world destined to
have a wide circulation and to be translated into many
languages. It was gracefully, even entrancingly written,
and here and there the author managed, not too conspicu-
ously, to touch upon a number of forbidden topics.

The book was written to appeal to two sorts of readers:
those interested in the simple description of animals and
those intellectuals who might wish to think about what
they saw. We need not expect complete candor on the
part of a man writing a century before Darwin. Buffon
had doubts, hesitations, and fears. He wrote at times
cryptically and ironically. He brought forward an impressive array of facts suggesting evolutionary changes and
then arbitrarily denied what he had just been at such
pains to propose. It is not always possible to determine
when he was exercising an honest doubt of his own and
when he was playing a game. In any case he could not
leave this dangerous subject alone. It fascinated him as,
a century later, it was to fascinate Darwin. He had devised a theory of "degeneration." The word sounds odd
and a trifle morbid today, because we are in the habit of
thinking of life as "evolving," "progressing" from one thing
to another. Nevertheless, Buffon's "degeneration" is nothing more than a rough sketch of evolution. He implied
by this term simply change, a falling away from some
earlier type of animal into a new mold. Curiously enough,
as his work proceeded, Buffon managed, albeit in a somewhat scattered fashion, at least to mention *every significant ingredient which was to be incorporated into Darwin's great synthesis of 1859*. He did not, however, quite
manage to put these factors together. Specifically they
may be analyzed as follows:

1. Buffon observed a tendency for life to multiply faster than its food supply and thus to promote a struggle for existence on the part of living things. "Nature," he said, "turns upon two steady pivots, unlimited fecundity which she has given to all species; and those innumerable causes of destruction which reduce the product of this fecundity. . . ."[10]

2. He recognized that within a single species there were variations in form. In domestic plants and animals these variations were often heritable, so that by careful selection the stock could be improved and the direction of the improvement controlled. "There is," he wrote, "a strange variety in the appearance of individuals, and at the same time a constant resemblance in the whole species."[11] He recognized "our peaches, our apricots, our pears" to be "new productions with ancient names. . . . It was only by sowing and rearing an infinite number of vegetables of the same species, that some individuals were recognized to bear better and more succulent fruit than others. . . ."[12] Similarly he noted that in the case of the domestic hen and pigeon "a great number of races have been lately produced, all of which propagate their kinds." "In order to improve Nature," he commented in another volume, "we must advance by gradual steps."[13]

3. Buffon was impressed by the underlying similarity of structure among quite different animals, an observation which is a necessary prelude to tracing out ancestral relationships in the fossil past. "There exists," he said, "a primitive and general design, which may be traced to a great distance, and whose degradations are still slower than those of figure or other external relations. . . ."[14]

He philosophized warily that among the numerous families brought into existence by the Almighty "there are

10 *Buffon's Natural History*, London, 1812, Vol. 5, p. 88.
11 Ibid., pp. 128–29.
12 Ibid., Vol. 2, p. 346.
13 Ibid., Vol. 4, p. 102.
14 Ibid., pp. 160–61.

lesser families *conceived by Nature and produced by Time*."[15] Such remarks, woven into the web of orthodoxy, at times grow bolder, as when he suggested "that each family, as well in animals as in vegetables, comes from the same origin, and even that all animals are come from one species, which, in the succession of time, by improving and degenerating, has produced all the races of animals which now exist."[16] "Improvement and degeneration," he had earlier remarked, "are the same thing; for they both imply an alteration of original constitution." Though Buffon was quick to add something to satisfy the ecclesiastical authorities after such a remark, it is interesting to observe that in repeating all creatures have really been specially created, he says *"we ought to believe* that they were then *nearly* such as they appear at present."[17] It is obviously a most grudging concession.

4. Buffon foreshadowed in some degree the uniformitarianism of James Hutton at the end of the century. Like De Maillet he sought natural explanations for the formation of the earth and for geological events. After having listed the innumerable effects of rain, rivers, winds, and frost he remarked perceptively, "We do not pay any consideration that, though the time of our existence is very limited, nature proceeds in her regular course. We would condense into our momentary existence the transactions of ages past and to come, without reflecting that this instant of time, nay, even human life itself, is only a single fact in the history of the acts of the Almighty."[18]

Buffon anticipated the need of a greatly lengthened time scale in order to account for the stratification of the planet and the history of life upon it. "Nature's great workman," he said, "is time." By modern standards, of course, his estimates of the antiquity of the globe are very con-

15 Op. cit., p. 162. (Italics mine. L.E.)
16 Ibid., Vol. 5, pp. 184–85.
17 Ibid., p. 185. (Italics mine. L.E.)
18 Barr's *Buffon*, London, 1797, Vol. 2, p. 253.

stricted but in his own time they were unorthodox. He thought that it had taken some seventy-two thousand years for the globe to cool from an incandescent state sufficiently to allow for the appearance of life. He assumed that the heat of the globe was imperceptibly diminishing. Further, he calculated that roughly another seventy thousand years would elapse before the planet was so chilled as to be unable to sustain life on its surface.[19]

5. He accepted the fact that some of the animal life of the earth had become extinct. This he ascribed to the cooling of the earth which had eliminated the warmth-loving fauna of an earlier day. He thought that many existing species would, in time, perish for the same reasons. He recognized the bones of mammoth as being those of extinct elephants and foresaw the value of paleontology. "To know all the petrifactions of which there are no living representatives," he remarked, "would require long study and an exact comparison of the various species of petrified bodies, which have been found in the bowels of the earth. This science is still in its infancy."[20] By this means, however, man, through the use of comparative anatomy, might be enabled to "remount the different ages of nature." It will eventually be possible, Buffon thought, to place milestones "on the eternal route of time."

6. Buffon also recognized the value of an experimental approach to evolutionary problems. The relations between species, he contended, could never be unraveled without long continued and difficult breeding experiments. "At what distance from man," he hinted slyly, "shall we place the large apes, who resemble him so perfectly in conformation of body . . . ? Have not the feeble species been destroyed by the stronger, or by the tyranny of man . . . ?"[21] Although in some passages he was careful to maintain the distinctive qualities of man, that his

19 Op. cit., 1812, Vol. 2, p. 337.
20 Ibid., p. 250.
21 Ibid., Vol. 4, p. 218.

"animal body" had been infused with a divine spirit, he also remarked at a convenient point: "You unjustly compare, it may be said, an ape who is a native of the forests with the man who resides in polished society. To form a proper judgment between them, a savage man and an ape should be viewed together; for we have no just idea of man in a pure state of nature."[22] Buffon then gives a revolting picture of the savage Hottentot so frequently described by the eighteenth-century voyagers and ends by commenting: "There is as great a distance between man in a pure state of nature and a Hottentot, as there is between a Hottentot and us."[23]

There can be noted in these passages a tendency which will be seen to descend into the Darwinian era and to find at least faint expression in Darwin's own work. I refer to the preference for continuing the use of the morphology of the living as a key to descent rather than to wait upon paleontology. This inclination was enhanced because of the long use of the Scale of Being, which, of course, had always involved only living forms in a permanently linked relationship. Furthermore, since the fossil past was still little known and its length inadequately perceived, emphasis naturally continued to lie upon existing animals and their relationships. Thus even the pioneer evolutionists tended to see closer phylogenetic relationships in the present than actually existed between European man, Hottentot, and orang. In a few passages Buffon seems to be struggling to free himself from the living comparative ladder, from living "ancestral forms." At moments he glimpses the value of family trees and collateral lines of descent. Nevertheless, though he had a premonition that paleontology would prove valuable, he was not in a position to realize its scope or extent; thus his evolutionism was essentially trapped within the present.

[22] Barr's *Buffon*, London, 1807, Vol. 9, p. 136.
[23] Ibid., p. 137. Compare with Darwin's remark cited on p. 261.

7. Buffon was one of the first biologists to sense the significance of animal and plant distributions. He observed marked differences between the faunas of the New and Old World tropics. He also perceived that the northern, Holarctic region was more nearly similar in its fauna and most similar where Asia and North America adjoined each other. As we have remarked earlier there were seventeenth-century writers who had puzzled over these differences between the fauna of the New and Old Worlds. Buffon, however, answered the question in a truly modern fashion. He said of the New World species which differed from those of the Old Continent: "They . . . have remote relations, which seem to indicate something common in their formation, and lead us to causes of degeneration [i.e., evolution] more ancient, perhaps, than all others."[24] Thus Buffon had glimpsed that animals, instead of diffusing from the ark on Ararat, had, partially at least, originated in the areas where they were now to be found. They had, in other words, arisen by modification from ancestral forms previously inhabiting the same region.[25] Here we can observe the first premonitory formulation of the Law of Succession which was to be demonstrated paleontologically by Clift, Owen, Darwin, and others, later on in the nineteenth century.

8. Last, we may note that Buffon also had distinguished, though briefly and uncertainly, something of that world of eternal imperfection and change which, later on, was to fascinate Darwin. He had seen "doubtful species," "irregular productions," "anomalous existences." He had stared into the magic mirror of nature and, like the gods, had seen for a moment the cloud forms streaming past. Perhaps in the end he and his great contemporary rival Linnaeus had not seen too differently—though

---

[24] Op. cit., 1812, Vol. 4, pp. 47–48.
[25] See Theodore Gill, "The Principles of Zoogeography," *Proceedings of the Biological Society of Washington*, 1884, Vol. 2, pp. 1–39.

Buffon had seen farther and been bolder about what he saw.

The count died in 1788, ten years after Linnaeus, although both had been born in the same year. It was a good time to go. The next year his son was to perish with other aristocrats in the fury of the Terror, proudly and reproachfully saying as he waited on the scaffold, "Citizens, my name is Buffon." It was the end of an age. Buffon like Linnaeus had had a world reputation, had had his specimens passed graciously through warring fleets, had corresponded with Franklin, had been one of the leading figures in a great country at the height of its intellectual powers.

It is a great pity that his ideas were scattered and diffused throughout the vast body of his *Natural History* with its accounts of individual animals. Not only did this concealment make his interpretation difficult, but it lessened the impact of his evolutionary ideas. If he had been able to present his thesis in a single organized volume, it is possible that he himself might have argued his points more cogently and perhaps seen more fully the direction of his thought. For one important idea was still lacking: Buffon had never wrestled satisfactorily with the mechanism of change. He seemed, at times, quite conscious of the value of selection in breeding experiments, and this, with his full recognition of individual variation, implies something very close to Darwin's later theories. Actually, however, Buffon never seems to have been able to get from artificial to natural selection. Instead he suggests "climate" as a leading factor in "degeneration." However, almost everything necessary to originate a theory of natural selection existed in Buffon. It needed only to be brought together and removed from the protective ecclesiastical coloration which the exigencies of his time demanded.

IV   Erasmus Darwin and Lamarck

There has been considerable difference of opinion
among students of evolutionary thought upon the origin
of the views of Erasmus Darwin (1731-1802) and Jean
Lamarck (1744-1829). Some have contended that Lamarck was stimulated by Erasmus Darwin's work, which
was published prior to his own. Others claim both arrived
at their ideas independently. Still another view would derive both men's ideas, in essence at least, from Buffon.
This latter position is the most plausible. The contention
for complete originality of thought on the part of both
authors can be least sustained, for by the end of the
eighteenth century the *idea* of unlimited organic change
had been spread far and wide. It certainly was not a popular doctrine, but it had long been known in intellectual
circles, largely through the popularity of Buffon.

Increasing interest in scientific breeding had also intensified public interest in the alteration of animal and plant
forms. There were many who might not have been willing
to say that all life arose from a single organic corpuscle,
but who were vaguely and uncertainly aware that living
forms might vary within limits. If pressed to name those
limits with precision, they would have evinced discomfort. Lamarck and the earlier Darwin should be seen
simply as continuing and enhancing a little stream of
evolutionary thought which, beginning with ideas of
purely specific or generic change—alteration, in other
words, within narrow limits—was growing steadily bolder
in the range of its thinking.

Of the two men, Lamarck was the more complete and
systematic thinker. Erasmus Darwin's importance lies less
in his scientific achievement than in his relationship
to Charles Darwin and in his indirect influence upon
Charles. (He died seven years before Charles Darwin was
born.) Nevertheless, the priority of Erasmus over Lamarck is clear. His *Zoonomia* was published in 1794, but

there is correspondence extant which indicates that its author was at work upon it as early as 1771.[26] He had as insatiable a passion for the odd facts of natural history as his grandson. Any serious reading of the footnotes attached to his long poems, *The Temple of Nature* (1803) and *The Botanic Garden* (1791), will yield them in great quantities. The elder Darwin was a keen observer of adaptations of all kinds, including protective coloration. Like his grandson he was a keen student of seed dissemination. He noted the intricate web of ecological relationships between different forms of life; he considered the possible survival of living fossils in the depths of the sea. He had some knowledge of rudimentary structures and the "wounds of evolution." He was aware that life, because of its ever changing aspect, is not always perfectly adjusted to its surrounding environment. He is the undoubted source from which his grandson drew the idea of sexual selection, and in Canto IV of *The Temple of Nature* he sketched a ghastly picture of the struggle for existence. He estimated the antiquity of the earth in terms of "millions of ages." In spite of the diversity of life he recognized through "a certain similitude on the features of nature . . . that *the whole is one family of one parent.*"[27] Though similar quotations expressing Erasmus Darwin's grasp of comparative morphology and stores of odd learning could be multiplied from his works, we may come directly to the point. He himself remarks in *The Botanic Garden:* "As all the families both of plants and animals appear in a state of perpetual improvement or degeneracy,[28] it becomes a subject of importance to detect the causes of these mutations."

What, then, is Erasmus Darwin's explanation of the

[26] Bashford Dean, "Two Letters of Dr. Darwin: the Early Date of His Evolutional Writings," *Science*, 1906, n.s. Vol. 23, pp. 986–87.

[27] Preface to the *Zoonomia*.

[28] Compare with Buffon's phraseology cited on p. 39.

mechanics of evolution? It lies essentially in "the power
of acquiring new parts, attended with new propensities,
directed by irritations, sensations, volitions, and associations; and thus possessing the faculty of continuing to improve by its own inherent activity, and of delivering down
those improvements by generation to its posterity, world
without end!"[29] The key here lies in the words "irritations," "sensations," and "volitions." Erasmus Darwin, in
partial but not complete contrast to his grandson, believed in the inheritance of acquired characteristics. Lamarck's philosophy was markedly similar.

Jean Baptiste Lamarck was intimately acquainted in
his earlier years with Buffon, but it was not until his late
fifties, in 1802, that he expressed himself as favoring
the evolutionary hypothesis. Like the other eighteenth-
century evolutionists, he had to recognize the necessity
of a greatly lengthened antiquity for the world; he speaks
so clearly of the dynamic balance of populations and the
struggle for life that it would not be surprising if he had
read the *Système de Animal* of his countryman Brückner. Like De Maillet and Buffon, and with some of the
same wariness as the latter, he hints in the *Philosophie
Zoologique* (1809) at an anthropoid origin for man. "It
could easily be shown that his special characters are all
due to long-standing changes in his activities and in the
habits which he has adopted. . . ." Noting that man tires
rapidly in an erect posture he suggests that further investigation would reveal in him "an origin analogous to
that of the other animals."

Lamarck believed in a constant, spontaneous generation, so far as low forms of life were concerned, and he
assumed a living scale of life which, in some respects, is
reminiscent of the old *Scala Naturae*, although he broke
partially away from the simple ladder arrangement. He
believed in alteration rather than extinction. Any miss-

[29] *Zoonomia*, Vol. 1, p. 572.

ing taxonomical links simply remained to be discovered. Thus, in so far as he studied man, he would have derived him from a living primate—probably the ever serviceable orang. As the world alters, as geographic and climatic areas change, new influences are brought to bear upon plant and animal life. In the course of long ages transformations in this life occur. These alterations are the product of use, of the *effort* which the animal makes to employ those parts which are most serviceable to it under the new conditions. As time passes related species may differentiate further and further from each other and these changes will be retained through heredity. Physiological need will promote the formation of new organs or alteration of old ones. Disuse, on the contrary, will promote their loss.

It should now be clear that Erasmus Darwin and Lamarck held rather similar theories as to the nature of the evolutionary process. Lamarck's views were sparsely represented in English literature until Lyell introduced him to the British public in 1830. The work of the elder Darwin, on the contrary, had earlier passed into French and German translations. It is this fact which has led to some suggestion that Lamarck drew his ideas from Erasmus Darwin. Charles Darwin seems to have been of this opinion, for he remarked to Thomas Huxley about the time the *Origin of Species* was published that "the history of error is quite unimportant, but it is curious to observe how exactly and accurately my grandfather gives Lamarck's theory."[30] This passage, unfortunately, reveals an attitude toward both Lamarck and his grandfather—both dismissed as "part of the history of error"—which, as we shall demonstrate later, was persistent on the part of Darwin.

There is, it may also be observed, no evidence that Lamarck plagiarized Erasmus Darwin. The long-continued and widespread belief in the inheritance of acquired

[30] MLD, Vol. 1, p. 125.

characters historically documented by Professor Zirkle of
the University of Pennsylvania makes it very likely, as we
have earlier remarked, that both men were simply working in the same climate of ideas. Lamarck's name has by
historical chance become so heavily associated with the
doctrine of acquired characteristics that it is often assumed he invented it. Yet after an exhaustive treatment
of the subject, running back through several centuries,
Zirkle remarks: "It is interesting for us to note how many
of Lamarck's contemporaries stated that such characters
were inherited and to note how completely these statements have been overlooked by modern biologists."[31]
Zirkle goes on to establish the presence of the idea in
medical, biological, and travel books. It was the commonly
accepted doctrine of the time and, indeed, the first apt to
be explored in the advance of biology. What Erasmus
Darwin and Lamarck both did was to apply a very ancient hypothesis, one might almost say a folk-belief, to
the explanation of continuing organic change and modification. Lamarck, whose work is the most thoroughgoing,
saw clearly the cumulative advantages of such change in
the creation of the higher organisms. Right or wrong,
there was nothing startlingly new about this—all the originality lay in its application to evolution.

As Professor Gillispie has pointed out, Lamarck was
a late eighteenth-century Deist. Evolution, in his eyes,
"was the accomplishment of an immanent purpose to perfect the creation."[32] Thus in his thought the old fixed ladder of being had been transformed into an "escalator."
Life, in simple forms, is constantly emerging, and, through
its own inner perfecting principle or drive, it begins to
achieve complexity and to ascend toward higher levels.

[31] Conway Zirkle, "The Early History of the Idea of Acquired
Characters and of Pangenesis," *Proceedings of the American Philosophical Society*, 1946, n.s. Vol. 35, p. 111.
[32] Charles C. Gillispie, "The Formation of Lamarck's Evolutionary Theory," *Archives Internationales d'Histoire des Science*, 1957,
Vol. 9, pp. 323–38.

In this way Lamarck accounted for the presence of simple forms of life at the present day. Except for the presence of the physical environment Lamarck seems to have felt that nature would arrange itself in a perfect ascending scale comparable to the old theologically conceived ladder of existence.

The physical environment, however, shifts with time and circumstance. This brings about changes in the life needs of the organism. The mutability of needs, argued Lamarck, brings about changes in behavior which in turn effect alterations of habit, which then by slow degrees involve the bodily structure of the organism. Because of this constant environmental adjustment the animal is diverted from achieving the pure, abstract perfection represented by the Scale of Being concept, and is forced into branching pathways of adjustment. The orang driven into the wilderness does not become man though he possesses this potentiality.

Certain conflicts in Lamarck's system were never totally resolved but need not concern us here. Both he and Erasmus Darwin placed, as we have seen, an emphasis upon volition, the "striving" of the organism for survival and adjustment. Nevertheless, it should be noted that with the rise of the romantic element in the literature of the early nineteenth century both Lamarck and Erasmus Darwin came to be somewhat misinterpreted—a misinterpretation which continues into the present.[33] Lamarck, in particular, has suffered from a certain obscurity of style and, in addition, from poor translation. It has been assumed that by constant, *conscious* wishing an organism secured the organ or bodily modification it desired. Actually neither of these early evolutionists meant this, but rather that the *unconscious* striving of the animal to adjust to the demands of the environment would promote

[33] G. R. Potter, *The Idea of Evolution in the English Poets from 1744 to 1832*, unpublished Ph.D. thesis, Harvard University, 1922, pp. 211–13.

physical modification and change through the use or disuse of organs. Professor Potter points out that the idea
of conscious willing fitted the romantic transcendentalist
doctrines of men like Emerson whose lines

> And striving to be man the worm
> Mounts through all the spires of form

are representative of the notion that the life force may
consciously determine its own destiny. It would appear
that Charles Darwin himself was somewhat influenced by
these confused interpretations of Lamarck.

V Early Glimpses of Ecological Adaptation

If, now, in retrospect, we cast an eye backward we
can make certain general observations. The struggle for
existence was known throughout the century and it is
well-nigh futile to attempt to assign this obvious and self-
evident fact to a definite individual. It was, however, regarded essentially as a pruning device keeping species
in dynamic balance and ensuring the survival of good
healthy stock. To quote a few examples, Mathew Hale
spoke of it in 1677, Rousseau was aware of it in 1755,
Lamarck remarked that "We know . . . it is the stronger
and the better equipped that eat the weaker, and that
the larger species devour the smaller."[34]

Since Lamarck's theory did not demand natural selection as its primary mechanism, however, he treated the
subject as it was, namely, a generally accepted fact of
natural history, but without the significance attached to
it by biologists today. It was part of the natural evil of a
world organized on the Scale of Being principle. Part
of that philosophy included the assumption that God
created up to the limit of His capacity which was infinite.
Only by the "war of nature" could so many unlike forms
of different habits and mutually contradictory natures ex-

[34] *Zoological Philosophy*, Eng. translation, Macmillan, 1914, p. 54.

ist. The very elements contended, and man, who at first glance seemed to have escaped this fate, struggled endlessly with his own kind. It is not necessary to have recourse to Malthus for this observation; it is omnipresent in the thought of the century.[35] Charles Darwin's later contribution lay, not in the application of the struggle for existence to the entire animal creation, but rather in his discovery that biological variation combined with the pruning hook of selective struggle might be the key to endless organic divergence.

If we examine the general status of evolution itself throughout the century, and the leading theological preconceptions which made up the intellectual climate of the times, it becomes easier to see why a society which was already practicing the selective breeding of plants and animals failed so signally, and for so long, to arrive at the heart of the Darwinian thesis. We have noted that the Scale of Nature doctrine implied fixity and instantaneous creation, even though there is a clear recognition of grades of organic complexity leading up to man and even beyond him. Nevertheless, naturalists, in actual practice, since the seventeenth century, had believed species capable of variation. It was assumed, however, without genuine proof, that these variations were restricted within certain limits. There was a type form of the species around which varieties might oscillate, but biological plasticity was circumscribed.[36] This notion accounted for the breeding successes of the gardener or pigeon fancier without raising serious issues which, in reality, could scarcely be faced until the fact of extinction and great geological

[35] See A. O. Lovejoy, "Optimism and Romanticism," *Proceedings of the Modern Language Association*, 1927, Vol. 42, pp. 930–33. An extensive discussion of this subject can be found in Conway Zirkle's "Natural Selection before the Origin of Species," *Proceedings of the American Philosophical Society*, 1941, Vol. 84, pp. 71–123.

[36] H. A. Nicholson, *Natural History: Its Rise and Progress in Britain*, London, 1886, p. 243.

age came to be accepted. The complex, interrelated web of life was appreciated long before Darwin, but the concentration on final ends, the theological argument for design in an immediate sense, was the really overpowering religious motif of the times. As a consequence of these factors natural selection, while recognized, was recognized only in a most limited sense.

One may venture that Lamarck, in particular, failed to grasp the possible significance of chance variation because he was unsure of extinction on any major scale. If he had been in a position to abandon the Scale of Nature concept sufficiently to accept the dying out of numerous species, Lamarck might have been led at least to consider some fortuitous element at work in life. Lacking this detailed knowledge of the past, but observant of change in the invertebrates he studied, he came to the conclusion that the lost species were not dead but only changed into living species. Thus his conception of organic development appeared so directively controlled that chance and extinction could play, at best, but little part in it.

The grip of the design argument was still strong. In fact, both Lamarck and Erasmus Darwin may be said to have been engaged in altering the divine fixed plan of the Chain of Being, the universal hierarchy, into what Bell has called a "composite of particular wills," a kind of open competitive society.[37] It is unlikely that the two men consciously realized this fact but it was curiously reflective of what was occurring in the social world about them.

The reaction, in England, to the French Revolution was destined to sweep Erasmus Darwin's ideas out of fashion, reinstitute religious orthodoxy, and lead to the derogation of Lamarck as a "French atheist" whose ideas were "morally reprehensible." In the end a conspiracy of

[37] Charles G. Bell, "Mechanistic Replacement of Purpose in Biology," *Philosophy of Science*, 1948, Vol. 15, p. 47.

silence surrounded his work.[38] As has happened many times before in the history of thought, an idea had become the victim of social events and its re-emergence was to be delayed accordingly.

Looking back, however, we can still observe a reasonably steady march toward a satisfactory evolutionary mechanism. Buffon had assumed direct organic change in response to climatic and similar environmental factors which was then inherited. Lamarck had denied that environment works direct changes. Instead, he contended it could do so only through altering the habits of the animal which, as we have seen, might then induce inheritable bodily changes. The views of Erasmus Darwin were similar.

In thus establishing the persistent adjustment of the animal to its environment both Lamarck and the elder Darwin were among the first to recognize the twofold ecological relationship between the organism and its environment—that when the one was altered the living creature persistently responded. Moreover, Lamarck appears to have been the first to grasp the importance of the concept of use and disuse in their effect upon individual organs. Later on this was to be appropriated by Charles Darwin and fitted into his own evolutionary system.

As one sees Lamarck fumbling over the problem of extinction, one realizes that the single key to the past contained in the comparative morphology of the living was insufficient to prove the reality of evolution. The time voyagers had to have vast eons in which to travel and they had, like the earlier voyagers, to bring back the visible spoil of strange coasts to convince their unwilling contemporaries. It is to the three great navigators who solved the secrets of that unknown ocean to whom we will now turn.

[38] Norton Garfinkle, "Science and Religion in England 1790–1800," *Journal of the History of Ideas*, 1955, Vol. 16, pp. 387–88. Also Gillispie, op. cit., 1957.

Chapter III

The Pirate Chart

The locks are rusty; the keys no longer fit, in
the mould of time they have become useless.

Max

I   Time and Organic Change

From the viewpoint of the historian of evolution the early
decades of the nineteenth century are difficult to organ-
ize. Seemingly unrelated events, diverse scientific discoveries, industrial trends, and religious outlook can all, in
historical perspective, be observed to revolve in a moment of seeming heterogeneity before they crystallize into
a new pattern with Darwinism at the center. It is like
looking into a chemical retort which is about to produce
some rare and many-sided crystal. One moment everything is in solution; there is a potentiality, no more—and
yet in the next instant a shape has appeared out of nowhere. It is difficult, as we have seen, to assess how much
the men of this period influenced each other, for they
were active contemporaries and, in many instances, were
putting forth their views, either verbally or in letters, long
before these were formally published. There is inevitable,
therefore, a certain arbitrary quality in the assignment of

honors though the leading books and thinkers are well enough known.

The thinkers of the eighteenth century were devoted to their correspondence. Much of what today goes quickly into scientific journals passed back and forth in letters and often did not formally emerge for decades. More than one original idea remained in manuscript until it was finally expressed by someone else. Since letters are less often preserved than published documents, a period such as we are discussing has more than its share of tantalizing minor mysteries even though, for the purposes of formal history, they are pretty generally ignored. Having taken note of our historic limitations I now intend in the pages that follow to examine the question of time in the pre-Darwinian era. No theory of evolution can exist without an allotment of time in generous quantities. Yet it is just this factor which was denied to the questing scientist by the then current Christian cosmology. A change as vast as that existing between the Ptolemaic and Copernican systems of the heavens had to be effected in Western thinking upon the subject of time before one could even contemplate the possibility of extensive organic change; the one idea is an absolute prerequisite to the other. Let us see, therefore, how it was that the change was brought about. We will observe in the process that it involved two demonstrations: first, a proof that the world is old and, second, but without reference as yet to evolution, a proof that there has been a succession of life forms throughout the past history of the planet.

II Pagan and Christian Time

Ever since man ceased to run like an uncaring beast through the sunlight of his living hours, he has dreamed of eluding time's shadow. He has sought fountains of youth in far lands, believed in some lost golden age before death came among men, some time of the ancestors when things were otherwise. But always the leaf has fallen from the tree, and man has seen his mortal generations descend into the dark. Three views, three insights may be said, therefore, to have characterized the human conception of time until the rise of stratigraphical geology. The first of these we may call primitive. It is the frail knowledge of the wandering hunter who drifts with the seasons but who knows no calendar and who leaves no record but his arrows in the earth. Among these men grayheaded elders may speak of many grasses or, perchance, of innumerable leaf falls, and then, speechless, they can only make a gesture and refer to the "dream time" or the "old ones." It is obvious that on this level of society man feels the touch of time emotionally but he cannot implement his feelings nor grasp the full significance of that vast waste across which today the astronomer and the geologist peer. Primitive man is confined to his own generation and some verbal memories of his father's time. The earth and the stars may be older but no one knows what that means and perhaps the question does not arise. Whether or not it does may depend on the creation myths of a given society.

In the area of the East, however, in the region of the first great cultures which rose and fell many times in the early millennia of civilized consciousness, a different conception arose: notions of vast cycles and undulations in a time stream where things became and passed, perhaps only to come again. In these philosophies one catches the weariness of old civilizations surrounded by the broken monuments of their predecessors and looking with cynical eyes upon the doings of the gods themselves. Marcus Aurelius, one of the last great voices out of the Greco-Roman past, discourses as follows:

"The periodic movements of the universe are the same, up and down from age to age. And either the universal intelligence puts itself in motion for every separate effect, and if this is so, be thou content with that which is the result of its activity; or it puts itself in motion once, and everything comes by way of sequence in a manner; or indivisible elements are the origin of all things.—In a word, if there is a god, all is well; and if chance rules, do not thou also be governed by it.

"Soon will the earth cover us all: then the earth, too, will change, and the things also which result from change will continue to change for ever, and these again for ever. For if a man reflects on the changes and transformations which follow one another like wave after wave and their rapidity, he will despise everything which is perishable."

With the rise of Christianity a sense of time totally unlike that entertained by the historically shallow primitive or the endless cycles over which Greco-Roman thought had brooded in antiquity took possession of the European mind. The Christian saw time, worldly time, as essentially the divine medium in which a great play—the drama of the human Fall and Redemption—was being played out upon the stage of the world. This drama was unique and not repetitious. Older pagan notions of eternal recurrent cycles were blasphemous to the Christian mind. "God forbid," protested St. Augustine, "that we should believe this. For Christ died once for our sins, and, rising again dies no more." Thus in the words of Professor Lynn White "the axiom of the uniqueness of the Incarnation required a belief that history is a straight line sequence guided by God. . . . No more radical revolution has ever taken place in the world outlook of a large area."[1]

Since man's historical knowledge of himself was incomplete, this great drama was estimated as consuming but a few trifling millennia terminated by a day of judgment. Worldly time, in other words, was of short duration. After the last judgment worldly time, historical time, would vanish, leaving that eternity which is the true home of God and the righteous in spirit. This interpretation of

[1] Lynn White, "Christian Myth and Christian History," *Journal of the History of Ideas*, 1942, Vol. 3, p. 147.

time and human destiny has gripped the imagination of the Western World for close to two thousand years. It was a philosophy which could only be sustained in its original version within a Ptolemaic cosmogony and in total ignorance of the facts of geology.

Christian scholars generally assumed for the age of the world a figure of around six thousand years. James Ussher, Archbishop of Armagh, placed the beginning at 4004 B.C., but, although his date attained particular acceptance after 1650, like figures had been current and had achieved widespread popularity long before Ussher's estimate. These dates were generally worked out on the basis of calculations involving the ages of the post-Adamite generations as recorded in the Bible.[2] The judgment day, ending earthly time, was assumed to be not far distant. Some, in fact, impelled by the symmetry of the "great play," contended that the advent of Christ occupied the precise center of earthly time and that the day of judgment would come as many years after the death of Christ as there had been years before His birth. Others calculated an even shorter duration, so that the more fanatical sects were constantly proclaiming that the hour was at hand and seeking portents and signs to prove their case. Occasionally, even today, such prophecies continue to be heard. Perhaps no other people have ever lived in such a curiously disparate time scheme as the Christian, whose material world was ephemeral, yet whose spiritual world, by contrast, was compounded of a kind of timeless eternal, beyond blemish and change.

The rise of the new science was beginning as early as the seventeenth century to erode the foundations of this Christian *mythos* and the several evolutionary debates of the nineteenth century represent only successive steps

[2] Paul Kocher in his *Science and Religion in Elizabethan England*, San Marino, California, 1953, p. 152, points out, however, that the orthodox were sometimes harried by atheistical or doubting mathematicians who, in the words of Thomas Nashe, "will proove men before Adam."

in its hastening decline. Although we may recognize the frailties of Christian dogma and deplore the unconscionable persecution of thought which is one of the less appetizing aspects of medieval history, we must also observe that in one of those strange permutations of which history yields occasional rare examples, it is the Christian world which finally gave birth in a clear articulate fashion to the experimental method of science itself. Many things undoubtedly went into that amalgam: Greek logic and philosophy, the experimental methods of craftsmen in the arts as opposed to the aristocratic thinker—all these things have been debated. But perhaps the most curious element of them all is the factor dwelt upon by Whitehead—*the sheer act of faith that the universe possessed order and could be interpreted by rational minds.*[3] For, as Whitehead rightly observes,[4] the philosophy of experimental science was not impressive. It began its discoveries and made use of its method in the faith, not the knowledge, that it was dealing with a rational universe controlled by a Creator who did not act upon whim nor interfere with the forces He had set in operation. The experimental method succeeded beyond men's wildest dreams but the faith that brought it into being owes something to the Christian conception of the nature of God.[5] It is surely one of the curious paradoxes of history that science, which professionally has little to do with faith, owes its origins to an act of faith that the universe can be rationally interpreted, and that science today is sustained by that assumption.

By the seventeenth century hints of geological antiquity no longer completely escaped the attention of devout but attentive thinkers. We can catch the glimmer of this dawning age of science in the remarks of Ray as he stood

[3] A. N. Whitehead, *Science and the Modern World,* Mentor Book ed., 1948, pp. 4–15.
[4] Ibid., p. 17.
[5] Ibid., p. 14.

at Bruges in 1663 marveling over a buried forest which had lain on the sea bottom and then become exposed on dry land once more. He saw "that of old time the bottom of the sea lay deep and that hundred foot thickness of earth arose from the sediments of those great rivers which there emptied themselves into the sea." It is a strange thing, he marveled, "considering the novity of the world, the age whereof, according to the usual account, is not yet 5600 years."[6]

If buried forests trouble him, so do mountains. They are figuratively duplicated in his mind with, as in the words of a Christian poet, all their

> cliffs of fall
> Frightful no man fathomed.

Since the world has changed but little in the time of recorded history and "if the mountains were not from the beginning, either the world is a great deal older than is imagined, there being an incredible space of time required to work such changes . . . or, in the primitive times, the creation of the earth suffered far more concussions and mutations in its superficial part than afterwards."[7]

A correspondent raises the same problem. In 1691 Mr. Edward Lhwyd wrote to him about the fall of a huge stone from a mountain in Wales:

"I gather that all the other vast Stones that lie in our mountainous Valleys have by such accidents as this fallen down: Unless perhaps we may do better to refer the greatest Part of them to the universal Deluge. For considering there are some thousands of them in these two valleys . . . whereof there are but two or three that have fallen in the Memory of any Man now living; in the ordinary Course of Nature we shall be compelled to allow the rest

---

[6] Charles E. Raven, *John Ray, Naturalist*, cited p. 421.
[7] Ibid., p. 425.

many thousands of years more than the Age of the World."[8]

Timidly Ray speculated as to whether certain shells might be those of creatures totally extinct, "a supposition which philosophers hitherto have been unwilling to admit."[9] But the cliff of fall yawns there before him. He cannot resist peering over: "Yet on the other side there follows such a train of consequences as seem to shock the Scripture—history of the novity of the world; at least, they overthrow the opinion generally received, and not without good reason, among Divines and Philosophers that since the first creation there have been no species of animals or vegetables lost, no new ones produced" (1695).[10] To what new world—vaster, more awe-inspiringly timeworn—these speculations were to lead, we have already begun to perceive as, on the threshold of the nineteenth century, we leave Lamarck fumbling uncertainly with the question of time and fossils—two parts of an unsolved puzzle.

III   The Chart

We have seen that as early as the middle of the seventeenth century Ray had concluded that "either the world is a great deal older than is imagined" or that at the time of creation the earth "suffered far more concussions and mutations in its superficial part than afterwards." Ray's insight here was almost preternaturally acute. In one small sentence he had unknowingly forecast the two lines of thinking which the geologist was destined to pursue throughout the next century and a half.

Three men it now appears—and all alive and active in that memorable last decade of the Enlightenment—pos-

[8] W. Derham, *Philosophical Letters Between the Late Learned Mr. Ray and Several of His Ingenius Correspondents, Natives and Foreigners*, London, 1718, p. 256.

[9] Charles E. Raven, *John Ray, Naturalist*, cited p. 425.

[10] Ibid., p. 437.

sessed essential fragments of the secret of the earth's past, but each was handicapped. They were like treasure hunters into whose separate hands had come pieces of a pirate's map. One, a great brooding mind that alone might have put the chart together, was old and died two years after his last volume was published; one wandered the roads of England for a lifetime showing his map generously in taverns and speaking of it so simply and practically that no one imagined he had part of the secret of time. The third, a high official and a darling of the greatest court in Europe, possessed the strangest part of the chart and published an eloquent description of it, but if he saw its purport and whither it led, he was bound by the ethics of his world, and unknowingly or willfully read into it a false latitude and longitude on a coast that never was. James Hutton (1726–97), William Smith (1769–1839), and the Baron Cuvier (1769–1832)—together they possessed the secret of the past but they never sat down in the same tavern to put the chart together. Only James Hutton brooding over a little Scottish brook that carried sediment down to the sea felt the weight of the solid continent slide uneasily beneath his feet and cities and empires flow away as insubstantially as a summer cloud.

IV   The Rise of Catastrophism

If there is one mind that deserves to rank between the great astronomical geniuses of the seventeenth century and Charles Darwin in the nineteenth, it is James Hutton. Though he is spoken of in histories of science as the founder of historical geology, the public has never known his name as it knows that of Newton and Darwin. He discovered an intangible thing against which the human mind had long armored itself. He discovered, in other words, time—time boundless and without end, the time of the ancient Easterners—but in this case demonstrated by the very stones of the world, by the dust and the clay over which the devout passed to their places of worship. And James Hutton reaped the rewards of that discovery—animus and charges of heresy—or, even more bitter, silence and disdain. If it had not been for his devoted friend and follower John Playfair, he might have suffered the fate of Mendel half a century later and been totally, if temporarily, forgotten. Even as it is, one cannot help feeling that this sad, long face which gazes remotely out of the single portrait that has come down to us already has weighed human fame against the forces that waste continents into oblivion and turned away from man to some nobler inner source of serenity. It is the face of one who has looked so far that man has ceased to interest him, save as one might turn to glance at a strange bird on a pleasant morning stroll.

Up to this point we have been primarily occupied with those who had been investigating the living world and the possible signs of animal transformation and gradation which could be observed there. Before Hutton's contribution can be properly assayed, however, it will be necessary to grasp what geological theory of the earth was held in Hutton's time. As one might have been led to suspect, it represented a compromise between the Biblical account of creation and the slowly growing observations of science. By the end of the eighteenth century catastrophism, as it came to be called, was the orthodox and accepted view of geology upon the past history of the earth.

This catastrophic or cataclysmic geology has two versions, one of which succeeded the other, but both, because of a slowly increasing public awareness of fossils, were forced to take some account of stratigraphy and thus of time. The name of Abraham Werner, a German geologist, is associated with the first version and that of Georges Cuvier, the French paleontologist, with the second. In Hutton's day it was the theories of Werner to which he found himself opposed. This "Neptunist" hypothesis accounted for the stratification of the earth's crust by the assumption that all the layers of rock had been precipitated out of a turbid universal sea which had once covered the entire planet. The primitive azoic rocks had been the first to be laid down, but had been shortly followed by the deposition of other materials containing fossils indicating a successive creation of forms of life. As the waters receded (where, no one was able satisfactorily to explain), advanced forms of mammalian life appeared. Gillispie has pointed out[11] that the scheme had a certain theological appeal because, depending upon one's beliefs, one could either claim a rapid or a slow succession of the Biblical "days of creation." In any case the appearance of life seemed to follow the order given in Genesis and to end with man.

The second catastrophic doctrine which gained public attention shortly after Hutton's death and for a time totally submerged his theories is associated primarily with the name of Cuvier—although Cuvier never urged successive creations but only migrations of fauna into new regions laid waste by geological upheaval. Catastrophism, so far as its biological aspect is concerned, is essentially a device to preserve the leading tenets of Christian theology and at the same time to give these doctrines a scientific cast. It preserves the assumption of special creation by assuming, instead of the one Biblical event, a multiple series of creations taking place successively in distinct geological epochs. It also, by implication, accepts the Noachian Deluge as the last in a series of tremendous upheavals or catastrophes which have separated one world of prehistoric life from another. At the close of each such revolution life was supposed to be created anew. As the progressive organic advancement in the rocks became better known and read, it was assumed that this stair of life, which was analogous with the Scale of Being in the living world, pointed on prophetically toward man who

[11] *Genesis and Geology,* Harvard University Press, 1951, p. 46.

was assumed to be the goal of the process of creation.

It will thus be seen that there was a powerful supernatural element in this conception which was actually enhanced in early nineteenth-century England. We must be careful to remember, however, that at the time Hutton wrote his *Theory of the Earth* in 1785 this "progressionist" aspect of catastrophism was by no means fully elaborated. It would reach its culmination only after the contents of the stratified earth became better known.

Peculiarly enough, French catastrophism seems to have arisen out of one of the earliest attempts to avoid supernaturalism in accounting for the past history of the globe. As we have earlier remarked, ideas of cosmic evolution were current in the mid-eighteenth century, mostly having derived from Descartes, and they thus achieved great popularity in France. Buffon in his *Théorie de la Terre* (1749) attempted to trace the history of our planet from the time when its substance escaped from the sun, through the successive "epochs of nature." He recognized that parallel strata "were not formed in an instant, but were gradually produced by successive sediments," and in spite of a greatly underestimated time scale, he recognized that erosion in its many forms "produced continual changes, which, in a succession of ages, become considerable." Insensible changes, he came to believe, may over long time periods "cause very great revolutions."

The word "revolution," as Dr. Tomkeieff pointed out a few years ago, meant to Buffon largely great changes and not the world-wide catastrophic upheavals into which it was soon to be translated.[12] Allowing for the state of information at the time he wrote, there is actually a Huttonian cast to Buffon's writing. By contrast, in the days following the French Revolution, Buffon's successor Cuvier gave a genuinely dramatic interpretation to the "revolutions" of the globe. Yet if one studies Buffon's use

[12] S. J. Tomkeieff, "Geology in Historical Perspective," *The Advancement of Science*, 1950, Vol. 7, p. 65.

of the term one can see that he uses it variously as a synonym for change. The work of rivers, for example, he speaks of as inducing very slow "revolutions," whereas a volcanic outburst may produce quick alterations of the landscape. Cuvier, however, because of his work with fossil vertebrates in the Paris Basin was becoming far more conscious of the problem of extinction than his predecessors. Also, working as he was with vertebrates in which it was not easy to trace continuous evolutionary change, he seems to have drawn from Buffon, whom he admired, a somewhat reinterpreted and elaborated series of epochs succeeded in each instance by world catastrophes. After each of these epochs a new fauna and flora were assumed to have appeared.

Although Cuvier himself left open the question of the origin of the new fauna it was not long before pure catastrophism was the reigning geological view. The last cataclysm was assumed to be represented by the Biblical deluge. The earlier epochs of life were generally regarded as equating figuratively with the days of creation. An enormous literature arose upon the subject and some writers projected over a score of successive creations and extinctions all based upon local disconformities of strata which were erroneously assumed to be world wide. The religious appeal of this system, particularly in the days of the conservative English reaction against the French Revolution, was bound to make it widely popular. It accounted for extinct animals and at the same time preserved the essential foundations of contemporary religious belief.

V James Hutton's World Machine and Uniformitarianism

There is a curious lag between the astronomical discovery of infinite space in the seventeenth century and the discovery of time in the last decade of the eighteenth century. Superficially it might have been expected that the one conception would rapidly force a recognition of the other. Actually, however, it appears that the Christian world retained a conception of the timeless Empyrean Heaven, even after its modification at the hands of science. The timeless Eternal of God was still not quite equated with the events of the mundane earth. Thus the realization of the scope of earthly time was resisted almost in the same manner that the concept of organic evolution lagged in acceptance behind the growing realization of cosmic evolution. Astronomical observations were too remote from reality, too dependent upon the mathematical calculations of a few virtuosi to bring the reality of time home to the average individual whose whole religious training was opposed to the idea. The man in the street, as in the days of the voyagers, was waiting for something he could handle and see with his own eyes —as he had seen talking parrots from the Indies come ashore on the shoulders of sailors whose caravels were moored at the London docks. With Cuvier he would be granted that final demonstration, but first a theory had to be prepared, a key, a part of the map of time had to be envisaged, else no voyage into that distant region would be possible. James Hutton's triumph was that he proved that vast invisible ocean to exist. He measured its dimensions. The way to its toothed birds and dragons would be provided by other hands.

The eighteenth century had seen, with the rise of the Newtonian doctrines in physics, the accompanying development of a philosophy in which God, the personal Divinity of earlier centuries, was more and more being relegated to the role of a spectator in His own universe. The Newtonian laws were such that the cosmic engine, once set spinning, was very largely self-regulatory. Miracles, providential interferences with the machinery, were no longer particularly acceptable. The passion for mathematical order was intense at the height of the Age of

THE PIRATE CHART 71

Reason. James Hutton had absorbed this atmosphere and the tone and the evident purpose of his book was to introduce into the history of the earth and the life upon its surface the same order and eternal perfection which Newton had perceived in the heavens. James Hutton, in other words, was the creator of a self-renewing world-machine whose laws of operation were as unswerving as the cosmic engine of the astronomers. In this respect he was following the scientific bent of his time. His misfortune lay in the fact that what had become acceptable in the heavens was still a heresy upon earth.

Before Hutton almost everyone who discoursed upon the configuration of the landscape had felt obligated to assume that its major features were the product of the flood. The strewn boulders of the glacial advances, often lying hundreds of miles from their point of origin, were thought to have been rolled and tossed by the turbulence of a giant sea. Since the earth was supposed to have lain almost, if not entirely, under water, it then became a point of ingenuity for these early students of geology to explain into what monstrous caverns beneath the surface the flood waters had withdrawn. Hutton, by contrast, proposed a reasonable but unorthodox solution. He did not attempt to "drain the pond." Instead he contended that dynamic forces in the crust of the earth created tensions and stresses which, in the course of time, elevated new lands from the ocean bed even as other exposed surfaces were in the process of erosion. There had never been a universal flood. There was observable in the buried shell-beds of the continents, which had long been taken as evidences of the Deluge, only the signs of subsidence and renewed uplift which were part of the eternal youth of the world.

"We may perceive," Hutton pondered, "the actual existence of those productive causes, which are now laying the foundation of land in the unfathomable regions of the sea, and which will, in time, give birth to future continents."[13] With a Newtonian joy in his discovery of the principles of a remarkable engine, he informs his audience that the destructive work of winds and frost and running waters would eventually engulf the continents were there not "a reproductive operation, by which a ruined constitution [might] be again repaired."[14] In these words, in his affectionate regard for his "beautiful machine," one can observe the full climate of the Age of Enlightenment, its distaste for "having recourse to any unnatural supposition of evil, to any destructive accident in nature, or to the agency of any preternatural cause, in explaining that which actually appears."[15] The world is made by nature to decay but it is also made to renew itself eternally. "This decaying nature of the solid earth," Hutton wrote in his later volumes, "is the very perfection of its constitution as a living world."[16]

The restorative force which Hutton visualized from his long examination of solidified strata, and the careful distinction between sedimentary and igneous rock which he drew, was the internal heat of the earth. He observed that tilted and distorted strata implied uplift and wrinklings of the earth's crust in a manner suggesting "a power which has for principle subterraneous heat." Active volcanoes confirmed his view that this force was not a thing of the past but continued as an active agent in the creation of new lands and mountain ranges. In the depths of the sea the materials brought down from the continents are solidified by the subterranean forces into stone only to be again upthrust and to endure once more the forces of erosion. The earth, "like the body of animal, is wasted at the same time that it is repaired."

Hutton's perception of the minute processes of decay is as keen as his eye for the vast movements of continental

13 *Essay of 1788*, p. 293.
14 Ibid., p. 216.
15 Ibid., p. 285.
16 *Theory of the Earth*, Edinburgh, 1795, Vol. 1, p. 208.

upheaval. So preternaturally acute was his sense of time that he could foretell in a running stream the final doom of a continent. Yet he saw also that in the long view this wastage foretold new worlds of life. "Thus . . . from the top of the mountain to the shore of the sea . . . everything is in a state of change; the rock and solid strata slowly dissolving, breaking and decomposing, for the purpose of becoming soil; the soil traveling along the surface of the earth on its way to the shore; and the shore itself wearing and wasting by the agitation of the sea, an agitation which is essential to the purposes of a living world. Without those operations which wear and waste the coast, there would not be wind and rain; and without those operations which wear and waste the solid land, the surface of the earth would become sterile." The man by the trickling brook had heard a roar like Niagara and seen a world go down into the torrent.

In this eternal hurrying of particles across the surface of the land, in the dissolution of previous continents with all their varied life, there emerges once more into Western thought the long shadow of illimitable time as it was known to the Roman thinkers. The result of our present inquiry, wrote Hutton, at the close of his book, "is that we find no vestige of a beginning,—no prospect of an end." Over sixty years after those words were written Sir Charles Lyell, addressing the annual meeting of the Geological Society of London, confessed that though "we have greatly enlarged the sphere of our knowledge, the same conclusion seems to me to hold true."[17] The way had opened for Darwin.

James Hutton read his *Theory of the Earth* before the Royal Society of Edinburgh in 1785. It was published in the *Proceedings* of that society three years later. In 1795 an amplified two-volume edition was issued. His theory had been at first well received in liberal quarters. As he

[17] Anniversary Address of the President, *Quarterly Journal of the Geological Society of London*, 1851, Vol. 7, p. lxxiv ff.

wrote in the edition of 1795: "When I first conceived my theory few naturalists could write intelligibly upon the subject; but that is long ago, and things are much altered since; now there are most enlightened men making observations and communicating natural knowledge. I have the satisfaction, almost every day, to compare the theory, which I had formed from my proper observations, with the actual state of things in almost every quarter of the globe."[18]

The fantastic catastrophism which was to be one of the first products of vertebrate paleontology was then about to obscure his work. Of what he thought of evolution there is no record save that he spoke with interest of De Maillet's "ingenious theory." Its lack of supernaturalism and appeal to natural forces intrigued his interest but he dismissed it as "only a physical romance" though "better founded than most."[19] Hutton's view of time, and this is the one crucial limitation in his work, is essentially cyclical. He recognized its illimitable extent, he knew that throughout the slow obliteration of continents other lands were rising to the surface so that there was no reason to assume complete extinctions and successive creations of life. In the end, however, he did not commit himself upon the nature of the past flora and fauna of the planet. He observed that it could "translate" itself from one locality to another as time and paleo-geography permitted, but like most of the writers of his period, he allowed the similarities existing in early marine shells to deceive him as to the stability of the forms of life from age to age.

Hutton was thus a total uniformitarian. "There are," he admitted, "varieties in those [ocean] species compared with the present animals which we examine, but no greater varieties than may perhaps be found . . . in the different quarters of the globe. Therefore the sys-

[18] *Theory of the Earth*, 1795, Vol. 1, p. 306.
[19] Ibid., Vol. 1, p. 271.

tem of animal life which had been maintained in the ancient sea, had not been different from that which now subsists. . . ."[20] In order to prepare the public for the acceptance of the evolutionary theory two more steps must be taken, two more fragments of the pirate chart must now be fitted to the piece supplied by Hutton. Animal remains must be observed to lie in stratigraphic sequences and to be different in kind for different ages. This in turn demands a kind of anatomical knowledge with which Hutton was unfamiliar.

VI William Smith

The astronomical theories which had so profoundly influenced Hutton and which had affected his philosophy of the world machine held, essentially, that in the celestial realm all perturbations of orbit tended to oscillate around a mean position so that even in the face of minor variation the solar system remained stable. It was this type of thinking which probably contributed to Hutton's indifference to the possibility of organic mutability. Evidences of change in marine forms were slight enough to be similarly dismissed as the minor variations of life around a standard type, a kind of thinking which, as we have previously seen, was a commonplace in Hutton's time. William Smith was a man of totally different background and a set of practical engineering needs.

We have had previous occasion to remark that several individuals in the eighteenth century, Buffon for one, had suspected that fossils might prove of some use in determining the age of deposits in which they were found. That there was a seeming difference to be observed in the fossils of distinct strata had been noticed by James Woodward as early as 1695,[21] but he had not correctly interpreted the phenomenon, ascribing it to gravitational

20 *Theory of the Earth*, 1795, Vol. 1, pp. 175–76.
21 *Essay Toward a Natural History of the Earth*.

effects at the time of the universal Flood. That strata themselves had been laid down successively had also been noted or implied by several.[22] There is no doubt that Abraham Werner's views on successive stratification, first promulgated in 1777, stimulated interest in the geological layers of the planet, but they contributed little to the rational solution of the problems thus raised, since Werner's explanations involved chemical deposition in a universal ocean.[23] Werner was instrumental, however, in promoting research to determine the similarity of strata over wide regions. Though his theories are long outmoded, they undoubtedly led to a more rapid recognition of the extent and relationships of certain formations.

This earlier research had largely revolved around the nature of the rocks involved rather than about the organisms contained in them. Smith introduced a totally new approach. The strata, he contended, can be identified by the fossils within them, and of any superimposed strata the lowest levels are also the oldest. This principle, which is now everywhere used in archaeology as well as paleontology, seems, like most great generalizations, amazingly simple once it has been stated. The fact that just as in the case of evolution itself many great minds had toyed unsuccessfully about the edges of the problem suggests what we have intimated so frequently before: an essential ingredient had been missing. Paleontology had lain undeveloped and interest had been less in time than in the mineral composition of deposits presumably laid down with great rapidity in a primeval ocean.

As we have seen, Hutton published his views on time and erosion in 1788. Three years later William Smith seems to have had the secret of stratigraphy worked out

[22] For a recent account of some of Smith's more obscure forerunners see C. J. Stubblefield's "The Relation of Paleontology to Stratigraphy," *The Advancement of Science*, 1954, Vol. 11, pp. 149–59.

[23] F. D. Adams, *Birth and Development of the Geological Sciences*, Baltimore, 1938, p. 221 ff.

though he did not publish his discovery until much later.

The origins of William Smith were quite different from those of the highly literate and philosophically minded Hutton. He was orphaned at an early age and cared for by an uncle who was a farmer. Always attracted to the open fields and to fossils, he became an apprentice surveyor in his youth. By the time canals were being projected for the widespread transport of coal and other goods in England, Smith had entered upon his professional career as a surveyor and engineer. Before the turn of the century and later, he traveled enormous mileages for canal companies. He reported upon coal deposits, drained swamps, laid out canal routes. He became, in other words, a practical field geologist much in demand for his unparalleled personal knowledge of ground waters and the complete composition of the English terrain. His entire living depended upon the accurate determination of strata and in tracing them successfully over wide areas. In examining exposed strata in commercial and natural deposits, Smith, "Strata Smith," as he came to be called, made the supreme observation that each individual stratum appeared to contain distinct organic ingredients. Smith, though it is unlikely that he fully realized what he had done, had discovered the strange historicity of life. In attempting to arrange sedimentary rocks which he would have been unable to classify on the basis of physical properties, he had selected and brought to attention the one thing on the planet which had consistently and identifiably altered itself throughout the long eras of the past, namely, life itself.

William Smith made no secret of his discovery. In fact it is remarkable, and only because of honest friends, that he received credit for his work at all. Always on the move and detesting, as he did, the process of formal writing, he talked with the freedom of a traveling salesman to any attentive listener about his fragment of the great secret. By 1799 he had circulated an unpublished manuscript on the order of the strata in the vicinity of Bath in which he made use of his new paleontological principle. By 1813 a friend, the Rev. Joseph Townsend, had written a book in which Smith's discoveries are lauded,[24] and by 1815 Smith's real life work, the first geological map of England, was published. There followed a few papers elaborating his views and setting forth the evidence upon which they are based. Probably the best known is entitled *The Stratigraphical System of Organized Fossils* which was published in London in 1817. Smith flourished in a time when there was an economic demand for his type of specialized knowledge. He himself spoke regretfully of the fact that "the theory of geology was in the possession of one class of men, the practice in another."[25] In the light of these remarks it is most interesting that Smith speaks respectfully of Lamarck's work on invertebrates "as most applicable to the arrangement of organized fossils." He was apparently familiar also with the work of Gustavus Brander and Daniel Solander, *Fossila Hantoniensia* (1766), which Lamarck had used in his pioneer effort to correlate the Tertiary fossil beds of Hampshire with those of France around the beginning of the century.

Smith disclaimed a concern with theory "for," he said, "I have none to support."[26] Yet in this he was not entirely consistent. With others I have the distinct feeling, without having been able to consult all of the original documents, that Smith carried on his early work under uniformitarian influences emanating from Hutton and Lamarck, but that in his later years he turned toward the catastrophism which had become so universally popular after Cuvier's rise to prominence. The stratigraphical essay of 1817, in spite of the disclaimer we have just quoted, assumes that

24 *The Character of Moses established for Veracity as an Historian, Recording Events from Creation to the Deluge*, Bath, 1813.
25 H. B. Woodward, *The History of the Geological Society of London*, London, 1907, p. 53.
26 Paper of 1817, cited above, p. vi.

"each layer of these fossil organized bodies must be considered as a separate creation, or is," he also speculates, "an undiscovered part of an older creation."

Although at one time he had evinced distaste for those who invoked unexplained "convulsions" to explain geological events, the conservative bent of the times and all the subtle pressures exerted by friends, position, and his own temperamental leanings led him finally to accept an unseen aspect to the geological past of the planet. "By the use of fossils," he contended, "we are carried back into a region of supernatural events."[27] In those words there is actually epitomized the reigning scientific climate of the early nineteenth century. It is a climate interested in science, increasingly interested in fossils, but firmly intent upon the preservation of religious orthodoxy.

When William Smith, characterized by a contemporary as "a plain and moderately lettered man," directed the attention of science to his law of the superimposition of strata and their contained relics of organic life, the world, for the first time, began to realize the nature of time. All about, in commercial excavations, on seacoasts, and among broken uplands with their exposed formations, had been lying, unknown and uninterpreted, the remnants of the past.[28] Now suddenly the pretty shells in curio cabinets began to take on a vast and mysterious significance. Smith may not have accepted evolution but he had accepted time—the time, essentially, of Hutton and Lamarck.[29] Nor was that time any longer abstract and without meaning to the layman. The curious thread of living matter ran through it, unique and always changing, for-

[27] F. J. North, "Deductions from Established Facts in Geology, by William Smith: Notes on a Recently Discovered Broadsheet," *Geological Magazine*, 1927, Vol. 64, p. 534.

[28] The English series of formations was, for so small an area, remarkably complete.

[29] Lamarck thought readily in terms of millions of years. See A. S. Packard, *Lamarck, the Founder of Evolution*, London, 1901, pp. 132–33.

ever unpredictable. Cuvier had found strange bones in the Paris Basin but even the less impressive marine shells were becoming a worthy object of attention for young ladies.[30] Some people complained that Smith, who had no particular gift for writing, did not fulfill his publishing engagements, and they chafed in an irritated fashion over the delays.

Once and for all the study of extinct life had been indissolubly joined to the rocks of the planet. The ladder into the past had been created and no phylogeny of a living creature could be worked upon again without checking against the story in the earth. If, because of the nature of his profession and his times, Smith chose to emphasize the breaks rather than the connections in the fossil record, the mistake would be remedied. He had been generous with his part of the great secret—generous in a hard, dogged life that might well have led him to behave otherwise.

In the year 1831 he was presented with the first Wollaston Medal of the Geological Society of London. It was given in recognition of the man who had found the way backward into time, and who had achieved that triumph while trudging over hill and dale in what many would have regarded as a grubby and not very genteel profession. The cloistered Scotch physician and the man whose face had been beaten by all the winds of England had done their solitary work. Apart from Smith but contemporaneous with him had labored a grander and more aristocratic figure, the inheritor of Buffon's mantle, the Baron Georges Cuvier. Hutton and Smith had been pri-

---

[30] Anonymous, "An Earnest Recommendation to Curious Ladies and Gentlemen Residing or Visiting In the Country, to Examine the Quarries, Cliffs, Steep Banks, etc., and collect and Preserve fossil shells as highly curious objects in Conchology, and, as most Important Aids in Identifying Strata in Distant Places; on which Knowledge the Progress of Geology in a principle degree if not Entirely Depends," *The Philosophical Magazine and Journal,* 1815, Vol. 45, pp. 274–80.

marily physical geologists. Cuvier, who held the third secret of our figurative pirate's chart, was a comparative anatomist. He was the real founder of vertebrate paleontology.

VII Cuvier: the Magician of the Charnel House

It is a casual piece of folklore among laymen today that a paleontologist can always reconstruct an entire animal from a single bone. Most students of the science, who know their limitations, would smile and say "it depends on the bone." The public, however, has, for over a century now, been vastly impressed by the huge articulated skeletons erected in museums, and by the restorations of vanished reptiles, winged or bipedal. Here is a magic with whose details the common man is little acquainted. Moreover, like the citizen on the London docks in the days of the voyagers, he can gaze upon these great bones, these spoils from the lost coasts of time, and believe more readily by beholding what it was he rejected when he turned away from Hutton and Lamarck. They, it is true, possessed the secret of time but it was lost like the sound of the sea in little shells. Only the huge bones, the saber teeth of cats, the tusks of giant elephants impress us with the marvelous organic diversity which strews the shores of continents that have vanished from the light. Man, convinced at first, in his naïve innocence, that the world was made for him, has now been told by the time voyagers that, at a period not very remote, geologically speaking, the human form is no longer to be found. The outlines of this story, even the rearticulation of those giant bodies, we owe to the anatomical diligence of Cuvier and his followers. It is from his exploits, which brought him the title "magician of the charnel house," that the story of the paleontologist and the single bone has descended to us.

Before scholars could go beyond the marine fauna and ascertain what type of life had roamed upon Hutton's lost continents, a method had to be perfected which would permit the investigation of a whole animal from a fragment. Land vertebrates, unlike shells, are infrequently found in total articulation. They are apt to have been torn to pieces after death by roving scavengers and birds, or, even if engulfed in muds and quicksands, the long erosion of time may have destroyed the larger part of the carcass before man comes upon it. Nature has no interest in the preservation of the dead; her purpose is to start their elements upon the eternal road of life once more. Thus out of innumerable vertebrate skeletons, here and there one is preserved under satisfactory conditions, and of these man may discover a few. The ability, as a consequence of this situation, to recognize a given form from fragments is tremendously important. It was this art which Cuvier carried to a high degree of perfection so that his exploits have come down to us as folklore.

The beginnings of comparative anatomy like a good many aspects of our subject can be traced all the way back to the Greeks. Aristotle, for example, knew that the large animal groups shared a unity of structure which, in different species, was modified for different ends.[31] The gradations of the Scale of Being itself contributed to the promotion and continuation of such ideas. This does not necessarily imply an understanding of actual physical descent with modification. Rather it had been comprehended that animals were formed on a "plan," or "plans," which extended across whole groups of differing organisms. The plan might thus be seen as immaterial, a kind of Platonic form, a divine order manifesting itself in nature.

As the eighteenth century drew on, however, unity of plan began to be considered as possibly indicating some kind of common physical origin for quite divergent forms. We have seen it emerge hesitantly in Buffon, and various

[31] E. S. Russell, *Form and Function*, New York, 1917, p. 3 ff.

shades or intimations of the same idea are not unknown to other French and German writers of the mid-eighteenth century,[32] considerably prior to Cuvier. Just as in the case of the theory of evolution itself, we may observe that there was a preliminary groping for the precise way in which this information might be used, considerably before the appearance of the master artist, Cuvier.

Without detracting from Cuvier's genius we may point out that by the time he was ready to turn the unity of plan which existed in the living world into a method for probing the past, several things had occurred: (1) Attention, particularly on the continent, was shifting from shells to bones. News of American remains of huge bones were beginning to sift back to the Old World and, in some instances, the bones themselves had been exhibited in Europe. (2) Smith's discoveries of a stratigraphic sequence in fossils, along with the obviously growing age of the world, heightened public interest as to what forms of land life might have existed contemporaneously along with the rather monotonously uniform invertebrate marine fossils. (3) The continually expanding geographical information upon other world areas now made it extremely unlikely that any large vertebrates were still hidden in unknown portions of the globe. Extinction, at last, was a reality. The past life of the earth, therefore, might offer marvels no living eye had beheld. (4) The rock formations of the Paris Basin were being quarried extensively in the days of the First Empire. There were strata interspersed with others containing fresh water forms, as well as later deposits containing numerous land animals of great size. An anonymous contemporary writer spoke in an awed tone of perished species and the mystery of how new species originated. "The mind is lost," he philosophized mourn-

[32] For a more lengthy account of these writers than can be attempted here the reader may consult E. S. Russell, op. cit., A. S. Packard, op. cit., pp. 136–39, and A. O. Lovejoy, "Some Eighteenth Century Evolutionists," *Popular Science Monthly*, 1904, Vol. 65.

fully, "amid uncertain lights and gigantic images that pass before it."[33]

It is in the lights and shadows of this vast, unfolding landscape that we find Cuvier like a modern Faust poring over the heaped bones recovered from these excavations. "I found myself as if placed in a charnel house," he once said, "surrounded by mutilated fragments of many hundred skeletons of more than twenty kinds of animals, piled confusedly around me. The task assigned me was to restore them all to their original positions. At the voice of comparative anatomy every bone and fragment of a bone resumed its place."[34]

It is particularly satisfying that this modern magician who resurrected the vanished dead to live once more in the mind of man should have named the Pterodactyls. Like imps the leather-winged flying reptiles would have been most appropriate circling the master magician's head. The scene would have made a suitable painting, for Cuvier had a deep sense of drama. He knew these creatures to be the most extraordinary and *outré* of any that the spade had then revealed; he knew that they belonged utterly to a long vanished world. Yet he makes no exception of them. They, too, bone by bone and tooth by tooth, are amenable to the discipline of science. Strange-bodied and strangely adapted though they were, they are allied to an ancient reptilian pattern, a plan, a unity, that has come down through the long cycles of change into the present. The biologist could therefore say "Pterodactyls are gone but the pattern remains. They were reptilian vertebrates highly specialized and adapted for flight. In structure, however, they show a clear relationship to modern reptiles."

The man who perfected and popularized this mode of penetration into the past was the son of a Swiss army

33 *Edinburgh Review*, 1812, Vol. 20, p. 382.
34 *Edinburgh Review*, 1837, Vol. 65, p. 23.

officer in moderate circumstances. His early education was obtained at Stuttgart where he came under the influence of Kielmeyer, one of the early German students of anatomy. From 1788 to 1794 he was employed as a tutor to the son of a French count in Normandy. He thus escaped the vicissitudes of the revolution but through a fortunate connection was able to go to Paris in 1795. Here he entered upon a brilliant career at the Jardin des Plantes. He came to occupy, in addition, important positions of state, and was a favorite of Napoleon. Beginning in 1800 he published his *Lessons in Comparative Anatomy* in which he set forth the views he was later to apply so brilliantly in the investigation of the Parisian bone beds which he carried out in association with Alexandre Brongniart.[35] He wrote extensively and such works as *Recherches sur Les Ossemens Fossiles* (1812), *Le Règne Animal* (1817), and his *Theory of the Earth* (1815), which received a wide circulation in English, had a leading role in diffusing knowledge of comparative anatomy. All of these volumes passed through many editions. We have already mentioned his role in the development of the second phase of catastrophic geology; we will here confine ourselves to his "principle of correlation."

Cuvier carefully pointed out that although vertebrate remains offered the hope of extensive insights into the past, they had been neglected because of their fragmentary condition. Few men were sufficiently equipped to read the meaning in bits of bone and their study had been neglected. It was just here that Cuvier, after long effort, produced his part of the lost map of time that fitted so well with the portions that Smith and Hutton had possessed. He said, in effect, "We will take what we have learned of the comparative anatomy of the living and we will use it as a ladder to descend into the past. All our information, scanty though it may be, leads us to assume

[35] *Essai sur la geographie minéralogique des environs de Paris,* 1811.

that the same unity of design of which we observe evidences in the modern world extends also across the enormous time gulfs of the past. My key, my principle, will enable us to restore the appearance of those long vanished beasts and relate them to the life of the present."

In order to perform his feats of identification and restoration Cuvier proceeded upon a principle that today might be labeled organismic or holistic. He regarded organs, in fact all anatomical structures, as so intimately related to the life of the entire creature that no one part can be fitted to perform a certain function without the modification of other related parts. Thus even a footprint may tell us a good deal about the structure of an animal of which we possess no other trace at all, or by a feather we may go on to infer many things about a bird simply because of known correlations of structure in all birds. "Thus," said Cuvier, "we procure astonishing results. The smallest fragment of bone, even the most apparently insignificant apophysis, possesses a fixed and determinate character, relative to the class, order, genus and species of the animal to which it belonged; insomuch, that when we find merely the extremity of a well-preserved bone, we are able by careful examination, assisted by analogy and exact comparison, to determine the species to which it once belonged, as certainly as if we had the entire animal before us."[36] So assiduously did Cuvier pursue his studies of the bones of both living and extinct animals that he was able to incite great wonder at his feats of identification.

To give but one example: A fossil-bearing slab which had been secured near Lake Constance had been described by Johann Scheuchzer in 1726 as containing the skeleton of a man who lived before the Flood. This specimen, exhibited at Haarlem, had attracted great interest because of its supposed religious background, but in 1811

[36] *Essay on the Theory of the Earth,* Edinburgh, 1815, p. 101.

Cuvier examined the bones and revealed the creature to be a gigantic extinct salamander. The day had clearly passed when any obscure bone could be ascribed to a human giant or set aside as a saintly relic.

Two other achievements of the Baron deserve mention here as having contributed to clearing the way for Darwin. One of these was his clear break with the Scale of Being hypothesis. It will be remembered that the eighteenth century was, on the whole, addicted to an ascending series of living forms shading by insensible degrees into each other and leading on to man. There was no consideration of the fact that this might be reading into Nature a greater unity than she actually possessed. It led inevitably to some highly questionable taxonomy produced in the effort to compress all life into positions upon a single stairway.

Cuvier broke with this conception by the simple expedient of demonstrating anatomically that certain broad groups represented such divergent anatomical organization that they could not be fitted into a single unilineal ascending system. Instead, he conceived of four great groups: the Vertebrates, the Mollusca, the Articulata, and the Radiata. The last has suffered the most alteration by later work but, in essentials, he greatly improved the taxonomical classification of animals and showed, even though he did not realize its evolutionary implications, that there were many stairways of life rather than one. The molluscan plan of organs and of adaptations could never be fitted successfully into a vertebrate sequence. Perhaps it was this sharp realization of distinct worlds of organization that caused him to reject evolution as savoring of the old Scale of Being whose clumsy morphology he detested.

At any rate, all unknowingly, Cuvier had opened the way to a conception of divergent evolution which, though glimpsed timidly by Lamarck, had not been logically pursued to its conclusion by the latter. Whatever might be learned later of the original source of all life, it was evident from Cuvier's time on that the Scale of Nature, useful though it may have been in stimulating interest in the natural world while theology still dominated science, was, to a degree, a myth. There were several plans of life on the planet and by no stretch of the imagination, within the world open to man's investigation, could they be placed in an ascending relation to each other. Instead, each was unique and ramifying along its own evolutionary corridor. Man was not the creature toward which the worm was striving. Life was a bush, not a ladder.

Finally, although averse to evolutionary explanations, Cuvier was the first to note of his Parisian studies, "There is a determinate order observable in the disposition of these bones in regard to each other, which indicates a very remarkable succession in the appearance of the different species."[37] He recognized clearly that the younger alluvial deposits contained creatures more similar to those of the present than strata representing more remote ages. He felt that the rocks revealed a gradual advance in the complexity of life through the several "revolutions" of the planet. This Deperet regards as "a fundamental idea," the merit of which has been too often forgotten.[38] Certainly it was the first clear evidence from the rocks of the organic advances in land life, the first satisfactory mammalian sequence from any quarry in the world.

It was Cuvier's discoveries that gave the impetus to biological progressionism which, as will be seen, was the clear prelude to nineteenth-century evolution. Moreover, Cuvier—and this is occasionally forgotten by twentieth-century critics—recognized the empirical quality of his law of correlation. He knew that increasing knowledge of the anatomy of extinct life would enhance our ability to pierce farther into the past and avoid the occasional

[37] Op. cit., 1815, p. 109.
[38] C. Deperet, *The Transformations of the Animal World*, New York, 1909, pp. 9–10.

mistakes which can be made with animal remains most distant from our common knowledge. It is perfectly true that a few of his correlations would not hold in the case of transitional or peculiarly divergent specimens we possess today. This does not, however, justify the dismissal of a method that has opened the doorway of the past.

A bird like Archaeopteryx with feathers and teeth he would not have anticipated, but his own philosophy would have quickly adjusted to such exceptions for, as he himself wrote in advance of his critics, "our theoretical knowledge of these relations of forms is not sufficient to guide us, unless assisted by observation and experience."[39] He himself identified most successfully creatures who had reasonably similar living relatives. Furthermore, the man who in youth had laboriously painted in color the animal pictures in a treasured set of Buffon may, like a quiet child, have retained some private thoughts. Once he wrote cryptically, "Observation alone, independent entirely of general principles of philosophy, is sufficient to show that there certainly are *secret reasons* for all these relations of which I have been speaking."[40] When he wrote those lines, "descent with modification" was still thirty-five years away. The Baron Georges Cuvier was a proud and sometimes arrogant man of state. He was discreet. He had come a long road since the quiet days on the Normandy shore while the heads were falling in Paris. Perhaps he had his moment of hesitation, perhaps not. In any case he was one of the first great time voyagers.

[39] Op. cit., 1815, p. 95.
[40] Ibid. (Italics mine. L.E.)

Chapter IV

Progressionism and Evolution

> How could Sir Charles Lyell . . . for thirty
> years read, write, and think on the subject
> of species and their succession, and yet con-
> stantly look down the wrong road?
> *Hewett Watson*

I Geological Prophecy

A bone, to Cuvier, was never just a bone, because it told,
in its curvatures and varied processes, the story of an organized being whose every other bone and organ could
be expected to be in harmonious proportion and accord
with the solitary fragment. Thus, within a certain degree,
a claw should ordinarily disclose a particular type of
tooth, or a tooth the necessary nature of a shoulder blade.
A landscape, to James Hutton, was not a given thing,
shaped once and forgotten, but rather a page from a continuing biography of the planet. The scene had been written by frost and a light wind that blew for ages, by the
hidden touch of subterranean fires, by a plant that grew
and held a little patch of soil from being carried away by
a stream. Whatever else it was also, this landscape was
natural. It had not been wrought by convulsive and
mythical events or by the hand of a wrathful Divinity. Instead, it was a part of the long intricate interplay between

the forces that waste away the land and the forces that produce uplift and renewal. A countryside is above all a biography, the only visible biography left by time. Similarly a stratum, to William Smith, was not a thick layer of indifferent rock, but a ladder descending into the unknown darkness of the past. Caught and preserved like insects in amber, there were, at every rung of that ladder, animals, to use Smith's own phrase, "materially different from those now in existence." As we survey these tremendous contributions to human knowledge, contributions to which we have grown so accustomed by long familiarity that the genius of the men who made them escapes us, we wonder what ingredient was still lacking to convince the general public that organic, as well as stellar, evolution was a reality.

We are, however, if we think in this manner, still unconsciously projecting back upon the first decade of the nineteenth century accumulations of information which did not then exist. Let us look a little more closely at this situation. In 1788 Hutton's first and most compactly literate account of his discovery had been published. It had come at a time when the German geologist Werner had been at the height of his teaching popularity and when the public, by its own Christian tradition, preferred stories of a great Flood. Hutton had grasped the significance of fossils, but unfortunately he came too early to quite realize the fact of animal difference and extinction on the scale science was later to discover. Extinction, by its nature, could not be inferred. It had to be found out by empirical means. As a consequence, though Hutton saw illimitable vistas of time and the natural forces which worked to mold the surface of the planet, his uniformitarianism is *total*. He did not visualize organic change; he was content with having perceived the main outlines of the way in which the world machine persisted and renewed itself. About life he asked few questions. There is thus an oriental flavor of eternal changelessness in his system. All things pass only to come round again in the great year, in the march of waves that are forever similar. A system of this sort does not, by itself, attract followers in a culture dedicated to a unique drama in the sense that the Christian world was so dedicated.

William Smith, shortly after Hutton's death, in feeling his way down through the strata began to recognize change, but it was, on the whole, petty molluscan change. Smith was working mainly in marine beds and was concerned with tracing similar strata over considerable areas of England. The ideal organisms for this purpose are marine molluscs and similar creatures, which appear in constant profusion. Vertebrate fossils tend to be too sparsely distributed to be useful. In addition, as we have seen, Smith was a practical engineer, not a student of philosophical anatomy like Cuvier. In later writings he speaks of vertebrate fossils but it is largely because of the work of Cuvier with which he had become acquainted. Though there is a genuine rise in public interest which heightened after Cuvier's brilliant exploits in vertebrate paleontology, of which he is the recognized founder, we can, if we look sharply, see pretty clearly that the true continuity of evolution has not quite been attained.

The reason lies in the fact that, though between the achievements of Smith and Cuvier the public had finally become excited and convinced that a past world existed, it was not, in actuality, impressed by the continuity of that past. It had accepted the sharply demarcated and successive organic worlds of Smith and Cuvier while, at the same time, it had rejected the continuous and permeating time flow of Hutton. It took the superimposed strata, just as Smith had taken them, to be as distinctly defined in time as they appeared in the rock formations.

Each stratum with an organic content differing in a major way from one above or below represented a distinct creation which was then, after a variable period of time, destroyed by convulsive upheavals and floods over

the surface of the globe. Instead of the smooth flow of
life through long eons in which certain forms became extinct and others evolved and changed, the public was
really enjoying, not a motion picture of the planet's past,
but a series of still photographs extracted from their
context.

The knowledge of the layman had been deepened and
broadened, but both he and most contemporary scientists
still preferred at least some aspects of a cosmology with
which they had been familiar since childhood. The genuine unity of organic design which could be traced from
the present into these worlds of the past was assumed to
be an immaterial, spiritual connection emanating from
the designer of the universe. It was not believed to represent in the least a physical connection. When Cuvier succeeded in demonstrating a progressive aspect, particularly to land life, this was quickly transformed in the
minds of the more traditional thinkers into an increasingly
complex prologue leading on toward man who in the
words of one of these thinkers was "foreknown and prefigured from the beginning."

One can note that this type of "progressionism," as it
was termed, has some of the qualities of the Scale of Being still lingering about it. For one thing the progressivist
doctrine is man-centered. Man is believed to be the goal
of the process and everything points in his direction or
prophesies his appearance. At the same time we may note
that the progressionist doctrine clearly demonstrates the
fact that it was possible to temporalize the Chain of Being and extend it into the past without making it a truly
evolutionary philosophy. Here, instead, we have a succession of organic worlds, each terminated by catastrophic
and probably supernaturally induced geological disturbances. The unity of design which connects the flora and
fauna of these worlds is, as one of the leading proponents
of progressionism states, "nothing like parental descent."
He makes it quite clear that the link is "of a higher and

immaterial nature."[1] Spiritual evolution, it might be said, thus precedes a belief in actual physical change.

Here, in the pre-Darwinian portion of the nineteenth century, we encounter what is really a combination of traditional Christianity overlaid by a wash of German romantic philosophy. Elements of the new science and the new discoveries are being fitted into what is regarded as the "foreordained design of the Creator." Much of this thought derives from late eighteenth-century German romantic writers, but in England the Christian element becomes pronounced. As Gode-von Aesch has pointed out, a whole philosophical school in Germany came to regard the world "as a gigantic system of hieroglyphics, as the language of God or the book of nature."[2]

Interesting in this connection is the fact that Karl Kielmeyer, Cuvier's early friend and anatomy instructor, seems to have been the earliest formulizer (1793) of the biogenetic law which was regarded by the romantic philosophers as the dawn of a new era in science.[3] It will be remembered that the biogenetic law, which in the post-Darwinian period is widely associated with the name of Ernst Haeckel, expresses the idea that there is a parallelism between the stages of embryonic growth in the individual and the succession of fossil stages in the phylogeny of the species. In its earlier pre-evolutionary idealistic expression among the German philosophers it reflected the conception that man was a microcosm or reflection of the rest of the organic kingdom and that his embryonic development reflected the fact that "animals are merely foetal stages of man."[4]

[1] Hugh Miller, *The Testimony of the Rocks*, Edinburgh, 1869, p. 192.

[2] Alexander Gode-von Aesch, *Natural Science in German Romanticism*, Columbia University Press, 1941, p. 219.

[3] Ibid., p. 121.

[4] Oken cited by Gode-von Aesch, op. cit., p. 122. For a detailed discussion of the German transcendental school of biology one should consult E. S. Russell's excellent work *Form and Function*, New York, 1917.

This conception can be found reflected in some of the racial thinking even of post-Darwinian days in which it is assumed that the Caucasian, as the highest type of man, reflects in embryonic or infantile stages the other lower races. This German philosophy is, of course, closely allied to, and in some degree is developed from, reflections upon the Scale of Being.[5] When, in the English progressionist philosophy, a revised scale of being was actually projected into the past, it was inevitable, under the circumstances, that there should emerge a system of "geological prophecy." The fossils were true hieroglyphs, signs from earlier ages as to God's intention and design. There is, moreover, a continuing unilineal trend to the whole scheme which ignores Cuvier's divergent classes. Everything points prophetically toward man. The fossil footprints of Chirotherium, an extinct reptile, had a vaguely human appearance. They are read as "mute prophecies of the coming being."[6] The philosopher James McCosh and his collaborator George Dickie argued that bipedal fossil footprints of birds (actually dinosaurs) were a sign of human appearance "in a subsequent and still distant epoch."[7]

It is obvious, as we find statements of this kind in the writings of eminent biologists, that this transcendental emphasis among the progressionists was bound to inhibit in some degree the understanding of ecology, divergence and adaptation. Instead, attention is concentrated upon the "prophetic scroll" of geology. The books of Hugh Miller went through numerous editions. Certain of his ideas were drawn from Louis Agassiz who survived to combat Darwin and remain to the end a convinced adherent of the progressionist point of view. Many passages reveal that this type of anthropocentric concentration made the assumption inevitable that with the appearance

[5] Russell, op. cit., p. 214.
[6] Miller, op. cit., p. 193.
[7] *Typical Forms and Special Ends in Creation*, New York, 1857, p. 330.

of man the geological story was complete. Thus as late as 1866 Louis Agassiz expressed himself as follows: "Coming to the noble form of Man we find the brain so organized that the anterior portion covers and protects all the rest so completely that nothing is seen outside, and the brain stands vertically poised on the summit of the backbone. Beyond this there is no further progress, showing that man has reached the highest development of the plan upon which his structure was laid."[8]

In another earlier volume he stated even more explicitly that "by anatomical evidence" man is "the last term of a series, beyond which there is no material progress possible *in accordance with the plan upon which the whole animal kingdom is constructed. . . .*"[9] The italics are mine. They are intended to draw attention to the typical transcendental implication of a prefigured order, and the emphasis placed upon man as the creature for whom, or toward whom, the entire creation had labored. The passage is, basically, merely another repetition of Oken's remark that animals are foetal stages of man. It should now be apparent that, in spite of certain interesting ideas carried into British biology from German sources, what had emerged was still not a true evolutionary system of thought. Rather it represents a type of biological supernaturalism linked with a similarly supernatural geology. It remained to be seen what the renewed attempt to introduce uniformitarian conceptions into this system would bring forth.

II   Sir Charles Lyell and the Re-emergence of Uniformitarianism

James Hutton, as we have seen, was one of the first men to ignore the flood hypothesis in a full-fledged and com-

---

[8] *The Structure of Animal Life*, New York, 1866, pp. 108–9.
[9] *An Essay in Classification*, London, 1859, pp. 34–35.

prehensive study of the mechanics of physical geology.[10]
He had argued that the continents were built from the
ruins of more ancient land surfaces and that these past
worlds had been continuous and unbroken in their history
with the eras which had succeeded them. Not many were
attracted by the vast impersonal spectacle he presented
and his followers were few. Among them, however, was
John Playfair who, in 1802, undertook to present to the
public in his *Illustrations of the Huttonian Theory of the
Earth* a lucid and less prolix account of his friend's work.
There is no doubt that this book—a very elegantly written
treatise—did something to keep Hutton's name faintly
alive in the thirty years during which catastrophism was
the reigning geological doctrine. The conservative English reaction to the French Revolution, however, submerged Playfair almost as effectively as his predecessor.

Then, at a time when Cuvier was at the height of
his fame, and the leading geologists of both England
and France were catastrophists, a young unknown man,
Charles Lyell (1797–1875), published a book, *Principles
of Geology*, which was destined to destroy the reigning
geological doctrine and introduce unlimited time and
the play of natural forces once more into geology. Lyell
must be accorded the secure distinction, not alone of
altering the course of geological thought, but of having
been the single greatest influence in the life of Charles
Darwin. Moreover, he introduced Lamarck's theories to
the British reading public and, although he opposed
them, he gave Lamarck a fair dispassionate hearing. Lyell
had originally been trained for the law. He knew how to
marshal the facts of an argument, to weigh evidence and
to present it well.[11] Stylistically his writing was distin-

---

[10] Among the propositions which Buffon had been forced to recant by the Sorbonne was the view that the surface features of the
earth were due to secondary causes which, in time, would destroy
them and produce others of similar character.

[11] Professor C. F. A. Pantin in speaking of the *Origin of Species*
says that its style reminds him of Lyell's *Principles of Geology*

guished. His book was widely read not only by professional geologists but by the cultivated public whose curiosity about the secrets of the earth was growing. Without the public revision of attitude on the subject of time and natural forces working over inconceivably long intervals Darwinism would have had little chance of acceptance. Moreover, it is unlikely that without the influence of Lyell's book Darwin would have conceived or put forth his theory.

Curiously, though Lyell won in the geological field a victory similar to the one Darwin was later to achieve in biology, he did not become an evolutionist until his last years, although today it seems to us that evolution was the normal consequence of the system he presented. It remained, instead, for Darwin to demonstrate that the successive organic worlds of the progressionists were actually moving with the steady invisibility of a clock hand. The astronomer Halley in 1717 had demonstrated our solar system to be adrift in some great star-swirl rather than anchored securely at a fixed spot in space. Darwin was about to reveal that, not man alone, but the whole world of life was similarly unfixed in position. Rising, falling, evolving, changing, it was anything but the stable system visualized by the reigning philosophy of the eighteenth century, or the directed progression toward man envisaged by the majority of thinkers in the early nineteenth century.

Before turning to Darwin, however, it is necessary to examine the nature of Sir Charles Lyell's biological thinking. He was eleven years older than Darwin and his great work was achieved at an earlier age. Darwin read the first edition of the *Principles of Geology* while on the voyage of the *Beagle* and became Lyell's devoted admirer upon

---

"to which unquestionably it was indebted." Lyell's early training as a barrister, he goes on to say, has certainly benefited mankind. "Darwin's Theory and the Causes of its Acceptance," *The School Science Review*, June, 1951, p. 313.

his return. In fact, as early as 1836 Darwin wrote to a
friend, "Amongst the great scientific men, no one has
been nearly so friendly and kind as Lyell."[12] Darwin
never made any secret of his debt to Lyell—he dedicated
the *Journal* to him—but there are few, nevertheless, who
realize the extent of this relationship. Geology and biology, in spite of certain mutual interests, are now far
more divergent and specialized than they were in 1830.
As a consequence, Sir Charles Lyell's biological writings
tend to remain unread because they are contained in an
old textbook of geology and his geological successors are
inclined to occupy themselves historically only with Sir
Charles's contributions to geology. In the course of time
a legend has arisen that Darwin drew his geological uniformitarianism from Lyell, but that his knowledge of biological matters is derived from other sources.

No one would deny that Darwin was an inveterate
reader and observer, but an examination of Lyell's early
writings reveals that in the *Principles* he came very close
to Darwin's position. Consequently, one can scarcely resist the observation that the *Origin* could almost literally
have been written out of Lyell's book, once the guiding
motif of natural selection had been conceived. Lyell cir-
cled again and again about the leading idea that eluded
him, but perhaps the fact that he was older than Darwin
by more than a decade produced in him, both by background and temperament, a greater aversion toward the
last inevitable step. His long reluctance to declare himself, which at times irritated Darwin, is suggestive of the
hesitation which may have partially blocked his insight
upon the matters which he discussed so thoroughly and
with such toleration and objectivity in the *Principles*.[13]
Later we shall examine this problem at more length.

[12] *Life and Letters of Charles Darwin,* ed. by Francis Darwin,
London: John Murray, 1888, Vol. 1, p. 277.

[13] Lyell himself once remarked, "You may well believe that it
cost me a struggle to renounce my old creed." *Life, Letters and
Journals of Sir Charles Lyell,* ed. by Mrs. Katherine Lyell, London:
John Murray, 1881, Vol. 2, p. 376.

In Darwin's first brief sketch of his theory, written in 1842, there is a phrase about Augustin de Candolle's "war of nature."[14] This reference to the French botanist also occurs in the *Origin*. Now it is often said that Darwin took the phrase "struggle for existence" from Malthus, and Malthus is accorded a high place by Darwin in leading him to his great discovery. Malthus, in Darwin's essay of 1842, is mentioned along with De Candolle, but not in such a manner as to suggest that Darwin was unaware of other writings upon the struggle for existence. Instead, Malthus's doctrine of geometric increase seems to have caught his fancy as graphically indicating the great pressure of life against its resources. When glancing at the reference to De Candolle I noted that Darwin gave no direct source and remembering Darwin's own admission that he did not read French with facility, I was curious as to where he had found this reference. Knowing that Darwin had occasionally drawn upon Lyell's *Principles* for facts, I re-examined my copy of the third edition (1834).

In the third volume (p. 35) I came upon the quote from De Candolle, the source again unindicated. "All the plants of a given country," remarked the French botanist, "are at war with one another." Lyell then quotes De Candolle at some length upon the struggle for living space until "the more prolific gradually made themselves masters of the ground. . . ." There can be no doubt then as to where the De Candolle reference was secured. Indeed, Darwin himself in the first edition of the *Origin* remarks that "the elder De Candolle and Lyell have largely . . . shown that all organic beings are exposed to severe competition."[15] Lyell, in another place, after speaking of unhealthy plants being the first to be destroyed and choked out by more vigorous individuals, uses the phrase which was afterwards to become world famous, "the struggle for

[14] *Foundations of the Origin of Species,* ed. by Francis Darwin, Cambridge University Press, 1909, p. 7.
[15] O, p. 53.

existence."[16] Tradition has often maintained that Darwin drew it direct from Malthus, but of this there is no evidence. Lyell himself in after years reiterated to the biologist Haeckel his early treatment of certain of the ideas which went into natural selection and once more gives credit to De Candolle for the idea of the struggle for existence.[17] "Most of the zoologists," he added a little wearily (this was 1868), "forget that anything was written between the time of Lamarck and the publication of our friend's *Origin of Species.*" We have, of course, already seen that the idea of struggle, and even selection within varietal limits, is far older than De Candolle, but it is equally clear that Darwin probably drew more heavily upon Lyell in regard to this subject than upon Malthus.

Lyell's work, directly concerned with animals as it is, contains much extensive ecological discussion. He speaks of the changes that can ensue from the introduction of a new species in a given region. He recognizes that "the changes caused indirectly would ramify through all classes of the living creation, and be almost endless."[18] There is clear evidence that Lyell actually anticipated Darwin in the recognition of ecological change which could promote extinction. The intricate relations between species, including the unconscious effects wrought by man, were all carefully considered and elaborated. Lyell was not prepared to recognize the creative aspect of the changes he observed in nature, yet he saw clearly that disturbances of natural balance might easily lead to extinctions and readjustments of the fauna over wide areas.

Such a succession of species did not have to wait upon geological convulsions but were a constant product of— natural selection! Ironically enough, *Sir Charles Lyell had fully recognized the negative aspects of the principle and had passed beyond Lamarck in recognizing its part*

[16] PG, 1834, Vol. 2, p. 391.
[17] LLL, Vol. 2, p. 436.
[18] PG, Vol. 3, p. 52.

in the elimination of species. His failure lay in his inability to grasp the principle in its full creative role. He was still under the Linnaean spell that the amount of variation which could be produced was limited.

There is much in Lyell's career that served as an outright model for Darwin's activities. In addition, Lyell accumulated in his book stores of information from some of the sources we have previously discussed. They were thus conveniently summarized and brought to the direct attention of Darwin, and Darwin's co-worker Wallace, by the hand of a man directly interested in the same problems which confronted them. In fact, one might well say he composed and set forth for them the problem which they eventually solved. He advocated a geological continuity based on Huttonian principles, but built upon much more extended geological information that had accumulated since the days of Hutton and Playfair. In successfully overthrowing by degrees the old catastrophic doctrine, he was inevitably destroying also the precise, serried, and advancing worlds of the progressive creationists. Instead, it became apparent, in the light of Lyell's careful examination of the struggle for existence and the interlinked web of nature, that the succession of species had always been going on throughout past time and was even now continuing.

No item was too small for its significance to escape him as it might relate to the demonstration of the persistence of natural forces similar to those active upon the globe today. He drew from Buckland's investigation of the eyes of trilobites the observation that "the ocean must then have been transparent as it is now; and must have given a passage to the rays of light, and so with the atmosphere; and this leads us to conclude that the Sun existed then as now and to a great variety of other inferences."[19] He was one of the first to investigate fossil rain marks, "the

[19] Sir Charles Lyell, *Eight Lectures on Geology*, New York, 1842, pp. 41–42.

drops of which resembled in their average size those
which now fall from the clouds." He argued on the basis
of this evidence "that the atmosphere of one of the re-
motest periods known in geology corresponded in density
with that now investing the globe."[20] It was this type of
long, careful mustering of evidence which led to the final
fading of the catastrophic doctrines. As one impressed reviewer put the matter as early as 1835, "the concession
of an unlimited period for the working of the existing
powers of nature has permitted us to dispense with the
comets, deluges and other prodigies which were once
brought forward, *ad libitum,* to solve every difficulty in
the path of the speculating geologist."[21]

It was from Lyell that Darwin drew his now well-
known argument as to the imperfection of the geological
record. It was to Lyell, as late as the writing of the *Descent of Man* (1871), that Darwin had recourse in the attempt to explain how a comparatively weak-bodied primate could have survived until his cultural development
made him a match for the formidable carnivores of the
primitive world. Here is Lyell's statement:

". . . for if a philosopher is pleased to indulge in con-
jectures on this subject [i.e., the birthplace of humanity],
why should he not assign, as the original seat of man,
some one of those large islands within the tropics, which
are as free from wild beasts as Van Dieman's Land or
Australia? Here man may have remained for a period peculiar to a single isle, just as some of the large anthropomorphous species are now limited to one island within
the tropics. In such a situation, the new born race might
have lived in security, though far more helpless than the

---

[20] Sir Charles Lyell, "On Fossil Rain-Marks of the Recent,
Triassic, and Carboniferous Periods," *Quarterly Journal of the
Geological Society of London,* 1851, Vol. 7, p. 247.

[21] Anonymous, "Lyell's *Principles of Geology," Quarterly Review,* 1835, Vol. 53, p. 410. The paper is unsigned but attributable
to William Whewell.

New Holland savages, and might have found abundance of vegetable food."[22]

A similar expression, save for the added element of natural selection, is to be found in the closing paragraph of Chapter II of the *Descent of Man*. Darwin had been attacked critically by the Duke of Argyll, and it is interesting that in this period of his mature scholarship Darwin still sought his old friend's speculations when he found himself in a tight spot.

Although such evidences of Lyell's influence upon Darwin as I have given here could be multiplied, their general bearing is plain: Lyell, far more extensively than Buffon, possessed in 1830 all of the basic information necessary to have arrived at Darwin's hypothesis but did not. Granted some emotional aversion to a family connection with Lamarck's orang (a relationship to which he jokingly referred), Lyell was, nevertheless, a cool, objective reasoner, as well informed biologically as he was geologically. Studies of his letters have led to a few accusations that he equivocated, that he assumed a conservative pose in public and speculated privately upon the possible mutability of species.[23] I think that this charge of timid vacillation is in some degree unjust to the man who marshaled the evidence and took the stand which eventually destroyed the catastrophic doctrine which, in the words of a contemporary historian of science, William Whewell, "held almost undisputed sway in geological circles."[24] It is true his work was later to become a conservative classic, but at the time it was launched Lyell stood courageously alone as much as Darwin did when the *Origin* was given to the press. Lyell cannot, therefore, be easily

[22] PG, Vol. 3, pp. 17–18.
[23] Darwin's pseudonymous biographer, Geoffrey West, has taken this point of view. See *Charles Darwin, A Portrait*, Yale University Press, 1938, pp. 103, 123.
[24] *Quarterly Review*, 1835, Vol. 53, p. 407.

called, in spite of a pleasant uncontroversial temperament, a truckler to public opinion.

As a matter of fact, even his biological observations received laudatory attention shortly after the publication of the second volume of the *Principles*—that volume which was so to excite Darwin when it reached him in South America. "Nothing," maintained Whewell, who reviewed it in the conservative *Quarterly Review*,[25] "can be more striking than the picture given by our author of the mutual wars of the different tribes of plants and animals, their struggles for food, their powers of diffusion . . . and the wide and sweeping changes which these phenomena have produced and are producing in the face of animated nature." Whewell dwells upon the "ingenious reasoning" by which Lyell accounts for extinctions. "The author," he says admiringly, "urges that when new species multiplying widely, and requiring large supplies of food, are introduced into a country, the older tenants of the soil *must* necessarily be reduced by want, and some classes must be destroyed." This is just how close to evolution Lyell was in 1830 and this is the way in which certain, though not all, of his ideas were being received by a leading scholar in a widely read review.

What then were the inhibiting factors which contributed to drawing Lyell's attention away from a subject to which he had devoted much space in his great book? I think they lie, much more than has been realized, in the philosophical background of uniformitarianism and, curiously enough, in the progressionism which, at first glance, seems to have been moving in an evolutionary direction. The situation is a complex one, demanding considerable analysis. Moreover, it has been further obscured through the unconscious simplification of motives activating those, including Lyell and Huxley, who survived the progressionist period to become full-fledged Darwinists. There is always a desire, after such a great intellectual triumph as

[25] 1832, Vol. 47, pp. 118, 120.

Darwinism represented, to submerge the account of one's past hesitations and to appear to have been a disciple who, from the first, had never doubted the direction events were to take.

In 1868, when Darwin was riding the full wave of his fame, Lyell wrote to the German biologist Ernst Haeckel acknowledging the gift of the latter's latest book. In a discussion of some of the historical background of the evolutionary philosophy and his own contribution to it, Lyell remarks, and the remark in and of itself is honest enough, "I had certainly prepared the way. . . ."[26] The intriguing thing about this statement, however, and a few others of comparable character, is the fact that right up to the time, almost, of the publication of the *Origin of Species*, Lyell was advocating, though with no great success and not by any really extended publication, a doctrine which he himself once termed "non-progressionism." In the commotion attendant upon the publication of the *Origin*, and in the ensuing debates, non-progressionism died quietly, never to be resurrected by its author. Lyell, as is evident from his later modest claims to have been one of Darwin's predecessors, was content to let his ill-starred theory perish without being acknowledged by its author.

Yet it is this theory which was actually expressed in his Anniversary Address given before the Geological Society of London in 1851. The speech is of particular interest because facts in this address were once referred to by Lyell in connection with his claims to having promoted the way for Darwin. Again he is not wrong in detail, but he chose not to be wholly candid about this forgotten episode. With the death of progressionism—and progressionism began to die more rapidly after the glacial theory was developed at the hands of Agassiz and others in

[26] LLL, Vol. 2, p. 436. See also LLD, Vol 2, p. 190.

the forties[27]—non-progressionism ceased to have meaning.
Since it is one of the obscurer and shorter-lived episodes
in nineteenth-century thought it has not been investigated nor its meaning in relation to larger events examined. This doctrine, however, irrational though it may
now seem, is perfectly consistent and logical for a Huttonian and a uniformitarian to have advocated. It is no ab-
erration on the part of Sir Charles Lyell. It is, instead, the
logical outcome of pure uniformitarianism when that system is kept fully divested of progressionist elements. Evolution, by contrast, is a system which contains material
derived from both philosophies. It is a hybrid, a product,
really, of two distinct lines of thought which had to merge
to become completely successful. All this the world has
forgotten and Lyell for very human reasons helped in
the forgetting. It is now necessary to examine non-progressionism and the intellectual atmosphere out of which
it arose.

III Non-progressionism

We have observed, in our discussion of James Hutton,
that he had seen the world as a self-adjusting, self-reno-
vating engine, surviving through illimitable vistas of time.
Cosmological speculation, theories of earth formation, of
which there had been many before him, he viewed with
distrust. They were, he felt, essentially speculative and
unverifiable. He wished to confine geology to its proper
province—the earth—and to the facts which could be
elicited from her formations and deposits. It was essential to the regularity of Hutton's system that there be no
mysterious and supernatural, or unaccountable, powers at
work in the earth. The erosive forces shaping the surface
of the planet were to be seen as those at work around
us constantly in the shape of winds and frost and running

[27] Ice advances explained away the glacial erratics which had
been previously used to bolster the position of the catastrophists.

water, along with the somewhat more mysterious but natural forces of heat in the earth's interior. Life did not particularly occupy his attention—he saw it merely as extending into the indefinite past. There was as yet no sure evidence of vast extinctions or the progressive advancement of living forms.

By the time Lyell came to write the *Principles of Geology,* he was, though drawn to the uniformitarian philosophy, presented with a somewhat different situation than had confronted Hutton in the 1780s. There were evidences pointing to extinction of animal forms, to the past existence of unknown animals, and, above all, there existed in the transcendental, man-centered progressionism of the catastrophists a philosophy which was the very antithesis of the Huttonian approach. Progressionism may very well be regarded today as a long step toward evolution. Looked at in another light, from Lyell's position in the 1830s, it could be viewed, like catastrophism itself, as a retreat from scientific principles and an introduction of supernaturalism into geology. Lyell, in defending the uniformitarian geology, could scarcely at the same time be expected to embrace progressionism which, as we have seen, is really the biological equivalent of catastrophism. As a consequence, from the very beginning Lyell's philosophical position was somewhat ambiguous if not contradictory.

In spite of his great victory over the "convulsionists" he was never entirely happy with the situation in which he found himself. He had come upon the scene too late to ignore the accumulated information upon organic change, but was philosophically committed to secondary causes and the reign of natural law. What was easy for the progressionist to account for by special creation and divine edict was a constant embarrassment to the man whose whole work had been opposed to epochs of extinction and re-creations of fauna. As a later writer has observed of this period, "The aim of naturalists seemed to be to create a world as unlike that of today as it was possible to have it."[28] Lyell, when he challenged the validity of catastrophism, was inevitably confronted with a far more unanswerable problem. Unlike Hutton he had to account in uniformitarian terms, *not alone for change in the inorganic world, but in the world of life as well.* If he was forced to admit supernaturalism in the successive creations of life, then his geological opponents could readily say, and they did say:

"When we find that such events as the first placing of man upon the earth, and the successive creation of vast numbers of genera and species, are proved to have occurred within assignable geological epochs, it seems to us most natural to suppose, that mechanical operations also have taken place, as different from what now goes on in the inorganic world as the facts just mentioned are from what we trace in organic nature."[29]

Lyell, in other words, was being challenged either to explain the mysterious changes in the world of life or accept the fact that the planet also has been shaped by unknown forces.

It was a shrewd and formidable challenge. Lacking the Darwinian principle only one recourse was possible. In taking this way out Lyell was not able to remain wholly consistent and his thinking on the subject wavered from time to time. In essence, however, he clung to a slightly modified Huttonian position: he accepted time as being boundless as space and he denied, admittedly in a rather cautious fashion, that major organic changes could be proved.

As part of his geological treatment of the subject he extended and elaborated Hutton's work upon erosion, but where Hutton had contented himself with physical geology, Lyell called paleontology to his aid. He pointed out that the unity of plan, which could be traced from

[28] *Science*, 1883, Vol. 1, p. 69.
[29] *Quarterly Review*, 1832, Vol. 47, p. 126.

living forms back into the past, itself bespoke an unbroken continuity and connection. He strove successfully to show that the catastrophic discontinuities supposed to be world-wide in extent were frequently local and that animal forms claimed for a single catastrophic interval could be traced, in many instances, straight though successive strata, thus raising serious questions as to the total obliteration of successive faunas. He made use of the argument from the imperfection of the geological record to claim that we do not have sufficient evidence to prove the type of biological progression which so many writers demanded.

"The only negative fact," Lyell contended in the *Principles*, "remaining in support of the doctrine of the imperfect development of the higher orders . . . in remote ages, is the absence of birds and mammalia. The former are generally wanting in deposits of all ages." Land mammals could not be expected in oceanic deposits. For the more remote ages, therefore, there was "scarcely any means of obtaining an insight into the zoology of the then existing continents."[30] Man, Lyell was forced rather unwillingly to admit, did seem to be a recent introduction and an exception to his system.

Lyell was not so foolish as to deny that there had been organic change of a sort on the planet. It is here that his system and his writings, scattered over some twenty or more years, are not always consistent. Essentially, however, his position, which, rather than weakening, was being more strongly asserted by its author at mid-century, can be summarized about as follows.

He recognized that faunas altered and changed, but by using inferences drawn from peculiarities of modern distribution he seems, like Cuvier before him,[31] to suggest that many of the differences between one age and an-

[30] PG, Vol. 2, pp. 396–97.
[31] The idea is implied in Hutton (1788) but was not developed.

other are not the result of newly generated species. Instead, they may represent influxes from other areas, influxes made possible by shifts in the position of land and sea along with climatic alterations. Thus he pointed out that even in the nineteenth century one could find a dominant marsupial fauna in Australia, a reptilian fauna in the Galápagos, and a bird fauna in New Zealand. If we knew of these facts only from geological evidences we might claim some kind of progressive succession which actually represents only geographical distinctions. In like manner there may have been periods in the past when reptiles, for example, dominated wider areas than today without there being a succession of forms "governed by any law of progressive development."[32] Similar arguments were used in the field of paleobotany.

By Lyell's time it was not, of course, possible to deny the extinction of certain forms of life, but the great geologist was intent upon discrediting the notion of progressive succession which constituted a threat to his uniformitarian geology. Nor, incidentally, can he be labeled as totally wrong. When the older catastrophic notions began to give way because it was being discovered that the supposedly separate creations overlapped, what was more natural at first than a reaction like Lyell's? Animals whose time of origin was supposedly known began to be found further back in time than had been anticipated. Even the most clearly established, recent form of all—man—began to be eyed with more suspicion.

Lyell dismissed the doctrine of successive development as untrue. "By the creation of species," he said, "I simply mean the beginning of a new series of organic phenomena, such as we usually understand by the term 'species.'" As to how these species came into existence he offered no conjecture, though he hinted that he did not believe "the renovating power" totally suspended.

[32] Anonymous, "Sir Charles Lyell on Progressive Development," *Edinburgh New Philosophical Journal*, 1852, Vol. 52, pp. 358–59.

It can now be seen, glancing back at the intellectual climate of Lyell's period, that a great deal of his energy, thought, and effort had to be devoted to the support of the Huttonian conception of time and natural process. The one idea of what we might call "evolutionary" advance which stood in popular favor was basically imbued with a supernatural aura which Lyell felt obliged to reject. This led him, ironically, into a position where he was in some danger of rejecting organic change at the same time that he tried to account for it by natural means. His position was, from the first, an uneasy and ambivalent one. It forced him into extended investigations which were of great value to Darwin and Wallace, for he had concentrated upon the forces making for organic change in order to explain these *naturally*. His comments upon animal distribution, the struggle for existence, extinction, and related topics were, on the whole, judicious and painstaking. Without them it may well be that neither Darwin nor Wallace would have stumbled upon the final secret. That this position was not purely an idiosyncrasy of Lyell's can be seen from Huxley's Anniversary Address of 1861 before the Geological Society of London.[33] In it he took a firm stand against the progressionist doctrine. There is, he admits like Lyell, "abundant evidence of variation—none of what is ordinarily understood as progression."

There is a sort of oscillation principle in some of this writing, a willingness to admit the fact that the great classes of life have thrown off variable forms in different ages and that these forms may become extinct and new ones arise by means unknown. The system, in principle, however, is too uniform for modern taste. It is almost like the self-correcting aberrations that occur in the cosmic systems of the eighteenth-century astronomers. This attitude stems naturally from the eighteenth-century influ-

[33] Frequently reprinted among his essays under the title "Geological Contemporaneity and Persistent Types of Life."

ence of Hutton. The uniformitarians were, on the whole, disinclined to countenance the intrusion of strange or unknown forces into the universe. They eschewed final causes and all aspects of world creation, feeling like their master Hutton that such problems were confusing and beyond human reach. The uniformitarian school, in other words, is essentially a revolt against the Christian conception of time as limited and containing historic direction, with supernatural intervention constantly immanent. Rather this philosophy involves the idea of the Newtonian machine, self-sustaining and forever operating on the same principles.

For this school to have introduced progressive biological change into its schema would, as we have seen, been an abandonment of its own principles. In terms of nineteenth-century science it would have smacked of the supernatural, of forces not susceptible to investigation and hence suspect. The only thing that the uniformitarian hypothesis did lend in the direction of evolutionary thought was *continuity of action*. Lyell augmented this Huttonian observation by attempts to account naturally for extinction, faunal shifts, and similar topics. He retained, however, a bias toward cyclic rather than indefinitely progressive change. Here, however, he is not always consistent. His position, and the facts, made total consistency impossible.

By contrast, the philosophy of catastrophism was frankly supernatural in essence, and progressive. The world was not regarded as always shaped by the forces of today, and the biological record in the rocks was read as progressive though its *material continuity* is interrupted. There is a mixture of both change and Platonism involved in this point of view. Life is prophetic from its first appearance and points on to man. Cosmology held no terrors for the catastrophist. Thus progressionism was better prepared, in a sense, to accept the mysterious origins of life and the apparition of new forms in the rocks than the uniformitarian who wanted to believe only in forces he could see and interpret in terms of existing knowledge.[84]

The final victory of uniformitarian geology over catastrophism, and the fact that Lyell, its leading proponent, became a Darwinian, has led to the unconscious assumption that uniformitarianism nourished the evolutionary hypothesis. Actually, however, this can be observed to be only a partial truth. Uniformitarianism was, in some respects, rigid and uncompromising. It was wary of anything which could be regarded as an upward trend in the organic world although it was soon obvious that the *fact* of such a trend, irrespective of its explanation, could not be evaded. Lyell felt pressed by this problem and it led to some of his ambiguous and uneasy evolutionary remarks, which, to use the words of his great pupil Darwin out of context, are "master wrigglings" rather than prophetic insights.

We may thus say briefly that evolution, to a very considerable extent, arose out of an amalgamation or compromise which partook largely of progressionism, but drew the important principle of continuity and adaptive response largely from uniformitarianism. Darwin, by an astute application of Malthusian selection, supplied the observable "natural" principle demanded by the uniformitarians and this relaxed their fears of supernaturalism. Progressionism and uniformitarianism in their extreme forms began to fade from men's minds. What emerged —Darwinism, developmentalism, evolutionism—was the intellectual offspring of two distinct schools of biological thought.

[84] It should be noted, of course, that it was possible, at least theoretically, to be a catastrophist without inclining toward supernatural forces. The bent of the school, however, runs otherwise.

Chapter V

The Minor Evolutionists

If man was to think beyond what the senses
had directly given him, he must first throw
some wild guess-work into the air, and then,
by comparing it bit by bit with nature, improve and shape it into a truth.
William Smith, Thorndale, 1859

---

1 Branching Evolution

One thing that contributed to the failure of the early attempts to gain consideration for evolution—even from scientists—was the arrangement of life in terms of a single
scale with man at its head. If one attempts to change the
scale into a moving chain one is confronted by gaps. Lamarck was not able to connect invertebrates to vertebrates. An attempt by Geoffroy Saint-Hilaire, an early
nineteenth-century transcendental morphologist and ten-
tative evolutionist, to span the gap between the invertebrates and the vertebrates by introducing the cephalo-
pods as a transitional form, a sort of "bent vertebrate,"
was easily refuted by Cuvier.[1] This famous controversy

---

[1] Étienne Geoffroy Saint-Hilaire's importance as an early evolutionist has been somewhat exaggerated. The English reader will
find a very able discussion of his views on morphology and evolution in Chapter V of E. S. Russell's *Form and Function*, New
York, 1917.

is sometimes described as an early, evolutionary debate. Actually, though the argument had some potential evolutionary overtones, it revolved about Geoffroy's transcendental unity of plan. Unity of structure did not then necessarily imply what it does today, namely, actual physical descent of related forms from a common ancestor.

The rising interest in the similarities and dissimilarities of structure existing in the animal and plant kingdoms stimulated philosophical discussion in both Germany and France. With the rise of the romantic movement in philosophy and literature this thinking was not slow in seeping into England. Though Cuvier is often castigated as having crushed the evolutionary position in his attack on Geoffroy, the truth is that his rejection of a universal plan for all organisms,[2] and his insistence upon unrelated structural types no longer arranged in a unilineal series with man at the head, was a necessary preliminary to the kind of branching evolutionary phylogeny which is now everywhere accepted. The attempts to fill in all the gaps represented in the old Scale of Being were bound to fail and to stand as an impediment to evolutionary thinking. Until the vast riches of the paleontological record were revealed, and until human embryology became better known, biologists were bound to regard the creation of man by successive slow transformations as, in the words of a contemporary thinker, "the most complex and circuitous method imaginable"—a "dream of the imagination."

One can understand this reasoning. The advocates of the development hypothesis were fond of speaking of the simplicity of nature, and the fact that the Deity, in the last analysis, controlled the powers behind nature. Why then, a devout scholar could reasonably argue, should God not have chosen to create man simply and immediately? So long as one accepted the premise that man was

---

[2] "There is, philosophically speaking," Geoffroy once wrote, "only a single animal." He aimed to link insects, crustacea, and molluscs with the vertebrates in terms of anatomical pattern.

preordained in the beginning it was difficult to account for the rationale of such a roundabout way of bringing him upon the scene. Only the emergence of a totally different way of looking at man and the forms of life related to him would offer a reasonable explanation for this seemingly unanswerable question.

II William Wells

The major tenet of Darwinian evolution, the struggle for existence, is, as we have seen, an old principle. For it to be comprehended as a leading factor in organic change, other assumptions are necessary. Among these, variation which is capable of indefinite extension beyond specific and generic bounds is paramount. Plenty of people, from the time of conscious improvement of domestic stocks, understood the value of artificial selection but few had attempted to apply that principle to wild nature. Fewer still had glimpsed that mutability over long time periods might cause the slow disappearance of one fauna and the rise of another genetically related to but continuing to diverge from the first.

The complex of ideas which later went to make up Darwinism was widely enough diffused in the eighteenth century that finding an unknown or forgotten evolutionist has about it something of the fascination of collecting rare butterflies. Moreover, writings involving the Scale of Nature and progressionism, both of which have faded out of general knowledge, are sometimes misinterpreted by naïve investigators as true expressions of evolution. The occasional similarity of phrases results from the fact that we, with our modern evolutionary ideas, have unwittingly inherited so much from this preceding era of thought. Thus the Darwinian precursors have to be scanned with some care. There remain a few, however, who present us with interesting minor problems and upon whom we have not touched. All wrote before Darwin published,

and of these men, four in England[3] and one in America
glimpsed at least faintly the principle of natural selection.
Alfred Russel Wallace, in no sense a minor figure, I shall
treat of later for purposes of convenience. He shares with
Darwin the leading role in the discovery and demonstration
of natural selection as a leading factor in organic change.

As one examines the second decade of the nineteenth
century—a time when catastrophism held the field and
Lyell was a young man quietly accumulating the data for
his book—one comes upon the name of an expatriate
American physician who was at that time resident in England. William Wells delivered before the Royal Society of
London in 1813 a paper which contains an almost complete
anticipation of Darwin's major thesis, natural selection.
The event is of particular interest for two reasons. The
paper was not given in obscure circumstances, yet its significance seems to have been totally ignored until it was
resurrected by a correspondent of Darwin's in the 1860s. A
reference to it was incorporated into the latter's historical
preface to later editions of the *Origin*.[4] Wells's paper was
entitled "An Account of a White Female, Part of Whose
Skin Resembles that of a Negro." There is no record that
the paper aroused any particular attention and it was not
published again until 1818 after the author's death. Nevertheless, there are some strange aspects to this story.

First of all, there can be no doubt that Wells did
clearly indicate in his discussion of the piebald woman
who was the subject of his discourse the relation between

[3] Wells, Blyth, Matthew, Wallace. For Grimes, the American, see
pp. 314–15. For Edward Blyth, a recent discovery, see my "Charles
Darwin, Edward Blyth and the Theory of Natural Selection" *Proc.
Am. Philosophical Society*, 1959, Vol. 103, pp. 94–158.

[4] For an excellent historical treatment of this episode the reader
is urged to consult Dr. Richard Shryock's "The Strange Case of
Wells's Theory of Natural Selection" in *Studies and Essays in the
History of Science and Learning in Honor of George Sarton*, Cam-
bridge, 1946. Charles Kofoid's "An American Pioneer in Science,
Dr. William Charles Wells, 1757–1817," *Scientific Monthly*, 1943,
Vol. 57, pp. 77–80, supplies some interesting personal details of
Wells's life.

artificial and natural selection. He put together, in other words, two essential ingredients of what was later to become Darwin's theory. "What is here done by art," he says, speaking of artificial selection in domestic animals, "seems to be done with equal efficacy, though more slowly, by nature, in the formation of varieties of mankind, fitted for the countries they inhabit." As a physician he visualized that some stocks might better resist disease and multiply at the expense of others in particular areas.

The case of Wells has aroused extensive discussion as to why his observations failed to attract the attention of scientists. He had gained considerable attention for some of his scientific work, including his memorable *Essay on Dew,* and was a member of the Royal Society. Darwin admitted that Wells's statement appeared to be the first published recognition of natural selection but he commented that so far as he could see Wells had applied the idea only to the human races. This objection of Darwin's has often been challenged of late years. It has been pointed out—for example, by Kofoid[5]—that Wells had in reality paid attention to animals since he had said that "amongst men, as well as among other animals, varieties of a greater or less magnitude are constantly occurring." Thus it has been generally argued that Darwin's restriction will not hold, and that Wells's briefly, though much too timidly, expressed conjecture is actually a full anticipation of the Darwin-Wallace thesis.

My own interpretation differs in some degree from that of other writers. I introduce it here simply because it serves to illustrate some of the more subtle and elusive aspects in the growth of the Darwinian hypothesis and how easy it is to read back into this material something that may not have been present in the mind of its author. Darwin, obviously and naturally a little on the defensive about his originality, couched his analysis of Wells in terms of the human races. In this he was bound to lose

[5] Op. cit., p. 78.

because it is perfectly true that Wells mentions that varieties of great or small magnitude occur in animals. Moreover, he is perfectly cognizant that what today we would call a mutation can descend to posterity. There is no doubt that he is perfectly informed upon selective breeding.

We have observed that Wells put together two essential ingredients of the Darwinian hypothesis—that he saw clearly the similarity between artificial and natural selection. There is, however, a third ingredient which has to be present before we are really dealing with a full-blown evolutionary system. It is the principle, or conception, of unlimited organic change in time. Try as one will, it is impossible from Wells's phraseology to make out whether this element had entered his thought. Darwin apparently sensed this lack but attributed it to Wells's treatment of human races alone. It is perfectly true that he mentioned animals, but, just as in the case of men, only in a varietal sense. There is no clear expression of unrestricted deviation in unlimited time.

Let us recall what we have learned previously of the seventeenth and eighteenth centuries. At that time there was considerable recognition of variation within circumscribed limits. Struggle, in nature, was supposed to be a sort of pruning device promoting strong and vigorous stock. It will now be seen that Wells's view, as expressed, is far more commonplace than it appears at first glance. His facts are set down with sharp analytical precision but without the specific expression of an extension of change through the species barrier; hence his remarks are not nearly so unique as they have been regarded as being.

Just to re-establish the conclusions which we have already drawn from Lamarck and others, and which could readily be fortified from Zirkle's study of the early history of natural selection,[6] it is perhaps worth mentioning Jo-

6 Op. cit.

seph Townsend.[7] Townsend's paper once more forecasts the Malthusian problem, clearly recognizes the struggle for existence and the selection of the fittest. He tells the story of dogs and goats introduced on Juan Fernández Island to illustrate his principles and describes how the weak under harsh conditions were destroyed while the fittest survived. As with most of the eighteenth-century writers there is no evidence that Townsend perceived that the perfecting principle could carry a stock beyond its normal range of variability. In the case of Wells there is no doubt that his statement, brief though it is, contains a very clear analysis of principles which in some of these other writers are loosely and diffusely stated. For this reason it catches the modern eye. In its essence, however, it still lacks a clear expression of the principle of endless deviation which lies at the heart of the evolutionary philosophy. Wells's remarks, therefore, sound more iconoclastic to us than they actually were. As a matter of fact, I strongly suspect that this is one of the reasons, though perhaps not the only one,[8] why the public was not stirred by Wells's paper. His sentiments simply were neither unusual nor startling to that public without the time factor. Almost one hundred and fifty years later we are reading back into Wells's essay, because of its apt presentation of two of the necessary points out of the possible three which constitute Darwinism, a full-blown anticipation of Darwin which cannot be established.

There is another curious side to the vicissitudes of this remarkable little paper which throws light on the labyrinthine ways of ideas and the way they may pass, like elusive and slippery fish, close to the hands that are groping for them and yet escape. Sir John Herschel's book, *A Preliminary Discourse on the Study of Natural Philosophy* (London, 1833), is one of the best-known treatises on sci-

[7] *A Dissertation on the Poor Laws, By a Well-Wisher to Mankind,* London, 1786.
[8] See Shryock for additional material and a very able discussion.

entific method of the first half of the nineteenth century. We know that Darwin studied this book assiduously. In it Dr. Wells's *Essay on Dew* is referred to as a very beautiful specimen of inductive scientific logic. Ironically, in the light of after events, Herschel earnestly recommended this work to the student of natural philosophy "as a model with which he will do well to become familiar."[9] The little volume contains, in its 1818 version, the case history which preserves Wells's account of natural selection. There is no record that Darwin took Herschel's advice.

Once more, however, and in a quite astonishing manner, this elusive essay was destined to pass across the Darwinian horizon. It came this time as Darwin was proposed by Hugh Falconer for the Copley Medal of the Royal Society in 1864. Falconer, the distinguished paleontologist, was just Darwin's age, but was destined to die shortly after his letter was dispatched to the secretary of the society. In it he drew up a list of Darwin's scientific achievements, among them mentioning the study of coral reefs. "It may be compared," said Falconer, "with Dr. Wells's 'Essay on Dew' as original, exhaustive and complete—containing the closest observation with large and important generalizations."[10]

Here was a foremost scholar lauding, among other papers, Darwin's "great essay" on the *Origin of Species*. Yet Falconer, acquainted with Wells's work, seems never to have read the supplementary essay or, if he had, not to have perceived that he held in his hand a partial anticipation of the very friend he was later to propose for the Copley Medal. Moreover, Sir John Herschel himself, friend and correspondent of Lyell and Darwin, as well as the admirer of Wells's incisive scientific logic, seems never to have realized, or at least never to have voiced, the fact that this interesting anticipation of Darwin existed in the papers of a man not unknown to British

[9] Op. cit., p. 163.
[10] MLD, Vol. 1, p. 254.

science.[11] Darwin, instead, received that information in 1860 from an unknown American.

William Wells's prize-winning *Essay on Dew* was, in a sense, perhaps, his downfall. It was regarded as a model of scientific method and it diverted attention from his all too brief formulation of natural selection. As Professor Shryock observes, Wells did not appear to grasp the significance of what he had done and this in itself suggests that the third important factor, time, had not received his serious consideration. Nevertheless, the lonely and embittered American royalist had come within a hairsbreadth of the greatest discovery of the age. The fact is revelatory of the endless flux of ideas which, in the social mind, await their moment of crystallization. Wells did not possess even a fragment of that pirate chart which was then in the possession of William Smith of Bath. Wells loved to visit suburban gardens at full moon to study and tramp in the wet dew. It is thus that he passes from our sight, an exile who saw some kind of elusive shadow by moonlight but was unsure of what he saw.

III   *Patrick Matthew and Robert Chambers*

In 1831 an obscure Scotch botanical writer, Patrick Matthew by name, published a book entitled *On Naval Timber and Arboriculture.* Although Matthew was a contemporary of Darwin nothing seems to be known of his life or of his birth and death dates.* This is unfortunate because Patrick Matthew is the first clear and complete anticipator among the progressionists of the Darwinian theory of evolution. Unfortunately his book is now exceedingly rare. This has led to a tendency merely to repeat what Darwin said in his introduction to the *Origin* and let it go at that. As has been remarked by many stu-

---

[11] It should be noted that there were several editions of the *Essay on Dew* which did not incorporate the evolutionary paper.

* Since the above was written Sir Gavin de Beer has established his dates as 1790 to 1864.

dents of the period, however, Darwin's little venture into the history of the subject is meager and not particularly generous. In addition, Darwin was not in a position to look at his subject with the perspective we can bring to it today.

Patrick Matthew was not, from all accounts, a very tactful man. He bristled over the failure of the world to recognize him, after the publication of the *Origin*. He had cards printed announcing himself as the discoverer of the principle of natural selection and he so nettled Darwin that the latter was obviously happy to announce, after the discovery of Wells, that Matthew had lost his own claim to priority. The truth is that Matthew never really lost his claim. One essential of the complete theory—indefinite divergence through time—was not expressed by Wells, whatever his personal thoughts may have been.[12] Matthew, on the other hand, is precise on this point, and his remarks, though briefly expressed in the appendix to his treatise on tree-growing, are clear enough to make any confusion impossible. Darwin, it is true, said in his historical sketch prefixed to the *Origin* that he did not understand some passages, and that Matthew "attributes much influence to the direct action of the conditions of life."

Nevertheless, Darwin was forced to admit that Matthew had anticipated both himself and Wallace. Matthew, he wrote to De Quatrefages in 1861, "most expressly and clearly anticipated my views."[13] In 1860 he had written similarly to Wallace, italicizing the statement, "He gives *most clearly* but very briefly . . . our view of Natural Selection. It is a most complete case of anticipation."[14] Wallace, in a letter to Samuel Butler, who ex-

[12] As a physician Wells was, of course, acquainted with the *Zoonomia*.

[13] MLD, Vol. 1, p. 187.

[14] James Marchant, *Alfred Russel Wallace: Letters and Reminiscences*, New York, 1916, p. 118.

plored the subject and gave an extended series of quotations from Matthew in his *Evolution, Old and New,* confessed, "To my mind your quotations from Mr. Patrick Matthew are the most remarkable things in your whole book, because he appears to have completely anticipated the main ideas of the *Origin of Species.* . . ."[15]

It is now important, if we are to understand Matthew and his role, to remember that his book was published in 1831 at a time when the catastrophist doctrine in geology was at its height. It tends to bear out my contention, expressed previously, that the intellectual climate of catastrophism and its accompanying biological analogue, progressionism, was peculiarly favorable to the eventual development of the idea of evolution. The only obstacle standing in the way of this modification was the physical break supposed to exist between one biological world and its succeeding one. It is, therefore, of great interest to observe that Matthew, a geological catastrophist, succeeded in evading this difficulty.

Darwin and the men who were to become his disciples and publicists, Wallace, Huxley, Hooker, and Lyell, were all uniformitarians who clung to continuity of action, but finally introduced a modified organic progressionism into their philosophy. Patrick Matthew, by contrast, clung to geological catastrophism but introduced a kind of faint uniformitarian continuity into his organic system. In both cases it is evident that some compromise between the two schools was necessary before a real evolutionary philosophy could emerge.

Matthew's system perished, not only because it had been published obscurely by an obscure man but because uniformitarian geology at the hands of Lyell was about to weaken and overthrow the catastrophist philosophy. Over and over in the works of the post-Lamarckian evo-

[15] A. R. Wallace, *My Life: A Record of Events and Opinions,* New York, 1905, Vol. 2, p. 84.

lutionists it is made abundantly clear that a compromise
on one or the other side of the two extreme wings of the
opposed geological schools was necessary in order for a
true evolutionary philosophy to emerge.

Patrick Matthew seems to have been the only genuine
evolutionist produced from the ranks of the English catastrophist school. It is thus regrettable that no published
information exists, beyond what we can gain from his
book, as to the intellectual life history of this crotchety but
perceptive man.

"As nature in all her modifications of life has a power
of increase," Matthew wrote, "beyond what is needed to
supply the place of what falls by Time's decay, those individuals who possess not the requisite strength, swiftness,
hardihood, or cunning, fall prematurely without repro-
ducing—either a prey to their natural devourers; or sink-
ing under disease . . . their place being occupied by the
more perfect of their own kind who are pressing on the
means of subsistence."[16]

Here, of course, we have, clear and well stated, what
the eighteenth century had already observed. Remove the
struggle for existence, Brückner had long ago commented,
and "a universal inundation would ensue."[17] So far we
are at the position of Wells almost twenty years before.

Matthew did not stop here, however, as did Wells,
leaving his evolutionary position unclear. Instead, he
turned directly to geology, and we are thus in a position
to see how a catastrophist attempted to handle the evolutionary succession in the rocks.

"Geologists," he maintained, "discover a like particular
conformity—fossil species—through the deep deposition
of each great epoch, but they also discover an almost complete difference to exist between the stamp of one species
or stamp of life, of one epoch from that of every other. We
are therefore led to admit either of a repeated miracu-

16 Op. cit., p. 365.
17 Brückner, op. cit., [as cited in text p. 38.] p. 149.

lous creation; or of a power of change, under a change of circumstances, to belong to living organized matter, or rather to the congeries of inferior life, which appears to form superior. The derangements and changes in organized existence, induced by a change of circumstance from the interference of man, affording us proof of the plastic quality of superior life and the likelihood that circumstances have been very different in the different epochs, though steady in each, tend strongly to heighten the probability of the latter theory."[18]

Matthew, to put the matter briefly, observed that species and varieties under artificial selection "soften into each other."[19] He took this as proof of the "plastic quality" of life and what he called the "circumstance-suiting power of organisms," that is, adaptability. He noted in his book several types of ecological adaptation and he went on to observe that when changed circumstances occur the struggle for existence may be enhanced. Under such conditions individuals of superior adaptive power and "greater power of occupancy" eliminate the less well adapted. All of this is very Darwinian; it is, in fact, pure Darwinism.

As a catastrophist, however, Matthew upheld the usual belief in periods of calm alternating geologically with great convulsions and upheavals of the earth's surface. His evolutionism is adjusted to the convulsionist doctrines in the following manner:

1. He appears to have believed in a vast destruction of fauna at each upheaval but with a few low forms surviving so that the chain of life remains unbroken.

2. At each such interval the destruction of life is so great that new corridors, new adaptive zones, to use a modern term, are opened for exploitation. There is thus a re-radiation and evolution of life, the world fills up once more, but the new forms are never precisely like the old. As a consequence, each great period in the rocks is dif-

18 Matthew, op. cit., pp. 381–82.
19 Ibid., p. 381.

ferent though the continuity of life on a low level remains. What Matthew upholds, therefore, is the comparative stability of life in the calm intervals when the world is filled up and, on the other hand, he appears to visualize marked rapidity of evolution by selective principles when the amount of life on the globe is greatly reduced by catastrophic events. The idea is really another version of Cuvier's notion of the new fauna, which replenishes a damaged area, coming from elsewhere. In Matthew's case this fauna evolves and there is even a hint, never developed, of spontaneous generation.

We may now observe that such a catastrophist evolution, if Matthew had ever gone on to elaborate it, would have had to account for an extremely rapid ability to evolve high forms within the course of a single geological epoch. He might also have been called upon to explain why the results differed so much from one era to another. Actually Matthew, in embryonic form, had answers prepared to both these questions. They are worth giving because they reveal a remarkable parallelism of thought existing between himself and Darwin on one point where Darwin, when he wrote his historical sketch, thought himself and Matthew to be the furthest apart.

Matthew, as Darwin was later to do, believed that natural selection operated "upon the slight but continued natural disposition to sport in the progeny."[20] Unlike the usual progressionist he does not appear to have been particularly man-centered, although he makes a kind of polite perfunctory exception in his discussion of the human race. With the exception of man, he observes, "there does not appear to have been any particular engrossing race, but a pretty fair balance of powers of occupancy, or rather, most wonderful variation of circumstance parallel to the nature of every species, *as if circumstance and species had grown up together.*"[21] Matthew, in other words,

20 Op. cit., p. 385.
21 Ibid., p. 387. (Italics mine. L.E.)

here intimated that life is in a kind of dynamic balance which is never twice the same from one era to another because the web of living things is both subject to chance, in the shape of fortuitous variation, and to natural law, in the guise of selective survival. In this respect life is undirected, chanceful, and will never emerge twice the same on the planet after any great catastrophe. Matthew thus ignores the supernatural metaphysics of the progressionists: geological prophecy and the conception of a divinely inspired series of events leading step by directed step to the human emergence. In all these respects Matthew appears to have had as purely a naturalistic outlook as Darwin.

"But," said Darwin, "it seems that he attributes much influence to the direct action of the conditions of life." This Lamarckian factor was played down in the first edition of the *Origin*, though as we will have occasion to see in a later chapter, Darwin was forced to fall back upon it when heavy criticism and a reduced allowance of geological time sorely beset him. Now Matthew, as we have observed, was confronted with a peculiar problem in developing his views. Unlike the uniformitarian Darwin, he had to account for, not the evolution of life upon one world, but in reality a succession of worlds. I say this because, if one had to explain the almost total rise of a new fauna and flora after each catastrophic episode in the earth's history, one was, in actuality, explaining the rise of life within a series of almost unrelated worlds. The continuity in Matthew's system is reduced, in other words, to a bare minimum of primitive organisms. His system, therefore, demands great and rapid malleability on the part of the organism, yet the selective aspect of the theory emphasizes slight but continuous variation.

It is apparent that Matthew, even though he did not feel impelled to justify himself to the extent that the writer of a longer work might have, felt some concern over the relation of time to his natural selection theory.

He needed, to put it briefly, an accessory principle which might speed the process of organic change. Thus we find that Matthew "does not preclude the supposed influence which volition or sensation may have over the configuration of the body."[22] At this point we are back with Erasmus Darwin and Jean Lamarck. This fact threatened for a time to make fortuitous and undirected evolution a logical impossibility. Darwin, after earlier dissociating himself from Matthew's thought along these lines, was forced to move in the same direction and for what was, basically, the same reason—a restriction of the amount of free time at his disposal.

One other interesting observation can be made: in some of Matthew's phrases, such as the familiar "millions of ages," and in his emphasis upon "volitions and sensations" one can perceive the ghost of Erasmus Darwin. There would seem to be an actual continuity of intellectual descent here, so far as the inheritance of acquired characters is concerned. There is, however, no doubt, also, of the genuine originality of Patrick Matthew's thinking. It is a great tragedy that he did not bring his views into the open because the amount of ground he was able to cover in a few paragraphs suggests that he might have been able to sustain a longer treatise. As the record stands, neither Matthew nor Wells can be said to have advanced the subject. Their words were obscure flashes in the dark, firefly indications that some kind of intellectual ferment was working behind the orthodox surface of things.[23] It was time for something weightier to appear.

The hour came in 1844 with the publication of *The Vestiges of the Natural History of Creation.* The book was written by a scientific amateur and published anony-

[22] Op. cit., p. 385.
[23] Grant Allen, one of Darwin's earliest biographers, wrote, in 1892, "Long before Charles Darwin published his epoch-making work, conjecture and speculation were rife in England as to the origin of species and the evolution of organic life." *Fortnightly Review*, 1892, Vol. 58, p. 799.

mously for reasons of discretion. Condemned by the critics as immoral and godless, it promptly took the public by storm. Four editions appeared in seven months and by 1860 some 24,000 copies had been sold.[24] Two hundred copies of the first edition were distributed to prominent scientists in the attempt to arouse interest. The result of this effort to bring attention to the subject is of extreme interest to the scientific historian.

Robert Chambers, the anonymous author, had hoped for a scientific hearing but was promptly shouted down. Thomas Huxley, who was later to become Darwin's chief defender, attacked the book with the utmost savagery. Phrases such as "foolish fancies," "charlatanerie," "pretentious nonsense," "work of fiction," "mean view of Nature" rolled from his pen. None of Huxley's reviews of anti-Darwinian opponents equal the ferocity of this onslaught upon the *Vestiges*. Ironically, the review defends men like Owen and Sedgwick who were later to assault Darwin mercilessly. Chambers was berated for every possible minor error—and they were admittedly numerous—that could be found in his work.

"It is surprising," remarked Persifor Frazer at a later date, "that the influence of the *Vestiges* . . . which appeared anonymously should be so rarely and slightingly alluded to (if not entirely ignored) by masters like Huxley."[25] Any reading of Huxley's review of the tenth edition of the *Vestiges* in 1854 will give one an idea of why he preferred later that the book be forgotten.

The scientists as well as the theologians, however, overdid their case. The disputatious and vindictive storm they aroused made evolution public property. Thus, as Draper commented many years ago, "happily the whole subject

[24] A. R. Wallace, *The Wonderful Century*, New York, 1898, p. 138.

[25] "Was the Development Theory Influenced by *The Vestiges of the Natural History of Creation?*" *The American Geologist*, 1902, Vol. 30, p. 262.

was brought into such prominence that it could be withdrawn into obscurity no more."[26] The increasing growth of literacy among the working classes was contributing to a widespread interest in the new ideas of science. While the critics fulminated, the public, in which Chambers had placed little faith, read his book with eagerness and enthusiasm. Years later Francis Darwin was to write, "My father's copy [of the *Vestiges*] gives signs of having been carefully read, a long list of marked passages being pinned in at the end." Francis Darwin points out that Charles, seeing the difficulties Chambers got into with certain attempts to explain phylogenetic lines, wrote, "I will not specify any genealogies—much too little known at present."[27]

It is customary among biographers of Darwin to speak of the excitement which greeted the appearance of the *Origin* and of Huxley's able defense of Darwin at Oxford in his clash with Bishop Wilberforce. Actually, however, by the time Darwin published, Robert Chambers had drawn much of the first wrath of the critics and the intelligent public was at least reasonably prepared to consider a more able, scientific presentation of the subject. Not least among the curious realignments of forces which took place in 1860 is the fact that it was Robert Chambers who persuaded Huxley to attend the meeting at which he became engaged with Wilberforce. Huxley had had no intention of listening to the bishop, and had expressed an aversion to being "episcopally pounded." Chambers had urged Huxley not to desert the evolutionists in their hour of need and as a consequence he had finally consented to go.[28] If it had not been for the urging of Chambers the episode which, more than any other, dramatized

[26] John W. Draper, "Evolution: Its Origin, Progress and Consequences," *Popular Science Monthly*, 1877, Vol. 12, p. 181.
[27] LLD, Vol. 1, p. 333.
[28] E. B. Poulton, "A Hundred Years of Evolution," *Report of the British Association for the Advancement of Science*, 1931, pp. 72–73.

Huxley's powers as a public speaker and defender of the Darwinian cause would never have taken place. In his willingness to forget the assaults to which he had been subjected, Robert Chambers showed a rare quality of mind for which he was little enough rewarded even by those whom he helped to defend. To understand more fully his position in the controversies of his time a short résumé of the leading ideas of the *Vestiges* is now necessary. Through all, it must be borne in mind that Chambers, as part owner of a successful publishing house, had to remain anonymous in order to protect the business interests of himself and his brother William. This is a measure of the damage which threatened a man who transgressed established views in the first half of the century.[29]

Robert Chambers (1802–71) was not a trained scientist but a philosophically minded journalist who had become convinced of the reality of both cosmic and organic evolution—another illustration, if one were needed, of the ideas which were beginning to emerge from the works of the geologists. Chambers had absorbed many diverse ideas and some of his own errors are partly the result of eclectic gatherings from a variety of sources. The essentials of his position are as follows: (1) He adopted from the progressionist philosophy the idea that there is an advance in the complexity of life as one traces it upward through the sedimentary rocks of the planet. (2) He rejected with the Huttonian geologists the idea of total breaks in stratigraphy and recognized that certain forms appeared to extend from one era to the next. He believed in the world's great age and rejected the notion that the entire surface of the planet had been under water. "Time,"

[29] Anyone interested in a full and sympathetic treatment of Chambers is urged to consult Milton Millhauser's unpublished doctoral dissertation, *Robert Chambers, Evolution, and the Early Victorian Mind* (1951), a copy of which is on file in the Columbia University Library. A microfilm copy of this thesis is also possessed by the Library of the American Philosophical Society in Philadelphia.

he said, "and a succession of forms in gradation and affinity, become elements in the idea of organic creation. It must be seen," he continued, "that the whole phenomena thus pass into a strong analogy with those attending the production of the individual organism."

It is only fair to recognize at this point something which, except for the observations of Professor Lovejoy,[30] has rarely been clearly assigned to Robert Chambers. It is this: He actually put the separate pieces of the lost chart of Hutton, Cuvier, and Smith together and came up with the idea that organic as well as cosmic evolution was a reality.

The time of his publication, and the fact that he was a highly intelligent amateur, justifies my comment that so far as the accumulation of ideas was concerned it was not necessary to sail around the globe to develop a theory of evolution. The voyagers had already provided much of the necessary information. Rather it was necessary to break out of a particular, man-centered way of looking at the world. Chambers has often been castigated for the uncritical acceptance of naïve ideas upon the spontaneous generation of such complex organisms as plants and insects. It should be said in fairness, however, that while he held such reports favorable to his hypothesis, he saw that these creations were not indispensable to a theory of evolution. Although this conception of spontaneous generation led to accusations of atheism the truth is that Chambers never totally escaped the religious aspects of the old progressionism. He took rudimentary structures, as did the transcendental French and German anatomists, merely as evidences of continuing plan, "evidences of the manner in which the Divine Author has been pleased to work."

On the other hand, like Lamarck, he believed that the

30 A. O. Lovejoy, "The Argument for Organic Evolution before the Origin of Species," *Popular Science Monthly*, 1909, Vol. 75, pp. 499–514; 537–49.

original life impulse could be modified or adapted to particular environmental circumstances. He recognized, in other words, that there may be numerous branches or radiations within the ascending phyla. The marked rises in organization, as when a more advanced class like the Vertebrata appears, Chambers thought (and we cannot differ from him on this today), were very rare events in the course of untold millions of years.

At the same time he believed that varietal and species differentiation was constantly occurring in a wild state. In this respect his botanical examples sound very much like the macro-mutations of De Vries, which will be discussed in a later chapter. Although Chambers was perfectly aware, like so many before him, of struggle in nature, he seems to have retained the eighteenth century teleological conception that it was a method of keeping the forms of life in proper balance. Carnivores were a necessary policing accompaniment "to the weaker tribes, the fertility of which would otherwise produce complete anarchy." Like Lamarck he saw two principles at work, an inner "gestative" or internal developmental principle which brought about according to divine plan the greater advances in organization, and a second "variative power connected with the will and . . . working to minor effects." The *Vestiges* retains also elements of geological prophecy. "It might have been seen, ere man existed," commented Chambers, "that a remarkable creature was coming upon the earth."

We may now observe that the *Vestiges* is a revised progressionism with Lamarckian and Huttonian elements. It was actually as progressionism that it was attacked by Huxley who was, prior to his Darwinian affiliation, apparently an adherent of Lyell's non-progressionism. The weakness of the *Vestiges* lay in the inability of its author to produce a *vera causae* for evolution outside the metaphysical field of final cause. He is, in detail, occasionally ambiguous and uncertain as to the precise method of emergence of new forms. Nevertheless, as both Millhauser and Lovejoy have observed, he had made out a very impressive case for the reality of evolution, irrespective of the precise nature of the process. He recognized unity of structure, the significance of the fossil record and its genuine continuity. He was intensely, even exaggeratedly, aware of variation. Pathetically he had personal reasons for this knowledge. Both he and his brother William had been born full hexadactyls, that is, with six digits on both hands and feet.

The attacks which the scientific world launched upon the *Vestiges* have, in retrospect, a quite unreal character. They belabor minutiae and amateurish minor errors as though there was some subconscious recognition that the heart of the thesis was unassailable. This attitude is revealed in the letter of an educator to William Whewell in 1846. "You have read," writes this principal of an English school, "the sequel to the *Vestiges*.[31] . . . It was well that he [Chambers] began to write in the fullness of his ignorance and presumption for, had he begun now, he would have been more dangerous."[32]

The principal was wrong on just one point. The work was destined to become more dangerous, not less so. With its publication and success as a best seller, the world of fashion discovered evolution. The restricted professional worlds of science and of theology both lost their ability to suppress or intimidate public thinking upon the matter. The cause lay partly in the very anonymity of the author. Public curiosity was aroused. Speculation as to the name of the author was widespread. As is always apt to occur under such circumstances, names higher and higher in the ranks of society began to be mentioned. Finally it was whispered about that Prince Albert, Victoria's con-

31 *Explanations: A Sequel to the Vestiges*, London, 1846.
32 *Popular Science Monthly*, 1874, Vol. 5, p. 247.

sort, who was known to be interested in science, had written the volume.

People who might never have read the book otherwise now did so. In the words of G. M. Young, the distinguished English historian, "*The Vestiges of Creation,* issued with elaborate secrecy and attributed by a wild surmise to Prince Albert, was a national sensation; translated into golden verses by Tennyson, evolution almost became a national creed."[33]

Darwin, as we have seen, pored carefully over the book. Wallace and his fellow collector Bates perused it before setting forth for the Amazon. Many an unconverted biologist had to scurry hastily through his papers seeking information to resist the harsh questions being asked by the uninitiated and irreverent public. There was a great bustling, and dusting off of half-forgotten facts and fossils.

By 1859, when the *Origin of Species* was published, an aroused and eager audience was considerably prepared for the revelations of Charles Darwin. The great amateur disputant and the great professional scholar should always be remembered as having together won the public mind to evolution. It was one of those events, beautifully timed by accident, which rarely occurs in the history of thought.

Those who are unwilling to accord Chambers a place in the history of evolution because he was not a professional biologist and because, in a confused time, he was guilty of errors should remember what Chambers himself remarked of his own work, "It may prove to be a true system, though one half the illustrations presented by its first explicator should be wrong."[34] Darwin himself asked for no more. "I have only opened a path," he once ventured modestly, "that others may turn into a high road."

---

[33] *Early Victorian England,* Oxford University Press, 1934, Vol. 2, p. 477.
[34] Cited by Millhauser, op. cit., p. 246.

Robert Chambers, who first drew the lightning upon himself in England, deserves, better than most men, the tolerance and affection of posterity. Even Huxley lived to express regret over the impetuous cruelty of his review.

Chapter VI

The Voyage of the *Beagle*

The force of impressions generally depends
on preconceived ideas.

Charles Darwin

I   *The Age of Giants*

When Thomas Huxley, young, ambitious and competitive, glanced around him in 1851, he saw two men who impressed him as standing head and shoulders above the rest of the English naturalists. Richard Owen and Edward Forbes, he observed to a friend, were of superior learning, originality, and grasp of mind. Of Darwin, his coming master, he added charitably, almost as an afterthought, that he "might be anything if he had good health."[1]

There is an element of humor in this impulsive judgment. Within three years, Forbes was dead and the saturnine and devious Owen lived on to become Huxley's and Darwin's mortal antagonist. "I have no reparation to make," Huxley said in reference to their quarrels, on the occasion of Owen's death in 1892; "if the business were to come over again, I should do as I did." Following

[1] *Life and Letters of Thomas Henry Huxley,* ed. by Leonard Huxley, London, 1913, Vol. 1, p. 137.

which, in the typical Huxley fashion, he aided in promoting a memorial for Owen. "The man did honest work," he said gruffly, "enough to deserve his statue, and that is all that concerns the public."[2]

In so speaking, he rang down the curtain on the age of giants. Darwin and Lyell were long gone. Huxley was about to go. On one point only, Huxley was mistaken: he had said, still speaking of Owen, "The thing that strikes me most is how he and I and all the things we fought about belong to antiquity. It is almost impertinent to trouble the modern world with such antiquarian business."[3] Huxley's deprecation of his role was unwarranted. He was, like his great associate Darwin, already a legend in his own lifetime. The little, brilliant band of men who by their united endeavor had swung world thought into a new channel had taken on something of the quality of myth, like the Knights of the Round Table. As long as Science lasts their story will be remembered. And because great deeds demand great obstacles, their enemies also stand immortal in the light of that legend—perhaps even a little more formidable than in life.

The period of hesitant groping, of the patient piling up of facts had ended in 1859 with the publication of *The Origin of Species*. The master synthesis had finally been achieved. Yet even here the historian must proceed cautiously. The *Origin* and its author have a history which runs silently and mysteriously through twenty years of ill health, lone effort, and corroding doubt. The sources of such long continued mental effort are not always easy to discern, and it is unlikely that Darwin himself preserved to the end of his life clear memories of all his multiform activity during the years when he was engaged upon his book.

Although we possess a great quantity of his correspondence, owing largely to the fact that he was rec-

[2] Op. cit., Vol. 3, p. 273.
[3] Ibid., p. 321.

ognized as a genius in his own lifetime, there are, unfortunately, serious gaps in the letters which he preserved from his circle of colleagues—Hooker, Lyell, Owen, and others. Some of these missing letters we know to be important from the responses which Darwin made to them, but we can only infer their content, and often not clearly, from Darwin's preserved correspondence. Though Darwin's life is far more elaborately documented than that of many world figures, there are, nevertheless, some annoying gaps in the huge mass of private papers. Even more material has apparently perished among associates whose family lines ended in the Victorian period and whose possessions were destroyed or dissipated long ago.

To the extent that it is possible, the student of the Darwinian epoch will want to know with what intellectual furniture or preconceptions Darwin began his task, what led him to undertake it, and, finally, what shape his hypothesis took after it had been subjected to the harsh critical battering of the theologians and his brother scientists. The evolutionary hypothesis known as Darwinism was not conceived in a day and Darwin himself was anything but a fanatical dogmatist. As a consequence, there is a certain amount of give-and-take, hesitations persisting through long periods, and, finally, a retreat toward the Lamarckian position. Darwin, as is apt to be the case with any thinker who has opened up extensive new horizons of thought, was in no position to explore personally all of the ramifications of his own discovery. It is an idea open at the peripheries and still being modified and reviewed, as its originator knew quite well that it would be. Our purpose is merely to examine the way in which the hypothesis was put together. To do so we must return once more to the early part of the nineteenth century among ideas with which we are now reasonably familiar. It is here that the youthful Darwin began the researches with which he was to transform the nineteenth-century world-view. We know also that scientific innovators are not born into a vacuum. We shall want to learn, therefore, something of Darwin's family background, his schooling, and the state of scientific thought at the time, in 1831, when young Charles Darwin made his memorable decision to accept the position of naturalist on H.M.S. *Beagle* for a five-year voyage around the world. Most of this story is common knowledge, but there are a few intriguing points of mystery remaining even today.

II   The Influence of Erasmus Darwin

There were two separate channels by which Charles Darwin was familiarized with the general idea of evolution in his youth. Though the little autobiography which he wrote at the urging of his children in his declining years is not particularly explicit upon such points as this, one such channel can be documented, and the other, though not extensively discussed by Darwin, can scarcely be ignored as an almost certain source of information.

One, the more certain channel, lies in the poetry and prose of grandfather Erasmus Darwin, which achieved sufficient world renown as to make it very certain that the ideas of Erasmus would be discussed in family circles. Moreover, the schoolboy who boasted of a fondness for Shakespeare would surely have tried the wares of a poet within the immediate confines of the family. In fact, Darwin himself tells us that he had read his grandfather's prose work, the *Zoonomia,* and though he maintains it had no effect on him, it is not without interest that Darwin's first trial essay on the road to the *Origin* he entitled *Zoonomia.* Furthermore, in one of the unconsciously revelatory statements of which Darwin was sometimes capable he tells us, right after disclaiming that the *Zoonomia* had affected him, that "at this time I admired greatly the *Zoonomia.*"[4]

We need not at this point, however, raise the question

4 LLD, Vol. 1, p. 38.

of what the youth believed—quite possibly he did not know himself. It is sufficient to establish the fact that such ideas were likely to have been assimilated early enough as to have had a familiar ring. The theory of evolution would thus have lost the shocking and heretical implications that it had for the uninitiated.

Darwin himself at one point confesses, albeit a little reluctantly, that "it is probable that the hearing rather early in life such views maintained and praised may have favored my upholding them under a different form in my *Origin of Species*." Believing or unbelieving, young Charles had been raised in a family of somewhat unconventional and free-thinking traditions. We know further that he had a passionate attachment to nature and an equal revulsion against the conventional classical education of the time. At length he was packed off to Edinburgh in the hope that he would follow a medical career as his father and grandfather had done before him. Luckily for science, the sensitive youth could not endure the more ghastly aspects of medical practice and his stay at Edinburgh was short. In that brief period, however, he made the acquaintance of Dr. Robert Grant (1793–1874). Their relation was for a short time pleasant, but subsequently a coolness arose which persisted throughout their later years.* Grant was something of an anomaly in the Scotland of that day. In Paris he had picked up an acquaintance with Lamarckian evolution and was immensely enthusiastic about it. One day, walking with Darwin, he expounded the Lamarckian philosophy. Once more young Darwin listened, so he says, "in silent astonishment," again disclaiming any effect on his mind. Yet he listened, and listened well enough apparently to remember the episode into remote old age. He was then but a youth of sixteen; the voyage of the *Beagle* was still six years away.

* P. H. Jesperson, "Charles Darwin and Dr. Grant," *Lychnos*, 1948–49, Vol. 1, pp. 159–67.

It is not without interest also that while Darwin was at Edinburgh savoring the joys of zoological observation with Robert Grant, a quite remarkable paper appeared in the *Edinburgh New Philosophical Journal*, a scientific magazine contributed to by some of Darwin's professors, and edited by one of them. There is little doubt that Darwin was acquainted with the journal in the year of its foundation. In his later life he made extended use of it.

The paper of which we speak is remarkable in that it upholds the evolutionary hypothesis in the year 1826.[5] That the unknown author knew his views to be extravagantly heretical there can be no doubt. One suspects that he must have been well known to the editors in order to secure even anonymous publication. We know of one such likely person in the Edinburgh of that day: Robert Grant. Curiously enough the paper, perhaps because of its misleadingly innocent title, seems to have gone unnoticed by scientific historians. The writer apparently lays no claim to originality but upholds Lamarck.

"The doctrine of petrifactions, even in its present imperfect condition, furnishes us with accounts that seem in favor of Mr. Lamarck's hypothesis. We, in fact, meet with the more perfect classes of animals, only in the more recent beds of rocks, and the most perfect, those closely allied to our own species, only in the most recent; beneath them occur granivorous, before carnivorous, animals; and human remains are found only in alluvial soil, in calcareous tuff, and in limestone conglomerates."[6]

Referring to Lamarck as "one of the most sagacious naturalists of our day," this pioneer evolutionist continues: "The distinction of species is undoubtedly one of the foundations of natural history, and her character is the propagation of similar forms. But are these forms as im-

[5] Anonymous, "Observations on the Nature and Importance of Geology," *Edinburgh New Philosophical Journal*, 1826, Vol. 1, pp. 293–302.
[6] Ibid., pp. 297–98.

mutable as some distinguished naturalists maintain; or do not our domestic animals and our cultivated or artificial plants prove the contrary? If these, by change of situation, of climate, of nourishment, and by every other circumstance that operates upon them, can change their relations, it is probable that many fossil species to which no originals can be found may not be extinct, but have gradually passed into others."[7] Here, early in English scientific literature—before Lyell had attempted to elucidate the theories of Lamarck for the English public—the suspicious changeability of domesticated forms has been drawn to the attention of the public. It will re-emerge in the succession of Darwin's writings.

Perhaps, considering that this essay was written in the heyday of catastrophism, one of its most astonishing features is its rejection of this point of view. "Out of the vast number of animal remains," our author tells us, "but few belong to species now living, and these only in the most recent rock formations. . . .[*] May this destruction, as is commonly received, have been the result of violent accidents and destructive revolutions of the earth, *or does it not rather indicate a great law of nature, which cannot be discovered by reason of its remote antiquity?*"[8]

The unknown author is sure that "petrifactions" contain the history of the organic world and that this science along with the study of plant and animal distribution—"organic geography" he calls it—will reveal whether the ancient populations were controlled by the same distributional laws as those of the present. The paper is restrained and well-reasoned. Darwin himself was later to pay the most precise attention to distribution. Of interest, further, is the fact that Darwin was actively associated with the scientific life of Edinburgh in the same year that the anonymous essay appeared. There can be no doubt that he was

[7] Op. cit., p. 298.

[*] An intriguingly similar remark in phrase and idea occurs in the next to the final paragraph of the *Origin*.

[8] Ibid., p. 298. (Italics mine. L.E.)

acquainted with the just launched *Edinburgh Journal.* His biographer West, while failing to note the magazine specifically, makes quite clear that the subject of evolution hovered in the Edinburgh air. It is West's belief, certainly not belied by the material we have quoted, that it was here at Edinburgh that evolution became for Darwin "a living and potentially credible doctrine."[9]

Yet this pleasant society was not to last. Tiring of the medical round, Darwin drifted to Cambridge with the thought of entering the ministry, but he continued to cultivate naturalists, to dabble in geology, and to fear the wrath of his exasperated father who had grown weary of his eternal hunting and his lack of scholarly application. One thing, however, is significant: the boy attracted and held the attention of distinguished older men. They sensed something unexpressed within him. Through the good offices of the botanist Henslow and the winning over of his father by his uncle, Josiah Wedgwood, he was permitted to go as naturalist on the voyage of the *Beagle.* The ship sailed in 1831.

III Darwin's Intellectual Background

One can, in a sense, regard the voyage of the *Beagle* as a romantic interlude. One can point out that every idea Darwin developed was lying fallow in England before he sailed. One can show that sufficient data had been accumulated to enable a man of great insight to have demonstrated the fact of evolution and the theory of natural selection by sheer deduction in a well-equipped library. All of this is doubtless true. Yet it is significant that the two men who actually fully developed the principle of natural selection, Charles Darwin and Alfred Russel Wallace, were both travelers to the earth's farthest reaches,

[9] Geoffrey West, *Charles Darwin, A Portrait,* Yale University Press, 1938, p. 66. See also J. H. Ashworth, "Charles Darwin as a student in Edinburgh 1825–1827." *Proceedings of the Royal Society of Edinburgh,* 1935, Vol. 55, pp. 97–113. Professor Ashworth's data fully corroborate the views expressed above.

and both had been profoundly impressed by what they had seen with their own naked eyes and with the long thoughts that come with weeks at sea. It cannot be denied, however, that both had the additional advantage of literary counsel.

Because of the impact their discovery made, there has been a tendency to think, in the case of Darwin in particular, that he personally devised all of the experiment and thought which went into the *Origin of Species*. Without wishing in the least to subtract from his greatness, let us continue our examination of the state of European thought in the year 1831.

Darwin, in after years, sometimes spoke contemptuously of his Cambridge education, forgetting apparently that despite his opinion of the formal course work, he had been privileged to know there some of the finest scientific minds of the day and that the botanist Henslow had made his voyage on the *Beagle* possible.[10] One of these men, Adam Sedgwick, whom Darwin had accompanied on geological field trips, gave a surprising presidential address before the Geological Society of London early in 1830. It was surprising in that Sedgwick, who remained opposed to the evolutionary hypothesis throughout his life, really forecast the eventual triumph of uniformitarianism in geology, and organic evolution in biology. His remarks, perhaps, did not go unnoted by the youthful scholar who was soon to become a disciple of Lyell.

Consider, for example, the following statement: "Each succeeding year places in a stronger point of view the importance of organic remains, when we attempt to trace the various periods and revolutions in the history of the globe. Crystalline rocks are found associated with the strata of almost every age; and the constant laws of com-

[10] It was not that Darwin was ungrateful to these men as individuals. He simply failed to realize that they had been selected and assembled by a great university, irrespective of whether one approved of the curriculum of the time.

bination which have produced a certain mineral form in the rocks of one era, may produce it again in another. . . . The great barriers, which the fancy or ingenuity of geologists has at different times set up between the mineral productions of successive periods, have been thrown down one after another. . . ."[11]

Here Sedgwick is confessing that one can no longer, as in earlier years, claim that the actual mineral composition of the strata differ from one past "world" to another. Instead, to discern accurately the nature of the lost creations one must rely upon the organic remains in the strata. It is at this point that Sedgwick, in a manner which he was to repeat more than once, comes to the very verge of the evolutionary abyss and then draws back. He writes: "When we examine a series of formations which are in contact, we constantly find them passing into each other: and *when we place the groups of fossils derived from the successive terms of the series in the order of superposition, their passage is still more striking.* I do not mean by this to vindicate the transmutation of species; because that doctrine is opposed by all the facts of any value in determining such a question. . . . *I only wish to state a fact of general observation.*" (Italics mine. L.E.)

First minerals had failed to differentiate separate, distinct episodes in the world of the past. Now, Sedgwick implies, the very fossils themselves suggest transitions rather than breaks in the record. From this he recoils, but feels constrained to venture: "I only wish to state a fact of general observation."

That observation, which Sedgwick and most of his generation could not face, was to lead directly to the only possible explanation; that is, uniformitarianism in both geology and biology, the recognition that the successive worlds of the past were one continuous world which had been changing and evolving since time began. Thus, in

11 *The Philosophical Magazine,* 1830, Series 2, Vol. 7, pp. 306–307.

one form or another, Darwin had unknowingly taken aboard the *Beagle* the three fragments of the lost chart of Smith, Cuvier, and Hutton. Particularly, he had taken them in the shape of Lyell's book, *The Principles of Geology*. The second volume containing the material on animal life and Lamarck's theories would reach him in South America.

One other thing happened before he left. An anonymous but learned reviewer wrote in June of 1831 (Darwin would not leave until fall) a lengthy account of Sir John Richardson's *Fauna Boreali Americani* for the *Edinburgh Review*. Entitled "The Geography of Animal Life,"[12] it gives in a succinct summary all that was then known about the mystery of life on oceanic islands. The *Edinburgh Review* was a Whig organ and the Darwin family espoused the Whig point of view. There can be little doubt that Darwin was acquainted with this article. It might also be noted by way of anticipation that the *Review* was a strong advocate of the views of Thomas Malthus, and that William Paley, whose *Natural Theology* had been extensively studied by Darwin, was a convert to Malthusianism. The significance of this will concern us later. Here it will suffice to examine the essay on animal distribution.

Although the anonymous writer, who obviously knows his subject, discreetly comments that the mode by which the distribution of animals has been effected "will probably remain forever concealed from human knowledge," he cannot resist encouraging a program to pierce this barrier of ignorance. He urges the assiduous collection of facts and he points out that it is most important to ascertain "the limits which nature has assigned to the variation in the specific characters of animals." He asks what may cause a peculiar variety of bird to be confined to the island of Madeira and what the significance of this fact may be. "Why," he continues, "are the pampas of the

[12] 1831, Vol. 53, pp. 328–60.

New World inhabited by quadrupeds entirely different from the species which occur in the plains of Tartary?"

Returning in fascination to the subject of islands he puzzles over how "a mere speck in the vast world of waters" has received its flora and fauna. He recognizes, using the Mascarene archipelago as an example, that certain of these islands are volcanic and younger than the continents nearest to them, yet they are clothed with life. He discusses the possibility of oceanic transport of living seeds, or the dissemination of seeds by birds—all subjects to be much written upon by Darwin. At last he confronts the puzzled reader with a total mystery. "Finally, that monstrous and extraordinary bird, the dodo, indigenous to the island under consideration, and which so greatly astonished the early settlers, could not have been carried from any other quarter of the world, because it was neither known previously, nor has it ever since been seen or heard of elsewhere."

To this mystery there is only one key: evolution under conditions of isolation. During the next few years Darwin would examine with fascinated interest every island he came upon. In the Galápagos he would find a similarly rare and localized fauna. He would grasp there facts essential to the development of his theory. This *Review* article makes quite plain the kind of questions beginning to be asked in biology as Darwin sailed away in the *Beagle*. Remote archipelagoes had been found to contain species and even genera not to be found on the continents, yet some of these islands had been found to be geologically of much more recent origin than the continents. "Some recent speculators," the anonymous author confesses, "have argued from this the necessity of admitting the possibility of a comparatively modern creation of animal and vegetable life." English thought, one observes, is still couched in terms of creation rather than change. The dodo, for example, has not yet been seen to be a strangely altered member of the pigeon family. Nevertheless, it is questions of this nature which will lead inevitably in the direction of an evolutionary hypothesis.

Among the other influences at work in young Darwin's mind was that of Alexander Humboldt. Humboldt was one of the last of the great travelers. As Ackerknecht has recently pointed out, Humboldt, to his contemporaries, was not a mere scientist, "he was the 'symbol' of science."[13] A man of wide-ranging intellect, he was an adept synthesizer and played a major role in the creation of what might be called the "religion" of science which came to dominate nineteenth-century intellectual circles. "In thus popularizing science," Ackerknecht maintains, "Humboldt created the atmosphere in which later scientific mass movements like Darwinism could thrive."[14] Darwin himself had been so impressed by the *Personal Narrative* that he had investigated the possibility of voyaging to Teneriffe before the *Beagle* opportunity had presented itself.

Humboldt's volume, in spite of its detailed observations, urges upon the reader a sweeping range of facts which can be systematically correlated. "The most curious geological phenomena are often," he says, "repeated at immense distances on the surface of the continents . . . the accidental concurrence of the same causes must have everywhere produced the same effects; and amidst the variety of nature, an analogy of structure and form is observed in the arrangement of brute matter, as well as in the internal organization of plants and animals."

Later the "rents on coasts," "the sinuosities of valleys," and the "aspects of mountains" will preoccupy Darwin in South America. Humboldt, also, is an observer of seed transport. He speaks of the Gulf Stream depositing on the western shores of Ireland and Norway "the fruit of trees, which belong to the torrid zone of America." "On these same coasts, various kinds of tortoises," he claims, "are

[13] Erwin H. Ackerknecht, "George Forster, Alexander von Humboldt and Ethnology," *Isis*, 1955, Vol. 46, pp. 83–95.
[14] Ibid., p. 92.

sometimes found that inhabit the waters of the Antilles."
Humboldt is also quite aware of the part played by man
in changing the face of the planet: "The naturalist is exposed to a thousand errors, if he loses sight of the changes
which the intercourse between nations produces on the
surface of the globe. We might be led to say, that man
expatriating himself, is desirous that everything should
change country with him. Not only plants, insects, and
different species of small quadrupeds, follow him across
the ocean; his active industry covers the shores with rocks
that he has torn from the soil in distant climes." Once
more we find Darwin at a later date observing in his
Journal the spread of huge Old World thistles on the
pampas, and the alteration of plant and animal life under
European contact.

Humboldt also called attention to the fact that the science of his day was "under great obligations to navigators
who have accumulated an immense number of facts."
"But," Humboldt adds, "[we] *must regret that hitherto
naturalists have made so little use of their journals, which
when examined anew may yield unexpected results.*"
(Italics mine. L.E.) When Darwin turned to the amassing
of factual material for his great work on the origin of species, he spent much time and effort combing in just this
way the accounts of the early voyagers for data bearing
on plant and animal diffusion and the peculiarities of island faunas. It is, therefore, perhaps not without significance that one of the books which the youthful Darwin
so much admired should have contained this excellent
advice.

Humboldt's narrative is really something of a model for
the *Naturalist's Voyage around the World*. We glimpse
this in Darwin's transports of delight over the tropical
scenery of Bahia. "I am," he wrote in his diary, "at present
fit only to read Humboldt; he like another sun illumines
everything I behold."[15] Curiously enough, Ackerknecht's

15 *Charles Darwin's Diary of the Voyage of H.M.S. "Beagle,"*
ed. by Nora Barlow, Cambridge University Press, 1933, p. 39.

observation that Humboldt's "great synthetic picture of the world . . . omits nothing but one single item: man" has also been expressed of his scientific descendant, Darwin. One such critic has said of Darwin, "His was a world of insects and pigeons, apes and curious plants, but man as he exists had no place in it." That Darwin attempted to treat of man physically, did treat him from the evolutionary point of view, we know, but there is, nevertheless, considerable justice to the charge that he was a poor ethnologist. Whether the parallelism to Humboldt can be sustained this far as more than fortuitous there is no way of estimating. Like Ackerknecht, one can only wonder what the history and influence of ethnology might have been if Humboldt, the scientific idol of the early nineteenth century, had expressed more interest in its welfare.

The writings which we have just examined have been selected merely to emphasize once more what we have observed in earlier chapters—that great acts of scientific synthesis are not performed in a vacuum. The influences, the books, the personalities surrounding a youthful genius are always of the utmost interest in terms of the way his own intellectual appetites come to be molded. Darwin's impact upon biology was destined to be so profound that much of what he absorbed from others was remembered as totally his own achievement. This happened because many of the biological works written before the *Origin of Species* became old-fashioned and ceased to be read.

The still widespread notion that Darwin drew all of his ideas from pure field observation has been furthered perhaps by Darwin's own seeming indifference to the history of the ideas with which he worked. Actually, however, he was a voracious and inquiring reader[16] as well as a good

[16] In a letter to Huxley written in 1858 Darwin confides: "I have so repeatedly required to see old Transactions and old Travels, etc. that I should regret extremely, when at work at the British Museum, to be separated from the entire library." MLD, Vol. 1, p. 111.

field observer. It was this combination that produced his master synthesis. Having glimpsed a youth already perfectly cognizant of the evolutionary hypothesis, whatever his own personal viewpoint may have been at the time he boarded the *Beagle*, we have every reason to assume that he was intellectually equipped to make the most of his opportunities from the start. There was the stimulus of an evolutionary tradition stemming from his own grandfather and, from across the Channel, the more extended speculations of Lamarck which he at least knew by hearsay. In addition, he was under the spell of a great voyager, Humboldt, who emphasized observation and the synthesis of related facts into broad generalizations wherever possible.

It would be easy to get the impression from the first edition of the *Origin of Species* that Darwin conceived of the evolutionary theory solely by field observation in South America. That his belief in its possible truth had been strengthened in this manner is likely enough, but it does not negate the fact that he went aboard the *Beagle* already aware of an existing hypothesis which he might have the opportunity of testing in the field. His genius lay in the fact that he was *willing* to test it; no preconceived emotional revulsion hindered him, no appetite for any existing evolutionary theory prevented his development of a more satisfactory mechanism by which to explain its effects. Having made this background clear, we can now proceed to an examination of the events of the voyage itself.

IV   The Voyage

The development of the theory of natural selection is often dated casually from the time of the publication of the *Origin of Species* in 1859. Actually, however, its inception occurred far earlier than this date. Since Darwin discussed the subject with his intimates over a long period and it was rather widely known in professional circles that he was working on the "species problem," it is even difficult in some instances to know how far his influence extended before he published. There are hints in the *Naturalist's Voyage* which might well have been pondered over by a thoughtful man. Wallace had read the *Voyage* and knew by personal correspondence with Darwin that he entertained original ideas on the subject. In fact, the more one examines the relationship of the two men the more one is impressed with the likelihood that without the stimulus of Darwin, there might have been no Wallace, just as, without the stimulus of Wallace, Darwin might never have got around to formal publication. This episode is less one of independent invention than of what A. L. Kroeber has called "stimulus diffusion." There is no question that Wallace worked out the idea of natural selection independently but he might be said to have sensed perspicaciously that Darwin was entertaining a new theory of his own—in fact, Darwin practically told him as much—and thus his own eagerness was whetted. Furthermore, like Darwin, his writing shows the influence of Sir Charles Lyell.

As a result of this web of relationships between Darwin and his friends, as well as some contradiction in the enormous array of documents which confront us, it is not always easy to pursue a simple and straightforward narrative of events. Another complication lies in the fact that Darwin, hurrying ahead at the last under the pressure of Wallace's competition, maintained, at least to himself, that the *Origin* was merely an abstract of a longer work which would contain names, documentation, and historical references which he did not have the time or space to include in the *Origin*. As a consequence, since the "real" *Origin* remained a dream, its "Abstract," the published *Origin*, is, by modern standards, inadequately footnoted.

In many instances we are left without a clue as to where Darwin secured his ideas, yet it is obvious in certain instances that there were sources close at hand upon which he might have drawn. Darwin was generous in expressions of appreciation to such men as Lyell, for example, yet since these mostly occur as book dedications or in letters, they often throw inadequate light upon the use of specific ideas. Beginning with the diary kept by Darwin on the voyage, therefore, we shall try to make out what influences from the world around him he specifically records. In doing so, however, we must keep carefully in mind that Darwin, the naturalist observer, is looking on with a mind fresh from the European geological and biological controversies of his just completed student days. He is not, in other words, to be considered as a lonely genius of the Hudson or Thoreau literary type. "Rat catcher" though his father may have exasperatedly called him, this young man had impressed professors of the stature of Sedgwick and Henslow; he had bathed his mind in the intellectual currents that were beginning to stir the society of his day. Solitary by nature, it is probable that he never consciously realized the full debt he owed to his Edinburgh and Cambridge background.

As we turn to the diary of the voyage and to Darwin's autobiography, we encounter almost immediately a contradiction between the statements contained in these documents and his late reminiscences to a correspondent of 1877. To this individual he had written, "When on board the *Beagle* I believed in the permanence of species, but as far as I can remember vague doubts occasionally flitted across my mind." Keeping this statement in mind let us examine both Darwin's little autobiography and the diary and notebooks of the voyage. They give quite a different picture. Captain Fitzroy of the *Beagle*, in addition, once said that he had often remonstrated with Darwin for expressing doubts upon the first chapter of Genesis.

Let us take first the actual day-to-day references in the diary. We need not look for evolutionary statements directly expressed. They would have annoyed Fitzroy, and

Darwin's log was part of the official record of the expedition and open by right to Fitzroy. Some of the entries, however, are most provocative. We must also bear in mind as we examine Darwin's remarks that they can be divided into two categories: *those bearing on the proof that evolution has occurred, and those concerned with the actual search for the mechanism by which organic change is produced.* It is the confusion between these two points which is probably responsible for some of Darwin's own contradictory statements of later years. Apparently he came to equate, in some instances, the discovery of natural selection with his belief in the reality of evolution. Actually, however, the diary and notebooks of the voyage, as well as one of Darwin's own remarks in his autobiography, suggest that he began with an evolutionary suspicion which grew stronger with his continued observations and led, finally, to the discovery of the principle of natural selection and its accompanying law of divergence.

Darwin's diary, as early as 1832, records observations which clearly indicate his concentration upon subjects of primary significance to an evolutionist. He observes a snake with rudimentary hind limbs marking "the passage by which Nature joins the lizards to the snakes."[17] A month later he examines a serpent whose tail "is terminated by a hard oval point" which it "vibrates as those possessed with a more perfect organ are known to do."[18] Again, he is quick to note the various modifications among "three sorts of birds which use their wings for more purposes than flying, the Steamer (duck) as paddles, the penguin as fins, and the Ostrich (rhea) spreads its plumes like sails to the breeze."[19] The close observation of the diverse uses to which the same organ can be put by modification absorbed his fascinated attention.

There can be little doubt, however, that Darwin's ac-

[17] D, p. 83.
[18] Ibid., p. 106.
[19] Ibid., p. 126.

ceptance of the uniformitarian geology of Lyell and, finally, in November of 1832, his reception in Montevideo of Lyell's second volume of the *Principles of Geology*, which dealt with biological problems, enormously influenced his further development. In fact, as we have earlier seen, Lyell comes so close at times to the evolutionary viewpoint, including natural selection, that one is almost exasperated by his failure to make the connection. It is no wonder that Darwin, years after, expressed agreement with Judd that without the *Principles of Geology* the *Origin of Species* would not have been written.[20]

Around Darwin as the voyage progressed were living illustrations of all his books had told him, along with many additional and unrecorded marvels to further stimulate his imagination. On the night watches aboard the *Beagle* or traveling through the thin desert air of the Andean uplands he tells us that "the whole of my pleasure was derived from what passed in my mind."[21] Five years in the great solitudes, shut out by the wall of illiteracy or prejudice from the possibility of being able to talk freely with his companions, whether the seamen of the *Beagle* or the *gauchos* amused by the mysterious doings of the *naturalista*, were destined to strengthen his patience and at the same time to promote those aloof and lonely habits which were to characterize him until the end of his life. Long afterward his son Francis was to speak of Darwin's winter morning walks in Kent—walks taken so early that he used to meet the foxes trotting home at dawn.

It is possible from the information Darwin has left us, and again making allowance for the educational background that as a naturalist he already possessed, to interpret the successive stages of his thought in the development of the evolutionary hypothesis. There are, as we have earlier shown, two aspects of the problem: the

[20] John W. Judd, *The Coming of Evolution*, Cambridge University Press, 1912, p. 73.
[21] H. E. Litchfield, *A Century of Family Letters*, 2 vols., Cambridge University Press, 1904, Vol. 1, p. 438.

demonstration of evolution itself as a process taking place in time and, second, the nature of the mechanism controlling it. So far as the voyage is concerned, Darwin succeeded in solving only the first aspect of the problem, that is, the actual demonstration of the likelihood that evolution had taken place. Nevertheless, as we shall see, he came, in the Galápagos, upon a key to the mechanism itself.

V South America

As the *Beagle* had proceeded southward from Brazil, Darwin had participated in numerous landings and had also made long journeys on more than one occasion into the interior. He had become impressed, he informs us in the autobiography, "by the manner in which closely allied animals replace one another in proceeding southwards."[22] He had come to see, in other words, a moderate amount of varietal distinction among animals upon a single time level and differing only in their geographical location. Such distinctions suggested quite powerfully the *local modification of a single species*, rather than the separate independent creation of a new form differing only in a quite moderate fashion, or in a few insignificant characters, from a previously observed species farther to the north. Later, this impression was to be powerfully intensified upon his examination of the Galápagos fauna.

Upon reaching and exploring the pampas, Darwin was struck by the presence in the Pampean geological formation of huge fossil Edentates possessing a kind of skin armor comparable to that of the existing armadillo from the same region.[23] In other anatomical aspects, also, these animals seemed to bear some mysterious resemblance to their existing relatives. Still later, after Owen's identifica-

[22] LLD, Vol. 1, p. 82.

[23] As bearing again upon the curiosity of the voyagers, it is interesting to note that almost one hundred years earlier Thomas Falkner had left us the following account of a glyptodont: "I myself found the shell of an animal, composed of little hexagonal bones, each bone an inch in diameter at least; and the shell was

tions, he noted that this principle seemed to hold as well in the case of an extinct llama whose remains he discovered in Patagonia. In the first edition of the *Journal of Researches* he commented that "the most important result of this discovery is the confirmation of the law that existing animals have a close relation in form with extinct species."[24]

Darwin in his *Journal* called this phenomenon "the law of the succession of types" and commented cryptically that it "must possess the highest interest to every philosophical naturalist."[25] His comment that this type of succession was first noted in Australia shows that he undoubtedly drew the idea from Sir Charles Lyell, who commented with interest on finds of extinct marsupials in Australian caves as proving that "the peculiar type of organization which now characterizes the marsupial tribes has prevailed from a remote period in Australia."[26] The idea itself originated with William Clift and was so acknowledged by both Lyell and Darwin.[27] Some confusion has arisen on this point because Wallace in his evolution-

---

near three yards over. It seemed, in all respects, except its size, to be the upper part of the shell of the armadillo; which, in these times, is not above a span in breadth. Some of my companions found also, near the river Parana, an entire skeleton of a monstrous alligator. . . . Upon an anatomical survey of the bones, I was pretty well assured that this extraordinary increase [in size of bones] did not proceed from any acquisition of foreign matter; as I found that the bony fibers were bigger in proportion as the bones were larger. . . . These things are well known to all who live in these countries; otherwise, I should not have dared to write them." Darwin has occasionally been accredited with the first discovery of these creatures. Thomas Falkner, *Description of Patagonia and the Adjoining Parts of South America*, Hereford, Eng., 1774, p. 55.

[24] *Journal of Researches* (1839), facsimile reprint of the first edition, Hafner Publishing Co., New York, 1952, p. 209.

[25] Ibid., p. 210.

[26] PG, Vol. 3, p. 421.

[27] MLD, Vol. 1, p. 133. Clift, however, probably had gotten the idea from John Hunter. See the latter's *Essays and Observations* edited by Richard Owen, London, 1861, Vol. 1, pp. 290–91. The paper referred to was published in 1794.

ary paper of 1855 made considerable use of this idea in terms of suggesting evolutionary relationships. As a consequence, the development of the idea of succession has sometimes been attributed to him.

There exists in the files of the *London and Edinburgh Philosophical Magazine* the summary of a paper given by Darwin before the Geological Society[28] shortly after his return from the voyage of the *Beagle*. Part of the summary contains the following: "The author [C.D.] finally remarked, that although several gigantic land animals, which formerly swarmed in South America, have perished, yet that they are now represented by animals confined to that country; and which though of diminutive size, possess the peculiar anatomical structure of their great extinct prototypes." This statement is followed by a footnote which reads: "The relation between the extinct and living animals confined to America was first noticed . . . by Mr. Brayley, in some remarks on a fossil vertebra from Eschscholtz Bay; probably referable to a species of Megatherium."

Brayley, contemporaneously with Clift, had grown interested in the regional succession of faunas and had raised the question "whether the Megatherium was coextensive on both continents with the extinct elephant or whether, like the sloths, and the ant-eaters . . . to which it is allied, it was confined to the New World, where, alone the bones of the Megatherium also have yet been discovered."[29] Darwin, when he wrote Lyell about the law of succession in 1859 protesting Owen's claim to having originated the principle,[30] had apparently forgotten his own early paper and the reference to Brayley. The latter

[28] "A Sketch of the Deposits Containing Extinct Mammalia in the Neighbourhood of La Plata," 1837, Vol. 2, pp. 206–8.

[29] E. W. Brayley, "On the Odour Exhaled from Certain Organic Remains In the Diluvium of the Arctic Circle, As Confirmatory of Dr. Buckland's Opinion of A Sudden Change of Climate at the Period of Destruction of the Animals to which they Belonged, etc. etc." *The Philosophical Magazine*, 1831, Vol. 9, p. 418.

[30] MLD, Vol. 1, p. 133.

cannot be said to clearly formulate a principle, but there is no doubt that in the time it was written, and considering the paucity of reliable paleontological data from the Americas, Brayley had raised a legitimate and important question.

Clift, in examining some cave remains sent him for identification from Australia, came to a more clear-cut decision. "New Holland [Australia] was, at a former period," he wrote, "distinguished from other parts of the world, by the same peculiarities in the organization of its animals, which so strikingly characterize it at the present day."[31] Clift points out in addition that certain of his marsupials were larger than present-day forms—a fact which Darwin later observed to hold true for South America.

We have seen that Darwin in his *Journal of Researches* (1839) had hinted cryptically that this phenomenon of successive related faunas in a given region was of great importance. He was aware of its evolutionary significance when he wrote, but at this early date chose to remain silent. In 1855, four years before the publication of the *Origin of Species* and before Wallace himself had discovered the principle of natural selection, the latter published "On the Law which has Regulated the Introduction of New Species."[32] It was the most elaborate statement of the principle that had been given up to that time, or, for that matter, since. Every species, Wallace says, can be shown to have "*come into existence coincident both in space and time with a pre-existing closely allied species.*" Though Wallace expresses himself cautiously, he makes

[31] William Clift, "Report by Mr. Clift of the College of Surgeons, London, in Regard to the Fossil Bones Found in the Caves and Bone Breccia of New Holland," *Edinburgh New Philosophical Journal*, 1831, Vol. 10, pp. 394–96.

[32] This paper, which first appeared in the *Annals and Magazine of Natural History* is today most generally accessible in A. R. Wallace's *Natural Selection and Tropical Nature*, Macmillan, London, 1895.

it plain that in the light of this principle, and taking due note of other phenomena such as rudimentary organs, new forms of life emerge *gradually* rather than by special creation. This paper, while not quite so original on the "law of succession" as some have imagined, is, nevertheless, an early indication of the direction in which Wallace's thought was flowing. Moreover, in its use of apt data upon animal and plant distributions and the significance of oceanic islands in relation to the geological past, it already reveals the interests which would bring fame to Wallace as one of the foremost students of animal distribution.

In going forward to 1855 we have been forced to anticipate in order to give the full history of the law of succession. Darwin in South America had earlier grasped the resemblance existing between modern animals and those extinct forms lying beneath them in geological time. He expressed it as a question in his unpublished essay of 1842, the first prelude to the *Origin*.[33] "Although [the] creationist can, by the help of geology, explain much, how can he explain the marked relation of the past and present in [the] same area?" Darwin had grasped this principle of relationship between living and dead faunas as early as 1837, for he says in his first unpublished notebook, "Propagation explains why modern animals same type as extinct, which is law almost proved."[34]

This question had become steadily more important as world research yielded evidence that the extinct faunas of the main continental areas differed from each other, but bore a marked relationship to the living inhabitants of the same continent. Brayley had raised the suspicion in connection with the Americas. Clift, using the cave discoveries of Major Thomas Mitchel, had demonstrated its reality in Australia.

In 1844, in his second essay prior to the *Origin*, Dar-

[33] FO, p. 33, fn. 1.
[34] LLD, Vol. 2, p. 5.

win gives a remarkably full exposition of the evolutionary significance of this principle: "This general and most remarkable relation between the lately past and present mammiferous inhabitants of the three main divisions of the world is precisely the same kind of fact as the relation between the different species of the several subregions of any one of the main divisions. As we usually associate great physical changes with the total extinction of one series of beings, and its succession by another series, this identity of relation between the past and the present races of beings in the same quarters of the globe is more striking than the same relation between existing beings in different subregions: but in truth we have no reason for supposing that a change in the conditions has in any of these cases supervened, greater than that now existing between the temperate and tropical, or between the highlands and lowlands of the same main divisions, now tenanted by related beings. Finally, then, we clearly see that in each main division of the world the same relation holds good between its inhabitants in time as over space."[35]

Darwin, during his South American experience, saw in the case of both geographical variation and paleontological sequence the possibility of *modification* by organic change, but not dramatic special creations by supernatural means. The evidence for change was reasonably clear but not the mechanism; of this the Galápagos would supply a subtle hint.

VI *The Galápagos*

After rounding the Horn the *Beagle* sailed a leisurely course northward along the west coast of South America. While Captain Fitzroy pursued the mapping and other observational activities for which the *Beagle* had been sent out by the Admiralty office, Darwin continued to

[35] FO, p. 176.

make geological and zoological observations. He visited offshore islands and made short, high journeys into the Andes. Collecting shells in the valley of Copiapó he commented: "It was amusing to hear discussions concerning the nature of the fossil shells—whether or not they had been thus 'born by nature,' carried on almost in the same terms as were used a century before in Europe."[36]

He noted that the Andean Cordillera constitutes a great natural barrier to life and that differences between the flora and fauna on opposite sides of the range were to be expected. By the time the *Journal* was published he was willing to hint obscurely in a footnote that "the changes might be considered as superinduced by different circumstances in the two regions during a length of time," provided one did not assume the immutability of species.[37]

In September of 1835 the *Beagle* reached the Galápagos Archipelago 600 miles off the coast of South America and directly upon the Equator. These burnt-out volcanic chimneys, parched and blackened as an iron foundry, made a profound impression upon Darwin. The sequence of his travels had been such that his arrival could not have been better timed to impress upon his mind a series of facts, both geological and biological, which were necessary to the formulation of his theories.

Many times over, in the later years, Darwin, in letters to correspondents and in his autobiography, was to emphasize the importance of the facts brought to his attention among the islands of this obscure archipelago. He wrote to his co-discoverer Wallace in 1859: "Geographical distribution and geological relations of extinct to recent inhabitants of South America first led me to the subject: especially the case of the Galápagos Islands."[38] He reiterated to Moritz Wagner in 1876 that "it would have been

[36] JR, p. 435.
[37] Ibid., p. 400.
[38] MLD, Vol. 1, pp. 118–19.

a strange fact if I had overlooked the importance of isolation, seeing that it was such cases as that of the Galápagos Archipelago, which chiefly led me to study the origin of species."[39]

What Darwin has to say in his autobiography will gain in emphasis if we first place ourselves under the conditions encountered by the young naturalist in 1835 and try, as nearly as we can, to see the Galápagos fauna as he first saw it. He came to the islands already impressed by the similarity of the extinct armored glyptodonts to their living relative, the armadillo. He had seen the slow variation in the form of related species as one moved along the great distances of the South American coasts, or passed from one side of the great Andean mountain barrier to the other. He had obtained an impression of creatures, both from times remote and from the diverse conditions of the present, showing surprisingly similar types of structure—surprising, that is, if one had to assume the orthodox view that they were all totally distinct creations and in that sense unrelated to each other. He had stared at a penguin's wing and had perceived that by certain modifications a wing could be made to beat its way through either water or air. Was it logical to suppose that all these clever adaptations to circumstance had been plucked out of a vacuum? Were not these remarkable structures built on what was basically the same plan? And could not this plan be, perhaps, pulled this way or that way, distorted, remolded, made to fit the animal to some difficult environment? But if so, what influence was at work? Did life in some manner respond to the environment? Did the climate, the surroundings of an animal, in some manner impinge upon his protoplasm and slowly draw these modifications of structure out of him? It seemed fantastic. How could climate, about which people talked so glibly, adapt a woodpecker for climbing trees or a hummingbird to probe into a flower?

[39] LLD, Vol. 3, p. 159.

By great good fortune we possess two letters which Darwin mailed from the west coast of South America shortly before the *Beagle* pressed on to the Galápagos. They give us some excellent glimpses into his state of mind just before entering upon his last great intellectual adventure of the voyage. Writing to his sister Susan from Valparaiso in the latter part of April 1835, Darwin describes some of his experiences in the high Andes. He tells her of procuring fossil shells at elevations of 12,000 feet. He is confident that specimens "will give an approximate age to these mountains, as compared with the strata of Europe." Furthermore, he is convinced that the Andes are young as mountains go in the world's time scale. "If this result shall be considered as proved," he continues, only half concealing his eagerness, "it is a very important fact in the theory of the formation of the world; because if such wonderful changes have taken place so recently in the crust of the globe, there can be no reason for supposing former epochs of excessive violence."[40] Here we see that young Darwin has totally abandoned the catastrophic doctrines which were still the orthodox viewpoint of English geology. There is no finer evidence of Darwin's many-sided abilities as an observer than his geological work among the Andes.

Two months later he wrote to his friend and cousin, the Rev. W. D. Fox, that he had "become a zealous disciple of Mr. Lyell's views, as known in his admirable book." Then, as if it did not content him merely to proclaim himself a uniformitarian in geology, he adds mysteriously, *"I am tempted to carry parts to a greater extent even than he does."*[41] What remains so intriguing about this cryptic remark is that only a sentence or two later we discern for the first time in his thought a slight falling away of interest in pure geology. "I have a considerable body of notes together; but," he says, "it is a con-

[40] LLD, Vol. 1, p. 261.
[41] Ibid., p. 263. (Italics mine. L.E.)

stant subject of perplexity to me, whether they are of sufficient value for all the time I have spent about them *or whether animals would not have been of more certain value.*"[42]

Charles Darwin, on that July day in Lima, had arrived at the crossroads of his career. With almost preternatural sensitivity he suddenly writes, "I look forward to the Galápagos with more interest than any other part of the voyage."[43] That he fully shared Lyell's views is evident, but what is of paramount interest is the fact that Lyell failed to go as far as Darwin at just one point in his system, and that was in the application of natural forces to explain the evolution of life. "I am tempted to carry parts to a greater extent even than he does," hinted Darwin and then, in the same paragraph of the same letter, his thoughts begin to turn to animals and whether he might better have devoted his attention to them. It is the only place in his writings where he shows signs of abandoning for a moment his lifelong interest in geology. This neglected communication is pregnant with the unspoken excitement which even after the passage of over a century can be felt hovering at the tip of Darwin's pen.

Darwin landed at Chatham Island in the Galápagos on the seventeenth of September, 1835. He had looked forward to the adventure with eagerness, but it was largely because, freshly impressed with the paleontological record in South America, he had hoped to find Tertiary fossil beds in the islands. The expectation proved short-lived.

The rocks of black lava were heated like a stove. "The country," he comments, "was compared to what we might imagine the cultivated parts of the Infernal regions to be."[44] In addition, the islands swarmed with reptiles. Meeting some Galápagos tortoises for the first time, he observes that "they were so heavy, I could scarcely lift them off the ground. Surrounded by the black lava, the

[42] LLD, Vol. 1, (Italics mine. L.E.)
[43] Ibid.
[44] D, p. 334.

leafless shrubs and large cacti, they appeared most old-fashioned antediluvian animals or rather inhabitants of some other planet."[45]

In this strange little isolated world Darwin set immediately to work collecting all the animals, plants, insects, and reptiles he could locate. He visited several of the islands and collected upon all of them. In this work he made one serious mistake: he did not, until late in his visit, attempt to keep similar species from individual islands separately labeled in his collections.

This situation quite clearly came about because Darwin—although impressed from his South American experience with the evidence pointing toward plant and animal evolution—had not as yet fully grasped the possibility of dissimilar paths of development being taken by related organisms in close proximity on nearby islets. Darwin was, in other words, still seeking for the key to evolution in the exterior environment, in climate, in the natural surroundings of a given area. He had not expected to observe, in this score of islands clustered together and containing less than 2,800 square miles all told, much in the way of regional distinctions. That the fauna might differ from that of the neighboring continent was to be expected, but scarcely this strange divergence over little patches of sea in a totally similar climate.

Slowly, as Darwin talked with the local inhabitants, a different and strange impression grew upon him—an impression destined to be confirmed and heightened after his return home, when the intensive examination of his specimens was to begin. In one of his notebooks of 1835 he dwells on the fact that the Spaniards could distinguish from which island the huge tortoises had been brought, and he similarly notes, "Islands in sight of each other . . . tenanted by . . . birds but slightly differing in structure."[46] From this time on, the full force of his wide-ranging mind is turned upon the archipelago. Such facts as these, he

[45] D, p. 335.
[46] *Charles Darwin and the Voyage of the "Beagle,"* ed. by Nora Barlow, Philosophical Library, New York, 1946, p. 246.

grows powerfully aware, "would undermine the stability of species."[47]

By the time that the first edition of the *Journal of Researches* was published, Darwin, when he came to the subject of the Galápagos, was willing to throw out several evolutionary hints. "There is a rat," he records, "which Mr. Waterhouse believes is probably distinct from the English kind; but I cannot help suspecting that it is only the same altered by the peculiar conditions of its new country."[48] The finches in particular fascinated him. They differed remarkably in the structure of their beaks. Some had small beaks like warblers, some had thick, massive beaks. In the end, Darwin wrote regretfully of his many species of finches that although he suspected certain of the distinct types were confined to separate islands, he "was not aware of these facts till my collection was nearly completed."[49] *"It never occurred to me,"* he explained, *"that the productions of islands only a few miles apart, and places under the same physical conditions would be dissimilar.*[50] I therefore did not attempt to make a series of specimens from the separate islands."

This statement is extremely revelatory. As we have previously intimated, Darwin had, up to this point, been looking at variation largely over the great vertical distance of past time or horizontally over wide geographic areas. Under such circumstances one was apt to invoke climatic change as the primary mechanism involved in evolution. Here, in the Galápagos, Darwin was brought up short by a new series of facts: variation in form under isolation with the physical environment remaining precisely the same. As Darwin himself was later to observe, "One might really fancy that from an original paucity of birds in this archipelago one species had been taken and

[47] N, p. 247. See also Nora Barlow, "Charles Darwin and the Galápagos Islands," *Nature*, 1935, Vol. 136, p. 391.
[48] JR, p. 460.
[49] Ibid., p. 474.
[50] Ibid. (Italics mine. L.E.)

modified for different ends."[51] Darwin at last was face to face with the greatest of the evolutionary mysteries. If life varied on the individual islands of an archipelago subjected to the same climatic conditions, what determined this variation?

Darwin did not come to this problem by any great flash of insight. It was not his way. He tells us, more particularly in the later editions of the *Naturalist's Voyage*, that the Vice-Governor of the islands, Mr. Lawson, an Englishman, first called his attention to this puzzling inter-island variation. "I did not for some time pay sufficient attention to this statement," he confesses. As a consequence, most of Darwin's collections had been assembled and he was almost on the point of departure when the full import of this observation struck his attention. "It is the fate of every voyager," he complained in his *Journal*, "when he has just discovered what object in any place is worth his attention to be hurried from it."[52]

Lest in the light of modern biology Darwin's reaction may appear slow, the following comment by Sir Joseph Hooker, one of England's outstanding botanists, may better reveal the state of knowledge upon species during this period. As late as 1843, having examined some of Darwin's plant collections, Hooker wrote to him, "I was quite prepared to see the extraordinary difference between the plants of the separate islands from your Journal, *a most strange fact, and one which quite overturns all our preconceived notions of species radiating from a centre. . . .*"[53]

It was upon that strange fact that Darwin was to meditate for the next twenty years after his return from the voyage of the *Beagle*. "It may be asked," he wrote in the

[51] Charles Darwin, *A Naturalist's Voyage Around the World*, 2nd ed., London: John Murray, 1889, p. 380. The *Journal* of 1839 does not contain so direct a statement though the implication is clear (p. 462).

[52] JR, p. 474.

[53] Leonard Huxley, *Life and Letters of Sir Joseph Hooker*, 2 vols., London, 1918, Vol. 1, pp. 436–37. (Italics mine. L.E.)

first edition of the *Origin of Species*, "how has it happened, in the several islands situated within sight of each other, having the same geological nature, the same height, climate, etc., that many of the immigrants should have been differently modified, though only in a small degree. *This long appeared to me a great difficulty, but it arises in chief part from the deeply seated error of considering the physical conditions of a country as the most important for its inhabitants. . . .*"[54]

No clearer statement of the significance of the Galápagos experience could have been made by Darwin. The subject, he confesses, "haunted me." It haunted him around the world and back to England, where he opened his first notebook on the subject in 1837. He had passed beyond the environmentalism of Buffon and the earlier evolutionists, but the island mystery, that "great difficulty" of bird beaks and turtle shells continued to baffle him. "I worked on true Baconian principles," he tells us, "and without any theory collected facts on a wholesale scale."[55] The result of those efforts would be the making of the *Origin of Species* and to that labor we will now proceed. The voyage of the *Beagle* had turned a pleasant, somewhat idle youth into a man. It had given the man of uncanny and perceptive insight a chance to exercise his thought upon armadillos and glyptodonts, stones falling and falling without end in the Andean torrents, turtles and volcanoes and bird beaks. At home in England he would piece them together into a new synthesis and the thought of the world would never be the same afterwards. It would come about because he had excavated the carapace of an Edentate, watched, in an earthquake, the Andes pumping themselves higher, and had also read Lyell and Humboldt. The origins of his thought were as diverse as the fragments of the puzzle which he at last fitted together. It could scarcely have been otherwise.

[54] O, p. 339. (Italics mine. L.E.)
[55] LLD, Vol. 1, p. 83.

Chapter VII

The Making of the *Origin*

> Though I shall get more kicks than half-
> pennies, I will, life serving, attempt my work.
> *Darwin*

I *"The Bridgewater Treatises"*

When Darwin's uncle, Josiah Wedgwood, had sought to obtain the permission of Robert Darwin that Charles might go upon the voyage of the *Beagle*, he had urged that "the pursuit of Natural History, though certainly not professional is very suitable to a clergyman."[1] This remark is strongly indicative of the esteem in which natural theology was held in early nineteenth century England. Wedgwood was not a biologist. He was simply an affluent, intelligent manufacturer trying to do his nephew a favor. His recourse to this argument is evidence of its strength and wide dissemination in cultivated circles. The traditional observance of life in nature had been part of the legitimate province of the English clergyman since the days of John Ray and Gilbert White. It is significant, therefore, that the devout Fitzroy had chosen to take a "naturalist" on the *Beagle* rather than a geologist.

The argument for design, that is, the contention that

[1] LLD, Vol. 1, p. 198.

all the multitudinous adjustments of organisms to their environment were evidence of the direct hand of God in earthly affairs, had been vigorously promoted through a long series of theological naturalists from John Ray and William Derham to William Paley. This viewpoint, while naïve in its more primitive expression, nevertheless led directly to a great deal of very careful observation of both plants and animals. The microscope in particular enhanced the feeling of wonder toward the works of God and increased human faith in Divine Providence.

This popular attitude is very well expressed in the following passage from Paley's *Natural Theology*, a book which, though partially derivative, as many such works were after the time of Ray, was very influential in the early part of the century. Paley says: "Nor ought we to feel our situation insecure. In every nature and every portion of nature which we can descry, we find attention bestowed upon even the minutest parts. The hinges in the wings of an earwig and the joints of its antennae, are as highly wrought, as if the creator had had nothing else to finish. We see no signs of diminution of care by multiplicity of objects, or of distraction of thought by variety. *We have no reason to fear, therefore, our being forgotten, or overlooked, or neglected.*"[2]

The italics are my own. They call attention to the way in which the study of natural history was at this time used to sustain Christian faith and comfort the bereaved. There was a general conception of God as a kind of master workman who had personally supervised the creation of even the tiniest organisms of the living world. In earlier centuries the church had largely based its system of theology upon the inspired word of the Scriptures. From about the latter half of the seventeenth century, however, the cultivation of science had led to a more intensive examination of the natural world. A feeling that religious insight could be obtained from the observation of God's works in the

2 William Paley, *Natural Theology*, London edition of 1836, Vol. 2, p. 201.

things about us led to a great proliferation of works upon natural theology. The telescope and the microscope widened man's comprehension and imagination. The tiniest infusoria, equally with the vast reaches of sidereal space, gave awe-inspiring glimpses of a world whose wonders were proclaimed as the most powerful evidence of God's design. The search for design in nature soon became a mania and everything was made to appear as though created specifically to serve man. There were Bronto- (thunder)theologies, Insecto-theologies, Astro-theologies, Phyto-theologies, Ichthyo-theologies, Physico-theologies. Insects and stars alike were seen both figuratively and literally through human spectacles. Man stood at the center of all things and the entire universe had been created for his edification and instruction: hills had been placed for his pleasure, animals ran on four feet because it made them better beasts of burden, and flowers grew for his enjoyment.

This essentially egocentric point of view reached its final if sophisticated expression in the famous *Bridgewater Treatises*. Francis Henry Egerton, the eighth Earl of Bridgewater, died in 1829 leaving a bequest of eight thousand pounds for a work or works to be written "on the power, wisdom, and goodness of God as manifested in the Creation." Between 1833 and 1836 a series of eight such books were published, through the co-ordinated efforts of Chalmers, Buckland, Whewell, Kirby, and other scholars of the time.[3] They had set out to prove like others before them that the evidence of design in the world about us implies an intelligent designer. The argument from contrivance had become a standard part of theology. The existence of God, the position of man, the truth of the Bible

[3] E. C. Massner, *Bishop Butler and the Age of Reason*, Macmillan, New York, 1936, p. 203. See also D. W. Gundry, "The Bridgewater Treatises and Their Authors," *History*, 1946, Vol. 31, pp. 140–52, and George Ensor, *Natural Theology: the Arguments of Paley, Brougham, and the Bridgewater Treatises on this Examined*, London, 1836.

were all to be "proved" by an examination of the natural world about us. Since evolutionary change went unrecognized and each species of plant or animal was assumed to be a special creation, a particular conscious act on the part of God, natural theology had assumed the impossible burden of demonstrating "the *final* intention of the Creator in respect to each structure."[4]

The theologian was thus forced into the embarrassing position of having to explain why a benevolent Deity had devised unpleasant parasites with which to torture His subjects. In addition, the static nature of the design argument failed to explain satisfactorily the presence of rudimentary organs. The whole idea had to be propped up by a scaffolding of tendentious theory which rapidly became unwieldly. In the end Darwin was to appropriate the design hypothesis and turn it to quite another purpose. At the time of his voyage, however, it was still the reigning biological doctrine and received pious expression in church and lecture hall alike. Darwin had been a diligent student of Paley's *Natural Theology*, but what he did to Paley's carefully selected evidences of design will only emerge by degrees as we follow Darwin's thought in the formulation of the *Origin*.

II   Darwin and Malthus

When Darwin reached home in 1836 he was anxious to dispose of his specimens and set about the reports of the voyage. "I am to have the third volume," he wrote to Fox in 1837, "in which I intend giving a kind of journal of a naturalist. . . . The habits of animals will occupy a large portion, sketches of the geology, the appearance of the country, and personal details will make the hodge-podge complete. Afterwards I shall write an account of the geology in detail, and draw up some zoological pa-

[4] L. E. Hicks, *A Critique of Design Arguments*, New York, 1883, p. 42.

pers.["5] London he characterized as "a vile smoky place."[6] It is obvious that he is already at this time contemplating the retreat to the country which he later carried out, but he records with pleasure that some papers given before the Geological Society "were favorably received by the great guns, and this gives me much confidence."[7]

His short sojourn in London preceding his marriage had advantages. It brought him a close friendship with Sir Charles Lyell and the opportunity of meeting some of the finest scientific minds of the age. He had scarcely been home eight months before he opened, as he tells us, his first notebook upon the subject of species and began his conversations with commercial breeders.[8] In a letter to Lyell dated September 13, 1838, he wrote as follows: "I have been sadly tempted to be idle—that is, as far as pure geology is concerned—by the delightful number of new views which have been coming in thickly and steadily—on the classification and affinities and instincts of animals—bearing on the question of species. Note-book after note-book has been filled with facts which begin to group themselves clearly under sub-laws."[9]

This statement is particularly intriguing for two reasons: first, it shows that the interest in animals expressed in South America to his sister Susan was continuing and second, and more important, this letter, written about a month before Darwin read Thomas Malthus in October of 1838,[10] already speaks of "facts" grouping "clearly under sub-laws." What Darwin meant by this cryptic statement it is impossible to say, though one cannot help wondering if he was already groping his way toward the principle of natural selection before he read Malthus on

[5] LLD, Vol. 1, pp. 279–80.
[6] Ibid., p. 282.
[7] Ibid., p. 280.
[8] A few excerpts were given by Francis Darwin in Vol. 2 of the LLD.
[9] LLD, Vol. 1, p. 298.
[10] Ibid., p. 83.

population. Nevertheless, Darwin informs us in his autobiography, when speaking of Malthus, that "being well
prepared to appreciate the struggle for existence, which
everywhere goes on, from long continued observation of
the habits of animals and plants, it at once struck me that
under these circumstances favorable variations would tend
to be preserved, and unfavorable ones to be destroyed.
The result of this would be the formation of new species."[11]

This remark is straightforward enough, but it has always seemed dubious to the present writer that Darwin
received his complete inspiration on the selective aspect
of the struggle for existence from Malthus, or from his
South American observations. The idea is clearly expressed in Paley and even more suggestively in Lyell,
both authors whom Darwin had studied with great care.
Lyell, for example, notes that "Every species which has
spread itself from a small point over a wide area must
. . . have marked its progress by the diminution or the
entire extirpation of some other, and must maintain its
ground by a successful struggle against the encroach-
ments of other plants and animals."[12] Again and again
Lyell reiterates the observation that "in the universal
struggle for existence, the right of the strongest eventually
prevails; and the strength and durability of a race depends mainly on its prolificness. . . ."[13]

Actually, as we have already seen, it would appear
that Lyell foreran Darwin in the recognition of ecological
change brought about by the struggle for existence and
pressure of population, but that he did not grasp its creative aspect in terms of limitless *organic alteration* induced by such means. Darwin's son Francis has himself
expressed surprise that his father should have regarded
Malthus as providing the necessary clue to natural selection for, as he points out, the Notebook of 1837 contains

[11] LLD, Vol. 1, p. 83.   [12] PG, Vol. 3, p. 67.
[13] Ibid., Vol. 2, p. 391. For a more extended treatment of my
views on Sir Charles Lyell see "Charles Lyell" *Scientific American*,
1959, Vol. 201, pp. 98–101.

a discussion which, while a trifle obscure in diction, really expresses the whole principle. "We can easily see that a variety of the ostrich may not be well adapted, and thus perish out; or on the other hand . . . being favorable, many might be produced. This requires the principle that the permanent variations produced by confined breeding and changing circumstances are continued and produced according to the adaptation of such circumstances, and therefore that death of species is a consequence . . . of non-adaptation of circumstances."[14]

The statement would be clearer if it read "adaptation *to* circumstances" instead of "adaptation *of* circumstances," but anyone acquainted with Darwin's sometimes awkward and hasty wording of ideas in his notebooks will not be inclined to discount this passage. There is, in addition, one other very intriguing notation in the Notebook of 1837: "View of generation being condensation, test of highest organization . . ." Francis Darwin inclined to the view that this somewhat cryptic statement means that "each generation is 'condensed' to a small number of the best organized individuals." If this is the case it constitutes additional evidence that Darwin had grasped what was to become the essential principle of his theory before reading Malthus. An added indication lies in the fact that in the same paragraph he refers to adaptation, and while putting in, in parentheses, the Lamarckian explanation, "wish of parents," he places two question marks after the statement. He is apparently beginning to write it off in his mind, but it is one more proof that Lamarck did play a part in his early thinking.[15]

It may well be that Darwin really received only an increased growth of confidence in his previously perceived

14 FO, p. xvi. An entry in the *Beagle* diary (p. 212) speaks of the cause of Fuegian warfare as involving the means of subsistence. This statement (1834) shows very early Darwinian concentration upon the struggle for existence.

15 LLD, Vol. 2, p. 8. The recent publication in full of Darwin's Notebook by Sir Gavin de Beer makes Darwin's interest in Lamarck even more apparent.

idea through reading the Malthusian essay. The geometric growth of life as expressed by Malthus greatly impressed him and may have turned his thoughts more intensively upon the struggle for existence. There is evidence in Darwin's essay of 1842 of his impressed reaction to the mathematical approach of Malthus. He comments almost as a memorandum to himself: "Study Malthus and calculate rates of increase [for various species]."[16]

Moreover, Malthus was very popular at this time and therefore a powerful ally. We know that Darwin spoke of him admiringly as a "great philosopher." Perhaps in the vigorous expression of his views Malthus acted as one catalyst in the final precipitation of Darwin's thought. It is at least interesting that both Darwin and Alfred Russel Wallace attribute their insight into the struggle for existence to Malthus, although we know both men had been profound students of Lyell's *Principles of Geology*. Perhaps it is the mathematical aspect of Malthus which partly explains this situation. It is picturesque and brief and it captured the imagination as its later widespread use by the Darwinists reveals.[17]

III The Law of Divergence

As Darwin pondered upon the forces at work in the natural world about him he came to see that over and beyond the pure struggle for life some factor or accessory law must have made for increasing organic diversity. Life,

[16] FO, p. 8.
[17] In addition it should perhaps not pass unnoted, as a speculative point, that to have referred to Lyell as a direct source of inspiration would have been, for both Darwin and Wallace, to quote a man publicly opposed to transmutation in support of that doctrine. Malthus, by contrast, was active in a totally different field, and had a popular following. Since he was the source of most of nineteenth-century England's thinking on the struggle for existence, nothing was more natural than to have recourse to him as the "authority," even if one had largely digested his ideas by way of intermediate sources.

in other words, was a vast ramification of protoplasm into innumerable shapes and forms adapted not alone to differences in climate or medium as, say, air or water, but also it had succeeded in achieving differences of adaptation in a single location. Thus Darwin was later to remark to Asa Gray, "The same spot will support more life if occupied by very diverse forms. . . . And it follows . . . that the varying offspring of each species will try (only a few will succeed) to seize on as many and as diverse places in the economy of nature as possible."[18] Since this Law of Divergence, as it came to be called, was regarded by Darwin as of the utmost significance in evolution, it is not without interest to observe that there are preliminary intuitions of it once more among Darwin's favorite authors.

Humboldt, in describing the tropical forest of South America, does not, of course, state an evolutionary principle, but he sketches exactly the kind of life-situation which was now preoccupying Darwin. "It might be said that the earth, overloaded with plants, does not allow them space enough to unfold themselves. The trunks of the trees are everywhere concealed under a thick carpet of verdure; and if we carefully transplanted the orchidiae, the pipers, and the pothoses . . . we should cover a vast extent of ground. *By this singular assemblage, the forests, as well as the flanks of the rocks and mountains, enlarge the domains of organic nature.*"[19]

Paley, however, whom Darwin practically knew by heart, comes very close to a full statement of the law itself except that he does not directly recognize the possibility of evolutionary change save for one cryptic phrase which implies the likelihood of secondary forces at work. This phrase I italicize in the passage that follows. "To this great variety in organized life, the Deity has given, *or per-*

---

[18] LLD, Vol. 2, pp. 124-25.
[19] A. von Humboldt, *Personal Narrative of Travels*, 3 vols., Bohn, ed., London, 1852, Vol. 1, p. 216. (Italics mine. L.E.)

haps there arises out of it, a corresponding variety of animal appetites. For the final cause of this we have not far to seek. Did all animals covet the same element, retreat, or food, it is evident how much fewer could be supplied and accommodated, than what at present live conveniently together, and find a plentiful subsistence."[20]

There is no doubt that this statement contains the germ or the essence, which, given life and motion by Darwin, was destined to become the Law of Divergence. This, in more modern terms, we would call adaptive radiation. Even Paley remarks that "[Superfecundity] allows the proportion between the several species of animals to be differently modified, as different purposes require, or as different situations may afford for them room and food."[21] The passage quoted, equally with some of Lyell's remarks in the *Principles,* shows a true grasp of dynamic ecological change as the quantity of a given species alters in the struggle for existence.

What is not clearly realized by these earlier writers is the possibility of the slow alteration, not alone of the proportionate numbers of animals and plants in a given environment, but of their actual physical forms as well. "The thought of each age," remarked Sir William Thiselton-Dyer on the occasion of the Darwin-Wallace celebration in 1908, "is the foundation of that which follows. Darwin was an admirer of Paley, a member of his own College. He swept in the whole of Paley's teleology, simply dispensing with its supernatural explanation."[22] The manner in which this gigantic reversal of the orthodox field of thought was successfully attempted may now occupy our attention.

[20] W. Paley, *Natural Theology,* London ed. of 1822, p. 229. Huxley, in fact, speaks of Paley in his recognition of secondary causes as "proleptically" accepting the hypothesis of evolution. LLD, Vol. 2, p. 202.

[21] Ibid., p. 317.

[22] *The Darwin-Wallace Celebration Held on Thursday, July 1, 1908, by the Linnean Society of London,* London, 1908, p. 37.

IV The First Essay Attempts

Darwin tells us in his autobiography that directly after his return to England he had set about collecting "facts which bore in any way on the variation of animals and plants under domestication and nature."[23] He had observed that selection was the key process in the creation of new domestic races of plants or animals, and by steeping himself in the lore of the practical breeder he hoped to discover the secret of change under the conditions of wild nature. He remarks that he spent hours in gin palaces talking to pigeon fanciers or combing the files of gardeners' magazines. Even after the discovery of Malthus he was not content to relapse into an armchair consideration of the subject but persisted in breeding experiments of his own, particularly upon pigeons. "In your letter," he writes to his friend Joseph Hooker, the botanist, as late as 1849, "you wonder what 'Ornamental Poultry' has to do with Barnacles; but do not flatter yourself that I shall not yet live to finish the Barnacles, and then make a fool of myself on the subject of species, under which head Ornamental Poultry are very interesting. . . ."[24]

Darwin nowhere states just what led him to feel that domesticated forms might have some relationship to the secret he sought, but we know that the selective breeding of cattle and sheep was widely practiced toward the end of the eighteenth century. Many of the modern breeds became established at this time.[25] Moreover, there was great interest among naturalists as to the causes of variation in living things.[26] The examination of the products of colonial America and the passion for classification

[23] LLD, Vol. 1, pp. 82–83.

[24] Ibid., p. 376.

[25] C. F. A. Pantin, "Darwin's Theory and the Causes of its Acceptance," *The School Science Review*, June, 1951.

[26] J. C. Ewart, "The Experimental Study of Variation," *Report of the British Association for the Advancement of Science*, Glasgow, 1901, p. 666.

which, guided and stimulated by Linnaeus, had made the latter a world figure, doubtless played a considerable role in the development of this interest on the part of the public. At any rate, it was in such an atmosphere that Darwin was immersed in his youth. We know, in addition, that he observed and speculated upon a peculiar breed of cattle he encountered on the pampas. From the self-conscious awareness of the eighteenth- and early nineteenth-century naturalists that man had successfully altered living things, Darwin, convinced already of the reality of evolution, must have passed rapidly to the suspicion that the effects of small, controlled variations might in reality be potentially endless. Finally, and perhaps most important of all for Darwin, the road had been pointed out by no less a man than Sir Charles Lyell himself, who had said in the *Principles:* "The best authenticated examples of the extent to which species can be made to vary may be looked for in the history of domesticated animals and cultivated plants."[27] By the time of his essay of 1844 Darwin is willing to write: "That a limit to variation does exist in nature is assumed by most authors, *though I am unable to discover a single fact on which this belief is grounded.*"[28]

This is a bolder expression of Darwin's views than he was willing to express even two years earlier. Since we possess two compositions which may be regarded as trial runs before the *Origin*, and which were not published in Darwin's lifetime, their careful examination may be expected to yield us information as to the progress of his thought. We owe their preservation and publication in 1909 to Darwin's eldest son, Francis. There are two of these essays, one written in 1842, the other in 1844. The trial attempt of 1842 was not known to be in existence until it was discovered hidden in a cupboard when the old house at Down was vacated by the family in 1896.

[27] PG, Vol. 2, p. 354.
[28] FO, p. 109. (Italics mine. L.E.)

Though roughly and rapidly composed for his own purposes and not for publication, the first essay, seventeen years before the appearance of the *Origin*, contains the essential essence of Darwin's developed thought. As Huxley wrote long afterwards: "The facts of variability, of the struggle for existence, of adaptation to conditions were notorious enough; but none of us had suspected that the road to the heart of the species problem lay through them, until Darwin and Wallace dispelled the darkness."[29] In the first essay of 1842 all of these factors dwelt upon by Huxley are clearly assigned the roles they will later play in the *Origin of Species*.

The essay begins with a discussion of variation under domestication and this approach persists through the essay of 1844 and reappears as the opening chapter of the *Origin* itself. One might say that there is simply a steady enlargement in scope, sweep of ideas, and precision of statement from the first essay to the completion of the *Origin*. As one studies these early essays, however, one cannot help observing the transitional nature of much of Darwin's thought—transitional, that is, in the sense of passing from outright Lamarckian inheritance toward the as yet unformulated genetics of the future.

Although Darwin was in the habit of repudiating violently any intimation that he had profited from Lamarck, we have already seen that he was acquainted at an early age with English versions of the latter's work and in 1845 there is a reference in an unpublished letter to Lyell[30] regarding "my volumes of Lamarck." His rather cavalier rejection of his distinguished forerunner is tinged with an acerbity whose cause at this late date is difficult to discover. Darwin, although he added a meager and needlessly obscure historical introduction to later editions of the *Origin*, was essentially indifferent to his precursors,

[29] LLD, Vol. 2, p. 197.
[30] In the possession of the American Philosophical Society, Philadelphia, Pennsylvania.

and doubtless resented Owen's sharply critical treatment of this fact in the latter's review of the first edition of the *Origin*.[81]

As we examine the early essays, however, it becomes apparent that Darwin's theory does not lack Lamarckian elements in spite of the removal of the idea of willed organic change. Darwin always maintained, and rightly, that he could not see how climate (Buffon) or the individual effort of the animal (Lamarck) could accomplish such peculiar organic adaptations as, for example, that of a woodpecker. Instead, Darwin introduced the principle of fortuitous variation but he retained the idea that environment, climate, domestication, or other similar exterior influences were a *stimulating factor* which might induce the variations which were then selected in the struggle for existence.[82] Moreover, he held to the Lamarckian conception of the genetic transmissal of characteristics acquired by the animal during its own lifetime. This fact, though somewhat muted in the first edition of the *Origin*, re-emerged more powerfully in later editions as the Darwinian position became difficult to sustain under the assault of the mathematicians and the physicists, which will be discussed later on in Chapter IX. A few remarks will serve to indicate Darwin's thinking upon these topics.

As early as the *Journal of Researches* (1839) and drawn from material which, judging from clues in the *Diary of the Voyage*, dates to late in 1833, Darwin remarks that "Nature by making habit omnipotent and its effects hereditary, has fitted the Fuegian for the climate and productions of his country" (p. 237). This statement is so strongly Lamarckian that it suggests again the young

81 Richard Owen, "Darwin on the Origin of Species," *Edinburgh Review*, 1860, Vol. 3, pp. 487–532.

82 In 1856 he stated explicitly to Hooker: "My conclusion is that external conditions do *extremely* little, except in causing mere variability." LLD, Vol. 2, p. 87. In this remark he parallels the belief of Maupertuis.

Darwin's intellectual antecedents during the earlier portion of his voyage. On the very first page of the essay of 1842 he mentions that "habits of life develope certain parts. . . . Most of these slight variations tend to become hereditary."[33] He expresses, in addition, the view that "when the organism is bred for several generations under new or varying conditions, the variation is greater in amount and endless in kind." He is then careful to maintain that variation is not the product of direct effect from external conditions but only as these influence the reproductive powers and thus induce mutative changes.

In the essay of 1844 essentially the same views are given though in a more clearly expressed and qualified fashion. Also we observe here a theoretic trend which was to give an opening to Darwin's opposition and later to bring advice and counsel from his friendly rival Wallace. I refer to Darwin's failure, in spite of his Galápagos' experience, to estimate properly the amount of individual variation existing in wild nature. Two things were apparently responsible for his conservatism on this point: first, his own innately cautious reluctance to advocate what he could not thoroughly document or see; second, his preoccupation with domesticated plants or animals whose variation was easily observable and superficially so much more evident than that of creatures existing in a state of nature.

As a result, Darwin came to associate marked variation with the domestic state and to comment that "the amount of variation [was] exceedingly small . . . in a state of nature, and probably quite wanting . . . in the majority of cases. . . ."[34] Domestication with its accompanying tendency to vary seemed, he thought, "to resolve itself into a change from the natural conditions of the species." If this, then, promoted a tendency to vary, "organisms in a state of nature must *occasionally* in the course of ages be ex-

[33] FO, p. 1.
[34] Ibid., p. 83.

posed to analogous influences." These "influences" he ascribed to climatic and other inexplicable causes of an external character which, along with geographical isolation, would promote evolutionary development.

It is evident from these observations that Darwin's search for the mechanism of change in wild nature had led him to seek for environmental rather than interior causes of change. His considerable belief that change in nature was to a degree the "occasional" product of accidental migration or climatic alteration led him directly to a need for enormous quantities of time for the development of the living world. In this reluctance to accept an internal mutative factor and in his preference for postulated changes occurring only in lengthy, sporadic intervals as the external world might dictate, Darwin was unconsciously placing a heavy load on the credibility of his doctrine of fortuitous improvement through natural selection. Though by the time the *Origin* was written Darwin placed considerable emphasis on variability in wild nature and never again was so pessimistic on this point as in the second chapter of the essay of 1844, a residue of this philosophy did not escape his critics. He still argued that under nature organisms varied in less degree and he contented himself with the rhetorical observation that since useful variations have been accumulated under domestication, others "useful in some way to each being in the . . . complex battle of life *should sometimes occur in the course of thousands of generations.*" This statement, whose pertinent portion I have italicized, reveals the timidity and caution with which Darwin approached the subject of variation under natural conditions. Obviously it opened the way for critics to point out that if advantageous variation was this rare, all of the many intricate organs, habits, and behavior manifested in the past and living worlds would have demanded fantastic lengths of time for their appearance and dissemination. Moreover, such a slow production of variations would be further retarded by the likelihood that they would not appear at a favorable moment in the life of the species.

Wallace, bolder by nature and perceiving the danger implicit in this hesitant line of reasoning, wrote to Darwin in July of 1866 urging him to abandon the sort of statements we have quoted above as tilting the scales too strongly against himself. Wallace pleads at some length: "Such expressions have given your opponents the advantage of assuming that *favorable* variations are *rare accidents,* or may even for long periods never occur at all and thus [the] argument would appear to many to have great force. I think it would be better to do away with all such qualifying expressions, and constantly maintain (what I certainly believe to be the fact) that *variations of every kind are always occurring in every part of every species,* and therefore that favorable variations are *always ready* when wanted. You have, I am sure, abundant materials to prove this, and it is, I believe, the grand fact that renders modification and adaptation to conditions almost always possible. I would put the burthen of proof on my opponents to show that any one organ, structure or faculty, does *not vary,* even during one generation, among all the individuals of a species; and also to show any *mode* or *way,* in which any such organ, etc. does not vary."[35] In making this statement Wallace showed less addiction to the echoes of Lamarckian thought than his master. He was moving toward a more modern point of view. It is worth noting that Darwin took his advice. In later editions the sentence in Chapter V of the *Origin* which originally spoke of favorable mutations occurring "in the course of thousands of generations" has been unobtrusively altered to "successive generations."

Curiously enough, some years after Darwin's death, Hooker writing to Huxley expressed the view that "Darwin has nowhere that I can think of dealt with the causes

[35] James Marchant, *Alfred Russel Wallace: Letters and Reminiscences,* New York, 1916, pp. 142–43.

of variation . . . and I doubt his assenting to the view that they were in any scientific sense limited or directed by external conditions. . . ."[36]

This statement has been rather widely and popularly accepted, yet Darwin himself wrote to Hooker in 1862 saying, "You speak of an inherent tendency to vary wholly independent of 'physical conditions'! This is a very simple way of putting the case . . . but two great classes of facts make me think that all variability is due to change in the conditions of life: finally, that there is more variability and more monstrosities . . . under unnatural domestic conditions than under nature; and, secondly, that changed conditions affect in an especial manner the reproductive organs."[37]

As the years went on Darwin wavered on certain points, altered sentences, blew hot and cold in letters to friends, including Hooker and Huxley, but there is no evidence he totally abandoned the beliefs we have outlined. He besieged Gray upon the variability manifested by newly naturalized plants and, in at least one instance, expressed surprise that such plants should not have proved variable. Nevertheless, he clung to his own point of view. As his surviving friends entered the autumn of their careers they seem to have been loath to remember before a later, critical generation this fading argument of the master. So much had been written, and the subject, even in Darwin's hands, had proved so elusive that it was left to die a natural death. But the widely held notion that Darwin totally abandoned it is false. It is true he hesitated, that much at least can be allowed. Far more than his younger colleague Wallace, however, or the brisk and aggressive Huxley, he never totally escaped the shadow of Lamarck, the man who had haunted him at Edinburgh and in Lyell's pages read on the *Beagle* long ago.

[36] *Life and Letters of Sir Joseph Hooker*, Vol. 2, p. 304.
[37] MLD, Vol. 1, p. 198.

V   Darwin and Design

Although Lamarck had been dismissed as a "French atheist" in England and his work maligned in the conservative English reaction to the French Revolution and its Napoleonic consequences, there is no essential difference in the publicly expressed theological outlook of either Darwin or Lamarck. Both acknowledge a Creator, a Divine Author of all things, but both contend that the appearance of life on the planet, and its subsequent enormous radiation into divergent forms, is the product of secondary law as unswerving as that which the astronomer reads in the heavens. God, in other words, has not personally superintended the emergence of every species of gnat, mole, and cricket. Instead, these have come about through the working out of the natural forces implanted in that highly complicated chemical compound known as protoplasm, and the response of this same protoplasm to the environmental world about it. "It is derogatory," says Darwin in the first essay of 1842, "that the Creator of countless systems of worlds should have created each of the myriads of creeping parasites and slimy worms which have swarmed each day of life . . . on this one globe."[38] The creation and extinction of forms, he goes on to contend instead, "is the effect of secondary means." On homological resemblances alone, he argued later, "I disbelieve in . . . innumerable acts of creation."[39] Species formation, he wrote to Lyell, "has hitherto been viewed as beyond law, in fact this branch of science is still with most people under its theological phase of development."[40] "For the life of me," Darwin maintained, "I cannot see any difficulty in natural selection producing the most exquisite structure, *if such structure can be arrived at by gradation,* and I know from experience how hard it is to

[38] FO, p. 51.
[39] MLD, Vol. 1, p. 173.
[40] Ibid., p. 194.

name any structure towards which at least some gradations are not known."[41]

As one studies these remarks, and many like them, one
can observe that the continuity in nature which had been
maintained by Sir Charles Lyell against the catastrophists
in geology has now been extended to the living world.
The stability of natural law, first glimpsed in the heavens,
had been by slow degrees extended to the work of waves
and winds that shape the continents. Finally, through the
long cycles of erosion and the uneasy stirring of the ocean
beds, it was beginning dimly to be seen that life itself had
passed like a shifting and ephemeral apparition across the
face of nature. Nor could that elusive phantom be divorced from man himself, "the great subject," as even
Darwin once remarked. If fin and wing and hoof led backward toward some ancient union in the vertebrate line,
then the hand of man and ape could be scanned in the
same light. Even had they wished, the scientists could not
stop short at the human boundary. A world, a dream
world which had sustained human hearts for many centuries, was about to pass away. It was the world of design.

"Now it appears," wrote one wistful philosopher, "that
Darwin has at last enabled the extreme materialist to attempt and carry the design argument, the last and hitherto impregnable fortress behind which natural theology
has entrenched herself."[42] President Barnard of Columbia
University declared in 1873 that if organic evolution were
true then the existence of God was impossible. "If," he
declared bitterly, "the final outcome of all the boasted discoveries of modern science is to disclose to men that they
are more evanescent than the shadow of the swallow's
wing upon the lake . . . give me then, I pray, no more
science. I will live on in my simple ignorance, as my fa-

[41] LLD, Vol. 2, pp. 303–4.
[42] William Graham, *The Creed of Science*, London, 1881, p. 319.

thers did before me. . . ."[43] Time and time again similar,
if not more outraged, expressions echoed in intellectual
quarters both in America and Europe. Man had first
gazed out upon the night skies and found himself and his
planet dwarfed by the immensities of time and space;
now, to his fear and chagrin, he was learning that his ancestry was that of an arboreal primate who in the long
course of Tertiary time had descended to the ground and
achieved some dexterity in the manipulation of stones.
The wonder of the human achievement was lost for a moment in the sick revulsion of the wounded human ego.
The fallen Adam had stared into the mirror of nature and
perceived there only the mocking visage of an ape. Frederick Engels looking on amusedly at the disintegration of
the philosophy of the *Bridgewater Treatises* commented:
"Until Darwin, what was stressed by his present adher-
ents was precisely the harmonious co-operative working
of organic nature, how the plant kingdom supplies animals with nourishment and oxygen, and animals supply
plants with manure, ammonia, and carbonic acid. Hardly
was Darwin recognized before these same people saw
everywhere nothing but *struggle*."[44] Papers poured from
the press denouncing and refuting the *Origin* but the time
for that was long past. Its mass of accumulated evidence
had the weight of a boulder. Criticism flowed around and
over it but the boulder in all its impenetrable strength
remained.

Philosophically Darwin had achieved several things.
Whether every aspect of his interpretation of the evolutionary process was to prove correct or not—and about
this he retained more fundamental doubts than his followers—his work had destroyed the man-centered romantic evolutionism of the progressionists. It had, in fact,

[43] Sidney Ratner, "Evolution and the Rise of the Scientific Spirit
in America," *Philosophy of Science*, 1936, Vol. 3, p. 115.
[44] R. L. Meek, *Marx and Engels on Malthus*, Lawrence and
Wishart, London, 1953, p. 186.

left man only one of innumerable creatures evolving through the play of secondary forces and it had divested him of his mythological and supernatural trappings. The whole tradition of the parson-naturalists had been overthrown. Mechanical cause had replaced Paley's watch and watchmaker. It was not possible to argue from special design to the Deity. If this were true it could also be observed that men no longer were forced to wonder privately by what road the parasitism and disease which had troubled Darwin had come to exist in the world. These, too, were part of the evolving life-web, but they did not represent preordained evil. Man could learn from the secondary laws which had brought them into being how they might be controlled.

The key change in the intellectual climate of the nineteenth century came with the recognition of adaptation, of the fact that creatures fit themselves to their environment. Lamarck and a few others had glimpsed this fact but most naturalists had gone on examining their universe blinded by a tradition of natural theology based on special creation. With Darwin we come to observe a very different world—a world with which he is already toying in the first essay of 1842; he is concerned with abortive organs as Lamarck was before him—rudiments, echoes from the past, traces of vanished limbs, soldered wing cases, buried teeth—all that conglomeration of useless organs that lie hidden in living bodies like the refuse in a hundred-year-old attic. "No one can reflect on this without astonishment," muses Darwin; "can anything be clearer than that wings are to fly and teeth to bite and yet we find these organs . . . in situations where they cannot possibly be of their normal use."[45]

The only reasonable explanation of this fact, which even Cuvier could not satisfactorily explain, lies in the evolutionary past of every species of organism—the ghostly world of time in which animals are forever slip-

[45] FO, p. 45.

ping from one environment to another and changing their forms and features as they go. But the marks of the passage linger, and so we come down to the present bearing the traces of all the curious tables at which our forerunners have sat and played the game of life. Our world, in short, is a marred world, an imperfect world, a never totally adjusted world, for the simple reason that it is not static. The games are still in progress and all of us, in the words of Sir Arthur Keith, bear the wounds of evolution. Our backs hurt, we have muscles which no longer move, we have hair that is not functional. All of this bespeaks another world, another game played far behind us in the past. We are indeed the products of "descent with modification."

Yet as we dip more deeply into the pages of the *Origin* and as we browse in that great body of commentary which grew up around it one thing becomes apparent: Darwin did not destroy the argument from design. He destroyed only the watchmaker and the watch. "Under my hearty congratulations of Darwin for his striking contributions to teleology," wrote Asa Gray to de Candolle in 1863, "there is a vein of petite malice, from my knowing well that he rejects the idea of design, while all the while he is bringing out the neatest illustrations of it."[46] Alone among Darwin's immediate associates Gray inclined toward a more theistic position. We need not pursue his line of thinking here except to note that he sensed very early the fact that only a *certain type of design argument* had been eliminated by Darwin, namely, the finalistic one. Design by special creation implies the creation of an animal or plant for a special purpose and for all time; it is, in other words, final design. That was the design of the early naturalists whose last echoes resound in Paley and the *Bridgewater Treatises*. The word "final," however, throws a tremendous burden upon the theologian. "It places him," to reiterate the remarks of Lewis Hicks, "in

[46] Jane Gray, *Letters of Asa Gray*, Boston, 1894, Vol. 2, p. 498.

the attitude of attempting to demonstrate, not merely a purpose but *the* purpose, the only, the ultimate, the exclusive, the *final* intention of the Creator in respect to each structure."[47] Obviously, in the light of the discovery that organisms change their bodies and the functions of their organs, Hicks's stricture becomes most pertinent. The design enthusiasts had assumed to define the intentions of the watchmaker only to discover that he had no final purpose which they could anticipate and that the watch, furthermore, was showing signs of turning into a compass through some self-directed reorganization of its inner structure.

The analogy is plain. The evolutionists discovered that nature "makes things make themselves" and thus succeeded in apparently removing the need of a Master Craftsman. The resulting excitement was so great that it was only later that the question began to be asked: Why *does* nature let things make themselves? Obviously this is a question science can only philosophize about but cannot answer. It can trace the organism down to the final cell; it may even be able someday, in its knowledge of biophysics and chemistry, to create simple life, but it will still not be able to answer the final why. For at that point science will have left the field of secondary causes in which it operates so successfully and, instead, will be asking the primary and unanswerable questions.

Darwin had delivered a death blow to a simple, a naïvely simple, form of the design argument but, as Huxley himself came to realize, it is still possible to argue for directivity in the process of life even though that directivity may be without finality in a human sense. The rise of a broad and more sophisticated teleology may well have played a part in the development of the organismic philosophies of later years. Cuvier's grasp of the body as a functioning whole was far greater than Darwin's. Cuvier

[47] L. E. Hicks, *A Critique of Design Arguments*, New York, 1883, p. 42.

was struck with the wonderful stability of the functioning organism; Darwin with a theory of change. In pursuit of the mechanism of that change he tended to forget or ignore the interior organizing ability of the body, the curious adjustments of which it is capable and which he passed over lightly with the word "correlations" and references to "complex laws." Not even today is it possible to describe satisfactorily what power controls the innumerable activities, not alone of a living body, but of just one functioning cell which has to assemble and activate within itself all the chemical components necessary for its existence.

The concern with exterior struggle which followed the publication of the *Origin of Species* diverted biologists for decades from the most mysterious aspect of the living organism—how its elaborate interior system is so subtly controlled and regulated. Cuvier differed from Darwin in his concern with the great organ systems underlying classes and phyla. As a comparative morphologist he was occupied with divergent, stable systems; Darwin, as we have seen, with adaptability and change. Both were men of great insight and if they could have been combined into one person, much later confusion might have been avoided. Human lives are limited in time, however, and a powerful mind, by its own interests, draws its particular followers down a diverging path for years. It was true of Cuvier who ignored Lamarck and it was true in a more subtle way of Darwin who ignored the organismic aspect of the thought of Cuvier.

VI *Darwin and Lamarck*

To conclude our philosophic discussion of the making of the *Origin* a short comparison of the major tenets of the Darwinian as opposed to the Lamarckian view of nature will prove useful. It should be emphasized that we are here examining the writings of Darwin and Lamarck, not the embellishments or alterations made upon their systems by later writers. It must also be remembered in fairness to Lamarck that he was writing a half century earlier than Darwin, and with far less accumulated knowledge at his command.

Both (and in this respect Lamarck was far ahead of most of his generation) recognized that vast intervals of time were involved in the process of organic change. Each visualized the process as continuous, not saltatory. Each saw clearly that it was the exceedingly slow tempo of evolution as contrasted with the development of the individual which gave the illusion of total organic stability. Both saw life as branching and ramifying into a diversity of habitats and becoming by degrees ecologically adapted.

Here, however, a difference can be observed which reflects Lamarck's closer association with the thought of the eighteenth century. It is, he maintains, the necessity of ecological adjustment, of adaptation, which interferes with the perfectly graduated scale of nature which would otherwise come about naturally by means of an inner perfecting principle within the organism. It is the environment, in other words, which, in concert with the modifying power within the living creature, induces modifications of animal structure. There is thus an ideal structure toward which the organism *would* evolve, but which is constantly reworked by the creature's efforts to maintain and adjust itself to the world around it. This adjustment achieved by *need*, by the effort of the individual, will remain static and unchanging so long as the environment remains unchanged. In spite of Darwin's rejection of Lamarck's inner perfecting principle and modification by need to the demands of the habitat, one can observe that his break with Lamarck is not complete. The struggle for existence, the *willingness* of the organism to struggle, a fact which Darwin does not attempt to explain, equates at least partially, though perhaps not quite so teleologically, with Lamarck's life-power, or perfecting principle.

Furthermore, as we have previously had occasion to note, the Darwin of the essay of 1844, and similarly in a somewhat modulated tone thereafter, underestimates variation in wild nature. He comes close to assuming Lamarck's view of the perpetual stability of a once adapted form. Something in the external environment, they both believe, must impinge upon the organism to cause further change. Where Lamarck would have demanded renewed interior *need* for adjustment as a modifying force, Darwin institutes an environmental change which produces germ cell modifications by influence from without. These new characters are then selected as the creature struggles for life in its new or altered environment. It is a reworked Lamarckism but the similarities are intriguing. Of course, the belief in the reality of acquired characteristics was shared by both men. In Darwin's case, for reasons to be explored in a later chapter, this type of inheritance was to be carried to great lengths in his later work.

We have previously noted that the concept of the struggle for existence has sometimes been described erroneously as one of Darwin's contributions to general biological theory. By his own words he drew upon Malthus's treatment of human population problems and applied this concept throughout the organic world. Here again it should be remembered that knowledge of the struggle for existence in nature is to be found in Lamarck, Paley, and Lyell. By the early nineteenth century it was a commonplace.

But to Lamarck the "war of nature" was a pruning device, holding life in order and restraining the limitless fecundity of nature. It was not needed in order to achieve the transformation of species, since for him another mechanism was available. As a consequence, Lamarck ignored its possible winnowing effect in the preservation of variation. Darwin, by contrast, recognized its possible role in the accumulation of favorable mutations—even if the latter emerged in a purely fortuitous fashion. We come here to an exceedingly interesting and neglected point: *What led Darwin to believe in the chance emergence of new characters?* This constitutes his major break with Lamarck and it is far more important than his recognition of the struggle for existence. The latter takes on renewed importance only after one believes that chance variations emerge and are inherited. After this is recognized, and only then, does the commonplace and widely recognized "struggle" become a genuine creative device.

Darwin at no point dates for us the time when this distinction emerged clearly in his mind, but one may suspect that the analysis of the Galápagos fauna with its variable products in isles not widely separated and climatically similar played its part. Here, "need," in the Lamarckian sense, should have produced similar results, but if one retained the idea that a new environment merely stimulated fortuitous variation which was than selected by struggle—one would be moving toward a new interpretation of evolution by way of Lamarck. This apparently is what Darwin did. Similarly the domestic breeding in which Darwin also took such deep interest offers examples of the development of odd, exotic, and quite useless or even detrimental characters preserved by artificial selection. These could hardly be regarded as teleologically implanted in the organism and Darwin uses this fact as an argument against the predetermination of animal form. Yet to promote the variation he has recourse again to the argument that domestication in some manner *stimulates* variability.

It is impossible, as one considers this subject in the context of Lamarck's thought, not to wonder why Darwin had to seek his inspiration in Malthus, or why in writing to Lyell long afterward he found it necessary to characterize Lamarck's as a "wretched book . . . from which (I well remember my surprise) I gained nothing." The surprise, one comes to feel, should not be Darwin's. Rather it should be the surprise of the historian who finds that the two men shared similar views on the significance of domestic breeding, even to the extent of similar observations upon pigeons, greyhounds, and bulldogs, upon the interpretation of rudimentary parts, even upon use and disuse and their effects upon individual organs. They shared also like views upon man's relationship to the primates, except that Darwin was in a position to see more clearly man's paleontological relationship to extinct anthropoids. They felt varieties and species to be shifting, nebulous, and ill-defined. Though Lamarck hesitated over the question of total extinctions, he shared with Darwin a belief that morphological similarities indicated continuity of descent. It may be said justly that they differed in their opinions upon spontaneous generation, which Lamarck favored, and that Darwin eschewed necessary progression. Yet Darwin on the final page of the *Origin* so far forgot his antipathy to the idea as to write: "All corporeal and mental endowments will tend to progress toward perfection." In this he could no more quite escape his antecedents than Lamarck could escape the Scale of Nature.

Lamarck, however, in his final pages offers a sage observation. He says: "It is not enough to discover and prove a useful truth . . . but that it is necessary also to be able to propagate it and get it recognized." For this effort Lamarck, as we have seen, was too old, too inept, too poor, too ahead of his time. Darwin is often pictured as similarly launching his frail bark upon the restless intellectual currents of his day. There is one difference. He had acquired Lamarck's bitterly learned wisdom by way of the worldly-wise geologist Lyell. His book was not launched alone.

Edmund Gosse in his autobiographical study, *Father and Son,* throws an unconscious light upon the way in which that great book, the *Origin,* entered the world. "It was the notion of Lyell, himself a great mover of men, that before the doctrine of natural selection was given to

a world which would be sure to lift up at it a howl of exe-
cration, a certain bodyguard of sound and experienced
naturalists, expert in the description of species, should be
privately made aware of its tenor. Among those who were
thus initiated or approached with a view toward possible illumination, was my Father. He was spoken to by
Hooker, and later on by Darwin . . . in the summer of
1857."[48] The great idea was being launched again, as Lamarck had foreseen. One wishes that Darwin and Huxley,
both of whom had decried the shouldering and pushing
for eminence among the scientists of their day, might
have been just a little kinder to that old man whose bones
are lost among the forgotten millions of the Paris poor. In
the end perhaps it does not matter, but it is ironic that
he who glimpsed so much truth should largely be remembered as the perpetrator of an error which was also shared
by his intellectual descendant, Charles Darwin—the belief in the inheritance of acquired characteristics.

[48] Wm. Heinemann, Windmill Library ed., London, 1928, p. 106.
Gosse's memory seems slightly at fault here. The date was most
probably the summer of 1858.

Chapter VIII

The Priest Who Held
the Key to Evolution

Great revolutions in science are scarcely ever
effected but after their authors have ceased
to breathe.

William Swainson, 1834

I *Gregor Mendel*

"On a clear, cold evening in February," so his biographer
states, for the record is clearer upon the weather of this
particular evening of 1865 than upon the momentous
event that occurred in it, "Father Gregor Mendel read
before the Brünn Society for the Study of Natural Science, his paper upon 'Experiments in Plant Hybridization.'"[1] Forty people were present in the room at the
schoolhouse where the lecture was given. They were not
ignorant people. Botanists, a chemist, an astronomer, a
geologist were among those present. In the next month
Mendel spoke again to the same audience recounting before them his new theory upon the nature of inheritance.
The audience listened patiently. At the end of the blue-
eyed priest's eager presentation of his researches, the still

[1] Hugo Iltis, *Life of Mendel,* New York, 1932.

existing minutes of the society indicate there was no discussion.

Stolidly the audience had listened. Just as stolidly it had risen and dispersed down the cold, moonlit streets of Brünn. No one had ventured a question, not a single heartbeat had quickened. In the little schoolroom one of the greatest scientific discoveries of the nineteenth century had just been enunciated by a professional teacher with an elaborate array of evidence. Not a solitary soul had understood him.

Thirty-five years were to flow by and the grass on the discoverer's grave would be green before the world of science comprehended that tremendous moment. Aged survivors from the little audience would then be importuned for their memories. Few would have any.

In the four huge volumes in which, at the end of the century, the scientific historian John Merz records a hundred years of discovery, the name Gregor Mendel receives only footnote mention. Yet with Lamarck and Charles Darwin he shares today the biological honors of the nineteenth century. It is *par excellence* the century that discovered time and change. Perhaps as a consequence there is something a little symbolic about the lives of these three men. Lamarck died in forgotten poverty, but above his grave rang his daughter's defiant outcry, "The future will remember you, my father." Charles Darwin had been more fortunate in the world's adulation, yet a decade after the publication of the *Origin* he was to hesitate and fall back upon a theory which weakened his life's work and which would have proved unnecessary had he known what was said on that winter evening of 1865 in Brünn.

Darwinism, after the rediscovery of Mendel, was to undergo a sea change. It was to be half dismissed by Mendel's first followers and then emerge once more strengthened, enriched, and rejuvenated by the discoveries which flowed from the work of the obscure priest who read the

Origin of Species and carried on queer experiments with peas which he affectionately referred to as his children. From peas, dwarfed, wrinkled, yellow, tall, short, he was to derive the laws which make modern genetics one of the most exact of the biological sciences. He had probed into the mysteries of the cell without a microscope. He had done it by infinite patience alone in the solitude of a monastery garden.

Although his observations were reported to the world, they lay unread. "My time will come," he said once to his friend Niessl, but it is doubtful if by then he really believed it. When he died in 1884, it was as a prelate of the church, worn out with the cares of office. His experiments had long since ceased. They had never aroused public attention and perhaps in the end, alone, confused, and ill-advised by the only botanist he knew, he had come to doubt their value. A few years after his election as prelate a visitor wishing to observe the experimental plants at the monastery reported simply, "I found that I had come too late." In a similar way fame came at last to Gregor Mendel.

There is perhaps no stranger story in the annals of science than the rise to international eminence of this solitary man sixteen years after his death and thirty-five years after the talk in the little hall at Brünn. It is a story which is worth perusal by all scholars, not alone because of what Mendel achieved, but also because the complete failure of communication in this particular instance was, to a major degree, the failure of professional science. It has its lessons, even though the world has changed greatly since 1865. No man who loves knowledge would want an episode like this to happen twice.

Some scientists have tried to argue that the journal in which Mendel published was obscure, but his tragedy is more profound than this. He was advised by one of the great European botanists of his generation and he was betrayed, not consciously, we may say in charity, but betrayed through condescension. Mendel was an amateur and the professional scientist whom he looked up to and admired saw in him no more than an instrument for the furtherance of his own researches. It is true that the intellectual climate of the time increased his difficulties, but it is also true that Mendel, this man of buoyant good will, was denied throughout his life the solace of a single sincere professional friend who would lend an understanding ear to the account of his experiments.

From first to last Mendel was dogged by ill luck in everything that mattered save just one thing: the choice of the edible pea for his experiments. Even this plant, with its luckily simple genetic structure, was eventually abandoned—once more by professional scientific advice. Indeed, at this late point in time one might readily wonder how much he really glimpsed of the significance of his own discoveries—one might, that is, if one did not know of the well-stocked monastery library with its annotated copy of Darwin. We know, too, that he tried experiments to test the Lamarckian principle. Alone in his garden he had wrestled with the two leading theories involving organic evolution, but where Darwin and Lamarck had been fascinated by change, Mendel was fascinated by stability. Instead of attempting, as did Darwin, to determine how the characteristics of the adult organism were transferred to, or compressed into, a minute germ cell, Mendel sought to determine how it came about that the germ cell contained and transmitted the characters of the living animal.

Mendel, in other words, had intuitively grasped what seemingly no one else of his generation understood; namely, that until we had some idea of the mechanisms which controlled organic *persistence* we would be ill-equipped to understand what it was that produced evolutionary change. The persistence of biological form in time is the first fact in our experience. Organic change is a far more subtle phenomenon whose detection, as we have had occasion to observe, is dependent upon a sophisticated knowledge of successive plant and animal transformations occurring throughout great stretches of the past. It is for this reason that evolution remained so long undetected, whereas the assumption of special creation of each species struck very few as being in the least illogical.

It was Mendel's virtue that he concentrated with more precision than anyone before him upon the way in which already existing characters emerged or failed to emerge in the offspring of a particular union. In examining the details of his unfortunate career it will be possible to see with greater clarity why Darwin by 1871 in the *Descent of Man* was expressly retreating from his bold stand upon natural selection as the major factor in the production of evolutionary change. In that volume Darwin, quite in contrast with his assurance of 1859, wrote as follows: "I now admit . . . that in the earlier editions of my 'Origin of Species' I perhaps attributed too much to the action of natural selection or the survival of the fittest."[2]

There was a reason for this wary retreat on the part of the master. Ironically enough, two years after Mendel had actually placed a possible answer to Darwin's problem on record, a very erudite Scotch engineer brought forward in the pages of the *North British Review*[3] a formidable challenge to the Darwinians. It was a challenge which only a Mendelian geneticist could have answered—and Mendel, immured in his monastery, was unknown to both parties.

Darwin never attempted a direct response to Jenkin— he always avoided public controversy—but there is ample testimony in his letters to the effect which Jenkin's criticism had upon him. "Fleeming Jenkin has given me much trouble . . ." he wrote to Hooker in January of 1869.[4] In

[2] C. Darwin, *Descent of Man*, 1871, Modern Library ed., p. 441.
[3] Fleeming Jenkin, "The Origin of Species," *North British Review*, 1867, Vol. 46, pp. 149–71.
[4] LLD, Vol. 2, p. 379.

February he confided to Wallace: "Jenkin argued in the 'North British Review' against single variations ever being perpetuated, and has convinced me. . . ." Finally, in the sixth edition of the *Origin of Species* one may read his open confession: "Nevertheless, until reading an able and valuable article in the 'North British Review' (1867) I did not appreciate how rarely single variations, whether slight or strongly marked, could be perpetuated. . . . The justice of these remarks cannot, I think, be disputed."[5]

The reader must now consider what is implied in the above statements. Fleeming Jenkin had, in actuality, well-nigh destroyed the fortuitous character of variation as it was originally visualized by Darwin. Jenkin set forth the fact that a newly emergent character possessed by one or a few rare mutants would be rapidly swamped out of existence by backcrossing with the mass of individuals that did not possess the trait in question. Only if the same trait emerged *simultaneously* throughout the majority of the species could it be expected to survive.

An admission that numbers of animals or plants mutate simultaneously in the same direction, however, greatly reduces the significance of natural selection and suggests either some interior orthogenetic drive which is affecting the individual members of the species, or an external environmental force of Lamarckian character producing a direct effect on the germ plasm of an entire group of organisms. In either case fluctuating fortuitous individual variation has to be abandoned and with it goes much of the importance of natural selection.[6] Jenkin's formidable mathematical attack, formidable, that is, in the light of the conception of blending inheritance prevalent at the time, seemed to Darwin largely unanswerable. The only recourse was to fall back toward the type of Lamarckian-

[5] Modern Library ed., p. 71.

[6] J. C. Willis, *The Course of Evolution*, Cambridge University Press, 1940, pp. 5, 165–66. Also H. J. Muller, "The Views of Haeckel in the Light of Genetics," *Philosophy of Science*, 1934, Vol. 1, p. 318.

ism around which he elaborated his theory of pangenesis. Darwin died with this difficulty unsolved and its consequences haunting his last years. The answer to Fleeming Jenkin had been standing on library shelves in the Proceedings of the Brünn Society for the Study of Natural Science since 1866. Jenkin, the hardheaded engineer, and the gracious, dreaming naturalist who had been forced to retreat before him would both be gone before anyone blew the dust from those forgotten pages.

Mendel is a curious wraith in history. His associates, his followers, are all in the next century: That is when his influence began. Yet if we are to understand him and the way in which he eventually rescued Darwinism itself from oblivion we must go the long way back to Brünn in Moravia and stand among the green peas in a quiet garden. Gregor Mendel had a strange fate: he was destined to live one life painfully in the flesh at Brünn and another, the intellectual life of which he dreamed, in the following century. His words, his calculations were to take a sudden belated flight out of the dark tomblike volumes and be written on hundreds of university blackboards, and go spinning through innumerable heads. Before their importance can be grasped, however, it is necessary to examine the state of genetics at the time Darwin wrote the *Origin of Species* and to gain some idea of the nature of the menace which confronted Darwin upon the publication of Jenkin's paper.[7]

II Pre-Mendelian Genetics

The earlier history of human genetics is an amazing assemblage of superstitious error and fallacious observation. Monstrous births were assumed to be the result of man-animal connections. Right down into the eighteenth century such reports continued to be printed. As I remarked

[7] It can also be found in his *Papers, Literary, Scientific, Etc.*, ed. by Sidney Colvin and J. A. Ewing, London, 1887, Vol. 1.

on an earlier page, the fixed precision of Christian speciation really represents in no small degree a late amalgamation of Linnaean scientific taxonomy with the increasing
Christian emphasis upon special creation.[8] Monstrous
hybrids between men, bears, and other animals which no
educated person would accept today were taken quite
seriously right into De Maillet's time—an added reason,
incidentally, for not dismissing as romantics, or as unscien-
tific, scholars who were merely repeating the common beliefs of their day.[9] Undoubtedly some of the floating
beliefs that plants could change their type—ideas which
survive in the pages of the *Vestiges*—were derived from
accidental cases of genuine plant hybridity and mutation.
Anecdote and tall tale were the common data of genetics
until well into the latter part of the eighteenth century.
At that time the rise of professional breeding and the
growing interest in the importation of valuable food and
drug plants began to place emphasis upon controlled experimentation. The idea of selective livestock breeding
arose in England during the early phases of the Industrial
Revolution when the multiplying towns began to demand
meat and dairy produce on a large scale. What emerged,
and stimulated practical improvement in livestock, was
the shift from purely local subsistence farming to the prof-
itable business of supplying the food and wool needs of
the new industrial towns. All of these purely economic
factors greatly stimulated experimentation among commercial breeders. Darwin, who had come from the country, early showed a shrewd instinct for merging the theoretical with the practical when he began his intensive
perusal of horticultural and livestock journals.

If we are to get clearly in mind the difference between
the genetics of Darwin's day and the sort of problems

[8] E. B. Poulton in *Essays on Evolution*, Oxford, 1908, p. 56,
suggests seventeenth-century Puritan influence.
[9] Conway Zirkle in *The Beginnings of Plant Hybridization*,
Philadelphia, 1935, gives an extended historical account of fantastic
animal combinations.

which began to emerge toward the close of the century we must remember that all the great cytological work upon cell mechanisms was unavailable to both Darwin and Mendel. Their observations were confined to direct breeding experiments, or what they could learn from others. Mendel, as we have intimated, approached the problem in a quite different way from Darwin and proved to be the better experimentalist. Perhaps he was fortunate, so far as his experiments went, in not being a famous man already laboring under a point of view.

We have already learned the general nature of Darwin's beliefs. Here we are concerned only with the contrast he was later to make with Wallace on the one hand and, later on and posthumously, with the Mendelians on the other. Just as in the case of Darwin's evolutionary thinking, it is not always easy to isolate, out of the vast mass of his accumulated examples, the precise outlines of his genetic ideas. It is very commonly stated that Darwin believed in blending inheritance, while Mendel succeeded in demonstrating the reality of particulate inheritance. This appears to me a mild oversimplification of a more complicated situation. The confusion is emphasized when one comes to remark that Romanes, in discussing Darwin's views a few years prior to the rediscovery of Mendel, classifies Darwin's theory of heredity as a particulate one.[10]

Actually it would seem that the case might be better put as follows. Prior to the emergence of the critiques of A. W. Bennett and Fleeming Jenkin it would appear that Darwin had taken a great deal of the genetics of his day for granted. His primary interest, because of his evolutionary studies, lay in the field of variation. In the first edition of the *Origin* he simply states that the laws governing in-

---

[10] G. J. Romanes, *Darwin and after Darwin*, Chicago, 1897, Vol. 2, p. 45. E. S. Russell in *The Interpretation of Development and Heredity*, Oxford, 1930, p. 63, similarly expresses himself and cites Johannsen to the same effect.

heritance are quite unknown, though he is vaguely aware of phenomena that today would go under such categories as sex-linked inheritance, or dominance and recessiveness. He confesses that variability is governed by unknown laws, but he realizes that this variability is without significance unless its benefits can be retained and accumulated through heredity. Drawing upon the forceful analogy of domestic breeding he professes to see no limit to the transmuting power of nature.

As one studies this first edition of the *Origin* one can see that in spite of the author's enthusiasm for natural selection he is rather careful to mention all factors which could conceivably play a part in organic change. As we have remarked, he remains, in this sense, a transitional figure. His genetics is essentially that of the shrewd out-of-doors observer. He is neither particulate in any precise sense, nor does he incline totally toward blending conceptions of inheritance. In reality he is occupied with just two things: variation and natural selection. He is thinking about evolution and his views have not yet been proved vulnerable by means of heredity. It was the attack launched by Jenkin and Bennett that forced Darwin into a more elaborate treatment of genetic mechanisms and led eventually to a retreat down one of the pathways he had left open for himself. The retreat was not dictated through Jenkin's criticism alone. His troubles were augmented by events in the field of geophysics which we will chronicle in the next chapter.

When Jenkin penned his attack on natural selection it is quite obvious that he had found a loophole which Darwin, who was not mathematically gifted, had entirely overlooked. In brief, Jenkin simply took the position:

1. That it was not possible in domestic breeding to push a strain beyond a certain point of maximum efficiency for a given character. In his analysis of this problem Jenkin appears to have theoretically anticipated the later discoveries of Johannsen in the field of fluctuating variation.

In this, however, he was ahead of his time and the debates which would later emerge around that subject. The attack which really shook Darwin was:

2. The argument that a favorable mutative sport would be "utterly outbalanced by numerical inferiority." Since the unblending character of Mendelian units was unknown, Jenkin's position was simply that a single favorable mutation would soon be swamped out and by degrees obliterated in any population group in which it occurred. Since the favored animal or plant would presumably be mating with its normal fellows, the rare variation would not long survive. As a potent example Jenkin advanced the hypothetical case of a single well-endowed white man being cast ashore on an island inhabited by Negroes. No matter how much power he might attain among them, the tribe would certainly not become white because of his presence. The only answer, ignoring for the moment Mendelian genetics, is to postulate a large group of animals mutating in a similar direction and contemporaneously. Jenkin points out this alternative, though, as he justly observes, it results in an evolution which is no longer the product of chance and selection but rather "a theory of successive creations." The fortuitous element involved in natural selection disappears and one is immediately confronted, not with accident, but an orthogenetic and controlled movement in a single direction. Darwin was sufficiently impressed by this argument that, although he did not abandon his book, he incorporated into it the Jenkin alternative suggestion and began at the same time a retreat toward habit and use-inheritance which it is obvious he now saw as a refuge from the corner into which he had been forced by Jenkin. A. W. Bennett pressed the same advantage in another paper three years later in *Nature*[11] and Herbert Spencer, one of England's pre-

[11] "The Theory of Selection from a Mathematical Point of View," *Nature*, 1870, Vol. 3, pp. 30–31.

Darwinian evolutionists, reiterated the Jenkin position as late as 1893.[12]

The final edition of the *Origin* contains, in the light of Jenkin's views, some quite surprising comment. "There must be some efficient cause for each slight individual difference," Darwin says, "as well as for more strongly marked variations which occasionally arise; and if the unknown cause were to act persistently, *it is almost certain that all the individuals of the species would be similarly modified.*"[13] (Italics mine. L.E.) In those lines Darwin has assumed the Jenkin argument which permits the retention of evolution but at the price of fortuitous variation. One line further, however, and we encounter the contention that he has underrated "the frequency and importance of modifications due to spontaneous variability."

Darwin with his gift for compromise has here accepted both a point of view which, if pursued, would be metaphysically fatal to his system and, at the same time, has stepped up the pace of variation to try to overcome the logic of Jenkin's argument. The number of these concealed contradictions makes the later editions of the *Origin* instructive but difficult reading. For clarity and reasonable consistency the first edition is by far the most satisfactory.

III *Pangenesis*

In 1868 Darwin published the *Variation of Animals and Plants under Domestication.* In it, for the first time, he set forth a theory of inheritance to which he applied the term "pangenesis." This theory actually implies a type of particulate inheritance, although Darwin's concern over Jenkin's paper quite obviously reveals that this assumption of blending inheritance raised no question in his

12 "The Inadequacy of Natural Selection," *Popular Science Monthly*, 1893, Vol. 42, p. 807.
13 Modern Library ed., p. 155–56.

mind in 1867. Pangenesis, however, is a theory of particulate inheritance beginning at the other end, so to speak, of the problem Mendel pursued. It begins, that is, with the assemblage of another potential individual from the body cells of an existing organism. It is not an idea originating with Darwin by any means; it runs all the way back to the Greeks,[14] but Darwin's elaboration of it is an indirect escape from such problems as Bennett and Jenkin had formulated.

Darwin assumed that the cells of the body throw off minute material particles and that these particles, "gemmules," he calls them, are gathered from all parts of the body into the sexual cells of the organism. Darwin thus assumes that the sexual cells contain only what is represented in the living body—or primarily so—and the particles they receive upon fertilization. Every character thus comes from the somatic, or body, tissues, and the germ cells contain only what is brought to them by the blood stream from all parts of the body. The germ is merely a device to create a new body out of the mingling of the particles of the parents' bodies.

Darwin's germ materials are thus developed anew with every living individual. This is in marked contradiction to later theories about the inviolability of the germ plasm. It permits any somatic modification during an individual's lifetime to be represented in his germ cells. It is, in other words, a Lamarckian device ensuring the inheritance of adaptive modifications in unending succession. That Darwin should have proposed this theory indicates, not alone how inadequate natural selection had come to seem to him, but how truly transitional, in retrospect, we can observe his thinking to be. He is half modern, half experimental, yet in times of difficulty he is capable of obscure retreats in the direction of eighteenth-century concepts. August Weismann (1834–1914), the man who reversed the trend of particulate studies, and who has been termed

[14] M. J. Sirks, *General Genetics*, The Hague, 1956, p. 49 ff.

the first original evolutionist after Darwin,[15] has himself remarked that he would probably never have been led to deny the inheritance of acquired characters if it had not been for the impossible complications involved in "the giving off, circulation, and accumulation of gemmules."[16]

In spite of the fact that Weismann remained sufficiently hypnotized by the omnipresent Darwinian shadow to postulate a "struggle" among the determiners in the germ cell, he actually diverted the study of evolution into the pathway which has led on to the great modern advances in the field of genetics. We have seen that Darwin's determiners were supposed to arise in the body cells and to carry, in some mysterious manner, the image of their particular body region compacted into a newly produced germ cell.

Weismann, on the other hand, reversed the attention which had been directed to the body as a source of variation, and concentrated his attention upon the germ itself as the source of emergent change. He postulated a germ plasm which was basically immortal and inviolable. By this he meant that the reproductive cells are isolated early and are passed along unchanged from individual to individual in the history of the race. By "unchanged" is meant unaffected by exterior environmental influences. All changes which emerge in the phylogeny of a given organism must therefore emerge from the alteration or elimination of particular hereditary determiners within the germ plasm itself, not from "messenger" determiners carried into the germ from sources in the adult body. It has been said by many modern writers that Weismann carried this inviolability principle too far, but it should be remarked in simple justice that since his works are no longer read in great detail, his own qualifications upon this point have been forgotten. He was willing to concede that the germ plasm was probably not totally isolable from

[15] Mendel, of course, being unknown.
[16] *Essays upon Heredity*, Oxford, 1892, Vol. 2, pp. 80–81.

influences penetrating it from the body, but that such influences "must be extremely slight."[17] It must be remembered that Weismann was combating Darwin's notion of a great stream of "messengers" entering the germ plasm from the body itself. There is no reason to think that Weismann, if he were alive today, would find it necessary to cavil over mutations produced in the germ plasm by radiation or by other similar powerful forces exerted upon the body.

In summary then, we may say that while it has long since been disproved that the determiners engage in a struggle for existence within the germ cell, the main features of Weismann's system have been retained as the actual basis of modern genetics. Germ cells come from other germ cells and are not derived from body cells. Germinal continuity is complete, but not somatic continuity. This is the reverse of Darwin's position, and Weismann's victory over the conception of pangenesis marked the declining influence of Lamarckian theories of inheritance. As Weismann himself commented, "The transmission of acquired characters is an impossibility, for if the germ plasm is not formed anew in each individual but is derived from that which preceded it, its structure and above all its molecular constitution cannot depend upon the individual in which it happens to occur. . . ."[18] He also correctly recognized that sexual reproduction with its reshuffling of hereditary characters in every generation is really a remarkable device for promoting variability—new character combinations which may have selective value in the struggle for life. This observation was made possible by the slowly growing knowledge of cell mechanics to which the German workers of this period made such notable contributions.[19] So greatly does the sexual division promote new

---

[17] Op. cit., edition of 1889, p. 170.
[18] Ibid., p. 266.
[19] The advances in cell-staining techniques in Germany were responsible for major advances in cytology. Roux had observed

and individual combinations of characters that, without including any new mutations at all, it still contributes greatly to the potential evolutionary variability of any species.

Weismann's centering of emphasis upon a germ plasm out of which arose variation which was manifested in the living organism, and the failure of experiment to validate Darwin's pangenesis, led directly to the renewed experimentation which eventually culminated in the rediscovery of the lost work of Gregor Mendel. Before discussing the nature of that work, however, it is necessary to examine in a brief way just what Darwin, Wallace, and Weismann meant by variation. As we will see a little later, modern genetics, beginning with Mendel, has envisaged this problem differently from the way it was treated earlier in the century. The truth is that the Darwinists lumped under the term "variation" a great range of bodily differences about which they knew nothing whatever. They assumed that these characteristics were heritable—natural selection has no meaning without such inheritance—and that "variation and heredity," as Hogben says, "were coextensive processes."[20] Offspring were always a little different from their parents, the line of evolution was constantly in motion and constantly subjected to the selective attrition of the struggle for existence. As someone cleverly remarked, the species was always swallowing its tail. The normal curve of distribution for a given character was constantly being advanced on one side toward greater efficiency, and similarly suffering erosion from the side of the less effective. A stable species, in other words, was merely an il-

---

the behavior of chromatin and examined mitosis. He believed that the secret of heredity was incorporated in a particulate manner within the nucleus. Following Roux's lead Weismann glimpsed the role of the chromosomes in carrying what today we would call genes. He also predicted in 1887 the reduction division which was late · on to be established for meiosis.

[20] L. Hogben, *Genetic Principles in Medicine and Social Science,* New York, 1932, p. 167.

lusion created by the constant, slow pruning effect of natural selection.

This idea, in spite of other differences, is common to Darwin, Wallace, and Weismann. There was no clear comprehension that not all somatic variation is heritable. Thus the Darwinists tended to conceive of evolution as a continuous process. Even an organism which appears to be standing still, like some living fossils, is actually in a kind of dynamic balance. Its apparent resting state is really produced by the fact that selection is holding the norm of the species at a given spot instead of thrusting it forward. The modern interpretation of evolution and variation does not totally equate with this point of view. When we use the term "variation," our meaning is somewhat different from that of the Darwinists.

IV Artificial Selection and the Evolutionists

All through the earlier portion of the nineteenth century, and indeed the latter portion of the eighteenth century as well, evolutionists had had recourse to domesticated animals and plants as suggesting the mutability of biological form. Special creationists, even, had had to recognize a certain degree of plasticity in life whether wild or tame, but they had regarded this plasticity as being confined and demarcated. Species, *sammelarten*, as the Germans would say, were receptacles containing a range of varieties, but the species was the original created entity. The evolutionists, by contrast, had insisted that the species barrier was an illusion, that given time and opportunity the species, in Wallace's convenient phrase, would "depart indefinitely" from its original appearance. Buffon hinted at the possibility; Lamarck expressed it; Darwin used the whole process of artificial selection from which to develop, by analogy, his principle of natural selection. "The possibility of continued divergence," he remarked, "rests on the tendency in each part or organ to go on varying in the same manner in which it has already varied; and that this occurs is proved by the steady and gradual improvement of many animals and plants during lengthened periods."[21] While Darwin was not unaware of what today we would call macro-mutations, or saltations, he was inclined to believe that in a state of nature, particularly, smaller changes operating by degrees were the main instrument of change.[22] Wallace, in a rather unguarded moment when he was attempting to counter the weight of the Jenkin-Bennett argument, speaks of the "powerful influence of heredity, which actually increases the tendency to produce the favorable variations with each succeeding generation. . . ."[23] The metaphysical implications of this remark are about as "unDarwinian" as some of Darwin's statements in this same period.

Neither Wallace nor Darwin had any experimental data which would enable them to distinguish between purely somatic, non-heritable variation and change of the genuine mutative variety. Darwin did have some notion of the complexities of inheritance, and it is not quite accurate to say that his notions of heredity were as simple as mixing water and ink. His knowledge, he well knew, was clouded and obscure:

"The germ . . . becomes a . . . marvelous object, for besides the visible changes to which it is subjected, we must believe that it is crowded with invisible characters, proper to both sexes, to both the right and left side of the body, and to a long line of male and female ancestors separated by hundreds or even thousands of generations from the present time; and these characters, like those written on paper with invisible ink, all lie ready to be evolved under certain known or unknown conditions."[24]

[21] Charles Darwin, *Variations of Animals and Plants under Domestication*, New York: Orange Judd & Co., 1868, Vol. 2, p. 300.
[22] Ibid., pp. 306–7.
[23] A. R. Wallace, "Natural Selection—Mr. Wallace's Reply to Mr. Bennett," *Nature*, 1870, Vol. 3, p. 49.
[24] VAP, Vol. 2, p. 80.

Arguments for a lessened antiquity for the globe began to mount as nineteenth-century physicists applied their calculations to the age of the earth. It is interesting to see that Darwin, who had once been quite casual as to time, shows an increasing interest in stories which suggest visible change in the present. He quotes, in the *Descent of Man,* the story of an American hunter who asserted that in a certain region male deer with single unbranched antlers were becoming more numerous than the normal variety. In reality the bucks were all yearlings with their first antlers, and the observer had been self-deceived.[25]

The story is less important than the glimpse it affords into Darwin's mind. Although he had written much about the minute, age-long increments involved in evolutionary change, it is clearly apparent that some of these apocryphal anecdotes possessed a strong appeal for Darwin. There was an understandable desire to show the process of evolution in operation, even as one tried to explain why it could not actually be seen. It is not surprising that Darwin occasionally succumbed to this temptation and was, in spite of a judicious temperament, a little too easily tempted by "spiked buck" stories. They fitted in well with his notions of the way in which domestic animals were altered. We come now, however, to a peculiar fact. It would appear that careful domestic breeding, whatever it may do to improve the quality of race horses and cabbages, is not actually in itself the road to the endless biological deviation which is evolution. There is great irony in this situation, for more than almost any other single factor, domestic breeding had been used as an argument for the reality of evolution. Its significance, however, is somewhat deceptive and capable of misinterpretation.

[25] J. T. Cunningham, "Organic Variations and Their Interpretation," *Nature,* 1898, Vol. 58, p. 594.

V Mendel's Contribution

In 1900 Correns, Tschermak, and De Vries, all working independently along the lines which Weismann and others had brought under examination, rediscovered the lost principles and lost paper of Mendel. The mere fact that three workers, after the long lapse of years, turned the little document up at the same time suggests that biological science was just reaching the point where Mendel's work could be appreciated. We have seen that Weismann had dealt with the germ plasm from "inside," that he did not accept pangenesis. Mendel, though cytological methods were unknown to him, had, years earlier, used essentially the same approach. By carefully controlled experiment he sought to trace particular characters of the adult through successive generations, to find out whether such characters remained the same, mixed, or disappeared. As he himself commented in the introduction to his paper, "Among all the numerous experiments made [prior to his time] not one has been carried out to such an extent and in such a way as to make it possible to determine the number of different forms under which the offspring of hybrids appear, or to arrange these forms with certainty according to their separate generations, or definitely to ascertain their statistical relations."[26] Bateson observed that these primary conceptions of Mendel were absolutely new in his day. There is a surgical precision about Mendel's procedures which is in marked contrast to the bunglesome anecdotal literature which fills so much even of Darwin's treatment of the subject. By selecting from a variety of pea plants a series of easily observable and identifiable characters, Mendel began his experiments with attention focused upon what happened to these characters in the course of their passage through several generations. The details of the experiments need

[26] Mendel's paper is reproduced in W. Bateson's *Mendel's Principles of Heredity*, Cambridge University Press, 1913.

not concern us here, but the results, from the standpoint of evolution, were spectacular.

Mendel had established for a series of plant characters the fact that they passed through the germ cell as *units*. Such units did not mix with other units, though it was found that certain characters might be suppressed in a heterozygous individual and re-emerge only in a homozygous one. All of these facts depended on gametic segregation. They had nothing to do with pangenesis, nothing to do with the kind of selection Darwin and Wallace had been largely concerned with. Jenkin's "swamping out" of a new mutant character could not take place so long as the individual had offspring. The units were particulate and unalterable except by actual mutation. A character could be carried and could be spread even if recessive. If it had survival value, its diffusion could be rapid.

Mendel challenged directly the Darwinian idea that cultivated plants had, in some manner, been made more "plastic" and variable. "Nothing," he says, "justifies the assumption that the tendency to the formation of varieties is so extraordinarily increased that the species speedily lose all stability." Instead of this assumption, Mendel draws upon his new discoveries to suggest that most cultivated plants are actually hybrids, mixing back and forth and showing the unit character ratios which such origins would suggest. The close proximity of domesticated forms promotes the opportunities for hybridism. Thus the fluctuating variability which Darwin sometimes attributed to the indirect factors of climate, soil, and other influences could not all be regarded as due to the emergence of new evolutionary characters. Much of the supposed new was old, but variable in its phenotypic expression. Mendel had shown that the vast array of living characteristics was controlled by mathematical laws of assortment, and biological units (genes) were transmitted independently. "The course of development," he remarked, "consists simply in this, that in each successive

generation the two primal characters issue distinct and
unaltered out of the hybridized form, there being nothing
whatever to show that either of them has inherited or
taken over anything from the other."[27] Heredity and variation in the old Darwinian sense could, therefore, not be
synonymous. The unit factors had a constancy which the
Darwinians had failed to guess.[28]

VI Johannsen and Variation

We have seen that the Darwinian evolutionary mechanism was one involving the constant selection of small
variations which were assumed to be numerous and inheritable. For a long time they were pretty much taken
as given, and little or no attempt was made to determine
what lay back of them, or whether all variation actually
arose from the same cause. William Bateson, one of the
first active Mendelian researchers, put the matter succinctly when he said: "The indiscriminate confounding of
all divergences from type into one heterogeneous heap
under the name 'variation' effectually concealed those features of order which the phenomena severally present,
creating an enduring obstacle to the progress of evolutionary science."[29] It was Mendel's contribution to have revealed that not all variation was new in the sense of just
emerging. Furthermore, the revelation that discrete unblending hereditary units existed which might be studied
cytologically as well as through breeding experiments
swung interest in new directions. Hugo De Vries, whom
we shall discuss in the following chapter, seized public
attention by his advocacy of rapid species alteration
through sizable changes, speciation really, by sudden
saltations or jumps. This doctrine in its extreme form was
fated to be modified, but it cannot be denied that his em-

[27] Cited by Hugo Iltis, *Life of Mendel*, New York, 1932, pp. 147–
48.
[28] Ibid., pp. 178–79.
[29] "Heredity and Evolution," *Popular Science Monthly*, 1904,
Vol. 65, p. 524.

phasis upon the distinction between minor "fluctuating variations" and "discontinuous" variability, to which he applied the term "mutation," greatly stimulated research. Among the results of that research was the discovery of the Danish scientist W. L. Johannsen that the more or less constant somatic variations upon which Darwin and Wallace had placed their emphasis in species change cannot be selectively pushed beyond a certain point, that such variability does not contain the secret of "indefinite departure."

The Belgian anthropologist Lambert Quételet (1796–1874) observed in 1871 that for almost any biological character, height for example, one could erect a frequency distribution curve, provided a statistically adequate sample was available. There would be a scattering of individuals on either side of the norm and the extreme variants would lie at either end of the frequency curve. There is, in other words, an oscillation in a given population group around a mean value for any biological characteristic that we may choose to examine. It was this type of fluctuating variation which the Darwinian school had assumed might be "selected," either artificially or naturally, by the simple expedient of eliminating organisms at the lower end of the curve and selecting the individuals at the upper end of the curve for breeding purposes until the norm was moved forward. The breeder, it is true, can do certain things in this regard, but his effects are limited in a way the Darwinians were not in a position to foresee.

By selecting pure lines of beans, Johannsen anticipated that by raising beans from large bean seeds and from small and intermediate types he would obtain a series of different norms of size from his several plants. In this he failed. Whatever the size of the bean used, the progeny continued to fluctuate about a norm. Selection had had no effect in modifying the character of the norm. These variations in bean size were purely somatic, that is, they had no connection with genetic factors, but instead apparently represented accidentally favorable or unfavorable growth conditions.

There is another factor which is concerned in the successful artificial breeding of both animals and plants. Johannsen did find that in spite of the somatic norm indicated by the frequency distribution of his pure lines of beans, there were also distinct means in separate lines of beans. This represented a true hereditary component. If we breed for large beans, say, or the fastest race horses, we are selecting out a stock which contains hereditary unit factors favorable to our intent. By constant selection we perfect a relatively pure line for the given effect we wish to produce. Through judicious mating we may even introduce new elements into the complex. Basically, however, our efforts are limited to what exists genetically in the stock. By careful manipulation we may draw certain characters to the surface or combine them with others.[30] We can, however, produce only what is potentially contained within a given line. Beyond this the breeder can do nothing but wait upon those incalculable events known as mutations, which appear spontaneously. For example, Johannsen at one point in his experiments observed that the range shifted in an unexplainable manner in one of his true lines. It was a true mutative event —a new factor had been introduced.

The result of Johannsen's studies of 1903 and later was to demonstrate conclusively (1) that organisms with the same *genotype* (i.e., genetic composition) could differ *phenotypically*, that is, in their physical appearance; (2) that the selection of phenotypic characters without a genetic base would not yield hereditary change; (3) that selection of hereditary characters could induce some degree of physical alteration but the effect would attenuate

[30] Raymond Pearl, "The Selection Problem," *American Naturalist*, 1917, Vol. 51, pp. 65–91.

and halt unless there were added mutations which are sometimes forthcoming and sometimes not.

For a time there was an understandable feeling that Darwinism was moribund. This was due partly to the discovery that certain of the variations upon which Darwin had depended were non-heritable, partly to the feeling that new changes emerged suddenly and were not the result of a slow accretion of characters. By degrees, however, the latter notion gave way. It began to be realized that there were small mutations as well as large, which would produce an effect not greatly different from the kind of continuous evolution Darwin had visualized. Thus the word "mutation" began to take on its modern meaning.[81] The word "macro-mutation" fits better today the kind of evolutionary leaps which, under De Vries's influence, were heavily popularized in the first few years of the twentieth century. In this period there was, for a brief time, a line drawn between the significance of large and small variations, but it was a line which could not be maintained.

As the century progressed, biological thought swung around to the opinion that however wrong Darwin may have been in certain details, he had been justified in his view that small changes are less apt to be detrimental to the organism and are the more likely mode of evolutionary change.[82] Nevertheless, in contemplating the Darwinian rejuvenation, it is well to remember a forgotten observation of Jacques Loeb, one of the finest experimental biologists of the early decades of this century. He commented that one of the greatest peculiarities of the Darwinian period was the seeming scientific indifference to the actual visible demonstration of specific change. The draft of

[81] T. H. Morgan, "For Darwin," *Popular Science Monthly*, 1909, Vol. 74, p. 375.

[82] H. J. Muller, "On the Relation Between Chromosome Changes and Gene Mutations" in *Mutation*. Report of Symposium held June 15–17, 1955, Brookhaven National Laboratory, Upton, N. Y., pp. 134, 142.

limitless time at the Darwinists' command led them to assume that the process was too slow to be observed at all. That this troubled Darwin, particularly after the time scale began to be shortened, we can see from stories such as the account of the spiked buck. The literature, however, remained largely polemical. It was therefore an enormous leap forward when Hugo De Vries proposed his "mutation" theory and demonstrated hereditary changes of form. The rediscovery of Mendel at this time with his evidence for the actual existence of specific hereditary determiners marked, as Loeb says, "the beginning of a real theory of heredity and evolution." Even though some of De Vries's thought was later to be repudiated, and though Loeb was writing in the period of uncritical enthusiasm for De Vries's discoveries, we may, I think, with little reservation, endorse this final remark: "If it is at all possible to produce new species artificially I think that the discoveries of Mendel and De Vries must be the starting point."[33]

In the next fifty years Mendel's principles were expanded to cover many organisms, both plant and animal. Mathematical tools elaborated by such men as Fisher, Sewall Wright, and others were introduced to handle the theoretical genetics of entire populations. It was discovered that certain types of mutations occur over and over again in particular stocks, and thus by inference it was possible to assume that a certain reservoir of variability was always at hand in particular species—a reservoir possibly contributing to organic change in times of shifting conditions. Certain kinds of genetic mutation were found more likely to occur than others.[34]

Cytology continued to press farther and farther into the

[33] "The Recent Development of Biology," *Science*, 1904, n.s. Vol. 20, p. 781.
[34] Thomas Hunt Morgan, "The Bearing of Mendelism on the Origin of Species," *Scientific Monthly*, 1923, Vol. 16, p. 247. See also W. E. Castle, "Mendel's Laws of Heredity," *Science*, 1903, n.s. Vol. 18, p. 404.

mysterious mechanics of the nucleus and the cytoplasm. Finally, today, mutations are being artificially induced by various types of radiation and chemical agents. All this, however, is a book-long story in itself. There is still much that is unknown: the cellular location and nature of the great mechanisms that control the structure of phyla and classes escape us still; we know far more about fruit flies than men. It is strange, now, to walk through the laboratories and encounter the warning signs before radiation experiments, and to think of Mendel among the droning bees and flowers in the monastery at Brünn. "My time will come," he had said to his friend Niessl. "My time will come." Perhaps, as others had heard the sound of change and the flow of waters in the night, Mendel had learned from those tiny intricate units that shape a flower's heart something of the elemental patience that holds a living organism to its course while mountains wear away. "My time will come," he said. It was the indefinable echo of another century in the air.

Chapter IX

Darwin and the Physicists

We have almost unlimited time.
                    Darwin, 1858

If the mathematicians are right, the biologists cannot have what they demand.
                    Lord Salisbury, 1894

I Kelvin and Residual Heat

We have seen, in our earlier discussion of Sir Charles Lyell and the uniformitarian hypothesis in geology, what a vast reversal in human conceptions of the age of the earth went on in the Christian world in the earlier part of the nineteenth century. We also observed in the course of that survey what visions of limitless time, "millions of ages," as Erasmus Darwin somewhere remarks, were a necessary preliminary premise before a satisfactory theory of evolution could be entertained. The slow organic change postulated by both Lamarck and Darwin demanded time far beyond anything conceived in the Mosaic account of Creation. The existence of time of such magnitude, beginning with the labors of Hutton, Playfair, and others, was pretty well demonstrated to the satisfaction of all objectively minded scholars by the mid-century. It formed, in fact, part of the necessary groundwork of the *Origin of Species.*

Strangely enough, however, within six years after the publication of that work an attack on the conception of unlimited geological time had been launched with such vigor that, by the end of the century, it was still one of two leading arguments entertained by many naturalists as casting doubt upon the principle of natural selection. It had shaken the confidence of Darwin himself, forced Huxley into a defense characterized more by sophistry than scientific objectivity, and placed geology in general in the position of an errant schoolboy before his masters. The attack had been launched by Lord Kelvin, contended by many historians of science to be the outstanding physicist of the nineteenth century. Today there is a tendency in some quarters to regard the physical sciences as superior in reliability to those in which precise mathematical adeptness has not been achieved. Without wishing to challenge this point of view, it may still be worth a chastening thought that, in this long controversy extending well over half a century, the physicists made extended use of mathematical techniques and still were hopelessly and, it must be added, arrogantly wrong.

By contrast, the geologists who appeared to their physicist colleagues as bumbling amateurs expressing themselves only in vague hunches, and who could produce few arguments that the great Kelvin would deign to notice or to answer, happen to have been remarkably right. But in those days of the seventies things were going badly for Darwin and his followers. If fortuitous variations were the source of the great diversity of planetary life, then time was of the essence of the matter. A contraction in the time scale, therefore, must inevitably force biologists to a rejection of fortuitous variation in favor of some type of more rapid orthogenetic and therefore possibly teleologically directed change.

Whether Lord Kelvin and his Scotch associate, Peter

Tait, saw this inevitable consequence of their thought one cannot but wonder, since they were devoutly religious men. At any rate, they pressed their advantage hard. In the words of Sir Archibald Geikie, "the physicists have been insatiable and inexorable. As remorseless as Lear's daughters, they have cut down their grant of years by successive slices, until some of them have brought the number to something less than ten millions."[1] Today when the antiquity of life on the planet is beginning to be conservatively estimated at close to three billion years it can readily be seen that calculations as low as ten to thirty million years for the elapsed time since life on earth would have been possible placed an enormous strain on the Darwinian theory. It became, in other words, increasingly difficult to see how an evolutionary theory operating primarily on the basis of fortuitous mutations occurring at lengthy intervals, and only then being selected by the winnowing process of natural selection, could possibly account for the diversity of existing organic life in the short interval of a few million years.

It can be observed from Darwin's letters that this new development in physics gravely troubled him. He refers to Lord Kelvin as an "odious spectre,"[2] and in a letter to an unknown correspondent in the collections of the American Philosophical Society he writes: "Notwithstanding your excellent remarks on the work which can be effected within a million years, I am greatly troubled at the short duration of the world according to Sir W. Thomson [Lord Kelvin] for I require for my theoretical views a very long period before the Cambrian formation."[3]

Let us now investigate, from the historical standpoint, how this peculiar situation had come about in the short time since Darwin had published *The Origin of Species*.

[1] "Twenty-five Years of Geological Progress in Britain," *Nature*, 1895, Vol. 51, p. 369.

[2] James Marchant, *Alfred Russel Wallace: Letters and Reminiscences*, New York, 1916, p. 220.

[3] Dated January 31, 1869. The correspondent was apparently J. Croll. See MLD, Vol. 2, pp. 163–64.

By the last decade of the nineteenth century Lord Salisbury, in his Presidential Address before the British Association for the Advancement of Science, was able to bring forward as the two strongest objections to the Darwinian hypothesis the insufficiency of time for evolution by such a method and, second, the impossibility of demonstrating natural selection in detail.[4] Though not at first glance obvious, the two points are actually interlinked in some degree as we will later be able to observe.

Though the nature of our major subject will not permit a lengthy analysis of the developments leading to Lord Kelvin's position, we may note in passing that they were the inevitable outcome of the cosmic evolutionism of the late eighteenth century. Temperatures taken in deep mines indicated an increase of heat as one went downward, and these observations were occasionally dwelt upon in scientific papers during the early nineteenth century. What began to be regarded as the secular cooling of the earth, its dissipation of heat from its original molten condition into the freezing space around it, began to occupy attention. The geologist George Greenough, for example, in his Anniversary Address before the Geological Society of London in 1834, remarked that "it appears certain that the surface of our planet has become cooler and cooler, from the period when organic life commenced to the Tertiary epoch."

The growing recognition in geological studies of the second law of thermodynamics would thus inevitably bring into question the implied eternities of the early uniformitarians. When to this problem of the residual heat of the earth was added the question of the age of the sun's heat and its influence upon the life of the earth, it was inevitable that there should be a demand for geological reform. "British popular geology," insisted Lord Kelvin, "is in direct opposition to the principles of Natural

[4] Report of the British Association for the Advancement of Science, Oxford, 1894, pp. 3-15.

Philosophy." "I take the sun much to heart," groaned
Darwin to Lyell in 1868.

It is interesting to note that although time in quantity
had been implied by many solar observations there had
been, prior to Kelvin, comparatively few attempts to relate astronomical to geological problems. The uniformitarian geologists, in fact, had in their earlier phase "discerned
neither a beginning nor an end." Darwin, in the first edition of the *Origin*, had ventured that "in all probability a
far longer period than 300,000,000 years had elapsed
since the latter part of the secondary period."[5]

Even today, with radioactive methods of checking time
in the rocks, this figure would be regarded as excessive.
The later editions of the *Origin* do not carry it. One may
suspect that, just as today the study of man in the Pleistocene has greatly intensified our efforts to define, sub-
divide, and date this epoch, so the emergence of the
evolutionary theory after 1859 as a leading aspect of
biological thought enormously enhanced the human effort
to date the past. The past had no longer the static or
cyclic quality of the classical Greco-Roman conception,
nor, by contrast, the six-thousand-year ephemeral duration accorded it by orthodox Christians. Change had entered the world; time was debatable and open to scientific examination.

Lord Kelvin had thrown down a direct challenge to the
geologists and, by indirection, to the evolutionists themselves. At the close of the century the two antagonistic
camps would still be in existence. A collected bibliogra-
phy of the subject through the period 1862 to 1902 would
be enormous. What concerns us here, however, is the
effect which Kelvin and his colleagues in physics had
upon both the geologists and biologists. It was impossible
to ignore Kelvin. Given the physics of the time there was
no way of escaping him. Many geologists capitulated and
revised their calculations of the earth's antiquity down-

[5] O, p. 245.

ward. Biologists, trapped in a more difficult impasse, tried to find their way out through various ancillary hypotheses.

Three papers written by Lord Kelvin and dating back to the early sixties may serve to indicate the major points which he was to emphasize, with elaboration of detail, until the close of the century. "On the Age of the Sun's Heat," written for *Macmillan's Magazine*,[6] expounds the view, also supported by Helmholtz and others, that the sun is an incandescent liquid mass which is dissipating its energy at a rapid pace. Lord Kelvin could see no way in which this loss of radiant energy could be compensated for by other mechanisms. Therefore, argued Kelvin, the sun's future life is limited, and, in its not too lengthy past, it must at one time have been sensibly hotter than at present.

"As for the future," said Kelvin in a similar paper which he delivered before the British Association in 1861, "we may say with . . . certainty that inhabitants of the earth cannot continue to enjoy the light and heat essential to their life for many million years longer, unless [he added with unconscious prophecy] new sources now unknown to us, are prepared in the great storehouse of Creation."[7] Atomic energy was not, of course, discovered until the twentieth century, but it was already warming the earth that Kelvin gazed upon so gloomily. Ten per cent less light and heat would destroy us, we know now, and ten per cent more heat would boil us alive. Throughout the whole great range of geological time, modern science now tells us, our sun can have changed only insensibly at best from its original state.[8] Otherwise there would have been no continuity of life upon earth.

[6] 1862, Vol. 5, pp. 388–93.

[7] W. Thomson (Lord Kelvin), "Physical Considerations Regarding the Possible Age of the Sun's Heat," *The London, Edinburgh and Dublin Philosophical Magazine and Journal of Science,* 1862, Series 4, Vol. 23, p. 160.

[8] Cecilia Payne-Gaposchkin, *Stars in the Making,* Harvard University Press, 1952, pp. 106–7.

In 1865 Kelvin turned directly to the geologists with a paper whose very title was a forthright challenge: "The Doctrine of Uniformity in Geology Briefly Refuted,"[9] which he read before the Royal Society of Edinburgh. It is an attempt to demonstrate mathematically, in terms of heat loss, that the earth's crust cannot have maintained its stability over such an enormous time range as that demanded by the theories of the uniformitarian geologists and the evolutionary biologists who relied upon them.

Later, in 1869, Thomas Huxley attempted a counter-blow which did not prove particularly convincing. Essentially, he attempted to evade the issue by the nonchalant pose that "Biology takes her time from Geology. The only reason we have for believing in the slow rate of the change in living forms is the fact that they persist through a series of deposits which geology informs us have taken a long while to make. *If the geological clock is wrong all the naturalist will have to do is to modify his notions of the rapidity of change accordingly.*"[10] (Italics mine. L.E.)

On an earlier page I have spoken of this as sophistry. At best it was a mere delaying action. For if evolutionary biology relied for change upon infinitesimal variations acted upon by natural selection through long time periods, it was difficult to see how the process could be "speeded up" to accord with the new facts of geology unless Huxley had a new theory to propose in place of natural selection. Huxley proposed nothing new. "It is not obvious," he went on, "that we shall have to alter or reform our ways. . . ."[11] With his old proud gladiatorial skill he referred to himself as a counsel who contrives to gain his cause "by force of mother-wit. . . ."[12]

This was not, however, a struggle which debating skill

[9] Reprinted in *Popular Lectures and Addresses* by Sir William Thomson, London, 1894, Vol. 2, pp. 6–9.

[10] Anniversary Address, *Quarterly Journal of the Geological Society of London*, 1869, Vol. 25, p. xlviii.

[11] Ibid., p. xlviii.

[12] Ibid., p. xxxviii.

alone could win. Though we know now that Lord Kelvin was wrong, he was, paradoxically, right in terms of nineteenth-century physics. Grimly he ignored the elusive footwork of Huxley. "A correction of this kind," he observed to the Geological Society of Glasgow, "cannot be said to be unimportant in reference to biological speculation. The limitation of geological periods imposed by physical science cannot, of course, disprove the hypothesis of transmutation of species; *but it does seem sufficient to disprove the doctrine that transmutation has taken place through 'descent with modification by natural selection.'*"[13] (Italics mine. L.E.) Squirm as he might, Huxley could not totally evade that point. It is no wonder that Darwin, beset simultaneously by both the Jenkin and Kelvin nightmares, began to fall back toward the familiar landmarks of his youth, toward the "inherited effects of habit," toward that shadowy biological borderland haunted by Lamarck and the ghost of his grandfather. In this instance the swashbuckling of Huxley did not impress him. Painfully and doubtfully he wrote to Wallace in 1871, "I have not as yet been able to digest the fundamental notion of the shortened age of the sun and earth."[14]

Kelvin pressed his advantage relentlessly. "We find at every turn something to show . . . the utter futility of [Darwin's] philosophy,"[15] he said in 1873. By 1893 he was willing to go along with the American Clarence King's estimate of the age of the earth as around twenty-four million years. "I am not led to differ much,"[16] said Kelvin. Today these twenty-million-year estimates of the earth's antiquity would take us only into the upper reaches of the Age of Mammals. This will give us some idea of the contracted time span that had been forced upon a science

13 *Popular Lectures and Addresses*, London, 1894, Vol. 2, pp. 89-90.

14 James Marchant, *Alfred Russel Wallace: Letters and Reminiscences*, New York, 1916, pp. 205-6.

15 S. P. Thompson, *The Life of William Thomson*, London, 1910, Vol. 2, p. 637.

16 Ibid., p. 943.

used to reveling in time vistas of which Hutton had spoken long ago as having "no vestige of a beginning, no prospect of an end." The great rout was on at last. The science of geology had ceased to be what it was to the early uniformitarians, "the science of infinite time."

Most of the geologists, though occasionally hedging, grumbling, and not averse to claiming a few extra million years for themselves, fell in line reluctantly with the physicists. Sollas confessed that "so far as I can at present see, the lapse of time since the beginning of the Cambrian system is probably less than seventeen millions of years. . . ."[17] By 1900 he was aware that "eminent biologists" besides himself were willing to settle for twenty-six million years as satisfying the needs of evolutionists.[18] Charles Walcott conceded geologic time could be measured by tens of millions of years.[19] Falling in with Huxley's position he remarks evasively, "I have not referred to the rate of development of life, as that is virtually controlled by conditions of environment." Sir Archibald Geikie, although protesting "a flaw in a line of argument which tends to results so entirely at variance with the strong evidence for a higher antiquity," was willing, nevertheless, to settle for 100 million years. This figure, he modestly maintained, would content the geologists whose errors he admitted.[20]

II   The Biological Retreat

The biologists, confronted in this manner by the defection of the geologists, began to grope for feasible solutions. This groping is important to observe because it is part of

[17] W. J. Sollas, "The Age of the Earth," *Nature*, 1895, Vol. 51, p. 543.

[18] "Evolution Geology," *Report of the British Association for the Advancement of Science*, Bradford, England, 1900, p. 722.

[19] "Geologic Time; As Indicated by the Sedimentary Rocks of North America," *The American Geologist*, 1895, Vol. 12, p. 368.

[20] "Twenty-five Years of Geological Progress in Britain," *Nature*, 1895, Vol. 51, p. 369.

the confused intellectual climate out of which emerged a momentary anti-Darwinian trend and which, at the same time, contributed to the stimulation of researches leading toward the rediscovery of Gregor Mendel. Darwin died before the new trend culminated. He admitted in the sixth edition of the *Origin* that the objection to natural selection raised by Lord Kelvin was a very formidable one.

A close examination of the last edition of the *Origin* reveals that in attempting on scattered pages to meet the objections being launched against his theory the much-labored-upon volume had become contradictory. In Chapter XI, surviving from earlier editions, we read: "There is some reason to believe that organisms high in the scale, change more quickly than those that are low."[21] Darwin dwells on the "slow and scarcely sensible mutations of specific forms."[22] Then, as we turn to another section, we suddenly discover a converse statement apparently inserted as a device to evade Lord Kelvin's mathematics. We perceive with mild astonishment that "the world at a very early period was subjected to more rapid and violent changes in its physical conditions than those now occurring; *and such changes would have tended to induce changes at a corresponding rate in the organisms which then existed.*"[23] (Italics mine. L.E.) The last repairs to the *Origin* reveal, both in connection with Lord Kelvin and Jenkin, how very shaky Darwin's theoretical structure had become. His gracious ability to compromise had produced some striking inconsistencies. His book was already a classic, however, and these deviations for the most part

[21] Modern Library ed., p. 256.

[22] Ibid., p. 270.

[23] Ibid., p. 253. This statement may also be contrasted with one which Darwin made to Hooker in 1856: "This power of selection stands in the most direct relation to time, and in the state of nature can only be excessively slow." At this date he categorically denied that time and altered conditions were "convertible terms." LLD, Vol. 2, p. 84.

passed unnoticed even by his enemies. The number of improvisations which had had to be marshaled to the assistance of natural selection remind one at times of the difficulties which Lamarck tried to meet by additional hypotheses.

Wallace had suggested that periods when the earth's orbit was less eccentric would give an impression of greater stability so far as the living world was concerned. Changes in the earth's orbit, on the other hand, would, he contended, stimulate climatic change and thus speed the process of evolution. This, he thought, would account for a more rapid rate of organic change and enable us to fit the main events of evolution within a shorter time scale.[24]

Adam Sedgwick, a younger relative of Darwin's old geology professor, proposed a theory that selection tends to diminish the variability of species. Therefore, he reasoned, "variation must have been much greater in the past than now. . . . This view, if it can be established, is of the utmost importance to our theoretical conception of evolution, because it enables us to bring our requirements as to time within the limits granted by the physicists."[25] "That variation," Sedgwick goes on to say, "was much greater near the dawn of life than it is now, and heredity a correspondingly less important phenomenon, is a deduction from the selection theory."[26]

Sedgwick here seems to have developed another version of the Darwinian argument that evolution proceeded rapidly at the dawn of life. Others, like Lloyd Morgan, found solace in repeating Huxley's argument that time is

[24] A. R. Wallace, "On a Diagram of the Earth's Eccentricity and the Precession of the Equinoxes Illustrating their Relation to Geological Climate and the Rate of Organic Change," *Report of the British Association for the Advancement of Science*, 1870, p. 89.

[25] Adam Sedgwick, "Variation and Some Phenomena Connected with Reproduction and Sex," *Report of the British Association for the Advancement of Science*, Dover, 1899, pp. 773–74.

[26] Ibid., p. 774.

the business of the geologist and that the biologist can adjust accordingly. No Darwinist could be long happy with this argument, however, which, as Kelvin had warned, left the notion of fortuitous mutation and selection in a most dubious position.

Nor, for that matter, were the geologists entirely happy. They were willing to admit that a false analogy had, in the past, "been set up between the boundless infinity of space and the vast immensity of past time,"[27] but the voluminous records of past life and the time ratios founded upon sedimentation did not fit easily into the strait jacket of the physicists. The geologists, shrewdly observed G. K. Gilbert, were "making as earnest an effort for reconciliation as had been made a generation earlier to adjust the elements of the Hebrew cosmogony to the facts of geology."[28] We might add that just as the earlier attempt had proved hopeless so, in the end, would this similar effort. Geological time, as foreseen by the eloquent Huxley, sprang irresistibly out of the facts. It was, as he had said, like the djin from the jar which the fisherman had opened. It was "vaporous, shifting, and undefinable, but unmistakably gigantic." In the end, for all their striving, the physicists would be unable to coax the monster back into the bottle. To this day it is continuing to expand.

III   De Vries and Saltatory Evolution

We have previously had occasion to examine the way in which the blending idea of inheritance held in Darwin's time led the author of the *Origin* into difficulties with the mathematically inclined engineer Fleeming Jenkin. We have, furthermore, noted Lord Salisbury's stricture at the end of the century that, along with the problem of time,

[27] C. L. Morgan, "Geological Time," *Geological Magazine*, 1878, n.s. Vol. 5, p. 155.

[28] G. K. Gilbert, "Rhythms and Geologic Time," *Popular Science Monthly*, 1900, Vol. 57, p. 346.

which we have just surveyed, the second point which left the status of Darwinian evolution inconclusive was the inability to demonstrate natural selection in detail. All in all, then, we may observe that Jenkin, and Lord Kelvin, along with a host of followers had forced Darwin, before his death, into an awkward retreat which mars in some degree the final edition of the *Origin*. As C. D. Darlington has ironically expressed it: "He panicked and ran straight into the opposite camp. . . . Lamarck became a posthumous Darwinian."[29] Within two years of Darwin's death a letter to Wallace insists: "It is impossible to urge too often that the selection from a single varying individual or of a single varying organ will not suffice."[30] Even his old colleague Wallace was constrained to remark in a letter to Professor Meldola fifteen years after Darwin's death that his addiction to notions of the hereditary effects of climate, food, etc., upon the individual "led to much obscurity and fallacy in his arguments, here and there."[31]

It is unnecessary to pursue further the inconsistencies of an outstanding and basically courageous thinker. As we have seen in a previous chapter, Darwin was essentially a transitional figure standing between the eighteenth century and the modern world. He had never entirely escaped certain of the Lamarckian ideas of his youth, whether they came by way of Lyell, or independently from his grandfather, or, as is more likely, from both. As a consequence it is not surprising that in a time of stress he grew doubtful that natural selection contained the full answer to the sallies of his critics. He fell back, therefore, toward ideas he had never totally repudiated but which, in the first edition of the *Origin*, had been allowed to remain in the background, masked, in a sense, while the

[29] "Purpose and Particles in the Study of Heredity," *Science, Medicine and History*, edited by E. A. Underwood, Oxford University Press, 1953, Vol. 2, p. 474.

[30] James Marchant, *Alfred Russel Wallace: Letters and Reminiscences*, New York, 1916, p. 249.

[31] Ibid., p. 322.

major emphasis had been placed upon natural selection. The inheritance of habit, incidentally, is indirectly an excellent device for speeding up evolution in a world where time is short. Darwin made use of it in *The Descent of Man*.

It is not Darwin but the younger generation of evolutionists who must now concern us. By and large they had accepted the evolutionary point of view, but they were oppressed by the confused and incoherent situation which they had inherited from the dead master. The relative value of natural selection against the Lamarckian approach was being reweighed. The nature of heredity was under debate and the rate of organic change was, as we have already observed, a matter of great concern. Weismann had overthrown Herbert Spencer's support of the Lamarckian position. In spite of Darwin's past hesitations, change appeared to be, not the result of climatic stimulation upon the germ cells, but the product of some imponderable chance, or so it seemed, emanating from those same germ cells. This development, more or less divorcing mutations from environmental influence, made even more impossible the attempt to assume rapid mutative change accommodating its emergence entirely to physical and climatic episodes upon the planet. The latter factors might in some degree select, but could not stimulate, the appearance of new variations.

It is now clear that evolutionary science in the last decade of the nineteenth century was drastically in need of a new approach. The old catastrophic cosmogony, by its short time scale, had made anything but the progressionist doctrine impossible. Darwin, to his great good fortune, had appeared when this hypothesis was in the process of being overthrown by Lyell. Thus Darwin, whose theories demanded a vaster grant of time than any previous worker had envisaged, wrote his book in the easygoing days of ultra-uniformitarianism, when time appeared as infinite as space. Once, for example, when Lyell in 1860 had raised some question about the slow change in insular faunas, Darwin had responded complacently, "We should . . . always remember that no change will ever be effected till a variation in the habits, or structure, or of both, *chance* to occur in the right direction . . . and this may be in any particular case indefinitely long."[32]

It can easily be seen that the harsh strictures of the physicists, if they had been voiced a few years earlier, might well have reduced Darwin to silence or, at the very least, have caused him to reject natural selection as an evolutionary mechanism. Fortunately, from the historical standpoint, this did not occur, physics instead, as represented by the devout Kelvin, probably having been stimulated to an examination of earth-time, by some degree of animus toward Darwin's new heresy. The results, viewed even partially in this light, are fascinating. It can be seen, for example, that the damage done by Kelvin's doctrine to Darwin's ideas of change as involving the selection of minute and almost imperceptible variations led to a renewed search on the part of the biologists. They badly needed some mechanism of rapid organic transformation. This became particularly true as the demonstrated inviolability of the germ plasm precluded further reliance on use-inheritance or similar Lamarckian mechanisms.

Thus, though the physicists originally appeared as the *bête noire* of this chapter, they became, wrong though they were, the indirect stimulation which played a considerable part in the emergence of the new genetics and the rediscovery of Mendel at the turn of the century. Discontinuous, saltatory evolution became the only apparent alternative to uniformitarian evolution, nor was it long in appearing. The doctrine of macro-mutations offered a way out of the Weismann-Darwin dilemma. Lest I seem to be reading connections into unrelated events long after their occurrence, the following quotation from Hugo De

Vries, one of the three independent rediscoverers of Mendel's work in 1900, may prove of interest.

"I have now to point out one of the weightiest objections against the conception of the origin of species by means of slow and gradual changes. It is an objection which has been brought forward against Darwin from the very beginning, which has never relented, and which often has threatened to impair the whole theory of descent. It is the incompatability of the results concerning the age of life on this earth, as propounded by physicists and astronomers, with the demand made by the theory of descent.

"The deductions made by Lord Kelvin and others from the central heat of the earth, from the rate of the production of the calcareous deposits, from the increase of the amount of salt in the seas, and from various other sources, indicate an age for the inhabitable surface of the earth of some millions of years only. The most probable estimates lie between twenty and forty millions of years. The evolutionists of the gradual line, however, had supposed many thousands of millions of years to be the smallest amount that would account for the whole range of evolution, from the very first beginning until the appearance of mankind. This large discrepancy has always been a source of doubt and a weapon in the hands of the opponents of the evolutionary idea. . . . The theory of evolution had to be remolded."[33]

When De Vries made this statement on a lecture tour of America he was being hailed as a second Darwin—much to the elderly Wallace's amazement—the latter having refused to express much confidence in the newfangled Mendelian genetics whose characters he regarded as in the nature of "abnormalities or monstrosities." The reaction of Wallace to the Mendelian discoveries was not purely the product of old age. There is in it a trace of

[33] Hugo De Vries, "The Evidence of Evolution," *Science*, 1904, n.s. Vol. 20, p. 398.

subconscious fear—the fear, perfectly understandable in the light of the times, that Darwin and he had, after all, not been right and that they might be losing their hold on posterity. This had become particularly apparent with the rise of the "new Darwin" who had momentarily captured the public imagination.

In 1886, about the time that Weismann was engaged upon his theory of the inviolability of the germ plasm, De Vries in Holland had begun to study an American plant, *Oenothera lamarckiana*, the evening primrose, which had escaped into the wild state in Europe. To his happy astonishment it seemed that he had discovered a plant actually giving birth directly to a new species—and this in considerable profusion. Furthermore, the plant appeared to be giving off new types every year. If this phenomenon could be verified and established, a macro-mutative method of establishing new species might be demonstrable. The evolutionary rate of change could be speeded up to accord with the time scale of the physicists and Darwin's minute variations could safely be disregarded. Natural selection would then cease to be as important as it was in the first edition of the *Origin*.

The idea of dramatic and considerable alterations at one step did not, of course, originate with De Vries. Darwin had been cognizant of the possibility so far as domesticated plants, or animals like the Ancon sheep, were concerned, but because of the problem presented by the conception of blending inheritance, he did not see how such breeds could be maintained except through the attention of the breeder. Theophilus Parsons in America, a few months after the first publication of the *Origin*, had dwelt on the possibility of the "hopeful monster" as a step in the creation of new species. Parsons even went so far (a courageous act in 1860) as to intimate that the earliest human beings were "children of Simiae nearest in structure to men, and were made, by some influence of variation, to differ from their progenitors. . . ."[84] This communication of Parsons's thus anticipates Kölliker's expression of similar views upon saltatory evolution in 1864.[85]

It was not until 1901, however, that De Vries, by now acquainted with Mendel's work, began to publish upon his discovery. He came to believe that states of mutability might alternate with periods of much greater stability in organisms which do not necessarily show such constant selection and change as had been propounded by Darwinians such as Wallace. His conclusions and the re-emergence of Mendel into the limelight brought De Vries world-wide fame. There are psychological aspects to this phenomenon. Thomas Case commented in *Science* that the new theory should appeal particularly to theologians. "If," he says, "we conceive that man originated abruptly by some unaccountable molecular change . . . there can be no doubt of the time when man became immortal, whereas there would be necessarily much, much uncertainty as to the time when this occurred among the successive infinitesimal increments of brain development necessitated by the Darwinian theory."[86]

For a short time it appeared that some of the more repugnant aspects of Darwinian thought—its constant emphasis upon struggle, its mechanistic, utilitarian philosophy which, to many, seemed as dingy as a Victorian factory—might vanish away in the light of the new Men-

[84] "A Communication upon Evolution," *Proceedings of the Am. Academy of Arts and Sciences*, 1860, Vol. 4, p. 416. Darwin was aware of Parsons's views and commented in the same year to Asa Gray that he had reflected on the possibility of "favorable monstrosities" playing a part in evolution. "It would be a great aid," he admitted, "but I did not allude to the subject, for, after much labor, I could find nothing which satisfied me of the probability of such occurrences." LLD, Vol. 2, p. 333.

[85] For a discussion of Von Kölliker and other early advocates of saltatory evolution see Philip Fothergill's *Historical Aspects of Organic Evolution*, Hollis and Carter, London, 1952, p. 172 ff.

[86] "The Mutation Theory," *Science*, 1905, n.s. Vol. 22, p. 309.

delian discoveries and particularly under the influence of the type of mutative change dwelt upon by De Vries. His work contained a vision in which even human evolution might appear to press forward more gracefully and rapidly than in the tooth-and-claw philosophies which had haunted Darwinian thinking. Then suddenly the dream, the popular enthusiasm, ended.

De Vries, who had held for a period a position of such unrivaled popularity that he had been brought to America to give personal addresses upon his theories, is now sometimes difficult to find in the indices of introductory works on genetics. It is no fault of De Vries, who was an honest worker. Instead, it was the simple irony of fate. The man who had sought to see creation at work in a simple flower, who had held in his own hands "a species which has been taken in the very act of producing new forms," the man who had been able to say "the origin of species is no longer to be considered beyond our experience," had been working with a plant hybrid whose genetic mechanism, because of unequal chromosome numbers, had a tendency to break down. In the words of two modern geneticists, "The mutants of *Oenothera* are therefore nothing more than symptoms of its peculiar hybridity and as such are of little significance in evolution."[37] The acclaim has long vanished. Even by 1907 Vernon Kellogg had seen fit to comment: "The lack of new observational data . . . of the origin of new species through mutations in nature, is significant. It is my belief that a reaction against the curiously swift and widespread partial to complete acceptance of the mutation theory . . . will soon occur." By "mutation theory," of course, Kellogg was referring to what today we would call a large or macromutation.

It would be ill to forget, however, that De Vries, like many another, had borne the heat of the scientific day.

[37] C. D. Darlington and K. Mather, *The Elements of Genetics*, London, 1949, p. 263.

He had pursued what seemed a reality and had found a phantom, but in the process had contributed like Mendel before him to the accumulating wisdom that might be used by other men after his name and his memory had vanished from the books. There can be no doubt that in dramatizing the large, the macro-mutation, rather than the small "fluctuating" variations of the Darwinists, De Vries so emphasized discontinuity in evolution as to promote a clarification of the problem by renewed research. Furthermore, his swift-changing kaleidoscopic evolution shifted attention from natural selection in the world of the adult organism to the processes at work in the egg or sperm cell. Cytology was coming into its own and the disproportionate emphasis upon natural selection was fading. There are still those who remember that in the thinly tenanted no man's land described by Bateson as the field of genetics in the first five years of this century, Hugo De Vries by this emphasis alone did notable work. As Bateson has remarked, it is in the seed bed, the poultry yard, and amid growing nature that variation may be found and its properties tested.[38] De Vries was to be found in these places. He was one of the very few theoretical evolutionists, after the old pigeon fancier died at Down, who did not confine himself to his study.

IV   Time and Radioactivity

We have now seen something of the subtle if mistaken pressures exerted indirectly upon biology from the field of physics. They had contributed to Darwin's discomfort almost from the time the *Origin* was published, and had played their part in his groping retreat toward Lamarck. Still, a few geologists remained suspicious. F. R. Moulton was among them. He was dubious that the contraction theory of the sun's heat was sufficient to give the neces-

[38] William Bateson, "Heredity and Evolution," *Popular Science Monthly*, 1904, Vol. 65, p. 525.

sary duration to energies radiated by that body. Finally he pointed out in 1899 that it was conceivable that some type of unknown atomic energy might contain the secret.[39] His words were indeed prophetic and were to be totally fulfilled within the next decade. In 1903 Paul Curie and Laborde demonstrated that radium steadily maintains its temperature above its surroundings. Both geology and astronomy were not slow to assess the significance of the newly discovered atomic energies. Kelvin's conception of the sun as a sort of figurative coal pile rapidly dwindling toward extinction was swept away; his harsh calculations became meaningless. Even here on earth the uranium content of the rocks was such that the doctrine of the loss of residual heat ceased to have significance. The way lay open for an enormous extension of the antiquity of the earth—an antiquity that would have delighted and astounded Darwin. The long tyranny of the physicists was over; the oncoming cold had been a phantom. Instead of a freezing and contracting earth whose fires were dying, men now saw a planet which, in terms of human years, was well-nigh forever young, prodigal of its heat in mountain upthrusts, green with some endless and undying spring whose source lay hidden at the atom's heart. Instrument of terror though the atom in our time has come to be, it may someday be remembered that the news of radioactivity came first among us as a message that the abysmal mechanics of nineteenth-century science had perished and had left us lifting our faces with renewed faith and understanding to the sun.

[39] A. C. Gifford, "The Origin of the Solar System," *Scientia*, 1932, Vol. 52, p. 154.

Chapter X

The Reception of
the First Missing Links

Must we suppose that the picture of the
original man has disappeared just as much as
that of the originals of domestic animals?
Christian Ludwig, 1796

I The Evolutionists Turn to Man

For many years philosophers had debated the nature of
man's relationship to the natural world about him. In the
year 1859 science discovered man was an animal—though
a most unusual one. Science arrived at this conclusion by
indirect deduction. The year 1859 is generally regarded
as the climactic point in the long, involved, and somewhat
sporadic efforts toward the development of a satisfactory
explanation of organic change. In that year Charles Darwin published the *Origin of Species* in which he dared
only one solitary and wary sentence upon the evolution
of man. "Light," he cryptically intimated in the conclusion of his epoch-making book, "will be thrown on the origin of man and his history." It was not until later editions
that he ventured to add the adjective "much" to his use
of the word "light." Nothing better illustrates the oppres-
sive theological atmosphere of the time than Darwin's re-

sponse to an inquiry from Wallace prior to publication of the *Origin* as to whether he intended to discuss man. Darwin rejoined as follows: "I think I shall avoid the whole subject, as so surrounded with prejudices, though I fully admit that it is the highest and most interesting problem for the naturalist."[1] In a similar vein he confessed to Jenyns, "With respect to man, I am very far from wishing to obtrude my belief; but I thought it dishonest to quite conceal my opinion."[2]

In the clamor that arose after his book appeared, Darwin, in spite of this last remark, was not to avoid insinuations of deceit in failing to elaborate upon the place of man in his system. It was, perhaps, partly in indirect answer to such slurs that he undertook the publication of the *Descent of Man* in 1871 when his position and that of his theory had ceased to appear so novel and revolting to the public mind. In the judgment of the present writer there can be no doubt, considering the temper of the times, that Darwin's caution was well justified, and probably had the salutary effect of broaching what was then an unpleasant topic by successive doses which were found assimilable rather than, as Lyell was accustomed to saying, "going the whole orang" all at once.

It is a matter of considerable historical interest that Darwin postulated his theory and extended it to man without having available as evidence a single subhuman fossil by which, on the basis of his theoretical views, he could have satisfactorily demonstrated the likelihood of man's relationship to the world of the subhuman primates. Yet, curiously enough, at least two early human fossils had been discovered and one, the Neanderthal skull, had been published upon. The historian of ideas should be attentive to the discussions of the closing half of the nineteenth century in order to observe, once the theory of evolution began its diffusion, the effect that the first paleontological

[1] LLD, Vol. 2, p. 109.
[2] Ibid., p. 263.

discoveries had, not necessarily upon the lay mind, which could be expected to discount them, but upon the minds of scholars and savants who were at that time either weighing or had committed themselves to a belief in human as well as animal evolution.

That our generation has accepted this commitment we know; evolution forms the guiding motif in all our biological studies. But no episode in science affords a better glimpse into the workings of even the cultivated mind than an exploration of that combination of motives which revolves about the scientific investigation of the first human fossils. The subject was one touching deeply upon human emotions, and it tended to become proportionately distorted. The reigning political prejudices, racial and religious shibboleths, are all caught up in an intellectual ferment which invaded staid congresses and cropped out in sober scientific pronouncements.

My remarks on this subject are offered, not in a critical spirit, nor to uphold our scientific fathers to ridicule, but to show with what doubt and withdrawal and hesitation, along with an almost morbid fascination, man discovered he was an animal. It is my genuine belief that no greater act of the human intellect, no greater gesture of humility on the part of man has been or will be made in the long history of science. The marvel lies not in the fact that the bones from the caves and river gravels were recognized in trepidation and doubt as beings from the half-world of the past; the miracle, considering the nature of the human ego, occurs in the circumstance that we were able to recognize them at all, or to see in these remote half-fearsome creatures our long-forgotten fathers who had cherished our seed through the ages of ice and loneliness before a single lighted city flickered out of the darkness of the planet's nighttime face.

That recognition did not come in a day, even with a Darwin to light the path. When it did come those wavering apparitional faces were masked by the projected fantasies arising in the minds of scientists themselves. They were ill seen, ill understood, and, above all, their numbers were pitifully few. The account which follows deals with the only two fossil men known from the nineteenth century—*Homo neanderthalensis*, ironically and indirectly named for a forgotten poet, and *Pithecanthropus*, who is really, in nineteenth-century terms, closest to a true missing link and who came closest to convincing the doubters. His earlier colleague from the valley of the Neander had no such success. The two forms together, however, cover almost a fifty-year span in the history of the search for human origins. In the words of Max Müller, "The skull as the shell of the brain has, by many students, been supposed to betray something of the spiritual essence of man. . . ."[3] Upon those fossil skulls, then just beginning to be wrenched from caverns and river drifts, the eyes of the world were now to be centered in horrified fascination. Man has probably never waited before in such a prolonged suspense of mingled hope and fear; his very faith in his uniqueness within the animal world was being shaken at last.

There is, however, a certain irony in the first results, for the bones were to be read ambiguously. In addition, ideas from the pre-Darwinian world of the eighteenth century were destined to shape much of the thinking of the nineteenth. Roaming Britishers at the world's far-flung margins were to see half-men slouch through the forests. Long-armed, bandy-legged, these nightmare creatures were subjective mental projections straight from the bookshelves of *philosophes* and Darwinists. Even now the last of them haunt the snow fields of the Himalayas or startle Malayan planters. The key to this labyrinth of ideas lies in picking up the separate thought streams which flow out of the eighteenth century and which mingle with true Darwinism in the nineteenth. Before examining the first genuine human fossils, therefore, it may be

[3] F. Max Müller, *Nature*, 1891, Vol. 44, p. 430.

well to ascertain with what preconceptions our Victorian predecessors entered upon their archaeological search and what it was, precisely, that they expected to see.

II Ape and Hottentot

Superficially it would appear that the growing number of archaeological discoveries bearing upon human antiquity which were made during the time Darwin was engaged upon his book aroused an interest which, after the publication of the *Origin*, simply coalesced about the theory of evolution. This is true, but there is a deeper substratum of ideas unconsciously carried over from the reigning philosophical doctrines of the eighteenth century, namely, the concept of the missing link as it flourished in that older pre-Darwinian atmosphere of the *Scala Naturae*. "Next to the word 'Nature,'" remarks Professor Lovejoy, "the Great Chain of Being was the sacred phrase of the eighteenth century playing a part somewhat analogous to that of the blessed word 'evolution' in the late nineteenth."

Let us refresh our memory by a quotation from Addison: "The whole chasm in Nature, from a Plant to a Man, is filled up with diverse Kinds of Creatures, rising one over another by such a gentle and easy Ascent, that the little Transitions and Deviations from one Species to another, are almost insensible."[4] This chain of organized beings is not, as we have seen, an evolutionary chain, but one instantaneously conceived at the moment of Creation. Everything holds its appropriate place and does not, or at least is supposed not to, aspire beyond its station. It is important, however, to take note of the fact that this widespread bio-theological doctrine had conditioned men, first, to the idea that one form of life passed insensibly into the next on the scale beneath it so that, in the words of a contemporary writer, "Man is connected by his nature and, therefore, by the design of the Author of all Na-

[4] *The Spectator*, No. 519.

ture, with the whole tribe of animals, and so closely with some of them, that the distance between his intellectual faculties and theirs . . . appears, in many instances, small, and would probably appear still less, if we had the means of knowing their motives, as we have of observing their actions."[5]

Second, this humbling thought had another corollary: it roused a high pitch of interest in those animals, such as the great apes, which appeared to stand close to man. The law of continuity, furthermore, implied that there might be "many degrees of intelligence found within the human species."[6] Though the vast majority of the eighteenth-century thinkers did not assume an actual genetic blood link between man and his nearest primate relatives, they were extremely conscious of the close position of the great apes to man on the Scale of Being. Moreover, when earlier the confusion as to whether exotic, little-known apes were actually men began to disappear, it was replaced or at least intensified by a search for some creature who, though speaking, would exemplify the imperceptible transition on the Scale of Being from an ape into a man. At this time the far-flung world of primitive cultures was being discovered, and Western man was being made increasingly aware of the vast gulf that seemed to yawn between his society and that of remote and, to his sophisticated eye, unquestionably benighted heathen peoples.

We find scattered through the accounts of voyagers of the late seventeenth and eighteenth centuries numerous accounts of the Hottentots of the Cape of Good Hope. Their low state of culture and the phonetic peculiarities of their speech, "a farrago of bestial sounds resembling the chatter of apes,"[7] led to great interest as to their po-

[5] H. Bolingbroke, quoted by Lovejoy, op. cit., p. 196.
[6] Lovejoy, op. cit., p. 197.
[7] R. W. Frantz, "Swift's Yahoos and the Voyagers," *Modern Philology*, 1931, Vol. 29, p. 55. See also Lovejoy, p. 234.

sition on the Scale of Nature. It is not surprising, therefore, to find "the brutal Hottentot" standing only an infinitesimal degree above the ape, nor did the American Indian escape similar attentions.[8] What is more interesting, however, is to find, long after the Scale of Being has lapsed out of existence as a serious philosophic concept, that this same "brutal Hottentot" is continuing to occupy his time-honored position in the minds of nineteenth-century scholars. Darwin, writing to Sir Charles Lyell in the year of the *Origin*, indicates with careful conservatism that "we have a very fine gradation in the intellectual powers of the Vertebrata, with one rather wide gap . . . between say a Hottentot and an Orang . . . even if civilized as much mentally as the dog has been from the wolf."[9]

We need not confine ourselves to Hottentots, however. The French anthropologist, Pouchet, by 1864[10] has faced up grimly to the implications of the new doctrine of evolution. "Let us no longer put *ourselves* on the stage," he exhorts his reader. "Let us descend boldly the steps of the human ladder. . . ."

"Examples are not wanting of races placed so low that they have quite naturally appeared to resemble the ape tribe. These people, much nearer than ourselves to a state of nature, deserve on that account every attention on the part of the anthropologist. . . . What will become of the unity of the human species, if we can prove that certain races are not a whit more intelligent than certain animals . . . ?"

Pouchet goes on to picture the Australian aborigine as existing "in a sort of moral brutality," surviving by means of "a kind of highly developed instinct for discovering the food which is always difficult for them to obtain. . . ."

Earlier than this, however, and unsullied by contact

[8] L. C. Rosenfield, *From Beast Machine to Man Machine*, New York, 1940, pp. 196, 204.

[9] LLD, Vol. 2, p. 211.

[10] *The Plurality of the Human Race*, London, 1864, p. 15.

with the *Origin of Species*, there is the eyewitness record of Henry Piddington published in the *Journal of the Asiatic Society of Bengal* in 1855[11] and relating, actually, to events of 1824.

"We have," he affirms, "upon three points of continental India the indubitable fact . . . that there are wild tribes existing which the native traditional names liken to the Orang-Utang, and my own knowledge certainly bears them out; for in the gloom of a forest, the individual I saw might as well pass for an Orang-Utang as a man."

"He was short," Mr. Piddington continues to reminisce, "flat nosed, had pouch-like wrinkles in semicircles around the corners of the mouth and cheeks; his arms were disproportionately long, and there was a portion of reddish hair to be seen on the rusty black skin. Altogether, if crouched in a dark corner or on a tree, he might have been mistaken for a large Orang-Utang."

The Geneva scholar, Carl Vogt, strives to be anatomically precise: "The pendulous abdomen of the lower races . . . shows an approximation to the ape, as do also the want of calves, the flatness of the thighs, the pointed form of the buttocks, and the leanness of the upper arm. . . ."[12] Giving particular attention to pubertal changes in the Negro, he comments with gloomy insight:

"It is a repetition of the phenomena occurring in the anthropoid apes. In them also the skull presents, until the second dentition, a remarkable resemblance to the human skull, the cerebral portion being arched and the jaws but little projecting. From that time the cerebral skull remains stationary, the internal capacity in no way increases. . . . Young orangs and chimpanzees are good-natured, amiable, intelligent beings, very apt to learn and become civi-

11 "Memorandum on an Unknown Forest Race," 1855, Vol. 24, pp. 207–10. See also "*Krao*, the So-called Missing Link," by J. P. Harrison, *Report of the British Association for the Advancement of Science*, 1883, p. 575.
12 Vogt, *Lectures on Man*, London, 1864, p. 128.

lized. After the transformation they are obstinate savage beasts, incapable of any improvement.

"And so it is with the Negro. . . ."[13]

Not content, however, with an attempt to show that the foot of the Negro makes ". . . a decided approach to the form of a hand," and that he "rarely stands quite upright," Vogt finally introduces an extreme statement which is unconsciously revelatory as reflecting attitudes in Western society of male superiority. He concludes, in short: "We may be sure that wherever we perceive an approach to the animal type, the female is nearer to it than the male, hence we should discover a greater simious resemblance if we were to take the female as our standard."[14]

After this new subdivision of the Scale of Nature, a less misanthropic observation like that of Robert Dunn before the British Association for the Advancement of Science in 1862 that "the American Indian is too dangerous to be trusted by the white man in social intercourse and too obtuse and intractable to be worth coercing into servitude"[15] is, for all its frank honesty about Caucasian intentions, a trifle anti-climactic. He does, however, succeed in a few succinct sentences in establishing his notion of a clear succession in the development of the white stock. The report of the conclusion of his address reads as follows:

"He observed that the leading characters of the various races of mankind have been maintained to be simply representatives of a particular type in the development of the highest or Caucasian; the Negro exhibiting permanently the imperfect brow, projecting lower jaw, and slender bent limbs of the Caucasian child some consid-

[13] Op. cit., p. 191.
[14] Ibid., p. 180.
[15] Robert Dunn, "Some Observations on the Psychological Differences Which Exist among the Typical Races of Man," *Report of the British Association for the Advancement of Science*, 1862, pp. 144–46. This idea is actually drawn from J. C. Prichard.

erable time before its birth, the aboriginal Americans representing the same child nearer birth, and the Mongolian the same newly born."

It is apparent from these statements, gleaned from a variety of sources, and which could be endlessly multiplied from the literature, *that long before the clear recognition of fossil forms of man there existed in the minds of western Europeans a notion of racial gradation, and a conception of that gradation as leading downward toward the ape.* Moreover, the less culturally advanced members of the human stock are increasingly seen as affording "a glimmer of the ape beneath the human envelope." These people are regarded as living fossils both culturally and physically; in fact, there is evident a lack of clear distinction between the two categories.

In the century of Enlightenment there had been philosophical admiration, at least in some quarters, for the "noble savage." The idea of progress as it had existed in eighteenth-century France had implied some notion of mankind's ability to absorb learning. Here, however, in nineteenth-century England the earlier Scale of Nature now classifies living men in terms of their cultural achievement by Western standards. The hopeful aspects of the idea of progress as they were entertained by the thinkers of Revolutionary France are denied fruition. Instead, a linear biology, so far as human kind at least is concerned, reigns in imperial England. Natives are incapable of achieving high culture. Humorlessly, in a dozen forms the philosophers of the Victorian Era repeat the story, "The Mongol and the Negro are but human saurians who reached long ago . . . their full development, and are now moral fossils."[16]

Darwin, gazing upon the natives of Fuegia, is appalled by the gap which yawns between savage and civilized man; yet it must be said in justice to his supreme observa-

16 *The Galaxy*, 1867, Vol. 4, p. 1881. See also W. B. Carpenter, *Nature and Man*, New York, 1889, pp. 406–7.

tional powers that, at the age of twenty-four, watching
the return of Captain Fitzroy's hostages to their own people, he comments:

"It was quite melancholy leaving our Fuegians
amongst their barbarous countrymen. . . . In contradiction of what has often been stated, three years has been
sufficient to change savages into, as far as habits go, complete and voluntary Europeans."[17]

His account of Jemmy Button and the last signal fire
lit by the latter in farewell to his white friends as the
Beagle stood out to sea contains the pathos of great literature. It is only in the later years as his constant concern with natural selection and the effort to explain the
rise of man weigh heavily upon his mind that he forgets
and speaks of Hottentots and Orangs. Charles Darwin
came close to envisaging the problem of culture as he
bade good-by to his Indian shipmates. It is perhaps too
much to expect of one man in an intellectually confused
period that he should have solved both sides of the human mystery, or have distinguished clearly between the
biological and the cultural. On that day in his youth, however, in a great surge of human feeling, he stood very
close to doing so. The fire from the dark headland stings
the eyes a little even now, and Jemmy Button's wistful,
forgotten face is an eternal reproach to those who persist
in projecting upon the bodies of living men the shadow
of an unknown vanished ape. Moreover, even the form
of that ancestral ape is illusory. The long arms, the bandy
legs, the pendulous belly, the semi-erect posture are conceived in imitation of the apes of today. Modern paleontology offers little encouragement to such notions and
none at all to the idea that the existing races represent
in the order of their emergence successive "missing links,"
mentally frozen, so to speak, at various stages of the human past.

[17] D, p. 136.

III   The Microcephali

It would appear from some of the material we have just reviewed that man had mentally so closed the gap between himself and the anthropoids that he would scarcely be conscious that there was a paleontological break in the evolutionary chain of ascent. Actually, however, we have to bear in mind that we are examining a ferment of opinion in which writers are not always consistent with their own more extreme statements, nor do they all represent the same point of view. The more religious-minded and the more sober-headed continued to cling to the views expressed by Adam Sedgwick in his Presidential Address before the Geological Society of London in 1831, just about the time young Charles Darwin was departing upon his memorable voyage. Sedgwick's speech was devoted to an attack on the uniformitarian hypothesis of Sir Charles Lyell. In it he called the appearance of man "a geological event of vast importance . . . breaking in upon any supposition of geological continuity, and utterly unaccounted for by what we have any right to call the laws of nature."[18]

It is obvious, of course, that so long as man was regarded in this fashion as "outside" of nature, a unique being divorced from any but the most recent past, he stood as a challenge to all scientific attempts to explain, not alone his own origins, but those of even the "natural" world about him. Only by establishing satisfactorily the continuity of human development and the relationship of man to his nearest primate relatives would it be possible to escape from the foggy atmosphere of supernaturalism which still lingered over the English scene. That atmosphere would not entirely pass away even from the more mundane aspects of geology until the nature of this strange emergent, man, could be more fully established.

[18] J. W. Gregory, "Problems of Geology Contemporary with the British Association," *Report of the British Association for the Advancement of Science*, 1931, p. 53.

It is not without interest as showing with what reluctance the task was carried out that as late as 1863 Sir Charles Lyell, whose geological doctrines form the very groundwork of the *Origin of Species* and who was Darwin's lifelong friend and confidant, was still speculating as to whether, in the case of man, he may not "have cleared at one bound the space which separated the highest stage of the unprogressive intelligence of the inferior animals from the first and lowest form of improvable reason manifested by man." Darwin, reading this remark in the first edition of the *Antiquity of Man* (p. 505), commented wryly that the sentence "makes me groan."[19]

It is plain, as one examines the more guarded statements of the leading evolutionists, that in spite of the tendency to arrange the existing human races in a sequence of stages, or to perceive even lower intermediates flitting through the unexplored forests of Africa or the Far East, the gap between living man and the animal world is still a source of embarrassment. After expressing hope that living apes may eventually be found which approach man in cerebral content, Vogt, for example, confesses that "in the absence of the fact, it would be foolish to form any conclusions."[20] That the evolutionists' hope was by degrees shifting to the fossil record is shown by his following remark: "There may, however, have existed *inter-*

[19] LLD, Vol. 3, p. 12. As indicating the vacillation of Lyell's thought on this subject, however, one might refer to a letter from Huxley to Lyell dated January 25, 1859, in which Huxley says in response to a letter now missing: "I do not exactly see the force of your argument that we are bound to find fossil forms intermediate between man and monkeys in the Rocks. . . . How do we know that man is not a persistent type?" (LLH, Vol. 1, p. 251.) Huxley at the time of this letter seems to have inclined, in the case of man, toward the possibility of some leap of the order of a macromutation taken very long ago. This hypothesis sounds rather similar to Lyell's publicly expressed view of 1863 and since it was written to Lyell, may have had some influence in leading his thought in this direction. Huxley's remark also shows the lingering influence of Huxley's only recently abandoned non-progressionism.

[20] Op. cit., p. 194.

mediate forms, which in the lapse of time have become extinct."[21] Vogt saw fit to italicize this statement, but he was not the man to be handicapped by any lack of the necessary fossils. Instead, he succeeded in commanding international attention with a very ingenious, if now outmoded, theory.

Undaunted by "the gulf which still exists between the Negro and the ape," Vogt turns to the abnormal. We have a right, he contends, when living forms fail us, to refer to the pathological. "I do not hesitate to uphold . . . that microcephali and born idiots present as perfect a series from man to the ape as may be wished for. . . ."[22] Since the evolutionary development of man from some lower primate inevitably seems to demand an increase in cranial capacity, what would appear more logical than that a modern microcephalic idiot "in its abnormity represents that intermediate form, which at a remote period may have been normal. This arrest . . . is the simian stage." Such an "arrested monstrosity of the present creation," argues Vogt, "fills up the gap which cannot be bridged over by normal types in the present creation, but may be so by some future discoveries."[23]

Vogt, in other words, has taken the notion of atavistic throwbacks and argued that his microcephali, of which he gives several examples, constitute just such returns to the ancestral human line. "The arms," he observes, "seem disproportionately long, the legs short and weak. The head is that of an ape."[24] Though he occasionally hedges upon the teeth and jaw, so far as the skull is concerned, every naturalist, if such a fossil specimen were found, would, he asserts, "at once declare it to be the cranium of an ape."[25] With careful deliberation he places the skulls of a Negro, an idiot, and a chimpanzee together

[21] Op. cit., p. 194.
[22] Ibid., pp. 194–95.
[23] Ibid., pp. 462–63.
[24] Ibid., p. 195.
[25] Ibid., pp. 198–99.

in order to show that the idiot "holds in every respect an intermediate place between them."[26]

The various breeding experiments of the Darwinians, along with their eagerness to observe traces of the evolutionary pathway, had led to great interest in what they termed "atavisms" or "reversions" in which a carefully bred and standardized form showed a tendency occasionally to produce descendants who resembled more remote ancestors. Since genetic mechanisms were not clearly understood by the Darwinists, these mysterious episodes were regarded with considerable awe.[27] Darwin himself once remarked that he regarded "reversion —this power of calling back to life long-lost characters— as the most wonderful of all the attributes of inheritance." Red Eye, the ferocious throwback in Jack London's *Before Adam*, is an interesting example of the atavism's appearance in popular literature well within the twentieth century. Today most so-called atavisms are explainable on Mendelian principles as the results of various types of gene segregation and recombination, alteration in growth rates, or even outright mutation in the gene system.

Vogt's cases of arrested brain growth, therefore, are certainly not to be regarded as the emergence of missing stages in the long history of humanity, and they bear little actual resemblance to recently discovered fossils of the hominid line. Vogt's idea was seriously received in the sixties of the last century, however, and Darwin devotes attention to it in the *Descent of Man* (1871). Huxley, in addition, commented that even the Neanderthal skull might be just such an accidental reversion, though he feels that the capacious cranial capacity suggests "the pithecoid tendencies, indicated by this skull, did not extend deep into the organization. . . ."[28]

[26] Op. cit., p. 198.

[27] M. F. Ashley Montagu, "The Concept of Atavism," *Science*, 1938, Vol. 87, pp. 462–63.

[28] T. H. Huxley, *Evidence as to Man's Place in Nature*, London, 1863, p. 137.

Arguments were occasionally brought against the theory of human evolution on the ground that man did not show "reversion" as he should if he had really evolved from an ancestor unlike himself. In 1872 we find Darwin responding serenely to one such criticism: "I do not think the absence of reversions of structure in man is of much weight. Carl Vogt, indeed, argues that [the existence of] Micro-cephalous idiots is a case of reversion."[29]

We may observe at this point that so long as the theory of microcephalics as "missing links" was seriously entertained, the claims launched by some writers against the first human fossils as merely representing idiots showing premature synostosis of the cranial sutures actually proved nothing at all. A follower of Vogt's views could simply have responded thus: "Certainly, this is what we have been saying all along. Modern idiots resemble a specific human level of organization in the past. *Now you have found genuine traces of that level in the past.*" Thus those who spoke of Neanderthal or Pithecanthropus in this way were, in actuality, merely begging the question, so far as the true nature of these specimens was concerned. In the light of the intellectual preconceptions of Vogt and his followers it was perfectly possible for a human calvarium to be both that of a true fossil hominid and to resemble in detail the skull of a modern idiot. With this observation, and having seen a slow shift from a belief in living *normal* links passing slowly to a notion of living microcephalic *abnormals* as in some manner *representing past normals no longer existent in the living world, we shall now turn to the final remaining alternative.* The archaeologist has been busy throughout the Darwinian period. It may be that he can supply the missing evidence from the ground. Let us see how his evidence was received.

29 LLD, Vol. 3, p. 163.

IV   The Descent into the Past

Up to the time of Cuvier's death in 1832 no remains of any primates were known from fossiliferous deposits. The great master of French biology died in the unshaken belief that man's advent upon the earth did not much exceed the common estimates of around six thousand years, and that probably the lower monkeys were little if any older. Only a few years later, in 1836, his own countryman, Edouard Lartet, unearthed the first fossil anthropoid in Miocene deposits near Sausan in the south of France. The report of the Siwalik discoveries of Falconer and Cautley soon followed.

Cuvier's theory had been breached in so far as man's simian relatives were concerned. There was a consequent feeling of alarm in many quarters, for the unearthing of ancient primates made it quickly apparent that the discovery of human fossils was made more probable. The weight of Cuvier's authoritative dogmatism was no longer able to stem the tide. In the words of Isidore Geoffroy Saint-Hilaire: "The question will soon be answered in the affirmative. There are already a sufficient number of facts which would be considered as conclusive, were the question confined to any other animal."[30]

Boucher de Perthes revealed the presence of ancient human artifacts along the Somme in the 1840s, and it is interesting to note that Darwin admitted years later that he had read de Perthes' book. Although this is well within the period when Darwin was developing his evolutionary interpretation of life, he confesses humbly, "I . . . looked at [de Perthes'] book . . . and am ashamed to think that I concluded the whole was rubbish. Yet he has done for man something like what Agassiz did for glaciers."[31] It was not until 1859, the year of the *Origin*, that de Perthes' efforts were finally vindicated.

[30] Quoted in the *Anthropological Review*, 1863, Vol. 1, p. 65.
[31] LLD, Vol. 3, pp. 15–16.

Three years before the antiquity of de Perthes' artifacts had been conclusively accepted, a skull cap of strange aspect had been discovered in a small cave in Rhenish Prussia. This skull, though not the first Neanderthal skull to be observed, was the first to come under the attention of science. It constitutes, therefore, the first genuinely extinct variety of man ever to undergo scientific scrutiny. Moreover, the date of its discovery, 1856, and the descriptions and discussions which followed were juxtaposed so closely upon the evolutionary debate as practically to have ensured attention from the leading Darwinians and their opponents.

As might have been expected, attempts to diagnose the age and nature of the skull range all the way from a sober, but very cautious, analysis by Thomas Huxley to claims that the bones represented only a rickety Cossack from the Napoleonic Wars. The individual was geologically old: he was not old. He was pathological: he was normal.[32] Notable names were entered in the lists on both sides of these questions. By way of extenuation it may be said that the confusion among the savants was augmented through the incomplete nature of the calvarium, and the lack of clear stratigraphical information from the Neanderthal Cave. No scientific eye, it must be remembered, had, before this, looked upon the remains of an extinct form of man.

Setting aside some of the more outmoded, if not ludicrous, treatments of the subject, the careful student is still, in the light of historical perspective, forced to conclude that the antiquity of man was as yet little understood, and his salient characteristics less so. In addition to the still heavy prejudice directed against belief in the existence of early man an accidental factor further confused the issue: the Engis skull from a cave along the banks of the Meuse, near Liége in Belgium, was regarded by many as

[32] Jacob Gruber, "The Neanderthal Controversy," *Scientific Monthly*, 1948, Vol. 67, pp. 436–39.

being of similar age. Professor Schmerling had found this skull under nearly five feet of osseous breccia in association with an extinct Pleistocene fauna. Discovered in the 1830s it long predated the Neanderthal discovery. Its significance in the present connection, however, lies in the words of Sir John Lubbock: ". . . there are, as yet, only two cases on record in which the bone caves have furnished us with skulls in such a condition as to allow of restoration. One of these was found by Dr. Schmerling in the cave of Engis . . . ; the other by Dr. Fuhlrott in the Neanderthal near Düsseldorf."[33]

There was as yet no clear stratigraphy separating the Middle from the Upper Paleolithic period. It was inevitable that these two skulls should be compared even though today we know that they are derived from widely separated time levels. Both lack totally the face and jaw, though the Engis skull is more nearly complete. In Neanderthal we possess one low-vaulted skull with a massive supraorbital torus, regarded by its describer, Schaaffhausen, as belonging to a period prior to the time of the Celts and Germans. The remains, he says, "were in all probability derived from one of the wild races of northwestern Europe, spoken of by Latin writers."[34] The Engis skull in contrast to the Neanderthal had no other interest than its fossiliferous associations. To quote Sir Arthur Keith: "There is not a single feature that marks this skull off from men of the Neolithic or of modern times."[35]

It has been pertinent to our discussion to make plain the fact that the facial character of Neanderthal man was then unknown. This unfortunate situation placed altogether too much emphasis upon the supraciliary ridges. Many writers, searching collections of skulls, thought the problem had been settled when they found a specimen

[33] John Lubbock, "Cave Man," *Natural History Review,* 1864, Vol. 4, pp. 407–28.

[34] H. Schaaffhausen, "On the Crania of the Most Ancient Races of Man," *Natural History Review,* 1861, Vol. 1, p. 155.

[35] *Antiquity of Man,* 2d ed., London, 1925, Vol. 1, p. 70.

of Homo sapiens with a massive supraorbital torus. Huxley, for example, after admitting the Neanderthal cranium to be "the most apelike . . . I have ever seen,"[36] contends that the creature was "in no sense intermediate between men and apes."[37] Taking note of the gradations to be found among recent skulls, he says "there is no ground for separating [Neanderthal] specifically, still less generically from Homo sapiens."[38] This view still finds emphatic expression in an anthropological text referring to the Engis and Neanderthal skulls, as late as 1890: "A number of other anatomical elements, thought to be peculiar in these fossil skulls, such as the superciliary prominences, the small and receding forehead, the form of the ciliary arcs, the amplitude of the occiput, are found to be but the individual and accidental varieties of men living among us."[39]

J. W. Dawson, writing with an eye to the modern races, comments: "that the characters for which this skeleton is eminent, are found, though perhaps in less degree, in the rude tribes of America and Australia. It is also doubtful whether this skeleton really indicates a race at all. It may have belonged to one of those wild men, half-crazed, half-idiotic, cruel and strong, who are always more or less to be found living on the outskirts of barbarous tribes, and who now and then appear in civilized communities, to be consigned perhaps to the penitentiary or the gallows, when their murderous propensities manifest themselves."[40]

This curious quotation not only shows the continuing application of the idea of racial gradation, but Dawson's "wild man" hypothesis seems to echo this tradition as it

[36] T. H. Huxley, "Further Remarks upon the Human Remains from the Neanderthal," *Natural History Review*, 1864, Vol. 4, p. 431.

[37] Ibid., p. 442.

[38] Ibid., p. 443.

[39] Thomas Hughes, *Principles of Anthropology and Biology*, 2d ed., New York, 1890, p. 69.

[40] J. W. Dawson, "On the Antiquity of Man," *Edinburgh New Philosophical Journal*, 1864, n.s. Vol. 19, p. 53.

exists in European folklore.[41] Neanderthal man is here quite close to being made one with those fallen, feral creatures who wander in the green forests of medieval romance.

Carl Vogt, as might have been expected, diagnoses the forehead of the Neander skull as "that of an idiot or microcephalus,"[42] though he accepts its antiquity and, as we have had occasion to note, this in no way prevents him from regarding it as "normal."[43] He takes, however, one further step which introduces to us the final vast confusion which can be wrought by archaeological ineptitude. Vogt finds "a great similarity between the Engis and Neanderthal skulls."[44] Moreover, recognizing the female skull to be smaller than the male and to possess less prominent supraorbital ridges, he arrives at the conclusion that both skulls belong to the same race. The Neanderthal skull belonged to a muscular, stupid male but the Engis specimen "belonged to an intelligent woman." The race, he assumes, resembled the existing Australian aboriginals. The cultural associations mentioned briefly in his writings suggest a similar confusion of different time levels. In this he was not alone. For over thirty years after its discovery and description *Homo neanderthalensis* was destined to remain the butt of idle speculation as well as the suspected product of disease.

In the meantime, a growing body of archaeologists continued to prowl through the caves and grottoes of civilized Europe. More discoveries of tools and artifacts were made. Additional human remains were discovered but they all proved to be those of big-brained upper paleolithic people. So consistent were these discoveries that for a time the Victorian uneasiness about ape-men began

[41] See R. Bernheimer, *Wild Men in the Middle Ages,* Harvard University Press, 1952.

[42] Op. cit., p. 304.

[43] Carl Vogt, "The Primitive Period of the Human Species," *Anthropological Review,* 1867, Vol. 5, p. 213.

[44] Carl Vogt, *Lectures on Man,* London, 1864, p. 304.

to fade. Perhaps the Darwinians had been wrong about man after all. The drift of thought can be glimpsed in this account by Gill of Riviere's discoveries at Mentone:

". . . the negative results afforded us indicate that fossil man was, in all respects, a typical man, perhaps even differing less from his successors in Europe than do some other existing races. It is at least very certain that he had no decided ape-like characteristics. Even more! He was man to excess. The proportions of the forelimb to the hind, and of the median and distal portions of each to the proximal, so far from proving a condition intermediate between man and the apes, or embryonic or juvenile humanity or even affinity to the Negro, indicate that he was more unlike the apes in such respects than are some existing races; nor is this evidence rebutted by the skull, the dentition or otherwise. . . ."[45]

Continuing in this vein, Dr. Gill goes on to assert that, in the light of such evidence as is revealed at Mentone, "the anxious may . . . contemplate with a happy serenity the explorations made, for every skeleton found, in its perfect manlike features, will not only disprove the existence of the dreaded intermediate link, but will add to the value of the negative evidence against such a link—that is in Europe or America."[46]

Apparently Gill is enough of an evolutionist to intimate that perhaps Africa or Asia may *sometime* yield a remote link to man, but he hastens to add comfortingly that "it is not likely to be of very recent origin, most likely Miocene." Another writer, A. S. Packard, similarly inclined, emphasizes ". . . anatomists of high authority have, we cannot but think too hastily, referred their [finds] to the most degraded of savage races."[47]

It may be added in extenuation of Professor Packard's

[45] Theodore Gill, "The Fossil Man of Mentone," *Popular Science Monthly,* 1874, Vol. 5, p. 644.

[46] Ibid.

[47] "The Hairy Mammoth," *American Naturalist,* 1869, Vol. 2, pp. 28–29.

point of view that the activities of confirmed evolutionists, as the Darwinian enthusiasm began to mount, are
sadly revelatory of a state of mind in its way as dogmatically fervid as that of those opposed to the evolutionary
point of view. Where some saw the big-brained upper paleolithic people, or even the big-brained Neanderthals, as
a denial of the possibility of evolutionary change, others
just as enthusiastically regarded these types as representing living races lower on the scale of life than the modern
Caucasian. Once more existing peoples were being arranged on the time scale of the fossil past. "If we uplift
the deposits of the earth's surface," writes a German
scholar in 1868, "there appears as the first inhabitant of
Central Europe a man whose protruding jaws and nearly
deficient forehead betray a savage animal character. The
elongated skull with its strongly projecting eyebrows reminds one of the Negro, the Mongol, the Hottentot and
the Australian."[48]

Others read into the fragmentary Neanderthal remains
something even more formidable. The jaw of La Naulette
found in 1866 in a cave in eastern Belgium is described
in one book as extremely apelike with huge projecting
canines." It does not seem to trouble the writers that the
teeth of this specimen are missing, having been lost from
the sockets after death. Instead, they go on to describe
the entire Neanderthal tribe with their "gorilla-like eye
teeth" as presenting an appearance "in the highest degree
hideous and ferocious."[49] No known form of fossil man
possesses gorilloid canines. These descriptions are the
product of imagination whether they visualize Neanderthal man as a Hottentot or a gorilla. In either case they

[48] R. Sweichel cited by L. Büchner, *Man in the Past, Present and
Future*, London, 1872, p. 261.

[49] J. Y. and F. D. Bergen, *The Development Theory*, Boston, 1884,
p. 196. Similarly the anatomist William King, in opposition to
Huxley, regarded the Neanderthal specimen as "eminently simian"
and its thoughts "those of the brute." See Keith, op. cit., Vol. 1,
pp. 188–89.

are simple projections into the past of living forms which the describer sincerely believes are links in the evolutionary scale leading to man. Once more there is an attempt to equate the past evolution of man with a graded *existing* scale of creatures running from the ape to man. Innumerable descriptions characterize natives as apelike in appearance and habits.[50] Similarly the effort to close the gap from the other, or anthropoidal, side leads to assumptions that the existing great apes may possess undeveloped or rudimentary linguistic ability. An anonymous article in *Chambers' Journal* speaks of the grunt of the orang as perhaps "some incipient form of speech capable of being cultivated and enlarged."[51] Ernst Haeckel, towards the turn of the century, characteristically proclaims that "the old doctrine that only man is endowed with speech" is outmoded. "It is high time," he says, "that this erroneous impression, resting on a lack of zoological information, should be abandoned."[52] Returning, however, to our more immediate point of discussion, it might have been thought that the discovery in 1886 of the Neanderthal men of Spy would have dissipated the mist of suspicion which had for so long lingered over the valley of the Neander. Certainly it led some to the belief that Neanderthal man could not be a diseased idiot or a distorted Lombrosian criminal. On the other hand, the recognition of the great cranial capacity of the type puzzled those who were still anticipating some sort of small-brained emergent.

As late as 1911, W. J. Sollas, the distinguished English geologist, wrote of this problem as follows:

"The Mousterian skulls are the oldest human skulls of

50 Büchner, op. cit., p. 314 ff.

51 "The Wild Man of the Woods," *Chambers' Journal,* 1856, Series 3, Vol. 6, p. 131. I am indebted to my colleague Dr. Gerald Henderson of Brooklyn College for calling this paper to my attention.

52 "On Our Present Knowledge of the Origin of Man," *Annual Report, Smithsonian Institution,* 1899, p. 466.

which we have any knowledge; but just as in the case of the Magdalenian and Solutrean, they indicate that the primitive inhabitants of France were distinguished from the highest civilized races, not by a smaller, but by a larger cranial capacity; *in other words as we proceed backwards in time the human brain increases rather than decreases in volume.*"[53]

Disregarding Pithecanthropus which even this great student believed diseased, he poses a final paradox: "Thus, as we proceed backwards in time Man departs farther from the ape in the size of his brain, but approaches nearer to the ape in the characters of his bodily framework."[54] It was a reasonably true statement so far as Neanderthal man was concerned, and it may have bolstered the hopes of those who had earlier followed the lead of Gill, Brinton,[55] and others. Nevertheless, it was a paradox and a paradox which could not be long sustained. Though Vogt's microcephals had not stood the test of time a few evolutionists, by pure extrapolation, saw clearly that at some point, however deep it might lie beneath us on the time scale, the transition from the animal brain had occurred.

V *The Java Ape Man*

With the discovery in 1891 of *Pithecanthropus erectus* by Eugene Dubois, the first human type of genuinely low cranial capacity was revealed. Some, with considerable reason, would regard it as the only real "missing link" produced in the nineteenth century. By this time much of the public outcry which had greeted Darwin's *Descent of Man* in 1871 had died down. The doctrine of evolution

[53] W. J. Sollas, "The Evolution of Man," *Scientia,* 1911, Vol. 9, p. 121.

[54] Ibid., p. 124.

[55] D. G. Brinton, "The Earliest Men," *Nature,* 1893, Vol. 48, p. 460.

had been widely disseminated, discussed, and accepted in intellectual circles. The time would have seemed ripe for a clinching paleontological demonstration of the pathway of human descent. Unfortunately, however, the face of the Java hominid was missing and almost the same distrust which had been directed at the first Neanderthal discovery emerged once more, though perhaps in a less aggravated form.[56]

At the Third International Zoological Congress which met in Leyden in 1895 Dubois exhibited and discussed his find. The zoologists present maintained that the skull was human and the human anatomists maintained it to be that of an ape. Once more the cry of microcephalic idiot was raised.[57] We have the testimony of Marsh that in the beginning, with the exception of Manouvrier in Paris and himself, no one took Dubois' claims at their full valuation. "Among a score or more of notices," he writes, "I do not recall a single one that . . . admitted the full importance of the discovery. . . ."[58] "M. Dubois," Manouvrier ironically observes, "can congratulate himself on seeing placed in relief at Berlin the reasons according to which his Pithecanthropus could not be a man and, in England, much better reasons according to which the same Pithecanthropus could not be a monkey."[59]

The situation, however, is not one in which the absurdities are all confined to one side. Nothing better illustrates the power of preconceived ideas than to discover Dubois contending that no good can arise from a comparison between his precious skull cap and that of the Neanderthals of Düsseldorf and Spy because these latter specimens

[56] O. C. Marsh, "The Ape from the Tertiary of Java," *Science*, 1896, n.s. Vol. 3, p. 790. Thomas Wilson, "The Beginnings of the Science of Prehistoric Anthropology," *Proceedings of the American Association for the Advancement of Science*, 1899, p. 327.

[57] R. Lydekker, *Nature*, 1895, Vol. 51, p. 291.

[58] O. C. Marsh, "On the Pithecanthropus erectus from the Tertiary of Java," *American Journal of Science*, 1896, Vol. 1, p. 476.

[59] L. Manouvrier, "On the Pithecanthropus erectus," *American Journal of Science*, 1897, Vol. 4, p. 218.

are pathological![60] Apparently it never crossed Dubois' mind that this argument was just as applicable to his own transitional man-ape calvarium. As for the Pithecanthropus femur, so deep are the preconceptions of the age that it is perhaps not surprising to find Dubois hinting of "indications in that bone of an arboreal habit, such as are not found in the human femur."[61] Today we know that the transition from the trees to the ground long preceded the rise of such true paleanthropic men as Pithecanthropus. At that time, however, constant morphological comparisons of man with the existing apes had left this point less clear.[62] It is with genuine pleasure and a little shock of surprise, therefore, that one encounters in a statement of the anatomist Cunningham a very clear modern grasp of the primate phylogeny and an unwillingness to confuse "missing links" with living collateral lines of descent. "Most certainly," he says, the Pithecanthropus fossils "are not derived from a transition form between any of the existing anthropoid apes and man; such a form does not and cannot exist, seeing that the divarication of the ape and man has taken place low down in the genealogical tree and each has followed . . . its own path. The so-called Pithecanthropus is in the direct human line although it occupies a place on this considerably lower than any human form at present known."[63]

With this precise and much ignored observation, Cunningham passes from the scene. It is left for Manouvrier

[60] D. J. Cunningham, "Dr. Dubois' So-called Missing Link," *Nature*, 1895, Vol. 51, p. 429.

[61] E. Dubois, "Remarks on the Brain Cast of Pithecanthropus erectus." Summary of a talk before the International Congress of Zoologists, *Nature*, 1898, Vol. 58, p. 427.

[62] Thomas Wilson, for example, writes in 1899 of paleolithic man as having crooked legs and projecting teeth. "It has been doubted whether he regularly assumed the upright position." "The Beginning of the Science of Prehistoric Anthropology," *Proceedings of the American Association for the Advancement of Science*, 1899, p. 330.

[63] Op. cit., p. 429.

to define Dubois' final contribution as it may now be also interpreted from the midpoint of our century. "He established the fact," comments the Frenchman, "that the craniologic inferiority of fossil human races, according to the specimens we know, increases with their antiquity. . . . We consider [Pithecanthropus] as one of the intermediate fossils theoretically foreseen."[64] Thus man, in his descent through time, had finally passed beyond the range of the big-brained men of the upper Pleistocene. The cerebral reduction was a reality, and the curious paradox of the anthropoidal big-brained Neanderthals could be carried no further. As we have noted, some did not at first accept this view, but by the 1950s it was a commonplace.

The whole of the nineteenth century and at least part of the eighteenth century had been devoted to the understanding not alone of man, but of his relationship to the only other living thing on the planet that looks like him—the monkeys. They had been with him since the beginning, grimacing at him from behind the curtain of leaves. Their faces were sad or evil little caricatures of the human face; bone for bone, tooth for tooth, they were built on the human pattern or the human on theirs. In the end, on that great scale of perfection which runs from the crystal to the noblest beings on the farthest worlds, they stood next to man, but the chain had been fixed in the moment of Creation. Nothing became extinct, everything was locked in an eternal order. In that order an ape crouched beside man and the two knew each other to be very close. There was only the breadth of a hair between them. They had come to know each other well. "Show me a generic character," cries Linnaeus, "by which to distinguish Man and Ape; I myself . . . know of none."[65]

Even the races ascended in that vast chain and the Hottentot knew best the touch of the ape. In the nineteenth

[64] Op. cit., p. 225.
[65] Cited by Gladys Bryson, *Man and Society*, Princeton University Press, 1945, p. 60.

THE RECEPTION OF THE FIRST MISSING LINKS

century the chain began to be forgotten, but fragments of it persisted in the minds of men and passed unconsciously into the new doctrine of evolution, where the wheel turned at last.

The nineteenth century drew from the eighteenth century an idea of necessary, constant progression which had arisen in the field of social studies. Every society in its own time and place would advance by necessary law even though historical chance and incident might promote or incommode that advance. In the nineteenth century aspects of this idea of progress were transferred to biology. Darwin, though he abjured the idea of necessary progression and mentions, as illustration, animals which had changed little, if at all, through long periods, shows signs of confused thinking on this point. He reveals in occasional passages that he is unconsciously transferring the concept of the eighteenth-century unilinear fixed scale of being to, as Teggart puts it, a "concept of a unilinear and continuous series in time, parallel with the classificatory series."[66] The classificatory series is, of course, the Scale of Being. Darwin speaks of the whole organic world as tending inevitably to "progress toward perfection." He pronounces that "among the vertebrata the degree of intellect and *an approach in structure to man clearly come into play.*"[67]

At least once more Darwin seems to imply that other primates would tend to evolve toward man if given the opportunity. In 1860 we find him writing to Lyell: "The simile of man now keeping down any new man which might be developed strikes me as good and new. The white man is 'improving off the face of the earth' even races nearly his equals."[68] Implicit also in this remark is

---

[66] F. J. Teggart, *Theory of History*, Yale University Press, 1935, p. 132.

[67] *Origin of Species*, New York, Modern Library ed., p. 93. (Italics mine. L.E.)

[68] LLD, Vol. 2, p. 344. Actually this idea was first advanced by Lamarck.

a growing need to explain the gap between man and his nearest relatives because natural selection can make each creature only a little more perfect than its competitors. Since the phylogenetic series is now historical the past must be searched and the man-creating, competitive intermediate links in the chain will be found there.

In the meantime, however, the concept "atavism," emerging out of the misinterpreted heredity studies carried out upon recent domesticated forms, promised a way of seeing the ancestor in the flesh without waiting for the laborious uncertainties of paleontological research. It is this which explains the popularity of Vogt's suggestion and the interest that the idea aroused in Darwin. By contrast, the big-brained Neanderthals, especially after the Spy discovery, must have seemed to the Darwinians at the very least anomalous, if not threatening, to their theories.[69] Neither Cro-Magnons nor Neanderthals showed the rapid mental regress which had been assumed, in the underestimated time scale of that day, to characterize the skulls of genuine primitives, particularly in the light of the assumptions which had been made about various of the living races of man. It disturbed the old ideas of continuity and progression and is undoubtedly one of the reasons why these first fossil forms were eyed with hesitation. Sollas's statement of his paradox of increasing brain size makes this quite clear.

At first, since by the law of the old Scale nothing became extinct, men had tended unconsciously to see their past story totally revealed among the living races hidden away in the forests. They had seen the half man pass in the jungle; they had interpreted lowly cultures as a sign of lowly brains. Later, as the forests were cleared and the

[69] Darwin, for example, seizes with eagerness upon Broca's suggestion that large cranial size in early man represents a more selected mean than among modern civilized peoples where the weak survive. This clashes, of course, with his cranial statistics aimed to demonstrate the superiority of Caucasians over other existing races. (*Descent of Man,* Modern Library ed., pp. 436–37.)

apes were seen in the sunlight, the gap loomed a little larger between man and his beasts.

It was then that his isolation struck him most clearly. He stared thoughtfully at the tiny-brained among his kind. He dug in the earth and found bones beneath it. He began to sense that the wondrous chain was moving, climbing, perishing. He found his own lost, bestial skull in the drift by the river, and the flints that his hands had tried to shape. At first he sought to run away from the sight of these things or to tell the tale differently. In the end it could no longer be done. The tale will tell itself and man will listen. He is quite alone now. In spite of claims that persisted into the beginning of this century, his brothers in the forest do not speak. Unutterably alone, man senses the great division between his mind and theirs. He has completed a fearful passage, but of its nature and causation even the modern biologist is still profoundly ignorant.

Chapter XI

Wallace and the Brain

The difference between the hand of a monkey and the hand of a man may seem small when they are both placed on the dissecting table, but in that difference whatever it may be, lies the whole difference between an organ limited to the climbing of trees or the plucking of fruit, and an organ which is so correlated with man's inventive genius that by its aid the Earth is weighed and the distance of the sun is measured.

Duke of Argyll

I The Darwinian Bias

"As evolution came to be the reigning hypothesis among men of science," remarked a contemporary observer, "it was to be anticipated that its central problem, the origin of the human mind, would demand consideration."[1] We have seen in the last chapter that one of the strongest unconscious motivations of the Darwinians was to draw human and animal nature, as well as anatomy, as close to each other as possible in the hope of thereby minimizing the evolutionary gap which mentally, at least, yawned between man and his existing primate relatives. There is

[1] Anonymous, "The Origin of Intellect," *Edinburgh Review,* 1889, Vol. 170, p. 359.

no need to read unscrupulous intentions into this situation. It was a natural response to the circumstances of an age of transition. Man, theologically, had for so long been accorded a special and supernatural place in creation that the evolutionists, in striving to carry their point that he was intimately related to the rest of the world of life, sought to emphasize those characteristics which particularly revealed our humble origins.

Today the intellectual climate has so changed that it is possible to find oneself totally misunderstood by cultivated people who assume that any serious examination of Darwinian ideas involves the repudiation of evolution or the principle of natural selection. Before entering further on this subject, therefore, let us examine certain detailed tenets of Darwin's thinking upon man. In subjecting certain of these ideas to critical scrutiny in the light of modern knowledge it is not implied that we are, in any sense, challenging the validity of Darwin's major thesis that man is both related to the existing monkeys and apes and has descended from some early and primitive group within the primate order. In attempting to bolster his scientific position, however, in a time when little in the way of paleontological materials was available, Darwin made use of hypotheses which we would be forced largely to repudiate today.

1. In making use of the living taxonomic ladder he implies marked differences in the inherited mental faculties between the members of the different existing races.[2] This point of view unconsciously reflects the old Scale of Nature and the tacit assumption that the races of today in some manner represent a sequence in time, a series of living fossils, with western European man standing biologically at the head of the procession.

2. Darwin assumed that "when at a remote epoch the progenitors of man were in a transitional state . . . natu-

2 *Descent of Man*, 2d revised ed., New York, 1874, pp. 30, 178. VAP, Vol. 2, p. 63. Also LLD, Vol. 2, p. 211.

ral selection would probably have been greatly aided by the inherited effects of the increased or diminished use of different parts of the body."³ This Lamarckian effect of habit he extended to such cultural activities as hunting and fishing techniques.⁴

3. He ascribes to the La Naulette jaw, which we discussed in the previous chapter, the "enormous" canines which the workers of this period frequently assumed would be found upon primitive specimens of man.⁵

4. Darwin assumes that in man the "vocal organs have become adapted through the inherited effects of use for the utterance of articulate language."⁶ Since language constitutes one of the most striking distinctions between man and the animal world about him, it was almost inevitable that the evolutionary school would seek to reduce its importance as confined to humanity alone. Thus at the very end of the century Haeckel was still insisting that animals were capable of incipient speech, and an enormous amount of poorly rewarded effort has gone into the attempt to teach the existing apes to talk or to formulate and use a few words.

Darwin and his followers actually obscured the whole problem by not differentiating clearly between the signal cries of animals and the symbolism of true speech.⁷ They tended to slur over a very difficult and complex question at the same time that they were successful in drawing attention to the fact that if man is a part of the rest of nature, language, too, must have evolved in some way. The obscurity and vagueness of the Darwinian approach to language lies in the fact that in spite of a certain use of signal cries of a largely instinctive nature, animals show no tendency to increase their vocabularies or to transform

³ *Descent of Man,* 2d ed., New York, 1874, p. 40.
⁴ Ibid., p. 37. See also LLD, Vol. 3, p. 90.
⁵ Ibid., pp. 46, 60.
⁶ Ibid., p. 56.
⁷ See, for example, Ibid., pp. 98–99.

vague emotional cries into specific symbols capable of manipulating the past and future. There is a recognizable gap here which the Darwinists in the first flush of their enthusiasm tried altogether to minimize. It is not necessary to belabor the point except to observe that there were attempts at first to equate living peoples with various levels of linguistic development which, in time, proved unsatisfactory.[8]

In the arguments which arose upon the subject of man, his animal relationships, his uniqueness or lack of uniqueness as various writers saw the story, the position of Alfred Russel Wallace came to differ markedly from that of Charles Darwin and most of his followers. The episode is a curious and dramatic one in the history of science —more particularly because certain of Wallace's observations were more perceptive than most of the writers of his own day—even though in other particulars he relapsed into a somewhat mystical approach. Moreover, the whole episode has been dramatically re-emphasized in modern times by the revelation of the Piltdown forgery. In pursuing the meaning of this somewhat involved series of events it will do no harm to examine Wallace's first contacts with Darwin. As is well known he arrived independently at the principle of natural selection and shares with Darwin a pre-eminent position in nineteenth-century biology.

II   Alfred Russel Wallace (1823–1913)

If any additional proof were needed that the first half of the "wonderful century" was stirring with half-

[8] Henry C. Chapman in his *Evolution of Life* (Philadelphia 1873) said that "the roots in the languages of the lowest races of mankind resemble the sounds made by monkeys" (pp. 172–73). Innumerable similar remarks exist in the literature of the period. "Even to this day," comments one writer as late as 1914, "there are said to be some low tribes in South America whose spoken language is so imperfect that they cannot converse in the dark." *Science Progress*, 1914, Vol. 8, p. 524.

formulated evolutionary ideas, the life of Wallace would supply such evidence. Born into modest economic circumstances and in his own words "shy, awkward and unused to good society,"[9] Wallace had, unlike Darwin, little in the way of educational advantages. Like so many Englishmen of the period, however, he acquired early a taste for nature. While working as a teacher at a private school in Leicester in 1844 he read Humboldt and Malthus, both of whom made a profound impression upon him. Earlier he had read Sir Charles Lyell's *Principles*, Chambers' *Vestiges*, and Darwin's *Journal of Researches*. Wallace was a convinced evolutionist with the same reading background as Darwin before he went to South America with his friend Henry Walter Bates as a beetle and butterfly collector in 1848. He spent four years wandering in the Amazon valley before going on a second collecting expedition to the Far East in 1854. It was here, on the island of Ternate in 1858, that Wallace, while suffering from an attack of fever, conceived the idea of natural selection.

Although he once generously compared his own part in the evolutionary story as one week to Darwin's twenty years, the truth was that Wallace had contemplated variation in wild nature for many years; moreover he was fully cognizant of, and sympathetic with, the evolutionary point of view. Somewhat like Darwin earlier, he had been mulling over his observations for some ten years before he was struck by this sudden flash of insight. It must be recognized, however, that although Wallace conceived his theory independently he had actually been stimulated not alone through perusing Darwin's *Journal of Researches* but also through direct correspondence with Darwin. Darwin had written to Wallace that he agreed heartily with an earlier (1855) paper expressing evolutionary views and that "they had thought much alike."[10]

Correspondence indicates that Darwin had told Wal-

[9] *My Life*, New York, 1905, Vol. 1, p. 433.
[10] LLD, Vol. 2, p. 95.

lace he was working on "the species problem." He generously urged Wallace on in his own speculations, but
politely declined to divulge his own theory prematurely.
There is thus clear documentation which, while establishing Wallace's own claims to originality, indicates at the
same time that this very astute and perceptive young
naturalist was running hot on Darwin's trail. His curiosity
must have been intense and there is every indication that
even if the memory of Malthus provided a spark, Wallace, like Darwin, had long pondered "the great work of
Lyell."[11]

When Wallace sent his theory to Darwin and there
occurred that mutual nobility of behavior so justly cele-
brated in the annals of science—a tolerance and recognition of their two claims which led to the reading of their
preliminary papers jointly before the Linnean Society in
1858—a new world had opened up for man. Even those
who loathe the very names of Wallace and Darwin today
seek out unquestioningly, when ill, doctors whose whole
medical training is postulated upon evolutionary principles, whose medical experiments are based upon the fact
that one form of life is related to another. As we examine
the skulls of primitive men which reveal the tremendous
physical changes man has undergone in the last million
years, the thought must inevitably cross our minds that
the unfixed but imminent future yawns before us; that
our acts may ensure the disappearance of our species from
the earth or, on the contrary, that we, like these small-
brained, massive-jawed forerunners of ours, may be the
bridge to a higher form of life than has yet appeared.
"Mother Nature," as Charles Kingsley, a nineteenth-
century minister once said, "lets things make themselves."
There is a great deal in that remark for the human species
to ponder.

Scarcely had the two leading exponents of natural
selection launched upon their evolutionary careers before

11 *My Life*, Vol. 1, pp. 354–55.

they came to differ, and to differ profoundly, upon the subject of human origins. Upon the development of the animal world alone Darwin and Wallace might have continued to agree. Man, however, is an elusive and, even to himself, mysterious subject. It was not long before these two great scholars had fallen into disagreement—though never into dislike of each other. The story is an interesting one—little told, almost forgotten in the dust of years—but emerging with renewed significance upon the discovery of the Piltdown fraud in 1953.

III Darwin and Human Evolution

As we have already had occasion to remark, Darwin, save for a passing sentence, reserved his opinions upon man when he wrote the *Origin of Species*. Later, in 1871, he published a selection of materials intended to demonstrate man's relationship to the higher animals "especially the anthropomorphous apes."[12] Although he expressed a general caution that "we must not fall into the error of supposing that the early progenitor of the whole Simian stock, including man, was identical with, or even closely resembled, any existing ape or monkey,"[13] it was inevitable that the dearth of human fossils would focus attention on the existing great apes. These animals were regarded by Darwin as being in an "intermediate condition" between a quadruped and biped.[14] It was not clearly foreseen in Darwin's time that the existing great apes, in many of their characters, reveal divergent specializations which need not necessarily be attributed to the early human forerunners. While it is a subject which we do not have space to pursue here, it may be noted that Darwin's conception of huge canine teeth in man's immediate ancestry has not been borne out by modern paleontological

12 *Descent of Man*, 2d ed., New York, 1874, p. 9.
13 Ibid., p. 176.
14 Ibid., p. 59.

discoveries and, in addition, it seems extremely unlikely that man ever passed through a modern chimpanzee- or gorilla-like postural stage in his achievement of the upright position.[15]

The question of the place of origin and the size of the human ancestor left Darwin divided between two possibilities: a large gorilloid type of primate whose homeland was very likely Africa, or some smaller, weaker anthropoid which might have inhabited a large island such as New Guinea or Borneo. In terms of his enthusiasm for "natural selection arising from the competition of tribe with tribe," Darwin, left to himself, might have been inclined toward the first hypothesis, as indeed his projection of huge canine teeth upon Neanderthal man and his suggestion of traces of a sagittal crest among male Australians strongly intimate.

There was, however, an obstacle to this approach. One of Darwin's opposition, the Duke of Argyll, in his volume *Primeval Man* published in 1869, had raised a very legitimate question. He had called attention to the fact that in comparison with many mammals man is physically weak, and, except for his brain, has no really specialized survival mechanisms. How then, contended the Duke, could the human ancestor according to the demands of natural selection "have been modified in the direction of greater weakness without inevitable destruction, until first by the gift of reason and of mental capacities of contrivance, there had been established an adequate preparation for the change?"[16]

Now although the Duke of Argyll's challenge was legitimate—he had raised a question based upon man's generalized physical attributes—it is clear he had drawn

[15] For more extended discussion of this subject the reader should consult R. I. Pocock, "The New Heresy of Man's Descent," *Conquest*, 1920, Vol. 1, pp. 151–57, and W. L. Straus, Jr., "The Riddle of Man's Ancestry," *The Quarterly Review of Biology*, 1949, Vol. 24, pp. 200–23.

[16] New York edition of 1884, p. 22.

something of a false contrast between intellect and physique, as well as equated the physical frailties of living savages with what fossil evidence now tells us were our more rugged Pleistocene ancestors. There was, in other words, another way of answering the Duke's objection, but Darwin, partly because of his very emphasis upon struggle, could not perceive it. As a consequence, he took refuge in his second hypothesis—that which conceived of the human forerunner as a less formidable primate. An ancestor like the gorilla, Darwin cautioned, "possessing great size, strength and ferocity" might never have become social. "Hence," he concludes, "it might have been an immense advantage to man to have sprung from some comparatively weak creature."

No sooner had Darwin given vent to this view, however, than it must have occurred to him that he was in danger of giving the Duke of Argyll another opportunity to attack him by means of the "weak creature" of rather un-Darwinian qualities which he had postulated. Darwin had once jokingly termed himself a "master wriggler" and these powers are not unobservable in the way he met the implied threat to his second hypothesis. It was quite conceivable, he contended, that the ancestors of man, "even if far more helpless and defenseless than any existing savages," had inhabited some safe island, or continent like Australia, until they had achieved sufficient intellect to be a match for the more formidable dangers of the major land masses. There is more than a hint of the Golden Age, of lost echoes from the Earthly Paradise, in this conception. Some of his German followers · added a final touch by suggesting that it was in Australia that man had learned to speak by listening to the beautiful voices of singing birds.[17]

This idyllic vision is quite in contrast with Darwin's usual emphasis on the major continents where, "in the

[17] W. J. Sollas, "The Evolution of Man," *Scientia*, 1911, Vol. 9, p. 136.

larger country, there will have existed more individuals and more diversified forms, and the competition will have been severer."[18] In a way, such maneuvers are rather characteristic of late Darwinian days before Weismann, Mendel, and the rise of experimental genetics. There was a great deal of theorizing on very little evidence and if one encountered a stiff argument it was easy to add an ancillary hypothesis or make out a special case. Since Darwin was making extensive use of *both* natural selection and inheritance of habit, there was really no way in which he could lose such an argument as that described above so long as it was not solvable by experiment. Slowly, however, a certain accumulation of paleontological and archaeological information was taking place. It was this fact, even as early as 1864, that had led Wallace to entertain a new conception of human evolution—an idea overlooked by Darwin—which was destined to influence profoundly all later thinking on the subject.

Before launching into a discussion of this conception it is important to make clear the fact that Wallace's original formulation of his ideas had nothing whatever to do with his religious beliefs. Wallace, in his later years, became interested in spiritualism. So greatly has our thinking shifted away from the religious interests of the nineteenth century that to consider, or express approval of, certain of Wallace's ideas is occasionally to find oneself labeled, along with Wallace, as a "mystic." This is particularly ironic because, anthropologically speaking, Wallace was somewhat in advance of his confreres, and made undisputed contributions to our common scientific knowledge, although some of these have been absorbed almost without notice. Modest and solitary by nature, Wallace, unlike Darwin and Huxley, left no scientific descendants to speak for him. A later generation has come to think of him as an old man who had outlived his time, a crotchety

18 O, 6th ed. Modern Library, New York, p. 152.

evolutionist who, in 1913, had refused to be impressed by the fossil skull from Piltdown.[19]

IV Degeneration or Development

When the Ice Age began to be investigated, profound changes in thinking about archaeological problems were brought about. We know, of course, that the abandonment of the idea of a universal deluge and of the conception of special creation forced great alterations in religious belief. Less well known, as observed in the chapter upon the missing links, is the fact that the evolutionists themselves were destined to have some of their own preconceptions shattered. So long as the emphasis upon the living scale of relationships had existed, there had been an unconscious tendency to rank the living races upon a succession of evolutionary levels, and to incorporate the existing anthropoids into the system.

Thus Haeckel at one time suggested that he had heard "remarkable clicking sounds" in the noises made by apes, and expressed the conviction that these sounds are still present in the language of the Bushmen.[20] Others maintained that the languages of savage nations were extremely simple, "often not rivalling even that of the children of the civilized."[21] "In trying . . . to show that man differs from animals only in degree, not in kind," wrote Henry Chapman, who reflects the typical ideas of his period, "we hope to have made out a series of transitional forms, beginning with the lower monkeys and ascending from them, through the higher apes and the lower races of mankind to the higher. Thus the skulls of the Chim-

[19] James Marchant, *Alfred Russel Wallace: Letters and Reminiscences,* New York, 1916, p. 347.

[20] See Walter Smith, "Why Is the Human Ear Immobile?" *Popular Science Monthly,* 1904, Vol. 65, p. 225.

[21] H. C. Chapman, op. cit., p. 172.

panzee, Idiot, Negro and Kalmuck offer a series of ascending forms."[22]

It becomes obvious, in the light of such views, that however much Darwin may have talked of the great length
of the time scale, such assumptions as those of Chapman,
Haeckel, and numerous others would stand in more or less
unspoken opposition to an extended history for man. If the
sequence of ascent was almost totally visible in the living
world, how could it, in reality, be very greatly extended
in time? There was, in other words, an unspoken contradiction between the geological demands upon the past
and the emphasis of the biologist, particularly in the case
of man, upon the living scale of life. The eighteenth century, it is evident, still possessed great power over men's
minds.

When, therefore, tools and implements began to be
traced into Ice Age gravels, and when, moreover, it was
seen that these tools were primitive, even though found
in an area of present-day high civilization, there was a
quickening of interest in evolutionary circles. It was already known that the Pleistocene fauna of Europe differed markedly from that of the present, and that several
huge beasts such as the hairy mammoth had completely
vanished. Awareness of these faunal modifications led to
the assumption that when man was found at such levels
he would prove to be very primitive—a real missing link
—of a kind mentally comparable to microcephals and Hottentots. If the big mammals had changed there seemed
no reason to suppose that man had not likewise altered
in appearance. In fact, so strong had this preconception
become that there arose a tendency to see, even among
remains that we would now classify as mesolithic, evidences of biological inferiority. Even when the form of
the skulls belied such a judgment it was argued that these
crania, though indistinguishable from those of modern

22 Op. cit., p. 169.

man, must have contained less gray matter and more interstitial tissue.[23]

Such a climate of thought caused the rejection, at first, of clues to the life habits of our upper paleolithic ancestors.[24] Many did not believe paleolithic men to have been mentally capable of burying their dead, and regarded their mural art with incredulity. As it began to be realized that the Engis skull and other Cro-Magnon specimens revealed no signs of biological inferiority, the notion that simple technological developments could be equated with inferior brains received a severe blow. European man was now looking upon the remains of his own ancestors, both physically and culturally. In physique and skull capacity they were his equals, if not superiors. Even the poorly understood Neanderthal calvarium had housed a large brain.

At this point there arose in English intellectual circles a considerable debate between the evolutionists and what we may term the "degenerationists." The "degeneration" school of thought has a long and interesting history which can be pursued into pre-evolutionary times as a pessimistic phase of Christian philosophy related to the doctrine of the Fall of Man and the idea of the sin of the microcosm (man) infecting the macrocosm (the universe).[25] In its new phase at the mid-nineteenth century it represented the last stand of the special creationists

[23] Rudolph Virchow, *Freedom of Science in the Modern State*, London, 1878, pp. 58–61. Virchow himself, however, did not accept this.

[24] Glyn Daniel, *A Hundred Years of Archaeology*, Duckworth, London, 1950, p. 97.

[25] Ronald W. Hepburn, "George Hakewill: The Virility of Nature," *Journal of the History of Ideas*, 1955, Vol. 16, pp. 135–50. The whole earlier history of the subject has been excellently treated in Ernest Tuveson's *Millennium and Utopia*, University of California Press, Berkeley, 1949, and in Victor Harris's *All Coherence Gone*, University of Chicago Press, 1949. E. S. Carpenter has devoted attention to its nineteenth-century aspect in his paper "The Role of Archaeology in the 19th Century Controversy Between Developmentalism and Degeneration," *Pennsylvania Archaeologist*, 1950, Vol. 20, pp. 5–18.

against human evolution. In brief compass, this school of thought regarded existing savages, not as surviving fossils representing the past condition of man, but rather as degenerate peoples fallen away from a more ideal condition. Richard Whately (1787–1863), Archbishop of Dublin, was a leading mid-century exponent of this point of view.[26] His influence in conservative circles was powerful, and he had, moreover, the effect of bestirring even his scientific opponents with the necessity of making a response.

Using the fact that modern natives often proved intractable and averse to the acceptance of cultural traits from Western society, the Bishop argued that savages were incapable of raising themselves to civilized levels by their own efforts. In the beginning, therefore, civilized man could not have achieved this status unaided, but must have received a divine revelation. Basically the Bishop was using the uninventiveness of man as a premise in a manner—minus its theological trappings—not too distinct from that of some of the more extreme diffusionists of the early twentieth century. A considerable debate arose and was continued over a score of years. Some, as Hugh Miller had earlier done, argued that "the farther we remove in any direction from the Adamic center [presumably Palestine], the more animalized and sunk do we find the various tribes or races."[27]

A writer in *The Contemporary Review* observed that "In the savage races of the present day we seem to find the human faculties, not in their fresh virgin state, tending to develop into something better, but arrested and benumbed by long acquiescence in grovelling habits. Therefore I think that we are justified in regarding these races as the swamps and backwaters of the stream of

[26] Richard Whately, "On the Origin of Civilization," *Miscellaneous Lectures and Reviews*, London, 1861, pp. 26–59. The paper dates originally to 1854.

[27] *Testimony of the Rocks*, Edinburgh, 1869, pp. 229–30.

noble humanity, and not as the representatives of the fountainhead from which it has been derived."[28] The fall of the ancient civilizations of the Near East and the more recently discovered remains of the Moundbuilders were all presented as clear-cut evidence that man was capable of relapsing from a civilized state.[29] The controversy echoed in the meetings of the British Association and prominent scholars aligned themselves on one side or another.[30] The entire dilemma was succinctly presented by C. J. D'Oyly when he remarked: "If the Caucasian appeared first, then a degenerating principle, which is observed in no other part of creation, has been allowed to operate, but if the Caucasian has appeared *last*, then the law of human life, like that of all other organized beings, has been progressive."[31] This remark, which contains three interesting items, is worth consideration. It is revelatory of the white, ethnocentric bias of western Europe in the nineteenth century, it reveals a general acceptance of the evolution of "all other organized beings," but it pauses over what was, given the intellectual climate of the time, an unanswerable question: were the traces of man in the earth a sign of feet going down or of footsteps ascending?

The degenerationists had neatly inverted the anthropological argument for evolution: man had not arisen from savagery; he had sunk to it, particularly in those regions most peripheral to Europe. To prove their point lay the Sphinx brooding over fallen Egypt. In the Guatemalan jungles the mathematical computations of the Mayan astronomer-priests lay lost and unread beneath the hungry rootlets of the rain forest. Who could say that

[28] A. Grant, "Philosophy and Mr. Darwin," *The Contemporary Review*, 1871, Vol. 17, p. 281.

[29] H. B. Tristram, "Recent Geographical and Historical Progress in Zoology," *The Contemporary Review*, 1866, Vol. 2, p. 124.

[30] For a contemporary analysis of some of the leading arguments and books see J. Hannah, "Primeval Man," *The Contemporary Review*, 1869, Vol. 2, pp. 161–77.

[31] "Man In Creation," *The Contemporary Review*, 1868, Vol. 8, p. 555.

whole nations had not fallen from their once high estate? Steps going up or steps coming down—but how was the archaeologist and ethnologist to judge which, particularly when he was considering peoples without written history, wandering, perhaps, on the bleak shores of Patagonia.

In reality both schools of thought were obsessed with one-way processes operating in diametrically opposed directions. The evolutionists, in addition, were struggling to align materials of a widely scattered and unrelated nature. So long as the paleontological record of man was almost lacking, his cultural remains could be read just as easily in terms of peripheral peoples fallen on evil days, and culturally deteriorated, as they could be interpreted in terms of stages in human advancement. This problem was stated with great objectivity by Rudolf Schmid. "Archaeology," he remarked, "seems to do no more than admit that its results can be incorporated into the theory of an origin of the human race through gradual development, *if* this theory can be shown to be correct in some other way, and that its results can just as well be brought into harmony with a contradictory theory."[32] No simple tool, of and by itself, would be sufficient to prove "that there was a condition of mankind lying near that of animals."[33]

Grant Allen had been forced to admit that the antiquity of man was growing more far reaching in its implications than had been at first imagined. Instead of being the "missing link," the cave man appeared to be "a mere average savage." The Darwinists seemed confronted either with no traces of man at all or with man essentially like that of the present day.[34] Having now reviewed the problem created by the discovery of the glacial antiquity of European man, let us examine its bearing on the thought of Alfred Russel Wallace.

[32] *The Theories of Darwin and Their Relation to Philosophy, Religion and Morality*, Chicago, 1883, p. 91.
[33] Ibid., p. 90.
[34] "Who Was Primitive Man?" *Fortnightly Review*, 1882, Vol. 38, pp. 308–9.

V Wallace and Human Antiquity

If one glances at the map of Wallace's eastern wanderings, one is immediately struck by the many lines which cross and crisscross among the innumerable islands of the Malay Archipelago.[35] They represent the journeys of Wallace over a period of eight years—eight years of passage, often by native *prau*, among the dangerous reefs and shoals of the eastern seas; eight years among the fevers, the leeches, the ten-inch scorpions; eight years among the solitudes of the great forests. Darwin and Huxley had seen natives in the days of their voyages, but neither had depended so completely or in such a fashion as Wallace upon their good will. It is interesting to observe that Wallace reveals scarcely a trace of the racial superiority so frequently manifested in nineteenth-century scientific circles. "The more I see of uncivilized people, the better I think of human nature," he wrote to a friend in 1855, "and the essential differences between civilized and savage men seem to disappear."[36]

When reviewing Walter Bagehot's *Physics and Politics* for *Nature* in later years, his old thoughts returned. "We find many broad statements as to the low state of morality and of intellect in all prehistoric men," he commented critically, "which facts hardly warrant."[37] So strongly did he differ from the major tendency to arrange natives on decreasing levels of intellect and to picture them as depraved in habits that Sir John Lubbock commented that Wallace's description of savage people differed greatly from that of earlier observers.[38] Somewhere on the seas or in the forests, accompanied by his faithful Malay, Ali, he had ceased to be impressed by the typical conception

[35] *My Life*, New York, 1905, Vol. 1, p. 368.
[36] Ibid., p. 342.
[37] "Modern Applications of the Doctrine of Natural Selection," *Nature*, 1873, Vol. 7, p. 277.
[38] "The Malayan Archipelago," *Macmillan's Magazine*, 1869, Vol. 19, p. 533.

of the native as a physical and mental fossil. With these attitudes and, paradoxically, being at the same time a confirmed evolutionist, he had returned to England. There he had encountered the degeneration doctrine in the early sixties.

Wallace was a man who went his own way. Evolutionist though he was, he had been impressed by some lectures given by a Mr. Albert Mott, the president of the Liverpool Philosophical Society. Mr. Mott appears to have regarded modern man as being basically in no way morally superior to his ancestors. In addition he had advanced the view that savages were often the descendants of more civilized races.[39] Although we do not possess the entire record of Wallace's thinking during the period just prior to 1864, when he published his first great addition to the theory of evolution, we can, nevertheless, discern certain stages in the development of his thought as it progresses through several successive contributions. We can begin with his statement of 1864, which received the approbation of Darwin.[40]

In this paper, which marks the beginning of Wallace's divergence from Darwin, we may note three things: (1) he seeks to account for the apparent long-time stability in the appearance of the human species as compared with the faunal variations observable in the upper Pleistocene; (2) he attempts to explain the racial varieties of man on another basis than that of successive stages; (3) he points out, for the first time, that with the rise of the human brain the whole nature of the natural selection process has altered.

[39] James Marchant, *Alfred Russel Wallace: Letters and Reminiscences*, New York, 1916, p. 335. I have been able to find a record of one paper of Mott's delivered before the Liverpool Philosophical Society on October 6, 1873. It is entitled "On the Origin of Savage Life." St. George Mivart quotes extensively from it in his *Lessons from Nature*, New York, 1876, p. 148 ff.

[40] A. R. Wallace, "The Origin of Human Races and the Antiquity of Man Deduced from the 'Theory of Natural Selection,'" *Anthropological Review*, 1864, Vol. 2, pp. clviii–clxxxvii.

It should be emphasized once more that there is nothing whatever of a mystical or theological point of view in this paper. It clings carefully to the basic Darwinian formulation of insensible variations selected for survival through the struggle for existence. Darwin himself received the paper with manifestations of pleasure and interest. In a letter to Hooker in May of 1864 he wrote: "I have now read Wallace's paper on Man, and think it most striking and original and forcible. I wish he had written Lyell's chapters on Man. . . . I am not sure that I fully agree with his views about Man, but there is no doubt, in my opinion, on the remarkable genius shown by the paper. I agree, however, to the main new leading idea."[41] Actually Darwin's point of difference with Wallace at this time revolved around comparatively minor matters involving racial differentiation which Wallace, in a letter to Darwin, clarified more fully and satisfactorily than in his paper.[42]

Wallace set out to explain the apparent stability of the human stock by pointing out that it was necessary to account for the fact that the bodily differences between man and the great apes were small but that the gap between them in mental and cranial characters was vast. Unlike some of the other Darwinists, he was not greatly impressed by the living taxonomic scale, nor did he regard modern primitives as almost filling in the gap between man and ape. In effect, what Wallace proposed would run somewhat as follows: he saw the evolution of man as occurring really in two stages. The first would have been represented by the series of physical changes which culminated in his achievement of bipedal posture and the freeing of the hands as implements to carry out the dictates of the brain. This earlier phase of human evolution, whatever the forces that promoted it, was the product of the same type of natural selection that had produced a

[41] MLD, Vol. 2, pp. 31–32.
[42] Ibid., pp. 35–36.

seal's flipper or the wing of a bird. It was, essentially, an evolution of *parts*, specializations promoting certain adaptive ecological adjustments of the individual. This type of evolutionary adjustment is omnipresent in the living world. It has led to the discovery of the principles of comparative anatomy and adaptive radiation. The investigation of the mechanisms involving the production of new organs and the alteration of living forms occupies the whole of the *Origin of Species*.

The second stage in human evolution, however—the stage which represents Wallace's original contribution to the subject, and which elicited admiring plaudits from Darwin—involves his recognition of the role of the human brain as a totally new factor in the history of life. Wallace was apparently the first evolutionist to recognize clearly and consciously and with a full grasp of its implications the fact that, with the emergence of that bodily specialization which constitutes the human brain, bodily specialization itself might be said to be outmoded. The evolution of parts, the evolution of the sort of unconscious adaptations which are to be observed in the life cycle of a complicated parasite or the surgical mouth parts of a vampire bat, had been forever surpassed. Nature, instead of delimiting through *parts* a creature confined to some narrow niche of existence, had at last produced an organism potentially capable of the endless inventing and discarding of parts through the medium of a specialized organ whose primary purpose was, paradoxically, the *evasion* of specialization.

The long dominance of partitive evolution, with its choking of life in blind alleys having no evolutionary outlet, was at last over. However imperfect this new brain might be, it had opened up new vistas which, if not limitless, were as yet beyond human experience. There had come into existence, Wallace emphasized, a being in whom mind was of vastly greater importance than bodily structure. For the first time there was offered to a complex living creature the possibility of escape from the endless paleontological story of a generalized animal becoming increasingly specialized until the destruction of its ecological niche foretells its own extinction. Man has the possibilities within him of remaining in the body he now inhabits while whole faunas rise and change or pass away. "We must look," said Wallace, "very far in the past to find man in that early condition in which his mind was not sufficiently developed to remove his body from the modifying influence of external conditions and the cumulative action of 'natural selection.'"[43]

Wallace, in other words, conceived of man's body, even though he made allowance for certain continuing minor selective effects, as having reached a kind of timeless aspect in the midst of universal change. "My argument is," he wrote to Darwin, "that this great cranial difference has been slowly developing while the rest of the skeleton has remained nearly stationary; and while the Miocene Dryopithecus has been modified into the existing gorilla, speechless and ape-brained man (but yet *man*) has been developed into great-brained, speech forming man."[44]

The order of time necessary to bridge the difference between the cranium of an ape and a man he suggested might be enormous and as quite possibly extending into the middle Tertiary. "While the animals which surrounded him have been undergoing modification in *all* parts of their bodies to a *generic* or even family degree of difference he [man] has been changing almost wholly in the head." Ten million years or more might be involved in this peculiar evolutionary development. It had been absurd from the first to expect to see the human phylogeny revealed among the historic races or among upper paleolithic Cro-Magnons. The major racial criteria, he was inclined to believe, dated to the infancy of the race before man was able successfully to protect his body from

[43] Op. cit., p. clxvii.
[44] *My Life*, Vol. 1, p. 419.

change.[45] In any case he thought the advantage of his theory lay in its perception of a heretofore unrecognized aspect of evolution and, along with this, a point of view which "neither requires us to depreciate the intellectual chasm which separates man from the apes, nor refuses full recognition of the striking resemblances to them which exists in other parts of his structure."[46]

While Wallace, like Darwin at this time, still conceived of human advance largely in terms of intergroup struggle, it is evident that the long phylogeny he had introduced for man lightened the emphasis upon a short unilinear succession of the modern races. Wallace's ideas had greater Christian appeal and, like the degenerationists, he recognized the fact that the decline of elaborate civilizations was sometimes possible. His "compromise," as in a sense it was, between the evolutionists and the degenerationists, was somewhat face-saving for the less fanatical elements in both parties. The Darwinians liked the new lease on time which had been given them. Huxley was willing to consider a Miocene date for man, and Lyell was intrigued by the new hypothesis. Time was still a commodity with which geologists could afford to be bountiful. Moreover, in a world which had yet to yield evidence of genuinely primitive hominids, Wallace had found a way around the big-brained men of the upper Pleistocene. Man might prove to be a very persistent and ancient type in his last, his intellectual phase.

Wallace, however, did not leave the subject alone. He persisted in returning to it in a succession of later papers. In doing so he ended by disturbing Darwin and drawing upon his own head accusations of mysticism. It is at this point that we must proceed with the greatest caution. The controversy is less than a century away and it is easy still

[45] See Stanley Garn, "Race and Evolution," *American Anthropologist*, 1957, Vol. 59, pp. 218–23 for a discussion of modern genetic views on race. Today, so far as racial characteristics go, man is seen as possibly more malleable than Wallace envisaged.

[46] *Anthropological Review*, 1864, Vol. 2, p. clxix.

to find oneself emotionally attracted to one side or the other. What one must do dispassionately is to realize that whatever one may think of certain of Wallace's philosophical interpretations of nature, the man recognized some genuinely unexplained phenomena.

It is an ironic aftermath of the Darwinian era that the two discoverers and popularizers of the theory of natural selection should both have found that doctrine inadequate when applied to man. Wallace made the more spectacular rejection and as a consequence, his own somewhat mystical religious convictions occupied more attention than the problems which he raised. Darwin, by contrast, escaped attention through a gift for being ambiguously inconspicuous. Yet it is plain that the Lamarckianism, which increasingly characterized his later years, is particularly evident in his treatment of man.

VI *The Concept of Latency*

We have already had occasion to observe that from the sixties onward there was a decline in geological prestige. Limitless earthly time was being subjected to the scrutiny of a physics which was intensely conscious of heat loss and the second law of thermodynamics. Kelvin, the odious specter who dogged Darwin's footsteps, threatened to compress the earth's history into something like twenty-five million years. There were physicists who argued for even less. Wallace's generous grant of ten million years, or even more, for the development of man would, according to this system, have taken half of the world's time and left the emergence of the rest of life to be dealt with in a compressed series of episodes remarkably similar to the old catastrophism. Keeping in mind this background of thought to which the Darwinists were being forced to give serious attention, let us now examine Wallace's later contributions to human evolution.

Wallace had always expressed himself as open to con-

viction on the subject of human antiquity, but in propos-
ing his theory that man was very old he had recourse to
no other possibility so long as he abided by strict Darwinian tenets. These included, first, organic change by
almost imperceptible increments, for the Darwinians on
the whole abjured saltatory macro-mutations. Second, for
intensive selection, a considerable emphasis on large populations. Thus Darwin remarked to Lyell in 1860: "Where
there are few individuals variation at most must be
slower."[47] In this same vein Wallace observed in 1876, after
he had begun to entertain other views, that, according to
Darwin's hypothesis, so "distinct a creature as man must
have risen at a very early period into the position of a
dominant race, and spread in dense waves of population
over all suitable portions of the great continent—for this
. . . is essential to rapid developmental progress through
the agency of natural selection." Third, and most important perhaps in its final effect upon the thinking of Wallace, was Darwin's heavy emphasis upon utility, upon
limited perfection. "Natural selection," he had contended
in the *Origin*, "tends only to make each organic being as
perfect as, or slightly more perfect than, the other inhabitants of the same country with which it had to struggle for existence. Natural selection will not produce
absolute perfection."[48]

It was just this reservation when applied to the problem
of the rise of the human brain which led Wallace to break
with the views of his distinguished colleague. In 1869,
much to the dismay of Darwin, he came to the conclusion
that natural selection and its purely utilitarian approach
to life would not account for many aspects and capacities

[47] MLD, Vol. 1, p. 143. Modern students of genetic drift, quantum evolution, and similar subjects will realize that small populations need not inhibit evolutionary change, but this fact was not
grasped in the Darwinian period, which lacked our present knowledge of genetics.

[48] O, pp. 172–73.

of the human brain.[49] Furthermore, he began to express concern over the difficulty of accounting for the absence of numerous human remains in the older geological deposits, if humanity had been indeed as numerous as the Darwinian theory demanded.[50]

Wallace contended in the *Quarterly Review* article, which soon drew the attention of Darwin and Huxley, that the brain of the lowest savages, or even of the known prehistoric races, was little inferior to that of Europeans. "Natural selection," he argued, "could only have endowed the savage with a brain a little superior to that of an ape, whereas he actually possesses one but very little inferior to that of the average member of our learned societies." Today, when careful distinctions are made between natural genetic endowment and cultural inheritance, such a remark does not sound particularly iconoclastic. In the time of Wallace, however, it was a direct challenge to Western ethnocentrism and the whole conception of the native as a living fossil destined to be swept away in the struggle for existence because of his feeble and archaic intellect. In contrast to the apocryphal stories of natives who spoke like monkeys, or were almost mute, Wallace pointed out "that, among the lowest savages with the least copious vocabularies, the capacity of uttering a variety of distinct articulate sounds, and of applying to them an almost infinite amount of modulation and inflection, is not in any way inferior to that of the higher races. An instrument has been developed in advance of the needs of its possessor."

In this last sentence we come upon the clue to all of Wallace's later thinking upon man. He had become firmly convinced that man's latent intellectual powers, even in a savage state, were far in excess of what he might have

[49] "Geological Climates and the Origin of Species," *Quarterly Review*, 1869, Vol. 126, pp. 359–94. Other papers followed. Most of them can be found in the uniform edition of Wallace's works issued by the Macmillan Co. of London.

[50] *Darwinism*, London, 1896, p. 458.

achieved through natural selection alone. "We have to ask," he said later, "what relation the successive stages of improvement of the mathematical faculty had to the life or death of its possessors, to the struggle of tribe with tribe, or nation with nation; or to the ultimate survival of one race and the extinction of another." Musical gifts, high ethical behavior, he had come to doubt as being ever the product of utility in the war of nature. They lay ready for exploitation as much among savages as among the civilized. They were latent powers. "It is a somewhat curious fact," Wallace remarked a little wryly, "that while all modern writers admit the great antiquity of man, most of them maintain the very recent development of his intellect, and will hardly contemplate the possibility of men, equal in mental capacity to ourselves, having existed in prehistoric times."[51] Wallace, in other words, had come to the conclusion that whatever the age of man might eventually prove to be, man's intellectual development had reached, biologically, a high level very long ago. Surveying such aspects of man's mental characters having no apparent relation to his material progress, his curious hairlessness, the structure of his larynx, his adept hand, Wallace was inclined to the belief that "some higher intelligence may have directed the process by which the human race was developed."[52]

"If you had not told me," wrote Darwin after the appearance of the *Quarterly Review* article, "I should have thought your remarks had been added by someone else. As you expected, I differ grievously from you, and am very sorry for it. I can see no necessity for calling in an additional and proximate cause in regard to man."[53] The two men remained friends, but the episode must have left

[51] "Difficulties of Development as Applied to Man," *Popular Science Monthly*, 1876, Vol. 10, p. 65.
[52] *Natural Selection and Tropical Nature*, London, 1895, p. 204. This particular paper, "Limits of Natural Selection in Man," was written in 1870.
[53] Marchant, op. cit., p. 199.

both of them—each in his own way a solitary thinker—a little lonelier. "I hope you have not murdered too completely your own and my child," sighed Darwin tolerantly, though he could never endure "miraculous additions at any one stage of ascent."[54] Others viewed Wallace's case more sympathetically. "If we do not admit that latent capacities in the savage brain were implanted for use at some time in the distant future," wrote one reviewer, "we can only say that they are the result of a force which we do not know, and of a law which we have not grasped."[55]

But the current of the times was running against mysticism and toward a positivist scientific approach. The Pithecanthropus skull cap and the discoveries at Piltdown gave a new impetus to the pursuit of the fossil history of man. The point raised by Rudolf Schmid—that the quarrel between degenerationists and evolutionists had to be settled in some other way than by archaeology—was at last answered by way of paleontology. The degeneration argument was difficult to sustain in the face of so pithecoid a fossil as Pithecanthropus or the ape-jawed creature (later found to be a hoax) from Piltdown.

Wallace's contributions to anthropology, on the other hand, the recognition that man had transferred to his tools and mechanical devices the specialized evolution which so totally involves the world of plants and animals, were absorbed into the general body of scientific knowledge.[56] Absorbed also, though in some degree reluctantly, has been the recognition that the higher intellectual and moral nature of man has been roughly stationary throughout the whole range of historic time and must be distin-

[54] LLD, Vol. 2, p. 211.

[55] Anonymous, "Darwin on the Descent of Man," *Edinburgh Review*, 1871, Vol. 134, p. 204.

[56] The idea was hailed by most of the leading thinkers of the period, including Darwin, Herbert Spencer, Chauncey Wright, James McCosh, Edward S. Morse, E. Ray Lankester, and many others. In the words of John Fiske "it seemed to open up an entirely new world of speculation." (*A Century of Science*, Boston, 1899, p. 104.)

guished from material progress. The Hottentot has ceased to be a step from the monkey people; the Negro's skull is no longer placed on the lecturer's table between that of the gorilla and the Caucasian.

Looking back from this vantage point in time we can recognize that some of the physical features of man which troubled Wallace in terms of the selective forces known in his day can now in some degree be accounted for in terms of pedomorphism—the retention of embryonic or infantile characters into adult life. That such forces have probably played a key part in human evolution is now generally recognized.[57] Wallace observed what he was not in a position to understand. If it led him, finally, away from his fellows toward a somewhat cloud-borne thought, it led him also toward the next century, toward a drama of which he would witness the beginning act before he died in 1913.

VII　Brains and Time

All through the nineteenth century the brain as the most mysterious of human organs had been under examination. It was then, as it is now, "the greatest enigma of modern science." Cuvier as early as 1804 called attention to the possibility of investigating the brains of extinct animals through natural endocasts.[58] Writing in his Notebook of 1837, Darwin foresaw that his theory would "give zest to recent and fossil comparative anatomy; it would lead to the study of instincts, heredity and mind-heredity."[59] In 1851 J. Stanley Grimes (1807–1903), a forgotten American evolutionist, produced a book which, falling

[57] See Gavin de Beer, *Embryos and Ancestors*, 2d rev. ed., Oxford University Press, 1951; also M. F. Ashley Montagu, "Time, Morphology, and Neoteny in the Evolution of Man," *American Anthropologist*, 1955, Vol. 57, pp. 13–27.

[58] Tilly Edinger, "Objets et Resultats de la Paleoneurologie," *Annales de Paleontologie*, 1956, Vol. 42, p. 97.

[59] LLD, Vol. 2, p. 8.

under criticism, he rapidly suppressed; it was entitled *Phreno-Geology: The Progressive Creation of Man, Indicated by Natural History and Confirmed by Discoveries which Connect the Organization and Functions of the Brain with the Successive Geological Periods* (Boston).[60] As the title indicates, Grimes attempted to correlate the various portions of the brain as they were then understood phrenologically with the different geological periods which rendered their emergence necessary.

It is evident that Grimes was acquainted with the work of Von Baer and other European naturalists. His evolutionary philosophy, though crudely entangled with phrenological ideas, contains glimpses of adaptive radiation and of mutations (he terms them "idiosyncracies") such "as to be able to sustain the shock of new circumstances and survive."[61] The book constitutes renewed evidence of the wide dispersal of evolutionary ideas after the success of the *Vestiges* and shows how infinitesimally close some of these writers came to the leading idea of the *Origin*. Grimes, as in so many other cases, did not have the technical background to deal with the ideas he had encountered or the ability to realize which of his own were important. His gropings upon brain evolution, however, are in a sense a prelude to the post-Darwinian recognition that the brain, like other bodily organs, has a history extending into the animal past. In this sense he is a pioneer forerunner of men like the neurologist J. Hughlings Jackson, who, later on in the century, observed that as evolution progresses the higher centers of the brain grow more complex and increasingly independent of the lower centers out of which they evolved.[62]

Two things, however, these students of the evolving brain were unable to say. They could give no answer to

---

[60] Later, in 1881, the work was republished under the title *Problems of Creation* (Chicago).

[61] Op. cit., [in text above] p. 135.

[62] *Evolution and Dissolution of the Nervous System*, London, 1888, p. 38.

the question of how long it had taken that organ to achieve its present status, nor could they be sure whether Wallace was right in his assumption that the human head had undergone its major alterations after a long period of upright terrestrial activity during which a completely non-prehensile foot had been developed. "We may suppose," Wallace had commented, "that when he had reached the erect form and possessed all the external appearance of man, his brain still remained undeveloped."[63] The one phase was merely a specialized adaptation in the old evolutionary sense; the second, involving the brain, had introduced a new power into the universe.

As the attack of physics upon geological time intensified, even Darwin had written to his friend Hugh Falconer: "I should rather like to see it rendered highly probable that the process of formation of a new species was short compared to its duration. . . ." Although he carefully dissociated himself in the same letter from any belief "that new species are suddenly formed like monsters," and emphasized again that species formation was a long process, it is evident that he was willing to consider the possible emergence of a new form in much less time than its after-survival as a species would suggest.[64] Similarly Wallace in 1876, although in the old terms of natural selection he had advocated a very lengthy history for man, was willing to venture that "if . . . continued researches in all parts of Europe and Asia fail to bring to light any proofs of his presence,[65] it will be at least a presumption that he came into existence at a much later date, and by a much more rapid process of development."

Wallace, at this point, could suggest as a "fair argument" only the possibility that man's evolution had been guided by "higher agencies."[66] Since this hypothesis re-

[63] *The Wonderful Century,* New York, 1898, p. 134.
[64] MLD, Vol. 1, p. 244.
[65] That is, in truly ancient deposits.
[66] "Difficulties of Development as Applied to Man," *Popular Science Monthly,* 1876, Vol. 10, p. 65.

moved the issue to the domain of metaphysics, it was not taken seriously in science, and the genuine question which he had raised about human antiquity faded from scientific attention. Although discoveries of fossil human material had been slight, the Pithecanthropus skull cap and thigh bone had suggested a development in which bipedalism, as Wallace had prophesied, preceded the full growth of the brain. Furthermore, the renewed grant of geological time, which emerged after the recognition of radioactivity, made the issue of human antiquity less pressing than it had begun to appear in the last decade of the nineteenth century.

Then in 1912 came the public announcement of the discovery of the Piltdown skull which precipitated the caustic remark from Wallace that "it does not prove much, if anything."* It was, perhaps, Wallace's last comment upon the fossil past of man. He died in November of the following year. It may reasonably be asked why he had dismissed in this cavalier manner the skull with which so many others were impressed—he, the last survivor of those who had fought and won the battle for evolution long ago, he who had lived to see the shadows which had haunted Darwin well-nigh dispelled. Did he have some inkling that the skull was an imposture?[67] It seems unlikely. Rather it may be suspected that in some degree he was actuated by the thought that the skull did not fit his own conception of human evolution.

The Piltdown skull had presented the contemporary workers with a most peculiar situation. Both Pithecanthropus and Piltdown, at the time of discovery, had been assigned very early datings around the Plio-Pleistocene border. Yet the disparity in appearance between the two specimens was such as to suggest quite different evolu-

* Marchant, op. cit., p. 347.
[67] For an account of the exposure of the hoax in 1953 the reader is referred to J. S. Weiner, *The Piltdown Forgery*, Oxford University Press, 1955.

tionary forces at work. The Java cranium, as we have noted, seemed to substantiate Wallace's view of a brain slowly increasing in size long after the attainment of the upright posture. Piltdown, by contrast, with its anthropoid jaw combined with a *sapiens* cranium suggested that the brain had advanced more rapidly than other parts of the body. Suggestions were also made that the creature had not even fully acquired an upright position.[68] So great was the resulting confusion introduced into human paleontology that all kinds of supporting hypotheses and ramifying family trees had to be elaborated to take care of this anomalous situation. Watson, after pointing out in 1928 that the specimens were of approximately the same age, commented that on the analogy of what we knew of evolution in other mammals it should be possible to discover "the characteristic structure of early Pleistocene man." The results of such a comparison, Watson had to confess, were "very disappointing." He found human variability "unusually great," and was only able to reduce the differences by attributing a small and primitive brain to the Piltdown fragments.[69]

Within the last two decades a new and striking series of developments have served to rearouse the long dormant interest in the antiquity of the human line. We here refer to Wallace's second phase of human evolution: that involving the emergence of the true culture-producing brain. In the first place there is a growing body of evidence—not at this writing conclusive, but far more weighty than at the time Wallace first raised the question in 1876—suggesting that in geological terms the evolution

[68] W. P. Pycraft, "The Jaw of Piltdown Man," *Science Progress,* 1917, Vol. 65, p. 391.

[69] D. M. S. Watson, *Paleontology and the Evolution of Man,* Oxford University Press, 1928, pp. 14–19. It should be said in justice to Dr. Watson that many other scholars found similar difficulties and made similar adjustments in dealing with the Piltdown material. His very complaints reveal an intuitive sense that something about the situation was abnormal. I merely use his work to illustrate a general trend of thought.

of the human brain has been extremely rapid. Dr. Tilly Edinger, distinguished paleoneurologist of Harvard University, has commented that enlargement of the cerebral hemispheres by fifty per cent seems to have taken place, geologically speaking, almost instantaneously, without having been accompanied by any marked increase in body size.[70] There are also suggestions, in terms of new dating methods, that the million-year age of the Pleistocene period may be shortened by new studies,[71] which would have the indirect consequence of further reducing the age of the fossil men now known to us. Pithecanthropus, once assigned a late Pliocene age, has long since been correlated with the middle Pleistocene, and a great many, in fact most, of the paleanthropic men remaining to us fall within the latter half of Pleistocene time. Below this level, and stretching backward into the mistier reaches of the lower Pleistocene, the researches of Raymond Dart, Robert Broom, J. T. Robinson, and others have revealed a curious series of anthropoids so close to the human border line that it remains a moot question whether they were already "tool users" in a very primitive way, or whether they are actually bipedal apes whose brains had not achieved even a low "human" level.

Numerous finds and accumulating information may settle these disputed points before long. Whether all of this rather variable assemblage now referred to as the Australopithecine man-apes is on the direct human line of ascent or not, it suggests the postulated earlier omnivorous ground phase of Wallace's twofold scheme of hominid evolution. The variability of the forms themselves unmistakably reminds one also of another aspect of Wallace's thought. In the tropics, he had theorized, perhaps in Africa, "we may trace back the gradually decreasing brain of former races, till we come to a time when the

---

[70] Op. cit., p. 5.

[71] Cesare Emiliani, "Note on Absolute Chronology of Human Evolution," *Science*, 1956, Vol. 123, pp. 924–26.

body also begins materially to differ. There we should reach the starting point of the human family. Before that period [man] had not enough mind to preserve his body from change, and would, therefore, have been subject to the same comparatively rapid modifications of form as other mammals."[72] Curiously enough, of all the ancestral primate relatives of man, these East African grassland apes, if apes they were, have come closest to filling those century-old speculations.

One asks inevitably, and asks again, what forces were at work, if indeed the human brain, as now seems likely, "exploded" so precipitously upon the world. Certainly competitive tribal struggle in the old Darwinian sense would seem to have little to do with man's pedomorphic nakedness and the other curious qualities that drew Wallace's attention long ago. This does not mean that we have to abandon natural selection as a principle, but it is obvious that we must seek selective factors of a sort that Darwin never envisaged, and which may be bound up with speech and social factors difficult to investigate paleontologically. As Watson has remarked, the most fascinating problems of human evolution may actually lie beyond the grasp of the paleontologist who must, of necessity, deal with the shapes of bone. It may be, as he says, that "those structures whose qualities can alone explain the meaning of man's evolution lie beyond his sight."[73] Even a great modern geneticist has confessed humbly: "The causes which have brought about the development of the human species can be only dimly discerned. . . ."[74] H. S. Harrison once put the matter: "Man did very well before he was a man at all, and no one has given any reason why he ceased to be an ape." We are

[72] Op. cit., 1864, p. clxviii.
[73] Watson, op. cit., p. 27.
[74] Theodosius Dobzhansky, *The Biological Basis of Human Freedom*, Columbia University Press, 1956, p. 9.

"trying to understand . . . the way in which natural man became unnatural."[75]

Can it be, one wonders, as one surveys this century-long discussion, that both Darwin and Wallace had within their grasp the general outline of a theory which, without the necessary addition of any metaphysical elements, might have answered some of the questions which so constantly baffled them? With man, as Fiske remarked, one is started upon a new chapter in the history of the universe. It is as though nature had chosen to bypass all her previous experiments in the making of limbs, paddles, teeth, and fins save for one thing: to place a manipulative forelimb under the conscious control of the brain, to totally encephalize the hand. The brain and hand alone will now order the environment that once ordered them. Trees will be cut, fires will be started, flint will fly.

But, asked Wallace, how did it come? Darwin "has taken care to impress upon us that natural selection has no power to produce absolute perfection, no power to advance any being much beyond his fellow beings, but only just so much beyond them as to enable it to survive them in the struggle for existence."[76] The power of natural selection is thus limited, but man, even savage man, sings and dreams, contains within himself vast latent powers that, properly educated, measure worlds and atoms. These powers are not the product of internecine struggle. From whence did they come? A brain a little better than that of a gorilla would have sufficed for man.

Hidden in a few obscure sentences in the *Descent of Man* is Darwin's answer, and it is a tremendous one, so far as his point of view and Wallace's are concerned. Yet in reality it is a sleepwalker's answer, the response of a man so deeply immersed in the thinking of his period

[75] H. S. Harrison, "Evolution in Material Culture," *Report of the British Association for the Advancement of Science*, 1930, p. 140.

[76] A. R. Wallace, *Natural Selection and Tropical Nature*, London, 1895, p. 187.

that his response is like that of an oracle who, in a trance, speaks a prophetic truth but does not envision its consequences. "In many cases," wrote Darwin, "the continued development of a part, for instance of the beak of a bird, or of the teeth of a mammal, would not aid the species in gaining its food, or for any other object; but *with man we can see no definite limit to the continued development of the brain and mental faculties, as far as advantage is concerned.*"[77]

In those words Darwin momentarily broke with his principle of relative or limited perfection because he had realized that the achievement of the reasoning brain swings open a possible door to perfection whose story is not told by the limited advantage of a butterfly's wing— though the life of man may yet prove as airy and as insubstantial as that delicate insect. For an instant, for just a solitary, musing instant as he wrote, the mind that had conceived in youth the whole vast evil and the good of life perhaps heard far-off an opening door. But Darwin was old, and the moment passed. He composed no essay, he made no answer. Across the pages of the selfsame book march struggle and habit, the war of tribe with tribe.

He did not realize, nor did Wallace, without appeal to special intervention, realize that with the shift from the evolution of parts to the evolution of the brain the principle of relative perfection did not rule. Once the higher qualities begin to emerge, man in his loneliness may well have felt drawn to them as even a dog prefers the kinder, understanding hand. Selection, then, to a certain extent, may have come under the guidance of man's nobler nature, just as he unconsciously selected for temperament the kind of animals he wanted. In the words of F. R. Tennant, "The human mind once having attained in the course of evolution to ideation, social intercourse and language, is in a position to develop spontaneously, no longer controlled by mechanical selection (which is but rejec-

[77] Op. cit., p. 169. (Italics mine. L.E.)

tion) but by its own interest and intrinsic potencies. From intelligence and emotional sensibility that are biologically useful it may proceed to disinterested science, to pure mathematics having no relation to the needs of life, to art, morality, and religion, no one of which products, rather than another, requires the *Deus ex machina* to cause its emergence."[78]

These remarks are not given to suggest that every aspect of the rise of the human brain, or the matter of how it came by the curious accelerated spurt which it shows at birth, is fully understood. Rather it is to reiterate that in the expanded cortex of man a new world has opened out. The precise instincts of the lower mammals have been replaced by a highly malleable and adaptive behavior controlled by the culture of the group.

This cultural phase of man, which has seemed to set him off so totally from other animals, has been recently re-examined by A. I. Hallowell, who comes to the conclusion that a false dichotomy has been erected by our tendency to regard existing man as the possessor of "culture," and the animal world, including our primate relatives, as totally lacking in such human traits. "The possession of culture," he writes, "has tended to become an all-or-none proposition."

By contrast he postulates what he terms a proto-cultural stage which might well have been reached early, "even before the development of speech." There may have been some slight degree of tool using, some learned behavior, but not the whole range of activities, including speech, which we now tend to regard as so uniquely human. Because Darwin and his associates pushed living apes too close to living men, a reaction set in which led anthropologists, even while rendering lip service to morphological evolution, to imply that culture is a whole with a "relatively constant categorical content." Culture and

[78] *Philosophical Theology*, Cambridge University Press, 1937, Vol. 2, p. 94.

"man," whatever this latter word might mean in the cloudy borderlands of prehistory, had presumably appeared together.[79] Obviously such a clear-cut artificial distinction interposed a barrier between man and his remote forerunners which would have baffled Darwin and his associates.

Ironically enough, a good bit of the responsibility for this artificial barrier must be attributed to the Darwinian circle. They had been too hasty in their assumption that animals possessed rudimentary speech and that living natives echoed the higher primates in their vocabularies. They had confused culture with biological endowment as thoroughly, perhaps, as later anthropologists have tended to assume that what we call "culture" is a single emergent without rudimentary preliminaries which may even precede language. They had, with such notable and infrequent exceptions as Wallace, contributed, though often unintentionally, to racial prejudice.

Perhaps there is something appropriate, in the end, about the fact that Wallace was a searcher after birds of paradise and that he was a butterfly hunter among the islands of the Coral Sea. He loved beauty, and among the many rarities he came to cherish was the potential moral beauty of man. He found it among simple people and it never passed away from his heart.

[79] A. I. Hallowell, "The Structural and Functional Dimensions of a Human Existence," *The Quarterly Review of Biology*, 1956, Vol. 31, pp. 88–101.

Chapter XII

Conclusion

Life can only be understood backward but
it must be lived forward.

Kierkegaard

I   Time: Cyclic and Historic

In the course of three centuries ideas, like the disintegrating face of Hutton's planet, evolve, erode, and change. Sometimes they are gone in a night without anyone's quite knowing what became of them, or why they had possessed momentarily a kind of demonic power. Again they may last for ages protruding, gaunt, bare, and uncompromising, from the soft sward of later beliefs. Sometimes, in the clouds that pass over the formless landscape of time, they will seem to shift and catch new lights, become transmuted into something other than what they were, grow dull, or glisten with a kind of sunset color reflected from the human mind itself. Of such a nature is that vast monument to human thinking which is now called evolution.

Something of its origins we have learned, a few of the many names that contributed to its substance have taken on a familiar appearance. The idea, the structure itself, however, looms ever vaster and more impenetrable. It is linked with the mysteries within the atom as it is also linked with that intangible, immaterial world of consciousness which no one has quite succeeded in identifying with the soft dust that flies up from a summer road. Evolution is an idea that has seemed to many to condemn man to the life of a beast and there are those who have ordered their days accordingly. Others have seen, in the long climb upward from the ooze, a law of progress, a reversal of the dour prophecies of an earlier Christianity which had viewed the human condition as one destined inevitably to worsen. The man of blood has had recourse to its arguments equally with the man of peace. In such circumstances we will do well to take a long second look at the history of this concept and at its moral implications.

It will be recalled that Adam Sedgwick spoke of the advent of man as "breaking in upon any supposition of zoological continuity—and utterly unaccounted for by what we have any right to call the Laws of Nature."[1] This is a typical progressionist remark from the early part of the nineteenth century. Compare it with the blithe and perhaps irresponsible gaiety of Huxley, going off to address a group of working men with the remark, "By next Friday they will all be convinced that they are monkeys." Or consider, coming down to our modern day, John Baillie's more measured observation: "The mark of modern unbelieving man is that he has felt astonishingly much *at home* in his earthly surroundings."[2] Between the first of these observations and the last a world has come and gone. It remains to ask, however, whether between the defiant supernaturalism of Sedgwick and the complacency of modern scientifically oriented man there may not lie other territories, other mysteries as great as those that intrigued Darwin long ago. To search out those last regions one must survey Darwin's century with care.

[1] Adam Sedgwick, *A Discourse on the Studies of the University of Cambridge*, 5th ed., London, 1850, p. xlv. Also *Proceedings of the Geological Society of London*, 1831, Vol. 1, p. 305.
[2] *Invitation to Pilgrimage*, Oxford University Press, 1942, p. 94.

II   The Pre-Darwinian Era

The first half of the nineteenth century may be roughly characterized as morphological in biology—the morphology being primarily derived from French sources—though paralleled to a degree in England by the somewhat inarticulate but magnificent anatomist John Hunter (1728–93). Great emphasis came to be placed upon the anatomical unities and connections between divergent forms. The work begun by John Ray and Linnaeus was extended to the most obscure portions of the globe, and the accumulated knowledge upon the world's faunas and floras had become tremendous. Though unity of biological type between great groups of animals had become evident, it was viewed by most thinkers as an immaterial, divinely ordained connection. While Germany and France had taken the lead in comparative biology, England had momentarily surpassed the Continental scholars in the field of stratigraphical geology. It may be that this latter episode was partly a result of the rise of industrialism in a circumscribed island area. At any rate, there met and merged in early nineteenth-century England a unique religious conservatism stemming from the reaction to the French Revolution, a recognized succession of faunas in geological time, and a similarly recognizable morphological resemblance, but not identity, between the faunas.

Out of this mixture the natural theologians, such as Sedgwick and others of like views, erected the concept of progressionism which, though based upon natural science, is essentially a metaphysical system. "It can be shown," wrote Agassiz, who subscribed fully to this viewpoint, "that in the great plan of creation . . . the very commencement, exhibits a certain tendency towards the end, betrays the issue toward which it is striving; and in the series of vertebrate animals, the constantly increasing similarity to man of the creatures that were successively called into existence, makes the final purpose obvious to-

ward which these successions are rising."[3] Progressionism
is really a system of evolution without either bodily or
geological continuity; it could be called, in fact, a theory
of spiritual macro-mutations. The rise of this romantic
"evolutionism," so vigorously opposed by the scientifically
minded uniformitarians with predilections for observable,
unchanging forces, led to the curious spectacle of scientific
geology actually opposing the idea of organic change. On
the other hand, progressionism was regarded approvingly
by Richard Owen, Louis Agassiz, and others who came
to detest the Darwinian viewpoint. The uniformitarian,
*so long as he had no natural explanation for the changes
in life patterns*, was dangerously exposed, philosophically,
if he admitted mysterious forces at work in life which
he refused to recognize when he rejected catastrophist
geology.

Living nature, in progressionist hands, was the very opposite of that calm, undeviating world machine envisaged
by Hutton as the quintessence of Newtonian world order.
To admit change and emergence into the world in the
miraculous fashion of progressionism[4] destroyed the reign
of scientific law. Paleontology, from the time in 1801 when
Cuvier announced to the world his discovery of twenty-
three species of animals no longer in existence, offered
just that threat to the scientific geologist. Without a natural explanation for change the dragons in the rocks were
in reality intellectual dragons. They threatened to impose
upon the rational Huttonian world order the unpredictable interposition of occult powers. Cuvier could indeed
have been regarded in some quarters as justly deserving

[3] Louis Agassiz, "A Period in the History of Our Planet," *Edinburgh New Philosophical Journal*, 1843, Vol. 35, p. 5.

[4] Care should be taken by the reader who consults the primary
documents of this period to distinguish between true "progressionism" and the phrase "progressive-development theory," which is
occasionally applied to genuine evolution, particularly the Lamarckian variety.

his satanic charnel house title and his impish halo of Pterodactyls.

Another aspect of thought developing slowly throughout the first part of the century has to do with the nature of time. We have seen that the growing knowledge of geology, even in the case of the catastrophists, had slowly strengthened the willingness of the public to accept a greater antiquity for the earth. In the case of Lyell and his followers time still has a sense of the illimitable about it. It is cyclical and in some degree repetitive. One can see the attraction of this old view in Lyell's waverings and advocacy of non-progressionism. Time of this character may be monotonous but it is safe, sane, and familiar. Throughout eternity the same waters hurry to the sea, the same basic animal forms expand or contract their habitat. All things pass and come again. The Newtonian world view, the eternal and balanced machine of the heavens, is repeated upon earth. Even life, crowded and struggling, remains in a dynamic, oscillating balance as much as perturbed planetary orbits correct themselves without supernatural interference. "Carnivorous animals," once remarked John Hunter, "are only to be considered the correctors of quantity. There is an equilibrium kept up among the animals by themselves." The struggle for existence he regarded as a "natural government."[5]

It should be noted that almost every eighteenth-century attempt to examine the struggle for existence ends upon this note of "equilibrium," "pruning," "policing," "natural government." Even Malthus's thesis is primarily a warning that man, too, cannot escape the limitation of numbers; perpetual progress is not possible. The observation of the creative aspect of this struggle waited upon the recognition of several interrelated clues. These clues are all really contained in one single basic proposition: historic as opposed to cyclic time. In the end it was not to be so much a demand for more time, as between catastrophists and

[5] *Essays and Observations*, London, 1861, Vol. 1, pp. 46–47.

uniformitarians, that introduced the true importance of the struggle for existence, but rather the unique character of the time which was beginning to emerge from astronomical and paleontological studies. It was time of enormous dimensions, true; in this men echoed the Greco-Roman past. For the first time, however, the historic ever-changing, irreversible, on-flowing continuum of events was being linked to galaxies and suns and worlds.

Laplace had been content, toward the end of the eighteenth century, to propose his nebular hypothesis as to how the planets might have been formed. That this in its turn suggested long lapses of astronomical time there can be no doubt.[6] Still, Laplace did not ask of the heavens the questions the nineteenth century was to ask; he did not debate the secular cooling of the earth or the rate at which the sun was consuming its own substance. In a way, by propounding a theory of the earth's origin, he was considering an historical event, but it was a remote and starry speculation.

In Darwin's century, however, the unique and unre-turning nature of the past began early to evince itself. The nature of energy began to be better grasped, with a consequent recognition of the importance of the second law of thermodynamics and the "heat death" which threatened potentially to chill the entire planetary system. In the rocks lay the evidences of a strange and unreturning fauna, rescued from oblivion by the arts of Cuvier. The gardens and paddocks of kings and nobles were revealing what curious, never-before-seen varieties, historic shapes in other words, could be tempted from the darkness of non-being by the selective hand of the breeder. Without anyone's being able to say just why, the struggle for existence which people had been examining for a century or more was suddenly seen by a few people almost simultaneously to be a creative mechanism. Basically—and this

[6] F. R. Moulton, "Influence of Astronomy on Science," *Scientific Monthly*, 1938, Vol. 67, p. 306.

reached great intensity after Darwin—man was adjusting himself, not just to time in unlimited quantities, but rather *to complete historicity, to the emergence of the endlessly new.* His philosophy was to include, henceforth, cosmic as well as organic novelty. It is not enough to say that man had come into possession of time, or even of eternity. These he had possessed before in other cultures, but never with this particular conception of on-goingness. To see and to re-create the past, to observe how it has come to mold the present, one must possess the knowledge that all things are new under the sun and that they are flowing in the direction of time's arrow never to return upon their course—that time is noncyclic, unreturning, and creative.

Instead of the "natural government" of the eighteenth century, the old principle of plenitude, of God's infinite creativeness, now led directly to a war of nature in which, through time, living creatures are jostled in or out of existence, expand or contract at one another's expense. The infinite creativeness remained as given, but the carefully balanced equilibrium was the illusion of an unhistorical outlook. The dreadful calculation of Malthus—that life tended to increase in geometric ratio against resources which at best could only be expanded on an arithmetic basis—cast a frightening shadow over public optimism. In spite of Lyell's transitional treatment of the struggle for existence (that he saw ecological contraction and expansion, we know), it may well be that the full import of the new conception demanded time for its complete import to sink home. As I have previously emphasized, it was possible—in fact is in large measure demonstrable—that Darwin and Wallace derived their applications of the Malthusian principle from Lyell, yet had recourse to Malthus as their inspiration. The paper in which Wallace first communicated his discovery bears, interestingly enough, the title "On the Tendency of Varieties to Depart Indefinitely from the Original Type." In Lyell's *Principles of Geology* occurs the following, directed toward the French evolutionists: ". . . let a sufficient number of centuries elapse, to allow of important revolutions in climate, physical geography, and other circumstances, and the characters say they, of the descendants of common parents *may deviate indefinitely from their original type.*"[7]

Wallace's title approximates so closely the italicized portion of Lyell's sentence that we may reasonably suspect it was Lyell he was primarily consulting as he worked upon his paper. Yet by his own testimony it was Malthus that brought the matter to his mind. One is thus inclined to observe that something about the Malthusian mathematical approach exercised an appeal to the first discoverers of natural selection comparable to the effect it had when the same idea was given to the public.[8] Irrespective of whether their major inspiration came from Malthus or from Lyell, they seem to have been impelled toward the former as the most powerful source of authority. With his acceptance of the phrase "to depart indefinitely," Wallace may be said, in 1858, to have epitomized the new time and the new world that Darwin and he were to leave as their heritage to the next century. Time was no longer the medium through which oscillated a self-adjusting and eternal world machine under a "natural government." It was instead a vast chaotic Amazon pouring through unimaginable wildernesses its burden of "houses and bones and gardens, cooks and clocks."

Just to make the change more emphatic, in that same year of 1859 the spectroscope was perfected. Even as the great scientific voyages had opened up the seas and continents, the long inviolable Empyrean heavens were now to be subjected to analysis. Until that instrument had been invented, astronomers might calculate from point to point

[7] Third ed., London, 1834, Vol. 2, p. 325. (Italics mine. L.E.)
[8] It is perhaps worth noting, since the biological observations of Malthus are little commented upon, that he recognized, like so many others, the effects of selective breeding in altering the appearance of plants and animals, but regarded such alterations of form as occurring within admittedly ill-defined limits.

the immeasurable distances of space, but the shining objects of their attention could be regarded only by dubious inference as being composed of the same matter as the earth. Ever since Newton's discovery of 1675 that the light of the sun is actually composed of a combination of colored rays which can be bent out of their course and separated by a lens, the solar spectrum, in principle, had been known. About 1815 Fraunhofer at Munich had succeeded in greatly improving the observational apparatus for examining the dark lines in the spectrum. The significance of Fraunhofer's lines was not cleared up until 1859 when Gustav Kirchhoff (1824–87) succeeded in establishing their relationship to heated metals here upon earth. Now, for the first time, it was possible to learn the composition of the outer universe, to dip a ladle into the roaring furnace of the sun and stars. Astrophysics had become a reality.

"All these marvellous and unexpected phenomena which have flashed, as it were, into the human cognizance within the last seven or eight years," writes a contemporary observer, "go far to establish the truth of Laplace's hypothesis, that the whole visible material universe *is an evolution of things,* arising from the condensation of vast tracts of gaseous or vaporous matter scattered through the regions of space."[9] By 1863 it had been pretty well established through this new "sidereal chemistry" that the matter of the entire visible universe was largely identical with the chemical elements known from our own solar system. In the fury of plutonic fires and wandering gases man began to seek the possibility of piercing "that hitherto impenetrable veil which seems to separate what we term inorganic from what we term organic and vital."[10] That the public was vastly interested can be shown by the number of popular articles devoted to the spectroscope and to

[9] C. Pritchard, "Spectrum Analysis," *The Contemporary Review,* 1869, Vol. 11, p. 487. (Italics mine. L.E.)
[10] Ibid., p. 490.

cosmic evolution. For a time the new cosmology rivaled the Darwinian controversy in interest, and there can be no doubt that it promoted and stimulated the willingness to accept Darwin. Stars and men and worlds emerged out of the interstellar vapor, flared briefly, and passed again into darkness. If the eternal stars transformed themselves, why should one quibble over the powers contained in a meadow mouse, or an ape who forgot to go back to his tree? Time was a different thing now. It was not even the old stable eternity of the stoics. It was, instead, irreversible and unreturning. As the life records in the rocks revealed, it was a loneliness, an on-going. Through the ruins of vanished eras one could trace the silver thread of genetic continuity winding on toward the always looming and unknown future.

III The Struggle of the Parts

With the fall of progressionism the sure and predetermined character of the human adventure appeared to melt away. The progressionist had seen the earlier stages of earth life prophetically—a great prologue whose sole purpose was to introduce man upon the scene, after which there would be no further alterations of life.[11] With the rise of natural selection and the philosophy of actual physical descent with modification, man becomes, along with all the other forms of life, "the child of chance." "The gist of Darwin's theory," wrote Ernst Haeckel, "is this simple idea: that the Struggle for Existence in Nature evolves new Species *without* design just as the Will of Man produces new Varieties in Cultivation *with* design."[12] All notion of preconceived Platonic ideal forms

---

[11] A few progressionists, such as Lord Brougham, were willing to entertain the possibility of a future development beyond man, but such ideas are not characteristic of this group of thinkers as a whole. The strong theological emphasis of this school of thought inevitably tended to overshadow such suggestions.

[12] *The Evolution of Man*, New York, 1896, Vol. 1, p. 95.

has vanished from this system. The fixed taxonomy of life is an illusion born of our limited experience. In reality every living thing is writhing from one shape into another in the way that we might witness the growth of a tropical forest in a speeded-up motion picture. Our long-assumed stability is only the illusion produced by the tempo at which we live.

So complete was the triumph of the new philosophy that the struggle for existence, the "war of nature," was projected into the growth of the organism itself. Darwin's shadow dominates, in this respect, the rest of the century. Moreover, it provides an apt illustration of the way in which a successful theory may be carried to excess. The co-operative aspects of bodily organization, the vast intricacy of hormonic interplay, of cellular chemistry, remained to a considerable degree uninvestigated. Instead, "struggle" was the leading motif of the day. "It is a probable hypothesis," said Huxley in 1869, "that what the world is to organisms in general each organism is to the molecules of which it is composed. Multitudes of these, having diverse tendencies, are competing with one another for opportunity to exist and multiply; and the organism, as a whole, is as much the product of the molecules which are victorious as the Fauna, or Flora of a country is the product of the victorious organic beings in it."[13]

Darwin commented, with what one cannot help suspecting was a private grin, "about natural selection amongst the molecules." He expressed admiration for Huxley's boldness—always easy to do—and then proceeded to add cautiously, "I cannot quite follow you."[14] The rage persisted, however. Wilhelm Roux, the distinguished German embryologist, developed a theory of internal struggle for nourishment between the parts of an organism.[15] Weismann went even further and extended

[13] LLD, Vol. 3, p. 119.
[14] Ibid.
[15] *Der Kampf der Theile im Organismus*, Leipzig, 1881.

natural selection to the smallest particles of the germ plasm. One could say in a somewhat figurative fashion that in a fertilized cell the very ancestors were struggling as to which might emerge once more into the light! "Each animal and plant," pondered Darwin, "may be compared to a bed of mould full of seeds, most of which soon germinate, some lie for a period dormant, whilst others perish."[16]

It is not necessary to pursue this subject at length. It fascinated good men, produced some able research in embryology, and faded with the rise of a better understanding of the complexities of cell mechanics. It does, nevertheless, express something about the period. So grim was the struggle for existence conceived to be that a single improved bristle, an inch longer horn was thought of as individually decisive in survival. Part of this mistaken emphasis lay in the attention paid to somatic variations which are now known to be fluctuating and nonheritable.

There can be no doubt that this utilitarian emphasis was in some degree misplaced. It diverted attention from other more imponderable mysteries, minimized the role of co-operation in animal life and, in its more absurd manifestations, left reason to wonder why, if the organism was nothing but a collection of struggling particles, it had ever managed to collect itself into a body in the first place. As we have observed in an earlier chapter, neither Darwin nor his immediate followers seem to have had any particular feeling for the internal stability and harmony of the organism. Their success with the concept of struggle in the exterior environment had led them to see everything through this set of spectacles. A whole generation of neo-Darwinians persisted in this point of view.[17]

16 VAP, Vol. 2, p. 483.
17 See E. S. Russell, "Schopenhauer's Contribution to Biological Theory," in Science, Medicine and History, edited by E. A. Underwood. Oxford University Press, 1953, Vol. 2, pp. 205–6.

IV Evolution and Human Culture

Coincident with the development of the evolutionary philosophy has been the rise of anthropology as a science. Although of late years there has been a tendency for social anthropology to pursue its tasks without reference to the field of biology, this specialization is not entirely desirable without at least some knowledge of the relationship of these two subjects in the past. We are in a position to see, after our lengthy survey of the history of biological evolution, that almost every mistake and folly which was perpetrated in the creation of a satisfactory theory of organic evolution was duplicated or had its analogue in the social field. On the other hand, steps which were taken to extricate biological theory from just such difficulties have, in certain instances, been utilized with equal success in anthropology.

In reality biological and anthropological thinking have influenced each other and have been part of the same intellectual climate for a long period of time. It has been man's curiosity about himself, extended to the origins of the world around him, that has led to the discovery of the evolutionary process. Although the Christian world had tended to take the Bible literally on Creation as a single act by divine fiat, it had, at the same time, never completely divorced itself from the ancient idea that simpler organisms are constantly arising by spontaneous generation. At the same time it had inherited from the Greek world of Aristotle a kind of taxonomic ladder, a sort of frozen evolution in the shape of the Scale of Being.[18] Since, before the rise of modern science, all three of these somewhat incompatible doctrines had persisted uncritically in the Western mind, the seeds of speculation lay ready to hand. One can note, for example, that Lamarck's evolution consists really in the utilization of spontaneous generation along with the unfreezing

[18] E. T. Brewster, *Creation: A History of Non-Evolutionary Theories,* Indianapolis, 1927, p. 81.

of the Scale of Being. When he came to man he made
use of a widely held eighteenth-century social theory;
namely, that man in a state of nature was in no way distinct from the existing apes; that we could see in the
orang outang of the voyagers a member of our own species
without language or other social proclivities, in short, a
living "cultural" as well as physical fossil. Man's history,
the French *philosophes* argued, is characterized by the
ability to unfold the higher mental attributes in a state
of society, to attain wisdom by degrees. He is capable of
perfectibilité, of progress.[19] That there was a submerged
element of biological thinking in some of the writing upon
purely social progress can be judged from Condorcet's
observation that "Organic perfectibility or deterioration
amongst the various strains in the vegetable and animal
kingdom can be regarded as one of the general laws of
nature. This law also applies to the human race."[20]

It has sometimes been ventured that it was the growth
and popularization of the idea of social progress that led
to the development of the idea of evolution. Without
wishing to ignore this influence it can still be observed
that both points of view seem to have arisen together,
and that from the first, particularly in France, there is
a considerable interplay of ideas between those whose
major thinking lay in one field or the other. In any case
only the extension of the earth's antiquity and increased
knowledge of the paleontological past, with its horde of
vanished animals, could remove a certain casualness from
the earliest expression of evolutionary ideas. The conception only becomes important when the full depth and
marvelous organic diversity of life become known.

In the seventeenth and eighteenth centuries the unilinear scale of nature, as we have earlier observed, placed

[19] A. O. Lovejoy, "Monboddo and Rousseau," *Modern Philology*,
1932–33, Vol. 30, pp. 277–78.

[20] Antoine-Nicolas de Condorcet, *Sketch for a Historical Picture
of the Progress of the Human Mind*, 1795, Noonday Press ed.,
New York, 1955, p. 199.

man at the head of the animal kingdom. Beneath him there descended a series of grades or steps to the lowest infusoria. This chain was regarded as a single unbroken stair. The existence of this idea led to conceptions of various racial groups as occupying positions on this ladder intermediate between Western Caucasian man and the great apes. The social thinkers, like Condorcet, tended to think of barbarians as educable; in fact, there were those who, right down into the nineteenth century, thought it might be possible to teach the orang to speak. As slavery and imperialism extended, however, the notion of existing races as lying fixed, biologically, upon levels inferior to Western man persisted, and was in some cases extended as a convenient rationalization. Cultural levels were often confused with biological potentiality. So powerful was the influence of the idea of the living scale of life that surviving human "links" were still being sought for in the nineteenth century.

In 1816 Cuvier broke with the conception of a single unilinear scale of life. He introduced in its place four great animal groups whose anatomical structure he regarded as impossible to correlate into a single ascending system of taxonomy, whether in terms of abstract unity of plan or in evolutionary terms. Karl von Baer (1792–1876) approached the problem through comparative embryology and demonstrated a little later that the egg of each of these separate groups undergoes a separate type of development showing no relationship to the developmental stages of the others. Neither Baer nor Cuvier was an evolutionist, but they were contributing heavily to the final triumph of the evolutionist cause. They were breaking away from a unilineal conception of organic relationship and enabling later workers to see the evolution of the Mollusca, for example, as being a separate branch of the tree of life related only in the most distant fashion, if at all, to the Vertebrates. They were not in the scale leading to man. The garden snail wandering in its little trail of slime over a leaf was not an ancestral vertebrate. Instead, it was following its own branching road of developments.

It is at just this point that we can observe an interesting analogy between the morphological revolution in biology and the later reaction toward unilinear schemes of cultural development which took place in the twentieth century. Just as the early Darwinians had to see man's relationship to living apes as closer than it was, so the nineteenth-century social evolutionists had shown a tendency to take the varied nonliterate cultures of modern primitives and arrange them in a sort of phylogenetic sequence leading to advanced Western culture. There was little attempt to examine the actual functioning of these communities. They were seen primarily much as the great apes appeared to the biologists: living ancestral social forms, surviving into the present.

Just as it had proved necessary for biologists to break away from the idea that existing apes are precisely similar to our Tertiary forerunners; just as it had been necessary to cease projecting upon unfamiliar racial types the features of existing gorillas and chimpanzees, so, similarly, it was necessary to break out of a particular habit of social thinking. Like the impact of Cuvier's reassessment of biological patterns in 1816, the questions raised by Westermarck in 1891 over the "origin" of given social institutions in terms of unilineal "advance" caused a mild flurry in English social anthropology. It began to be clear, and to be emphasized in twentieth-century anthropology, that "every culture in the world has had its own unique history and we can not therefore say that any culture observable in the present day world is an earlier form of any other."[21] Cultures contemporaneous in time have, like men, monkeys and apes, their own unique historical pathways. To

21 C. W. M. Hart, "Social Evolution and Modern Anthropology," *Essays in Political Economy*, edited by H. A. Innis, University of Toronto Press, n.d. p. 114.

recognize this fact is not to deny that men have a genuine morphological kinship to apes, nor that small isolated societies may not throw some general light upon human psychology under such conditions. This is a far cry, however, from the more rigid and ethnocentric extrapolations indulged in by both biologists and anthropologists in the Victorian past.

There is still another interesting analogy between theoretical developments in the biological world and events in anthropology. It will be recalled that I have touched upon the subject of Darwin's primary interest: the modification of living forms under the selective influence of the environment. I have been at some pains to point out that Darwin, by the very nature of his interests, was a student of the individual characteristics of animals and plants. He is concerned essentially with differences and their inheritance, with all that is unfixed, shifting, and subject to change. Magnificent as his grasp of this aspect of biology is, it is counterbalanced by a curious lack of interest in the nature of the organism itself. Perhaps this partly explains his indifference to his forerunners and their abstract ideas. Occasionally, when he is confronted by the problem of explaining a variation which demands simultaneous alterations in other parts in order to be successful, he faintly echoes Cuvier by referring to a "mysterious law of correlation."

It is obvious, however, that Darwin is uncomfortable among these inner mysteries of the body and does not, of his own volition, enjoy pursuing them. We have already noted the tendency of some of his followers to attempt to project the war of nature directly into the body, to make the method which had explained so much on the "outside" account for the organization within. Pursued to its *reductio ad absurdum* every living creature would simply be reduced to a sack of struggling molecules in some manner creating order out of individual chaos. One may suspect that having committed himself to a principle of fortuity in the emergence and evolution of life, he was made uncomfortable by temperament when issues implying bodily organization and co-ordinated behavior beyond the range of his theory were brought to his attention.

He was far too intelligent to ignore them completely, but, as in the "mysterious law of correlation," he had a way of relegating such subjects to a brief phrase, or paragraph, and hastily returning to his favorite subject. It is thus very difficult to discover what he really thought on the subject of biological organization. It is quite conceivable that he thought very little about it, that he took the body "as given," and proceeded from there. Darwin had an excellent sense for the sort of investigations which offered the possibility of solution with the means at his command. There is no use blaming him for a shrewd empirical good sense in evading what were then problems insoluble or likely to prove metaphysical and abstract. Nevertheless, it is difficult to find in Darwin any really deep recognition of the life of the organism as a functioning whole which must be co-ordinated interiorly before it can function exteriorly. He was, as we have said, a separatist, a student of parts and their changes. He looked upon the organism as a cloud form altering under the winds of chance and it was the permutations and transmutations of its substance that interested him. The inner nature of the cloud, its stability as a cloud, even as it was drawn out, flattened, or compressed by the forces of time and circumstance, moved him but little.

It is intriguing to find Huxley, on the other hand, fascinated by the stability of the great classes just before he surrendered to the Darwinian hypothesis.

"Not only are all animals existing in the present creation organized according to one of these five plans; but paleontology tends to show that in the myriad of past ages of which the earth's crust contains the records, no other plan of animal life made its appearance on our planet. *A marvellous fact and one which seems to present no small obstacle in the way of the notion of the possibility of fortuitous development of animal life."*[22]

Even later, in 1862, he expressed wonder "not that the changes of life . . . have been so great, but that they have been so small."[23] One has the feeling with some of this early writing of Huxley's that his interests were rather different from Darwin's, and that his later conversion to the latter's theory was more of a change of sides than any marked change in the store of facts he had available. He was interested, it is apparent, in the stability of form, in what kept the great basic plans of organization so steadfast throughout whole eras and epochs. Later his long warfare on behalf of Darwin drew him aside from this quite justifiable field of speculation.

In the domain of anthropology we may observe once more that after a period of pursuing the geographical diffusion of cultural traits and complexes over wide areas, after a time of conceiving cultures as things of "shreds and patches" made up of miscellaneous assemblages of traits derived from many sources, it began to become apparent that whatever the original derivation of these traits, they had been taken into a functioning society and reshaped by inner organizing forces. Just as Darwin had been partitive so these earlier studies in the social field had, to a considerable degree, concerned themselves with the picked bones of institutions and beliefs. The inner consistency, living society, had escaped attention. It was the day of the purely descriptive ethnographer just as, in post-Darwinian biology, several decades were consumed in the descriptive embroidery of evolution. It is not my intention to decry the value of these studies; it is merely to remark that in the end they were found, both

---

[22] "On Natural History as Knowledge, Discipline and Power" (1856), *Scientific Memoirs of Thomas Huxley*, 1898, Vol. 1, p. 306. (Italics mine. L.E.)

[23] Anniversary Address, *Quarterly Journal of the Geological Society of London*, 1862, Vol. 18, p. 1.

in biology and social anthropology, to be inadequate to the problems presented.

It was then, in the words of Ruth Benedict, that cultures began to loom like individual personalities "cast large upon the screen, given gigantic features and a long time span." To list or discuss the various views and contributions to this subject of such pioneers as Malinowski, Radcliffe-Brown, Mead, Hallowell, Kluckhohn, and numerous others would go beyond the limitations of this book. What I wish to indicate here is simply that the holistic, organismic approach which finally emerged in biology when the intricacy of inner co-ordination and adjustment began to be realized has, once more, its analogue in the social field.

Like organisms, societies ingest or reject materials which come to them. Often, like organisms, what is ingested is reworked in such a manner that when it reappears as a part of the social body it has been molded to fit a purpose other than what was envisaged in another time and place where the trait arose. Sometimes the psychological set or bent of a given society will long outlast its political independence or even its material technology. There is an inner cohesiveness which is a product of the social mind, just as in the body the persistence of a physical trait or an instinct is part of the co-ordinated behavior of an organism. With the rise of the human brain, however, and the emergence of societies in which social tradition constitutes a new form of heredity, another world is opening up for man—a world he has possessed for only a few seconds in terms of the geological clock. It is important that his new powers and limitations should be properly assessed because only so can hope be entertained for his future. It must be remembered that in geological terms we are living perhaps at the very dawn of complex human society and this is most unfortunate because man, in coming to understand his genetic history, continues to look toward the past. This is the burden which science, and particularly evolutionary biology, has placed upon man's shoulders even as it has tried to free him from the shackles of superstition. Man is, in short, in danger of acquiring a feeling of inferiority about his past. It provides him with rationalizations for things undone and dreams defeated.

How did this situation come about? "That man is an animal is the great and special discovery of natural science in our generation," reported a contemporary of Darwin.[24] In that remark is epitomized the whole Darwinian concentration upon the past. It is natural, it is normal, it is the reaction to be expected of a world discovering the historic continuity of life for the first time. It is, however, a literal fixation upon the past. It accounts for our too great feeling of "at homeness" in a world where man, ever eager to transcend himself, should have other aspirations by reason of his very nature.

He has been convinced of his rise from a late Tertiary anthropoid stock. Through neurological and psychological research he is conscious that the human brain is an imperfect instrument built up through long geological periods. Some of its levels of operation are more primitive and archaic than others. Our heads, modern man has learned, may contain weird and irrational shadows out of the subhuman past—shadows that under stress can sometimes elongate and fall darkly across the threshold of our rational lives. Man has lost the faith of the eighteenth century in the enlightening power of pure reason, for he has come to know that he is not a consistently reasoning animal. We have frightened ourselves with our own black nature and instead of thinking "We are men now, not beasts, and must live like men," we have eyed each other with wary suspicion and whispered in our hearts, "We will trust no one. Man is evil. Man is an animal. He has come from the dark wood and the caves."

As Huxley said, it is easy to convince men that they are

[24] William Graham, *The Creed of Science*, London, 1881, p. 161.

monkeys. We all know this in our hearts. The real effort lies in convincing us that we are men. Yet somewhere in the past a group of apes—gross, brutal, violent-tempered, with a paucity of words—started to act like men, and now they are men, but not far enough, not nearly far enough. There may be an animal limit within us but Darwin established no such limit. It is complacent to settle for material progress in machines while we stifle the spiritual aspirations for the "kingdom within" that all the world's great moral teachers have sought to instill into their followers.

It was natural enough, in the eagerness to communicate a great scientific truth, that Darwin's followers, more dogmatically than Darwin, told and retold the tale of the past or tried to press across the barrier that still lay between cosmic and organic evolution. Haeckel, in a statement of 1877, contended that "the cell consists of matter called protoplasm, composed chiefly of carbon, with an admixture of hydrogen, nitrogen and sulphur. These component parts, properly united, produce the soul and body of the animated world, and suitably nursed become man. With this single argument the mystery of the universe is explained, the Deity annulled and a new era of infinite knowledge ushered in."[25] This, it can readily be observed, is a very large order indeed.

No reasonable scientist today would assume, even if he succeeded in creating simple life in a test tube, that the mystery of the universe was explained thereby. Haeckel's remark was dictated by anti-theological bias and a desire to settle man into the kind of "natural" world in which he now finds himself. As a recent student of evolution, the naturalist W. H. Dowdeswell, has remarked, "Studies centered exclusively on the past tend inevitably to obscure the present and future, thus fostering the idea that evolution has come to a comparative standstill at the present

[25] Cited by W. S. Lilley in the *Fortnightly Review*, 1886, Vol. 39, p. 35.

time or is proceeding too slowly to be detected."[26] From the moral and ethical standpoint, unless balanced by some consideration of the emergent aspects of the human psyche, these studies can lead in unenlightened hands to a certain complacent acquiescence in everything but the desire for more and more material progress in goods, comforts, and sensual enjoyment.

Evolution, if it has taught us anything, has taught us that life is infinitely creative. Whether one accepts Henri Bergson's view of the process or not, one of the profoundest remarks he ever made was the statement that "the role of life is to insert some *indetermination* into matter." An advanced brain capable of multiple choices is represented on this planet only by man. He is a "reservoir of indetermination" containing infinite possibilities of good and evil. He is nature's greatest attempt to escape the blind subservience of the lower world to instinct and those evolutionary forces which, in all other forms of life, channel its various manifestations into constricted nooks and crannies of the environment. Wallace saw, and saw correctly, that with the rise of man the evolution of parts was to a marked degree outmoded, that mind was now the arbiter of human destiny.

The Darwinians, however, were essentially biologists. They were accustomed to dealing with the lower animals, with instincts, with inherited habit, with the study of organisms responding to change rather than the observation of creatures controlling their own environment. They tended to confuse cultural behavior with the inherited behavior with which they were far more familiar. They could speak seriously of other races seeming "less human than our dogs and horses," but about the social attitudes which led to these revelatory statements they were remarkably unperceptive. The Mendelian developments of the early twentieth century intensified a severe trend toward a delimitation of human psychology in terms of in-

[26] *The Mechanism of Evolution*, Heinemann, London, 1955, p. 1.

stinct.[27] Much of what we would call acquired behavior patterns were labeled as inherited instincts by William James, Thorndike, and others. The triumphs of biology were influencing other fields in a manner resembling the triumphs of atomic physics today. Selfishness, acquisitiveness, opposition to women's rights were all at one time or another justified on the basis of instinct, of "human nature." To seek for the amelioration or removal of social ills such as war was to "oppose instinct." And to oppose instinct was, of course, to interfere with the evolutionary process and the inscrutable selective wisdom contained in the struggle for existence.

In this attitude, in this unwillingness to interfere with "primeval nature," it is possible to perceive the greatest persistent blind spot in the thinking of the nineteenth century. Darwin himself is not guiltless in this respect, though there is no reason to blame him for the grosser philosophical sins of his followers. In making out his case for natural selection, and the fortuitous character of evolution as opposed to the metaphysical beliefs of the progressionists, Darwin incorporated into the *Origin of Species* a powerful expression of the utilitarian philosophy of his time. His emphasis lay to a very considerable degree upon selfish motivation, although he admitted that social animals would perpetuate adaptations which benefited the community. On the whole, however, he devoted little attention to the co-operative tendencies in life which later drew the attention of Prince Kropotkin.[28] It was, in actuality, part of that same curious indifference he showed to the co-operation manifested within the body itself. Yet this body we inhabit is composed of millions of selflessly toiling and co-operating cells. Cells have joined to individual cells in the long ages of evolutionary advance, have

[27] Merle Curti, "Human Nature in American Thought: Retreat from Reason in the Age of Science," *Political Science Quarterly,* 1953, Vol. 68, pp. 495–96.
[28] *Mutual Aid,* 1902 (various editions).

even sacrificed themselves to build that vaster individuality of which they can have no knowledge. The cell itself is, in turn, a laboratory where chemical processes are being carried on in an amazingly co-ordinated fashion. One generation, as Bergson somewhere remarks, bends lovingly over the cradle of the next. All of these thing₃ imply other aspects of life than those to which the Darwinians devoted the greater part of their attention. Professor W. C. Allee expressed the more modern viewpoint succinctly when he said, not long ago,

"The subsocial and social life of animals shows two major tendencies: one toward aggressiveness, which is best developed in man and his fellow vertebrates; the other toward unconscious, and in higher animals, toward conscious cooperation. With various associates I have long experimented upon both tendencies. Of these, the drive toward cooperation . . . is the more elusive and the more important."[29]

V   The Role of Indeterminism

The blind spot we have dwelt upon in Darwinian thinking is not confined to a confused weighing of the relative aspects of co-operation and struggle in the long history of life. There is another phase of evolutionary thought which it is of the utmost importance to clarify. We have spoken of the brain of man as a sort of organ of indetermination. We have seen through Wallace its ability to escape from mechanical specialization, its creation of a freedom unknown to any other creature on the planet. Ironically enough, that freedom, that power of choice on the part of man, represents in a curious way the belated triumph of Erasmus Darwin and Lamarck.[30]

[29] "Biology" in *What Is Science?* ed. by James R. Newman, New York: Simon & Schuster, 1955, p. 243.

[30] David Bidney, *Theoretical Anthropology*, Columbia University Press, p. 82.

Here at last volition has taken its place in the world of nature. It was not perhaps quite the place these evolutionists had foreseen, but in the end its part in the cultural drama of man could not be gainsaid by their scientific successors. The mind of man, by indetermination, by the power of choice and cultural communication, by the great powers of thought, is on the verge of escape from the blind control of that deterministic world with which the Darwinists had unconsciously shackled man. The inborn characteristics laid upon him by the biological extremists have crumbled away. Man is many things—he is protean, elusive, capable of great good and appalling evil. He is what he is—a reservoir of indeterminism. He represents the genuine triumph of volition, life's near evasion of the forces that have molded it. In the West of our day only one anachronistic force threatens man with the ruin of that hope. It is his confusion of the word "progress" with the mechanical extensions which represent his triumph over the primeval wilderness of biological selection. This confusion represents, in a way, a reversion. It is a failure to see that the triumph of the machine without an accompanying inner triumph represents an atavistic return to the competition and extermination represented in the old biological evolution of "parts." In the case of man the struggle is, of course, veiled and projected into his machines, but the enormous wealth now poured by modern governments into the development of implements of war reveals a kind of leviathan echo from the Age of Dinosaurs. Nor is this attitude confined to the exigencies of defense. It persists in the notion that something called gracious living is solely associated with high-powered automobiles and the social amenities available in the very best clubs. It is the twentieth-century version of the Victorian idea that men of simple cultures are "moral fossils."

A few years ago, in a desert and out-of-the-way region of Mexico, the writer and a companion wandered lost and exhausted into the camp of a Mexican peon. This man, whose wife and newborn child were sheltered in a little hovel of sticks into which one could only creep on hands and knees, supplied our needs graciously. To our amazement he gently refused any payment, and walked with us to the edge of his barren lands in order to set us on the right path. There was a dignified simplicity about this man and his wife, in their little nest of sticks, that was a total antithesis to gracious living in the great land to the north. It demanded no mechanical extensions, no stewards with shining trays. We had drunk from a common vessel. We had bowed and spoken as graciously as on the steps of a great house. I had looked into his eyes and seen there that transcendence of self is not to be sought in the outer world or in mechanical extensions. These are merely another version of specialized evolution. They can be used for human benefit if one recognizes them for what they are, but they must never be confused with that other interior kingdom in which man is forever free to be better than what he knows himself to be. It is there that the progress of which he dreams is at last to be found. It is the thing that his great moral teachers have been telling him since man was man. This is his true world; the other, the mechanical world which tickles his fancy, may be useful to good men but it is not in itself good. It takes its color from the minds behind it and this man has not learned. When he does so he will have achieved his final escape from the world which Darwin saw and pictured.

One last thing, however, should be said of Charles Darwin, the man who saw the wrinkled hide of a disintegrating planet, glyptodonts and men, all equally flowing down the direction of time's arrow: he was a master artist and he entered sympathetically into life. As a young man somewhere in the high-starred Andean night, or perhaps drinking alone at an island spring where wild birds who had never learned to fear man came down upon his shoulder, Charles Darwin saw a vision. It was one of the most tremendous insights a living being ever had. It combined the awful roar of Hutton's Scottish brook with a glimpse of Smith's frail ladder dangling into the abyss of vanished eras. None of his forerunners has left us such a message; none saw, in a similar manner, the whole vista of life with quite such sweeping vision. None, it may be added, spoke with the pity which infuses these lines: *"If we choose to let conjecture run wild, then animals, our fellow brethren in pain, disease, suffering and famine—our slaves in the most laborious works, our companions in our amusements —they may partake of our origin in one common ancestor —we may be all melted together."*[31]

Darwin was twenty-eight when he jotted down this paragraph in his notebook. If he had never conceived of natural selection, if he had never written the *Origin,* it would still stand as a statement of almost clairvoyant perception. There are very few youths today who will pause, coming from a biology class, to finger a yellow flower or poke in friendly fashion at a sunning turtle on the edge of the campus pond, and who are capable of saying to themselves, "We are all one—all melted together." It is for this, as much as for the difficult, concise reasoning of the *Origin,* that Darwin's shadow will run a long way forward into the future. It is his heritage from the parson-naturalists of England.

[31] LLD, Vol. 2, p. 6. Notebook of 1837.

Glossary

Uniformitarianism, that scientific school of thought generally associated with the names of James Hutton and Sir Charles Lyell which assumed that geological phenomena were the product of natural forces operating over enormous periods of time and with considerable, though not necessarily total, uniformity. With modifications it has become the geological point of view of the twentieth century. In the early nineteenth century it stood in considerable opposition to

Catastrophism, a geological approach which interpreted the stratigraphic features of the planet as representing a succession of sudden, violent, and cataclysmic disturbances in the geologic past interspersed between long periods of calm. These disturbances were often regarded as world wide and totally, or almost totally, lethal in their effect upon the life of the globe. The theory implies the work of forces unknown in the present era and there thus lingers about the doctrine a certain aroma of the supernatural even though not always directly expressed or avowed by its more scientific proponents. The fact that life was supposedly created anew after each such episode enhances this aspect of the theory. Essentially catastrophism represents a compromise between the Mosaic account of creation and the increasing geological knowledge of the late eighteenth and early nineteenth centuries. The biological analogue of catastrophism is

Progressionism, the assumption that life has risen from simple to more complex forms throughout the successive eras of the geological past. The doctrine does not imply actual phylogenetic descent from one form to another, but rather a succession of more and more advanced creations until finally man appears as the crowning achievement. The unity of biological form is thus not the product of "descent with modification" but rather a succession of creations linked only by an abstract unity existing in the mind of God. Opposed to this point of view was the short-lived

Non-progressionism of Lyell which was the biological equivalent of extreme uniformitarianism. Non-progressionism opposed the theory of successive and advancing creations by seeking to demonstrate that the higher and more complex forms of life such as the birds and mammals were actually to be found in ancient deposits. The theory was expressed somewhat ambiguously and with qualifications. It did not long survive but essentially it represents a pre-Darwinian attempt to avoid the supernaturalism so abhorrent to the uniformitarian geologists with their preference for natural rather than unknown mysterious forces. In the end

Developmentalism, later to be called evolution, arose out of the merging of progressionism with the natural philosophy of uniformitarianism. This could only take place when Charles Darwin supplied, through the principle of natural selection, a natural (i.e., uniformitarian) explanation for the past changes which had taken place in the flora and fauna of the world.

Suggested Reading

An exhaustive list of the sources consulted in preparation for the writing of this book would occupy too much space to be presented here. The reader is referred to the individual footnotes extended throughout the book. What follows consists primarily of a list of what might be called "basic" material bearing upon the major progress of evolutionary thought. As can be gathered from the text it does not include the variety of papers, published and unpublished, which the author has consulted in the composition of this volume.

Agassiz, Elizabeth Cary
    (1886) *Louis Agassiz: His Life and Correspondence*, 2 vols., Houghton Mifflin, Boston.
Agassiz, Louis
    (1894, 1896) *Geological Sketches*, 2 vols., Houghton Mifflin, Boston.
Barlow, Nora
    (1935) "Charles Darwin and the Galápagos Islands," *Nature*, Vol. 136, p. 391.
Barlow, Nora (editor)
    (1933) *Charles Darwin's Diary of the Voyage of H.M.S. "Beagle,"* Cambridge University Press.
    (1946) *Charles Darwin and the Voyage of the "Beagle,"* Philosophical Library, New York.
Bateson, William
    (1913) *Mendel's Principles of Heredity*, Cambridge University Press.
Blyth, Edward
    (1835) "An Attempt to Classify the Variations of Animals, etc.," *Magazine of Natural History*, Vol. 8, pp. 40–53.
    (1837) "On the Psychological Distinctions Between Man and All Other Animals," *Magazine of Natural History*, Vol. 1, n.s., Parts I, II, III.
Buffon, Georges Louis Leclerc, Comte de
    (1797–1807) *Buffon's Natural History* (Barr's translation), London.
    (1812) *Natural History, General and Particular*, 20 vols., translated by William Smellie.
Cannon, H. Graham
    (1955–56) "What Lamarck Really Said," *Proceedings of the Linnaean Society of London*, 168th Session, Parts I, II.

Chambers, Robert
>(1844) *Vestiges of the Natural History of Creation*, London.
>(1846) *Explanations: A Sequel to the Vestiges*, London.

Clark, John Willis and Hughes, Thomas M.
>(1890) *Life and Letters of the Reverend Adam Sedgwick*, 2 vols., Cambridge University Press.

Cole, F. J.
>(1930) *Early Theories of Sexual Generation*, Oxford University Press.

Condorcet, Antoine-Nicolas de
>(1955) *Sketch for a Historical Picture of the Progress of the Human Mind* (1795), Noonday Press, New York.

Cuvier, Georges, Baron
>(1802) *Lessons in Comparative Anatomy*, 2 vols., London.
>(1815) *Essay on the Theory of the Earth*, second ed., Edinburgh.

Darlington, C. D.
>(1959) *Darwin's Place in History*, Blackwell's, Oxford.

Darwin, Charles
>(1952) *Journal of Researches*, facsimile reprint of first edition (1839), Hafner Publishing Co., New York.
>(1951) *Origin of Species*, reprint of first edition (1859), Philosophical Library, New York.
>(1868) Variation of Animals and Plants Under Domestication, 2 vols., London and New York.
>(1874) *The Descent of Man*, second edition, New York.
>(1881) "Inheritance," *Nature*, Vol. 24, p. 257.
>*The Origin of Species (sixth edition 1872) and the Descent of Man*, Modern Library, New York, n.d.

Darwin, Erasmus
>(1791) *The Botanic Garden*, London.
>(1794–96) *Zoonomia*, 2 vols., London.
>(1803) *The Temple of Nature*, London.

Darwin, Francis
>(1888) *Life and Letters of Charles Darwin*, 3 vols., John Murray, London.

Darwin, Francis and Seward, A. C. (editors)
>(1903) *More Letters of Charles Darwin*, John Murray, London.

Darwin, Francis (editor)
>(1909) *The Foundations of the Origin of Species*, Cambridge University Press.

De Beer, Sir Gavin (editor)
>(1960) Darwin's Notebooks on Transmutation of Species, *Bulletin of the British Museum of Natural History*, Historical Series, Part I, Vol. 2, No. 2; Part II, Vol. 2, No. 3; Part III, Vol. 2, No. 4. London.

Derham, W. (editor)

(1718) *Philosophical Letters Between the Late Mr. Ray and . . . His Correspondents*, London.

Dupree, A. Hunter

(1959) *Asa Gray 1810–1888*, Harvard University Press.

Ellegard, Alvar

(1958) *Darwin and the General Reader*, Göteborg, Sweden.

Falconer, Hugh

(1856) "On Professor Huxley's Attempted Refutation of Cuvier's Laws of Correlation in the Reconstruction of Extinct Vertebrate Forms," *Annals and Magazine of Natural History*, second series, Vol. 17, pp. 476–93.

(1868) *Paleontological Memoirs*, 2 vols., London.

Geikie, Archibald

(1901) *The Founders of Geology*, Baltimore.

Gillispie, Charles C.

(1951) *Genesis and Geology*, Harvard University Press.

Glass, Bentley, O. Temkin, and W. L. Straus, Jr.

(1959) *Forerunners of Darwin 1745–1859*, Johns Hopkins Press, Baltimore.

Gray, Asa

(1876) *Darwiniana: Essays and Reviews Pertaining to Darwinism*, Appleton, New York.

Gray, Jane Loring

(1894) *Letters of Asa Gray*, 2 vols., Houghton Mifflin, Boston.

Grimes, J. Stanley

(1851) *Phreno-Geology*, Boston.

Gruber, Jacob

(1960) *A Conscience in Conflict: The Life of St. George Jackson Mivart*, Columbia University Press, New York.

Gunther, Robert W. T. (editor)

(1928) *Further Correspondence of John Ray*, The Ray Society, London.

Hagberg, Knut

(1952) *Carl Linnaeus*, Jonathan Cape, London.

Hunter, John

(1861) *Essays and Observations on Natural History*, 2 vols., London.

Hutton, James

(1788) "Theory of the Earth; or An Investigation of the Laws Observable in the Composition, Dissolution, and Restoration of Land Upon the Globe," *Transactions of the Royal Society of Edinburgh*, Vol. 1, pp. 209–304.

(1795) *Theory of the Earth with Proofs and Illustrations*, 2 vols., Edinburgh.

Huxley, Leonard
(1913) *Life and Letters of Thomas Henry Huxley*, 3 vols., London.
(1918) *Life and Letters of Sir Joseph Dalton Hooker*, 2 vols., Murray, London.

Huxley, T. H.
(1898) *The Scientific Memoirs of Thomas Henry Huxley*, 4 vols., edited by Michael Foster and E. Ray Lankester, and a supplement, Macmillan, London.

Iltis, Hugo
(1932) *Life of Mendel*, W. W. Norton, New York.

Jenkin, Fleeming
(1887) *Papers, Literary, Scientific, Etc.*, 2 vols., edited by Sidney Colvin and J. A. Ewing, London.

Jenyns, Leonard
(1862) *Memoir of the Reverend John Stevens Henslow*, John van Voorst, London.

Joly, John
(1925) *The Surface History of the Earth*, Oxford University Press.

Lord Kelvin (William Thomson)
(1894) *Popular Lectures and Addresses*, 3 vols., London.

Kramer, Herbert H.
(1948) *The Intellectual Background and Immediate Reception of Darwin's Origin of Species*, Doctoral Dissertation (unpublished), Harvard University.

Lack, David
(1957) *Evolutionary Theory and Christian Belief*, Methuen, London.

Lamarck, J. B.
(1914) *Zoological Philosophy* (1809), Macmillan, London.

Litchfield, Henrietta
(1904) *A Century of Family Letters*, 2 vols., Cambridge University Press.

Lovejoy, A. O.
(1942) *The Great Chain of Being*, Harvard University Press.

Lyell, Sir Charles
(1834) *Principles of Geology*, 4 vols., third edition, London.
(1842) *Lectures on Geology Delivered at the Broadway Tabernacle in the City of New York*, New York.
(1850) Anniversary Address of the President, *Quarterly Journal of the Geological Society of London*, Vol. 6, pp. xxvii–lxvi.
(1851) "The Theory of the Successive Geological Development of Plants, from the Earliest Periods to Our Own Time,

as Deduced from Geological Evidence," *Edinburgh New Philosophical Journal*, Vol. 51, pp. 213–26.

(1851) "On Fossil Rain-marks of the Recent Triassic and Carboniferous Periods," *Quarterly Journal of the Geological Society of London*, Vol. 7, pp. 238–47.

(1851) "The Theory of Successive Development in the Scale of Being both Animal and Vegetable, from the earliest Periods to Our Own Time, as Deducted from Paleontological Evidence," *Edinburgh New Philosophical Journal*, Vol. 51, pp. 1–31.

(1851) Anniversary Address of the President, *Quarterly Journal of the Geological Society of London*, Vol. 7, pp. xxxii–lxxi.

(1863) *The Antiquity of Man*, John Murray, London.

Lyell, Katherine M.

(1881) *Life, Letters and Journals of Sir Charles Lyell*, 2 vols., London.

(1890) *Memoir of Leonard Horner*, 2 vols., London.

Malthus, Thomas Robert

(1798) *An Essay on the Principles of Population as it Affects the Future Improvement of Society with Remarks on the Speculations of Mr. Godwin, M. Condorcet and Other Writers*, London, facsimile of the first edition, Macmillan, 1926.

Marchant, James

(1916) *Alfred Russel Wallace: Letters and Reminiscences*, Harper, New York.

Matthew, Patrick

(1831) *On Naval Timber and Arboriculture*, Edinburgh.

Millhauser, Milton

(1959) *Just Before Darwin: Robert Chambers and the Vestiges*, Wesleyan University Press, Middletown, Conn.

Montagu, M. F. Ashley

(1943) "Edward Tyson, M.D., F.R.S., 1650–1780, and the Rise of Human and Comparative Anatomy in England," *Memoirs American Philosophical Society*, Vol. 20.

Nicholson, H. Alleyne

(1886) *Natural History, its Rise and Progress in Britain as Developed in the Life and Labours of Leading Naturalists*, London.

Owen, Rev. Richard

(1894) *The Life of Richard Owen*, 2 vols., New York.

Packard, A. S.

(1901) *Lamarck: The Founder of Evolution*, Longmans, Green & Co., London and New York.

Paley, William

(1822) *Natural Theology*, London.

Pantin, C. F. A.
(1950–51) "Darwin's Theory and the Causes of Its Acceptance," *School Science Review,* 3-part paper, October, 1950, March and June, 1951.

Playfair, John
(1802) *Illustrations of the Huttonian Theory of the Earth,* Edinburgh.

Potter, George Reuben
(1922) *The Idea of Evolution in the English Poets from 1744 to 1832,* Doctoral Dissertation (unpublished), Harvard University.

Pulteny, Richard
(1805) *A General View of the Writings of Linnaeus,* London.

Raven, Charles E.
(1942) *John Ray, Naturalist: His Life and Works,* Cambridge University Press.
(1953) *Organic Design: A Study of Scientific Thought from Ray to Paley,* Oxford University Press.

Roppen, George
(1956) *Evolution and Poetic Belief,* Oslo.

Russell, E. S.
(1916) *Form and Function: A Contribution to the History of Animal Morphology,* John Murray, London.

Sears, Paul B.
(1950) *Charles Darwin: The Naturalist As a Cultural Force,* Scribner's, New York.

Sedgwick, Adam
(1850) *Discourse on the Studies of the University of Cambridge,* fifth edition, London.

Smith, Sir James Edward
(1821) *A Selection of the Correspondence of Linnaeus and Other Naturalists,* London.

Smith, William
(1817) *Stratigraphical System of Organized Fossils,* etc., London.

Trow-Smith, Robert
(1959) *A History of British Livestock Husbandry 1700–1900,* Routledge and Kegan Paul, London.

Wallace, Alfred Russel
(1905) *My Life: A Record of Events and Opinions,* 2 vols., New York.

Weismann, August
(1892) *Essays upon Heredity,* 2 vols., Oxford.

Wells, William Charles
(1818) *Two Essays: One upon Single Vision with Two Eyes; The Other on Dew,* etc., London.

"Account of a White Female . . ." (Wells), 120–21

Ackerknecht, E. H., 153, 154, 155

Acquired characteristics: Erasmus Darwin, Lamarck views on, 48, 50; misinterpretation of Erasmus Darwin, Lamarck views, 51–52

Adaptive radiation, 184, 315

Adaptive zones: Matthew on, 129–30

Addison, Joseph: on Scale of Nature concept, 259

Agassiz, Louis, 271, 327–28; approves of progressionism, 328; Miller takes ideas from, 96; on prefigured order of evolution, 97

Albert, Prince: rumored author of Vestiges, 138–39

Allee, W. C., 349

Allen, Grant, 132n

American Indians. See Indians, American

Ancon sheep, 249

Andes: barrier to life, 167; Darwin on age of, 169

Anthropology: and developments in biology, 337, 340–44; rise of as a science, 337; Wallace contributions to, 313–14

Antiquity of Man (Lyell), 267

Apes, 340, 341; and language, 260–61, 278, 289, 290n, 297; and man in nature, 338; and Scale of Nature, 8, 260; Buffon on relation to man, 42–43; characteristics imagined in fossil finds, 276, 277, 278; Darwin on relation to man, 293; Lamarck hints as man's origin, 48; Vogt on, 268

Archaeopteryx, 89

Archbishop of Armagh. See Ussher, James

Argument for design: and rudimentary organs, 178; defined, 175–76; used by Darwin, 178

Argyll, Duke of, 288; challenges Darwin, 105, 294–95

Armadillo, 161, 162n, 168, 174

Artificial selection, 221–23; Buffon on, 40, 45; Matthew on, 129

Ashworth, J. H., 148n

"Atavism": in fiction, 269; popularity of explained, 284. See also "Reversion"

Atkinson, Geoffroy, 28n, 29n

Atomic energy, 253

Augustine, Saint, 60

Aurelius, Marcus: on time, 59–60

Australopithecine man-apes, 319–20

Bacon, Sir Francis, 13; and "polar dominance," 10–11; Darwin and principles of, 174

Baer, Karl von, 339

Bagehot, Walter, 303

Baillie, John, 326

Banks, Sir Joseph, 22, 23

Barlow, Nora, 172n

Barnard, Henry, 194–95

Bates, Henry Walter: and Vestiges, 139; and Wallace, 291

Bateson, William, 252; on loose use of "variation," 226; on Mendel's contributions, 224

Beagle, 221–44; Darwin's beliefs while on, 158–63, 166–74; Darwin reads Principles while on, 99

Beer, Gavin de, 314n

Before Adam (London), 269

Bell, Charles G., 54

Benedict, Ruth, 344

Bennett, A. W., 213, 214, 215, 217; Wallace attempts to refute, 222

Bergen, F. D., 277n

Bergen, J. Y., 277n

Bergson, Henri, 347, 349

Bernheimer, R., 275n

Bidney, David, 349n

Biogenetic law, 95

Blyth, Edw., 120

Boerhaave, Hermann, 18

Bolingbroke, Henry: on Scale of Nature, 259–60

Botanic Garden (Erasmus Darwin), 47

Boucher de Perthes, Jacques, 271, 272

Brain: and time, 314–24; Agassiz on, 97; Cuvier suggests endocasts of, 314; Grimes on, 314–15; latent capacities of human, 309–14, 321–22; Wallace on, 287–324

Brander, Gustavus, 78

Brayley, E. W.: and succession of types, 163–64, 165

Brewster, E. T., 337n

Bridgewater Treatises, 13, 177–78, 195, 197

Brinton, D. G., 279

British Association for the Advancement of Science: Dunn addresses (1862), 263–64; Lord Kelvin addresses (1861), 238; Lord Salisbury addresses (1894), 236

Broca, Pierre Paul, 284n

Brongniart, Alexander, 85

Broom, Robert, 319

Brougham, Lord: and progressionism, 334n

Browne, Sir Thomas: on animals in America, 3; on individual variation, 14; on nature, 12–13; on Scale of Nature, 7; on time, 2

Brückner, John, 38, 48; on struggle for existence, 128

Brünn Society for the Study of Natural Science, 205, 206

Bryson, Gladys, 282n

Büchner, L., 277n

Buckland, Dean William: and *Bridgewater Treatises*, 177–78; Lyell draws from, 103

Buffon, Georges Louis Leclerc, Comte de (1707–88), 16, 89, 105; and climate and change, 55, 188; and Cuvier, 68–69; and earth's age, 36, 41, 42; hints species barrier an illusion, 221; hints at anthropoid origin of man, 42–43, 48; livestock partial source for ideas of change, 37; ideas and work of, 39–45; Maupertuis impresses, 38–39; Sorbonne forces to recant, 98n; use of term "revolutions," 68–69

Butler, Samuel, 127

Button, Jemmy, 265

Cambridge: and Darwin, 148, 149, 158

Canals: influence on geological studies, 76, 77

Candolle, Augustin de, 197; and Darwin, 101–2

Carpenter, E. S., 299n

Carpenter, W. B., 264n

Case, Thomas, 250

Cataclysmic geology. *See* Catastrophism

Catastrophism, 98, 112–20, 329; and Buffon, 67–68; and Cuvier, 67–69; and Darwin, 169; and Lyell, 103, 104, 109–15, 194; and Matthew, 127–31; and Smith, 78–79; and supernaturalism, 114, 115n; and time scale, 246; and uniformitarianism, 114–15; as device to preserve Christian theology, 67; defined, 353; public attitude toward, 93–94; rejected in *Edinburgh Review*, 147

Cautley, Sir Proby, 271

Celestial Worlds Discovered (Huygens), 12

Chain of Being. *See* Scale of Nature

Chalmers: and *Bridgewater Treatises*, 177–78

Chambers, Robert (1802–71):

ideas of, 132–39; Darwin reads, 134, 139; Wallace reads, 291. See also Vestiges . . .

Chambers' Journal, 278

Chapman, Henry C., 290n; on search for transitional forms, 297–98

Chatham Island, 170

Chirotherium, 96

Clift, William, 44; and succession of types, 162, 164

Collinson, Peter, 17

Comparative anatomy: Buffon sees value of, 42; debt to Cuvier, 82–88; Huygens recognizes principles of, 12; of extinct forms, 5–6, 9; of living forms, 5

Comparative morphology: failure of, 55

Condorcet, Antoine-Nicolas de, 338, 339

Convulsionism. See Catastrophism

Cook, Capt. James, 22

Copernican system, 58

Correlation, law of. See Law of correlation

Correns, C., 224

Correspondence: importance of, in early science, 58

Cro-Magnon, 284, 299

Cunningham, D. J., 281

Cunningham, J. T., 223n

Curie, Paul, 253

Curti, Merle, 348n

Cuvier, Baron Georges (1769–1832), 65, 66, 91, 98, 136, 151, 196, 328–29, 340; achievements of, 80–89, 330; advocates endocasts, 314; and catastrophism, 67–69; and Lamarck, 199; and law of correlation, 88–89, 341; and Matthew's version of ideas, 130; and progressionism, 88–89, 94; breaks with single Scale of Nature concept, 339; dates man's appearance, 271; contrasted

to Darwin, 198–99; effect of work on public, 70, 93; refutes Geoffroy Saint-Hilaire, 117–18

Daniel, Glyn, 299n

Darlington, C. D., 251n; on Darwin, 245

Dart, Raymond, 319

Darwin, Charles (1809–82): Personal: Cambridge, 148, 149, 158; early essays, 186–92; Edinburgh, 145–46, 147; ethnologist, 155; Galápagos, 152, 166–74; Fuegians, 264–65; influence of field observation, 155–56; influence of intellectual background, 148–55; influence of isolation, 160; influence of literary tradition, 155n; influence of youth, 145–48, 186, 240, 245; philosophical achievements, 195–96; pigeon breeder, 185; separatist, 342; transitional figure, 245

Ideas: anticipated by others, 54; artificial selection, 221–23; catastrophism abandoned, 169; change fascinates, 208, 247; cytology, 213; design argument, 178, 193–99; "favorable monstrosities," 250n; formation of new species, 316; genetics, 213–23; gradation, 193; human evolution, 255–57, 283, 293–96; natural selection and inherited effects, 288–89; Neanderthal man, 289, 294; La Naulette jaw, 289; law of correlation, 341–42; law of divergence, 182–84; law of succession, 162–63, 164, 165–66; limited perfection, 310, 321–22; Natural Theology studied, 151; Ornamental Poultry, 185; Pangenesis, 216–21; parasites, 193; phylogeny, 134; "polar dominance," 10–12; researches, 178–79; "reversion," 269, 270;

Scale of Nature, 261, 288, 283; struggle for existence, 53, 181–82, 182n; sun's age, 240; time scale, 223, 233, 234, 235–37; variation, 185, 186–92, 201, 220–23; vocal organs, 289; zoology, 169–70

Individuals: Agassiz, 96; Argyll, 294–95; Boucher de Perthes, 271; Buffon, 39–44; Candolle, 101–2; Chambers, 134, 139; Cuvier, 198–99; De Quatrefages, 126; Erasmus Darwin, 46, 47, 55, 144, 240, 245; Herschel, 124; Humboldt, 153–55; Huxley, 141, 187, 335; Jenkin, 209–10, 214–16; Kelvin, 235, 245; Lamarck, 49, 52, 55, 131, 143, 156, 174, 181, 182n, 187–92, 193, 199–204, 217–18, 240, 245, 288–89; Malthus, 101, 102, 115, 179–82, 185, 201, 202; Matthew, 125–26, 130–31, 132; Mendel, 206, 208; Paley, 178, 180, 184; Wallace, 120, 157, 291–92, 304–9, 312–13; Wells, 120; White, 14. *See also* individual entries

Darwin, Erasmus (1731–1802), 51, 52, 54, 233; achievements, 55; and doctrine of acquired characteristics, 48, 49–50; belated triumph, 349; ideas of, 46–48; ideas of in Matthew, 132; influence of French Revolution on, 54; influence on grandson, 144, 240, 245

Darwin, Francis, 14n, 160, 186; on father's use of *Vestiges*, 134; on influence of Malthus on father, 180–81

Darwin, Robert, 175

Darwin, Susan, 179; letter from brother, 169

Darwinians: bias of, 287–90; challenged by Jenkins, 209–16

Dawson, J. W.: on human fossils, 274

Dean, Bashford, 47n

Degeneration, 304; Buffon's use of term, 39, 41, 45; and Wallace, 308; and Lamarck, 50–51; described, 299–302; difficulty of sustaining in face of fossil evidence, 313; influence on study of nature, 37

De Maillet, Benoit (1656–1783), 36, 41, 48, 212; Hutton on, 74; ideas and work of, 29–35

Deperet, C., 88n

De Quatrefages, J. L. Armand: Darwin on, 126

Derham, William: argument for design promoted by, 176

Descartes: and cosmic evolution, 68; influence on De Maillet, 32

Descent of Man, 279, 293; Lyell's ideas in, 104, 105; on deer in U.S., 223; on inheritance of habit, 246; on limited perfection, 321–22; on natural selection, 209; on Vogt's ideas, 269; reasons for writing, 256. *See also* Darwin, Charles

Developmentalism, 115, 328n; defined, 354

De Vries, Hugo (1848–1935), 224, 229, 230; achievements, 251–52; ideas and work, 226–27, 248–51

Dickie, George, 96

Diffusion: of plants and animals, 44

Divergence, law of. *See* Law of divergence

Dobzhansky, Theodosius, 320n

Domestic animals: alteration of, 147

Dowdeswell, W. H., 346–47

D'Oyly, C. J., 301

Draper, John W., 133–34

Dubois, Eugene, 279, 280, 281, 282

Dunn, Robert, 263–64

Earl of Bridgewater. *See* Egerton, Francis Henry

Earth: age of, 31; Buffon estimates age of, 36, 41–42; physicists challenge age of, 234–53

Echelle des êtres. See Scale of Nature

Ecology: recognition of by Lamarck and Erasmus Darwin, 55

Edentates: fossil, 161, 174

Edinburgh New Philosophical Journal: early evolutionary paper in, 146–47

Edinburgh Review, 151–52

Edinger, Tilly, 314n, 319

Egerton, Francis Henry, eighth Earl of Bridgewater, 177

Ellis, John, 22–23

Emerson, Ralph Waldo, 52

Emiliani, Cesare, 319n

Engels, Frederick, 195

Engis skull, 272–73, 274, 299

England: and Linnaeus, 17, 18; first geological map of, 78; intellectual influence on Sweden, 18; reaction to Malthus doctrine, 37

English clergymen: and nature, 175–76

Ensor, George, 177n

Environment: Buffon and Lamarck on effect in evolution, 55

Epigenesis, 37

Essay on Dew (Wells), 121, 124–25

Essay on the Principles of Population, 37. *See also* Malthus

Evolution: discontinuity in, 251; discovered by public, 138–39; early mention in *Edinburgh Review,* 151–52; Buffon suggests experimental approach to, 42

Evolution, biological: De Maillet attempts to link with cosmic, 30–31

Evolution, cosmic, 35–36, 68; and Chambers, 135–36; and De Maillet, 30–31, 32; and Kelvin, 230; and spectroscope, 332–34; growing realization of, 70

Evolution, organic: and Sedgwick, 149–50; and Chambers, 135–36

Evolution of brain, 234–53

Evolution of man: Darwin on, 255–57; Lyell on, 256, 267

Evolution of parts, 305–6

Evolution Old and New (Butler), 127

Evolutionary theory: and the church, 23–24; importance of time scale to, 233, 234–44; in need of new approach, 246; Lyell resists, 100n, 100–15; moral interpretation of, 326; techniques for studying, 5–6; De Vries on, 248–52; voyagers' effect on, 1–2. *See also* individual entries on related subject matter

Ewart, J. C., 185n

"Experiments in Plant Hybridization" (Mendel), 205

Explorers: impact on western thought, 1–2

Extinction, 8, 33, 92; and Lamarck, 48–49, 55; and Lyell, 106

Falconer, Hugh, 124, 271, 316

Falkner, Thomas, 161n–62n

Father and Son (Gosse), 203–4

Fauna Boreali Americani (Richardson), 151

Finalism, 197–98

Finches: in Galápagos, 172

Fisher, R. A., 230

Fiske, John, 313n, 321

Fitzroy, Capt. Robert, 159, 175, 265

Flying fish: theories about, 33

Fontenelle, Bernard Le Bovier de, 1

Forbes, Edward, 141

Fossil rain marks, 103–4

Fossil shells, 31; and Smith, 93;

nature of questioned, 167; procured in Andes by Darwin, 169; Ray on, 64

Fossil skulls, 256, 258–59

Fossil vertebrates, 82–88, 93

Fossils: and De Maillet, 30, 31; Buffon suspects value for determining age strata, 75; Edentates, 161; eighteenth century attitude on, 31, 36; primate and human, 271–85; Sedgwick's interpretation of, 150; Smith on importance of, 79

Fothergill, Philip, 250n

Fox, Rev. W. D., 169, 178–79

France: and catastrophism, 68; shares lead in comparative biology, 327; intellectuals of, and nature, 37; intellectuals of, and voyagers, 29

Franklin, Benjamin, 45

Frantz, R. W., 260n

Fraunhofer, Joseph von, 333

Frazer, Persifor, 133

French Revolution, 10, 68; and Buffon's son, 45; and English reaction to, 69, 193, 327; effect on Erasmus Darwin's ideas, 54; effect on Lamarck's reputation in England, 54–55; effect on Playfair's and Hutton's ideas, 98

Fuegians, 264–65

Fuhlrott, Dr., 273

Galápagos, 112, 152, 161; and Darwin, 166–74, 202

Garfinkle, Norton, 55n

Garn, Stanley, 308n

Geikie, Sir Archibald: and physicists' conception of time scale, 235, 241

Genetic drift, 310n

Genetics: Darwin's ideas on, 213–23; pre-Mendelian, 211–16; Weismann's achievements, 217–21

Geoffroy Saint-Hilaire, Étienne, 117–18

Geoffroy Saint-Hilaire, Isidore, 271

Geological prophecy, 91–97; elements of, in Vestiges, 137; and Matthew, 131

Geological Society of Glasgow: Lord Kelvin addresses, 240

Geological Society of London, 73, 80; Darwin addresses (1837), 179; Greenough addresses (1834), 236; Huxley addresses (1861), 113; Lyell addresses (1851), 107; Sedgwick addresses (1830), 149–50

Geological time: attacks on, 234–53. See also Time scale

Geology: and catastrophism, 66–69; and Lyell, 98–108; and physicists' attacks on time scale of, 234–53; early speculations on, 31–32; Moulton suspicious of physicists on time scale, 252–53; Matthew's use of, 128–31

Germany: contributions to knowledge of cell mechanics, 219; shares lead in comparative biology, 327; Romanticism in, and effect on evolutionism, 95

Germ plasm: inviolability of, 218, 219, 247

Gifford, A. C., 253n

Gilbert, G. K., 244

Gill, Theodore, 44n; on fossil man, 276, 279

Gillispie, Charles C., 50, 55n, 67

Glacial theory: developed, 107–8

Glass, Bentley, 38

Glyptodent, 161n–62n, 168, 174

Gode-von Aesch, Alexander, 95

Gosse, Edmund: on launching of Origin, 203–4

Graham, William, 194n, 345

Grant, A., 301n

Grant, Dr. Robert (1793–1874): and Darwin, 145–46

Gray, Asa, 250n; on Darwin and idea of design, 197; Darwin questions on plant variation, 192

Great Chain of Being (Lovejoy), 6

Greenough, George, 256

Gregory, J. W., 266n

Grimes, J. Stanley, 314–15

Gruber, Jacob, 272n, 357

Gundry, D. W., 177n

Gunther, R. W. T., 31n

Habit: inherited, 240

Haeckel, Ernst, 278, 298; and biogenetic law, 95; and Lyell, 102; explains mystery of universe, 346; on linguistic ability of apes, 289, 297

Hagberg, Knut, 18

Hakewill, George, 299n

Hale, Matthew: and struggle for existence, 52

Haller, Albrecht von, 21

Halley, Edmund, 99

Hallowell, A. I., 323–24, 344

Hannah, J., 301n

Harris, Victor, 299n

Harrison, H. S., 321n

Harrison, J. P., 263n

Hart, C. W. M., 340n

Heat, residual. See Kelvin, Lord

Helmholtz, H. L. F. von, 238

Henderson, Gerald, 278n

Henslow, J. S., 158; and Darwin, 148, 149

Hepburn, Ronald W., 299n

Herschel, Sir John, 123–24; unaware of Essay on Dew, 124–25

Hicks, Lewis E., 178n, 197–98

Historicity, 77, 331

Hogben, L., 220

Holarctica region, 10; Buffon's perceptions on, 44

Homo duplex, 7

Homo neanderthalensis. See Neanderthal man

Hooker, Sir Joseph, 127, 145; and launching of Origin, 203–4; Darwin to, on variation, 192; Darwin to, on ideas of Wallace, 305; on Darwin and variation, 191–92; on Galápagos plants, 173

Hottentots, 3, 265, 282, 298; and fossil finds, 277; Buffon on, 43; cease to be step from monkey people, 314; Darwin puts in Scale of Nature, 261; language of, and apes, 260–61

Hudson, William H., 13, 158

Hughes, Thomas, 274

Humboldt, Alexander von: hints at law of divergence, 183; influence on Darwin, 153–55; Wallace reads, 291

Hunter, John, 327; and succession of types, 162n; on equilibrium in animal world, 329

Hutton, James (1726–97), 65, 67, 68, 80, 85, 93, 136, 151, 235, 325, 328, 352; ideas of, 69–75, 91, 108–9, 113; ideas of and non-progression, 108; ideas partially rejected by Chambers, 135–36; ignores Noachian Deluge theory, 97–98; influence of ideas, 113–14; Lyell uses principles of, 103; on time, 241; Playfair presents ideas of, 66, 98; publishes news of discovery, 92; Smith influenced by, 78, 79; uniformitarianism of, 41, 92–93

Huxley, Leonard, 141n, 173n

Huxley, Thomas (1825–95), 4, 8, 49, 106, 127, 192, 296, 311, 326, 345; and attacks on time scale, 234, 239, 240, 241, 243, 244; and directivity in life, 198; and natives, 303; and

Wilberforce clash, 134–35; against progressionism, 113; Chambers attacked by, 133–34, 137; Chambers attack regretted, 139; considers Miocene date for man, 308; Darwin on his interpretation of struggle for existence, 335; on Darwin, 141; on Darwin and Wallace and variation, 187; on Neanderthal skull, 272, 274, 277n; on Neanderthal skull as a reversion, 269; on Owen and Forbes, 141–42; on struggle for existence, 335; similarity to Lyell's views on evolution of man, 267n; stability fascinates, 342–43

Huygens, Christian: recognizes principles of comparative anatomy, 12

Idiots. See Microcephali
Illustrations of the Huttonian Theory of the Earth (Playfair), 98
Iltis, Hugo, 205n
Indians, American, 3; Dunn on, 263; in Scale of Nature, 261
Industrial Revolution: effect on livestock breeding, 212
Innis, H. A., 340n
Islands: De Maillet on, 33–34
Isolation: its role in evolution, 172–74

Jackson, J. Hughlings, 315
James, William, 348
Jardin des Plantes, 85
Java Man. See Pithecanthropus erectus
Jenkin, Fleeming, 240, 244; challenges Darwin, 209–11, 213, 214–16, 217, 225; Wallace attempts to refute, 222
Jenyns, Rev. Leonard, 13; Darwin to, on publishing evolutionary views on man, 256
Jesperson, P. H., 145n

Johannsen, W. L., 213n, 214; and variation, 227–28
Journals of Researches, 154, 162, 172; Wallace reads, 291. See also Darwin, Charles
Juan Fernández Island, 123
Judd, John W., 160
Judgment day: and historical time, 60–61

Kalm, Peter: in America, 17
Keith, Sir Arthur, 197; on Engis skull, 273
Kellogg, Vernon, 251
Kelvin, Lord (Sir W. Thomson), (1824–1907), 309; attitude toward Darwin's philosophy, 240; attacks Darwinian conception of time, 238–44; Darwin's attitude toward, 235; residual heat and ideas on, 236, 238; residual heat, De Vries on, 248
Kendall, Abraham, 1
Kielmeyer, Karl, 85; and Romanticism, 95
King, Clarence, 240
King, William: on Neanderthal skull, 277n
Kingsley, Charles, 292
Kirby, William: and Bridgewater Treatises, 177–78
Kirchoff, Gustav, 333
Kluckhohn, Clyde, 344
Kocher, Paul, 61n
Kofoid, Charles, 120n, 121
Kölliker, Albrecht von, 250
Kroeber, A. L., 157
Kropotkin, Prince Peter, 348

Laborde, 253
Labrador: reports of mammoths in, 9
Ladder of Perfection. See Scale of Nature
Lamarck, Jean Baptiste (1744–1829), 46, 54, 78, 79, 87, 105, 122, 132, 283n; achievements, 55; abortive organs concern,

196; acquired characteristics doctrine, 49-50; as "French atheist," 193; belated triumph of, 349; Chambers shares beliefs of, 136-37; change fascinates, 208; Cuvier and, 199; Darwin and, 143, 199-204; Darwin influenced by, 181, 182n, 187-92, 245; Darwin on, 202; Darwin passes beyond environmentalism of, 174; Darwin plays down ideas of in first edition of *Origin*, 131; Darwin uses ideas on effect of habit, 288-89; denies environmental influence in evolution, 55; Grant and, 145-47; effect of French Revolution on English reputation, 54-55; hints at man's anthropoid origins, 48; ideas of, re-evaluated, 246; Lyell introduces into England, 98; Lyell passes beyond ideas of, 102-3; Lyell puts theories of, in *Principles*, 151; "posthumous Darwinian," 245; recognizes adaptation, 196; Scale of Nature and, 337-38; Smith praises, 78; species barrier and, 221; struggle for existence and, 52-53, 200-1; time scale and fossil questions puzzle, 64; time scale's importance to theory of, 233

Lamarckianism: and Mendel, 208; and "progressive-development theory," 328n; and theory of pangenesis, 211; Darwin retreats toward, 217, 240, 252; Jenkin forces Darwinians to fall back on, 200-1; Weismann challenges ideas of inheritance, 219

La Naulette jaw, 277; Darwin on, 289

Language: Darwinists obscure problem, 289-90; Haeckel and linguistic ability of apes, 289,

297; Wallace on that of natives, 311-12

Lankester, E. Ray, 313n

Laplace, Pierre S.: his nebular hypothesis, 330, 334

Law of continuity, 260

Law of correlation, 86, 88-89, 341-42

Law of divergence, 182-84; Darwin accepts, 159

Law of succession, 161-66; Buffon hints at, 44

Lawson, Vice-Governor, 173

Le Regne Animal (Cuvier), 85

Lessons in Comparative Anatomy (Cuvier), 85

Lewis, Wyndham, 27

Lhwyd, Edward, 16, 63-64

Life: De Maillet on theories of origin, 34

Lilley, W. S., 346n

Limited perfection: Darwin's principle of, 310; Darwin abandons in case of man, 321-22

Linnaeus, Carolus (1707-78), 29, 37, 39, 44, 45, 327; ideas and work, 16-26; influence on contemporaries, 17-19; on distinction between man and ape, 282; on science, 15; prestige in England, 18

Linnean century, 27, 28

Linnean Society: Wallace and Darwin address (1858), 292

Linnean taxonomy: and effect on pre-Mendelian genetics, 212

Litchfield, H. E., 160n

Liverpool Philosophical Society, 304

Llama, extinct, 162

Loeb, Jacques: on rediscovery of Mendel, 229

Lombrosian criminal, 278

London, Jack, 269

Lovejoy, Arthur O., 6, 53n, 83n, 136, 138, 338n; on Great Chain of Being, 259

Lubbock, Sir John: on significance of fossil finds, 273; on Wallace's view of savages, 303

Ludwig, Christian, 255

Lydekker, R., 280n

Lyell, Sir Charles (1797–1875), 75, 91, 120, 127, 142, 143, 147, 192, 305; and catastrophism, 194, 246; and law of divergence, 184; and non-progressionism, 137, 329; and *Origin*'s launching, 203–4; and "polar dominance" theory, 11–12; and struggle for existence, 182n, 331; and succession of types, 162; and uniformitarianism, 233; biological ideas of, 99–115; Darwin and, 98, 113, 151, 160, 169, 179, 246; Darwin on, 100; Darwin to, on Lamarck, 202; Darwin to, on research, 179; Darwin to, on Scale of Nature, 261; Darwin's debt to, 158, 162; ideas and work of, 98–115; Lamarck's views presented by to British, 49; on natural selection, 102–5, 180; on evolution of man, 267; on evolution of man being discussed publicly, 256; on variation and domestic breeding, 186; questions rate of change in insular faunas, 246–47; Sedgwick attacks uniformitarianism of, 266; Wallace hypothesis intrigues, 308; Wallace influenced by, 157, 291, 292. See also *Principles of Geology*

McCosh, James, 96, 313n

Macmillan's Magazine, 238

Macro-mutation, 248–52; Darwin's ideas on, 222; doctrine, 247; modern meaning of word, 229

Malinowski, B., 344

Malthus, Thomas Robert (1766–1834), 37; and struggle for existence, 53, 181–82, 182n;

biological observations of, 332n; blights public optimism, 331; Darwin and, 101, 102, 115, 179–82, 185, 201, 202; *Edinburgh Review* approves doctrines of, 151; limitations of numbers concept as warning, 329; Lyell as probable source for Wallace-Darwin ideas on, 331–32; Paley a convert to ideas of, 151; predecessors of, 38–39; Townsend forecasts Malthusian problem, 123; Wallace influenced by, 291, 292

Mammoths: Buffon recognizes as extinct elephants, 42; reports of in Americas, 8–9

Man: and interpretation of creation, 118–19; belief in animal crosses with, 28; Lyell on origins of, 104–5

Manouvrier, Leonce: on Dubois find, 280, 281–82

Marchant, James, 126n, 240n

Marsh, O. C., 280n

Marsupials, extinct, 164

Massner, E. C., 177n

Mather, K., 251n

Matthew, Patrick (1790–1874): ideas and work of, 125–26

Maupertuis, Pierre de (1698–1759), 38–39

Mead, Margaret, 344

Meek, R. L., 195n

Megatherium, 163

Meldola, R., 245

Mendel, Father Gregor (1822–84), 38, 66, 211, 217, 218n, 220, 296; and cytology, 213; and *Origin*, 206, 208; contributions, 224–26; ideas and work of, 205–9; Loeb on rediscovery of, 230; principles of explain atavisms, 269; principles of and delimitation of human psychology, 347–48; reception of idea, 248–49; re-emergence of, 250; re-emergence tied to physicists' attack on time scale, 242, 247

Merz, John Theodore, 206

Microcephali, 266–70, 279

Microscope: and natural theology, 176, 177; Mendel lacks, 207; significance of, 36–37

Milhauser, Milton, 135n, 138

Miller, Hugh, 95n, 96, 300

Missing link, 9; belief in, 258; and Pithecanthropus, 279; and Scale of Nature concept, 259; and theory of microcephalics, 266–70

Mitchel, Dr. John, 17

Mitchel, Major Thomas, 165

Mivart, St. George, 304n

Mollusca, 339–40

Mongols: as moral fossils, 264

Montagu, M. F. Ashley, 269n, 314n

Morgan, Lloyd, 243

Morgan, Thomas Hunt, 230n

Morse, Edward S., 313n

Mott, Albert: impresses Wallace, 304

Moulton, F. R., 330n

Mountains: Ray ponders age of, 62

Müller, F. Max, 258

Muller, H. J., 210n

Mutation: modern meaning of word, 229. See also Macromutation

Napoleon: Cuvier favorite of, 85

Nashe, Thomas, 61n

Natural government, 329, 330, 331

Natural history: study of sustains Christian faith, 176–77

Natural History (Buffon), 39, 45

Natural History of Selborne (White): influences Darwin, 14

Natural selection: and artificial selection, 221–23; and inherited effects, 288–89; and timing of physicists' attack, 247; Argyll challenges it in man, 294–95; Buffon and, 45; Darwin and, 214, 295–96; Darwin on, in Descent of Man, 209; Darwin on, in Origin, 310; Darwin sees inadequacies in, 217, 245–46, 309; endless biological deviation, 223; Jenkin influence on ideas of, 209–16; Kelvin attacks, 238, 240; Lamarck and, 52; Lyell's use of, 102–3, 104–5, 180; Malthusian influence on Darwin's ideas of, 179–82; Matthew and, 126–32; Paley and, 180; pre-Darwinian development of theory, 155–66; pre-Darwinians glimpse theory, 120; Salisbury on failure of Darwinians to demonstrate, 236, 244–45; Scale of Nature and, 53; Townsend on, 123; Wallace conceives idea, 291; Wallace on, 310–14; Wallace sees inadequacies in, 309; Weismann extends, 336; Wells and, 120–25

Natural Theology (Paley), 15: Darwin studies, 151, 178; on argument for design, 176

Natural theologians: and progressionism, 327

Naturalist's Voyage, 173; natural selection theory hinted in, 157. See also Darwin, Charles

Nature: influence of Deism on study of, 37; influence in study of, 13

Neanderthal man, 278, 280, 284; and Darwin, 289, 294

Neanderthal skull, 256, 299; discovery of, 272; described, 273; comments on, 274–75

Negro, 264, 314; characteristics imagined in fossil finds, 276, 277, 278; Dunn on, 263–64; Vogt on, 262–63, 268

"Neptunists," 66–67

Newman, James R., 349n

Newton, Isaac, 65, 333

Newtonianism: and Hutton, 70–72; and uniformitarianism, 114

Newtonian world, 328, 329

Nicholson, H. A., 53n

Niessl, Gustav von: friend of Mendel, 207, 231

Noachian Deluge, 31, 63, 76, 297; and catastrophism, 67, 69; Hutton's ideas on, 71, 97–98; public prefers as interpretation of past, 92; supposed skeleton from, 86–87

Noah's Ark, 44

"Noble savage," 264

Non-progressionism, 107–15, 137; abandoned by Huxley, 267n; and Lyell, 329; defined, 354. See also Progressionism

North, F. J., 79n

North America: Buffon perceives distinctive species in, 44

"Observations on the Nature and Importance of Geology" (Grant?), 146–47, 146n

Oenothera lamarckiana, 249, 251

Oken, Lorenz, 97

On Naval Timber and Arboriculture (Matthew), 125

"On the Age of the Sun's Heat" (Kelvin), 238

"On the Tendency of Varieties to Depart Indefinitely from the Original Type" (Wallace), 331–32

Orangutan, 3, 34, 43, 265; Lamarck's place for in evolution, 49, 51; eighteenth-century view of, 338; linguistic ability of, Condorcet on, 339; linguistic ability of suggested, 278; Lyell averse to connecting with man, 105; men similar to in India, 262; Vogt on, 262–63

Organic change: and Mendel, 208–9; and Wells, 122

"Oriental Sage," 29

Origin of Species, 14, 15, 142, 163, 174, 306; Chambers' Vestiges prepares public for, 134–35, 139; considered abstract by Darwin, 157; De Candolle and "war of nature" phrase in, 101–2; Falconer lauds, 124; Gosse on launching of, 203–4; groundwork of others in, 233–34; Huxley defends, 133, 134–35; ideas in background, 245–46; influence of field observation on, 156; influence of youth on, 145; inheritance laws in, 213–14; Jenkin noted in, 210; Mendel reads, 207, 208; Lamarckian ideas played down, 131; Lyell's style similar to, 98n–99n; Matthew noted in, 125–26; on man, 255; revisions create contradictions, 216; revisions on natural selection, 209, 310; revisions to meet attacks, 242–43; time scale's importance to, 234; time scale in first edition, 237; utilitarian philosophy in, 348; Wallace on, 127; Wells noted in, 120. See also Darwin, Charles

Ornamental Poultry: Darwin on, 185

Orthogenesis, 210; and time, 234

Owen, Richard, 44, 143, 162; and Huxley, 141–42; approves of progressionism, 328; claim to originating law of succession, 163; reviews Origin, 188

Packard, A. S., 79n, 276–77

Paleontology, 5; and achievements of Cuvier, 81–89; answers quarrel between degenerationists and evolutionists, 313; as threat to Huttonian world, 328; as used by Lyell, 110–11; Buffon forsees value of, 42; debt to William Smith, 76; effect of Cuvier's exploits on public interest in, 93; effect of first discoveries on scholars, 256–57; effect of Piltdown skull on, 318; offers little encouragement to racial gradation, 318

Paley, William, 15, 196, 197; and Darwin, 178, 184; and law of divergence, 183–84; and natural selection, 180; argument for design promoted by, 176; doctrines approved by *Edinburgh Review*, 151

Palm prints, 14

Pampean formation, 161

Pangenesis, 216–21, 224, 225

Pantin, C. F. A., 98n, 185n

Parasites, 178, 193

Paris Basin: and Cuvier, 69, 80, 83

Parsons, Theophilus, 249–50

Parson naturalists, 13–14, 354

Payne-Gaposchkin, Cecilia, 238n

Pearl, Raymond, 228n

Pea plant: Mendel's use of, 207, 208, 224, 225

Pedomorphism, 314

Penguin, 159

Pennant, Thomas, 14

Personal Narrative, (Humboldt): impresses Darwin, 153–55

Philosophical Survey of the Animal Creation (Brückner), 38

Philosophie Zoologique (Lamarck), 48

Phreno-Geology . . . (Grimes), 315

Phylogeny: and Darwin, 134

Physics: effect of on geology and biology, 234–53

Physics and Politics (Bagehot): Wallace reviews, 303

Piddington, Henry, 262

Pigeons: bred by Darwin, 185; origin of, 14

Piltdown skull, 293, 297, 313; Wallace's views on, 317–18

Pirates: dangers of, to scientists, 17

Pithecanthropus erectus, 258, 279, 313; age of, 319

Planets: water content of, 35

Plants: Buffon on variations of, 40; Erasmus Darwin on variations of, 47

Platonism, 114

Playfair, John, 103, 233; presents Hutton's ideas, 66, 98

Pocock, R. I., 294n

"Polar dominance" theory, 10–11

Population: early studies of, 37–38; Lamarck on, 48

Pouchet, G., on Scale of Nature, 261

Poulton, E. B., 134n, 212n

Preformation: doctrine of, 37

Preliminary Discourse on the Study of Natural Philosophy (Herschel), 123–24

Pritchard, C., 333

Primeval Man (Argyll), 294

Primrose: variations in, 249, 251

Principles of Geology (Lyell), 11, 109; and law of divergence, 184; as probable source for Malthusian ideas of Wallace and Darwin, 331–32; Darwin influenced by, 98n–99n, 99–106, 151; Darwin receives on *Beagle*, 160; ideas in, 98–106; on variation and domestic breeding, 186; style similarity to *Origins*, 98n–99n; Wallace influenced by, 291, 292. *See also* Lyell, Sir Charles

Progress, idea of: and *philosophes*, 338; denied by Scale of Nature, 264; transferred to biology, 283

Progressionism, 334; and Chambers, 135, 136, 137; and Cuvier, 88–89, 94; and Lord Brougham, 334n; and Lyell, 106–15; and Matthew, 125, 127–31; and natural theologians, 327; and Scale of Nature, 94–95; and time scale,

246; defined, 328, 353; Darwin destroys, 195–96; misinterpreted, 119
"Progressive-development theory," 328n
Pterodactyls: named by Cuvier, 84
Ptolemaic cosmogony, 61
Ptolemaic system, 58

Quantum evolution, 310n
Quételet, Lambert (1796–1874), 227

Racial gradation: affects judgment of fossil finds, 274–75, 276, 277, 278; in European thought, 260–64
Racial idea: and evolution, 96
Radcliffe-Brown, A. R., 344
Radioactivity, 253; and dating methods, 237, 238
Radium, 253
Rain marks, fossil, 103–4
Ratner, Sidney, 195n
Raven, Charles E., 15n, 63n
Ray, John (1627–1705), 13, 24, 25, 36, 175, 327; achievements, 14–16; argument for design promoted by, 176; death of, 18; on earth and water, 31; suspects Biblical accuracy of time scale, 16, 62–63, 64
Recherches sur Les Ossemens Fossiles (Cuvier), 85
Religio Medici (Browne), 2
Reptiles: Darwin's observation of, 159; Lyell's theories on, 112; on Galápagos, 170, 171
"Reversion": defined, 269; used in arguments against human evolution, 270. See also "Atavism"
"Revolution": as used by Buffon and Cuvier, 68–69, 88
Rhea, 159
Richardson, Sir John, 151

Riviere, Emile, 276
Robinson, J. T., 319
Romanes, G. J., 213
Romanticism: effect on evolution, 95
Rosenfield, L. C., 261n
Rousseau, Jean Jacques: and struggle for existence, 52
Roux, Wilhelm, 219n–20n, 335
Royal Society of Edinburgh, Kelvin addresses (1865), 239
Royal Society of London: Darwin proposed for Copley Medal of, 124; Wells addresses (1813), 120
Rudimentary organs: and argument for design, 178
Russell, E. S., 82n, 95n, 117n, 213n, 336n

Salisbury, Lord, 233; objection to Darwin theory, 236, 244–45
Scala Naturae. See Scale of Nature
Scale of Being. *See* Scale of Nature
Scale of Nature, 6–10, 28, 43, 260, 284–85; and catastrophism, 67; and German philosophy, 96; and Lamarck's ideas, 48, 51, 52, 54, 337–38; and racial groups, 338–39; and similarity of progressionism, 94–95; Addison on, 259; Bolingbroke on, 259–60; Cuvier breaks with, 87, 88, 339; Darwin transfers to biology, 283; Darwin's ideas on, 288; effect on comparative anatomy, 82; effect on nineteenth-century thinking, 259–65; effect on evolutionary theory, 117, 118; Lovejoy on, 259; misinterpreted as expression of evolution, 119
Schaaffhausen, Hermann, 273
Scheuchzer, Johann, 86
Schmerling, P. C., 273
Schmid, Rudolf, 302, 313

Secondary period: Darwin's dating of, 237

Sedgwick, Adam, 158, 326, 327; attacks Lyell's uniformitarianism (1831), 266; forecasts triumph of uniformitarianism and organic evolution (1830), 149–50; Huxley defends, 133

Sedgwick, Adam (the younger), 243

Selection, artificial. See Artificial selection

Selection, natural. See Natural selection

Seward, A. C., 14n

Sexual selection, 47

Shakespeare: Darwin's fondness for, 144

Shryock, Richard, 120n, 123n, 125

Singer, Charles, 32n

Sirks, M. J., 217n

Siwalik discoveries, 271

Smith, Sir James, 15n, 23n

Smith, Walter, 297n

Smith, William (1769–1839), 65, 85, 125, 136, 151, 352; ideas and work, 75–81; meaning of a stratum to, 92; recognizes change in marine beds, 93

Smith, William, author of Thorndale, 117

Solander, Daniel (1736–82), 78

Sollas, W. J., 278–79, 295n; on time scale, 241

Sorbonne: and Buffon, 98n

Species: doubt about fixity of, 28–29; fixity of, 23–26

Spectroscope: and importance to cosmic evolution, 332–34

Spencer, Herbert, 313n; reiterates Jenkin position, 215–16

Spengler, J. J., 38n

Spontaneous generation, 130

Stability: fascinates Mendel, 208

Stratigraphical System of Organized Fossils (Smith), 78

Stratigraphy: and William Smith,

76–77; public interest in, 83; Sedgwick's use of, 149–50; significance of, 79–80

Straus, W. L., Jr., 294n

Struggle for existence: Brückner on, 128; Chambers on, 37; Darwin's contribution to theory, 53; Darwin's debt to Lyell for theory, 101–5; Darwin's early thoughts on, 181, 182n; Darwin's source for ideas on, 181–82; early believers in, 52; eighteenth-century attempts to examine, 329; Haeckel on Darwin's idea, 334–35; Huxley on, 335; Lyell's transitional treatment, 331; Malthus and, 37, 53; Malthus's influence on Darwin and Wallace, 182; Townsend on, 123; Wells and, 119–25

Struggle of the parts, 334–36

Succession, law of. See Law of succession

Supernaturalism, 27–28; and catastrophism, 94–95, 114, 115n; attempts to avoid in France, 68; lack of in De Maillet's theory, 74; Matthew ignores, 131; Sedgwick's version, 326

Swainson, William, 205

Sweden: influence of England in, 18

Sweichel, R., 277n

Systema Naturae, 15, 18, 20, 25, 26. See also Linnaeus

Système de Animal (Brückner), 48

Système de la Nature (Maupertuis), 38

Tait, Peter, 234–35

Taxonomy: stimulation of, 10; Linnaeus's views on, 21–22

Teggart, F. J., 283

Telescope: and natural theology, 176–77

Telliamed (De Maillet), 29–35
Temple of Nature (Erasmus Darwin), 47
Tennant, F. R., 322–23
Tennyson, Alfred, 139
Ternate, island of, 291
Theology: and effect on attitude toward nature, 6; appeal of new evolution to, 250
Theoria generationes (Wolff), 36
Théorie de la Terre (Buffon), 68
Theory of the Earth (Cuvier), 85
Theory of the Earth (Hutton), 68, 73–74
Thermodynamics, second law of, 236, 309, 330
Third International Zoological Congress (1895), 280
Thiselton-Dyer, Sir William, 184
Thomson, Sir W. *See* Kelvin, Lord
Time: cyclic and historic, 325–26, 329–30, 334; nature of, 329–34; Sir Thomas Browne on, 2
Time scale, 234–53; and catastrophism, 246; and Christian conception of, 2; and importance to evolutionary theory, 233, 234, 235–37; and organic change, 57–58; and pre-Christian era, 58–59; and pre-Darwinian era, 60–64; and progressionism, 246; and radioactivity, 252–53; and stratigraphy's effect on concept of, 79–80; and uniformitarianism, 236–37; Buffon sees need for lengthening, 41–42; Chambers' views on, 135–36; Darwin's interest in after physicists' attack, 223; De Vries on, 248; Hutton's view of, 74; Lamarck sees need for lengthening, 48; Matthew senses importance of, in evolutionary

theory, 126, 128–31; Matthew's relation of, to natural selection theory, 131–32; Mendel's re-emergence tied to physicists' attack on, 247; Moulton suspicious of physicists' findings, 252–53; Salisbury on insufficiency of, for evolution, 236; Wallace's view of, 307, 309–10; Wells fails to consider fully, 125; Wells's view of, 122
Tomkeieff, S. J., 68
Tortoises: in Galápagos, 170–71
Townsend, Joseph: recognizes struggle for existence, 122–23
Transcendentalism, 96, 136; and Agassiz, 97; and evolution, 52; and Geoffroy Saint-Hilaire, 117, 118
Trilobites, 103
Tristram, H. B., 301n
Tschermak, E. V., 224
Tuveson, Ernest, 299n

Uniformitarianism, 35, 63–64, 233, 328; and Buffon, 41; and Darwin, 160; and De Maillet, 33; and Hutton, 41, 69–75, 92–93; and Lyell, 106–15; and Matthew, 127–31; and Smith, 78–79; alternatives to, after physicists' attack on time scale, 247; contribution to evolutionary thought, 144; defined, 353; non-progressionism affected by, 108; Sedgwick attacks Lyell's views, 266; Sedgwick forecasts triumph of, 149–50; time scale's effect on, 236, 237
Uranium: and residual heat, 253
Ussher, James, 61

Variation: Bateson on loose use of word, 226; Buffon on, 40; Chambers' awareness of, 138; Darwin's ideas on, 161, 168, 172–73, 185, 186–92, 213–14, 220–23; Darwin-Lamarck ideas on compared, 200–3; Erasmus Darwin on, 47; Darwinists' meaning of term, 220–21; De Vries on, 226–27; early discussion of in *Edinburgh Review*, 151–52; Hutton on, 111n; importance of time scale to Darwinian conceptions of, 233, 234–41; in domestic forms, 187, 189–90; in nature, Darwin's views on, 186, 188, 189, 190; in nature, Wallace's views on, 189, 191, 192, 291; Jenkin on, 214–16; Johannsen's ideas on, 227–28; Lamarck fails to grasp significance of chance variation, 54; Lyell on, 111–12, 186; Mendel's ideas on, 225–26; Quételet on, 227; recognized by pre-Darwinians, 122; Sedgwick (the younger) on, 243; somatic, 219–21; Weismann's views on, 220–21; Wells on, 122

Variation of Animals and Plants under Domestication, 216. *See also* Darwin, Charles

Venus Physique (Maupertuis), 38

Vestiges of the Natural History of Creation (Chambers), 132–37; and Darwin, 134; fallacious genetics in, 212; influence of in America, 315; Wallace reads, 291

Virchow, Rudolph, 299n

Virginia: Dr. Mitchel collects plants in, 17; reports of mammoths in, 9

Vogt, Carl, 279; on evolution of man, 262–63, 267–70; on Neanderthal and Engis skulls, 295

Volition, 350

Voyagers: accounts of Hottentots, 260–61; curiosity of, 161n–62n

Voyages of exploration: their impact on western thought, 1–2

Wagner, Moritz, 167–68

Walcott, Charles: on geological time, 241

Wallace, Alfred Russel (1823–1913), 120, 126, 250, 287–324, 349; and De Vries, 248–49; and earth's orbit, 243; and human antiquity, 290–93, 296, 303–9; and Mendelian ideas, 248–49; and somatic variation, 221; and succession of types, 162–63, 164–65; and *Vestiges*, 139; contributions of, 306–9; contributions to anthropology, 313–14; Darwin on ideas of, 305; Darwin queried on whether he will discuss man in *Origin*, 256; Darwin to, on age of sun, 240; Darwin to, on Galápagos, 167; Darwin-Wallace relationship, 157, 291–92, 304–9, 312–13; diverges from Darwin, 304–9; epitomizes the new time, 332; influence of Lyell on, 103, 113, 157; influence of Malthus on ideas of struggle for existence, 182; influence of travels on ideas, 148–49, 291, 303; metaphysical views of human origins, 316–17; on Darwin's idea of heredity, 245; on human evolution, 310–11; on Matthew, 127; on primitive man, 303; on variation and heredity, 222; on variation in nature, 189, 191, 192; sees evolution of parts outmoded with rise of man, 347

War of nature, 331, 335; Darwin takes phrase from Candolle, 101

Waterhouse, G. R., 172

Watson, D. M. S., 318, 320

Watson, Hewett, 91

Web of life: appreciated before Darwin, 54

Wedgwood, Josiah: and Darwin, 148; and natural history, 175

Weiner, J. S., 317n

Weismann, August (1834–1914), 224, 246, 247, 249, 296; extends natural selection, 336; ideas and work, 217–21

Wells, William Charles (1757–1817), 126n, 128, 132; ideas and work, 119–25

Werner, Abraham, 66, 92; significance of work, 76

West, Geoffrey, 105n; on evolutionary ideas at Edinburgh, 148

Westermarck, Edward, 340

Whately, Richard, Archbishop of Dublin, 300

Whewell, William: and *Bridgewater Treatises*, 177–78; on Lyell, 105; on Lyell's biological doctrines, 106; receives letter on *Vestiges*, 138

White, Gilbert, 13, 14, 15, 175

White, Lynn, 60

Whitehead, Alfred North, 62

Whitney, Lois, 62

Wilberforce, Bishop Samuel, 134

Willis, J. C., 210n

Wilson, Thomas, 280n

Wisdom of God (Ray), 16

Wolff, C. F., 36

Woodward, James, 75–76

World machine, 70–75, 332; and Hutton, 92–93

Wright, Chauncey, 313n

Wright, Sewall, 230

Young, G. M.: on *Vestiges*, 139

Zirkle, Conway, 50, 53n, 122, 212n

Zoonomia (Erasmus Darwin), 46–47, 126n; and Darwin, 144

LOREN EISELEY was professor of anthropology at the University of Pennsylvania, where he taught since 1947. His other books include *The Immense Journey, Firmament of Time, Francis Bacon and the Modern Dilemma,* and *Mind as Nature.*